Robert S. O'Loughlin

The Delineator

Robert S. O'Loughlin

The Delineator

ISBN/EAN: 9783337817817

Printed in Europe, USA, Canada, Australia, Japan

Cover: Foto ©ninafisch / pixelio.de

More available books at **www.hansebooks.com**

The Delineator.

...THE WOMAN'S FAVORITE MAGAZINE...
Circulation—Over Half a Million Copies Monthly.

THE DELINEATOR is Issued Monthly, and covers the Field of Fashion, Women's Work and Recreation. Each Issue contains over One Hundred and Fifty Pages of Interesting Reading on the Fashions, Fancy-Work (including special contributions on Lace-Making, Knitting, Crocheting, Tatting, etc.), Household Management, The Toilet, The Garden, etc., etc., and has in addition each month Articles by Distinguished Writers on the Topics of the Time, Women's and Children's Education, Women's Handcrafts and Occupations, Suggestions for Seasonable Entertainments and a Variety of Other Matter Instructive and Helpful to all Women. The DELINEATOR is the Cheapest and Best Woman's Magazine published.

Subscription Price, $1.00 a Year.
Price of Single Copies, 15c. Each.

DELINEATORS sent on Subscription or by Single Copy to any Address in the United States, Canada, Newfoundland or Mexico are post-paid by the Publishers. When the Magazine is ordered sent on Subscription to any other country, Sixty Cents for Extra Postage must be remitted with the Subscription Price. Persons subscribing are requested to specify particularly the Number with which they wish the Subscription to commence. Subscriptions will not be received for a shorter term than One Year, and are always payable in advance.

NOTE THIS OFFER. To Any Person residing in the United States, Canada, Newfoundland or Mexico, sending us $1.00 for a Subscription to THE DELINEATOR, with Ten Cents additional to prepay transportation charges, we will also forward a Copy of the METROPOLITAN CATALOGUE of the current edition, until the same shall be exhausted. The METROPOLITAN CATALOGUE will also be furnished to Persons residing in other countries, providing the Ten Cents transportation charge is remitted us, in addition to the Subscription Price and the extra postage on the Subscription. The Catalogue is furnished on the above conditions only when ordered at the same time with the Subscription, and is subject to the transportation charge if ordered to be delivered at any point outside our Office. If the Current Edition of THE METROPOLITAN CATALOGUE is exhausted at the time we receive the Subscription, we will send a copy of the succeeding number immediately upon its publication. See Advertisement of THE METROPOLITAN CATALOGUE elsewhere in this issue.

The Delineator for February

CONTENTS.

FAR AWAY IN ROSELAND. Agnes S. Buck.	122
DRESSMAKING AT HOME.	129
ARTISTIC HOUSE FURNISHING AND DECORATION.	131
FASHIONABLE HATS.	133
LADIES' FASHIONS. (Illustrations and Descriptions.)	134–168
STYLES FOR MISSES AND GIRLS. (Illustrations and Descriptions.)	169–181
STYLES FOR LITTLE FOLKS. (Illustrations and Descriptions.)	182–187
STYLES FOR MEN AND BOYS. (Illustrations and Descript'ns.)	187–190
ILLUSTRATED MISCELLANY.	191–196
TATTING. Illustrated.	197
FANCY STITCHES and EMBROIDERIES. Emma Haywood.	198
SEASONABLE DRESS GOODS.	199
FASHIONABLE GARNITURES.	200
MIDWINTER MILLINERY.	202
MEXICAN STAMPED LEATHER. Illustrated. M. C. Frederick.	203
ADULTERATED AND DETERIORATED FOODS. A. B. Longstreet.	206
CROCHETING. Illustrated.	208
NETTING. Illustrated.	210
THE CHILDREN'S VALENTINE PARTY. H. C. Wood.	212
SEASONABLE COOKERY. Blair.	213
DRAWN WORK. Illustrated.	215
A FAN WITH A HISTORY. Illustrated.	216
ECCLESIASTICAL EMBROIDERY. Illustrated.	218
MEDICINE. (Professions.) Aimée Raymond Schroeder, M.D.	219
KINDERGARTEN PAPERS. No. 18. Sara Miller Kirby.	221
NEW STYLES IN SLEEVES, COLLARS, ETC.	224
ORIENTAL RUGS.	227
THE SOCIAL CODE. (Conclusion.) Mrs. Roger A. Pryor.	229
AROUND THE TEA-TABLE. Edna S. Witherspoon.	231
AMONG THE NEWEST BOOKS.	232
THE SOFT ANSWER.	235
THE CARE OF THE TEETH. Illustrated.	236
HOUSEKEEPERS' DEPARTMENT.	237
PUBLISHERS' DEPARTMENT.	240
ANSWERS TO CORRESPONDENTS.	V.

THE BUTTERICK PUBLISHING CO. (Limited), 7 to 17 West Thirteenth Street, New York.

Our Cloaks will this Season more than maintain their great reputation for Beauty.

Our New Special Catalogue

NOW READY.

MAILED FREE

On a Postal Card Request.

Representing about one hundred styles of the most beautiful

Cloth, Plush and Fur Capes and Jackets

we have ever shown.

The reason we sold over 75,000 Cloaks by mail last season is because of our original and

**Beautiful Styles,
Worthy Fabrics,
Faultless Fit,
Matchless Finish**

No. 319.   No. 416.   No. 320.

No. 319. Rich Black Bouclé Jacket, a beauty at $16.50. Price only $10.
No. 416. Fancy Scotch Brown Mixed, Inlaid Velvet Collar, Very nobby, only $10.
No. 320. Extra Fine Black Beaver, Very stylish. Worth $16.50, for only $10.

and because we **save you almost Half. They're not like other cloaks** — they lend the wearer a distinctive grace. With a **Stevens' Cloak** you always feel well dressed.

See our Catalogue for a hundred other equally unmatchable offerings from $5.00 up. It is mailed free. Write for it to-day.

Money Back on any Garment if you are Not Pleased.

CHAS. A. STEVENS & BROS., 111 TO 115 STATE ST., CHICAGO.

Better than Theory!

RESULTS from the Use of

Superior to Medicine.
CAPON BRIDGE, W. VA., Nov. 15, 1895.
"Since testifying in favor of the Electropoise two years ago, I have had the most gratifying results from its use in neuralgia, indigestion and in the rebuilding of broken-down females. We use it for all ailments and find it superior to medicine and doctors."
MRS. MINNIE A. BEALL.

Simple Remedy.
Prof. Totten, of Yale College, writes:
"But thanks be to God, there is a remedy for such as lie sick—some single, simple remedy—an instrument called the Electropoise. We do not personally know the parties who control this instrument, but we do know its value."

An **Oxygen**

Home **Remedy**

Without Medicine

Effective—Economical.
139 FIFTH AVE., N. Y., April 3, 1891.
"... My confidence in the merits of the Electropoise — simple, convenient, economical and effective as it be—has constantly grown with my increasing observation and experience."
W. H. DE PUY, A.M., D.D., LL.D.,
(Editor Peoples' Cyclopædia.)

An Invalid Twenty Years.
FREEPORT, MICH., March 11, 1895.
"For twenty years I had been an invalid with a combination of troubles; female weakness, spinal complaint, liver, kidney and stomach badly affected. Two years use of the Electropoise has given me health as never before, and I cannot praise it too highly."
MISS LENA NAGLER.

Often cures Cases pronounced "Incurable."

The Theory is Scientific.

An illustrated booklet of 112 pages contains it, together with the reports from 200 other users of the Electropoise, price of same, etc., mailed you free for the asking.

ELECTROLIBRATION CO.   1122 Broadway, New York.
346 Fulton Street, Brooklyn.

"**How?**" By its new method of introducing oxygen directly into the entire circulation.

General Harrison's National Articles

"This Country of Ours"

For the first time in our history an ex-President of the United States takes up the pen to write a successive series of magazine articles. In them he crystallizes a lifetime of study and observation of our country. Begun in the Christmas (December) number of

The Ladies' Home Journal

SEND ONE DOLLAR FOR A YEAR'S SUBSCRIPTION

Wanted—A First-class Man or Woman

To look after our subscribers, secure renewals and new names. The coming season will be the greatest in the history of THE LADIES' HOME JOURNAL. Profitable employment offered. Write for particulars.

The Curtis Publishing Company, Philadelphia

THE DELINEATOR.

BOOKS AND PAMPHLETS
ON SOCIAL CULTURE AND THE DOMESTIC SCIENCES AND ARTS,
Published by THE BUTTERICK PUBLISHING COMPANY (Limited).

If any of these Works cannot be obtained from the Nearest Butterick Agency, send your Order, with the Price, direct to Us, and the Publications desired will be forwarded to your Address.

METROPOLITAN BOOK SERIES.
Sold at the Uniform Price of $1.00 per Copy.

Good Manners. This is an Exhaustive Common-Sense Work, uniform with "Social Life," also advertised on this page, and fully explains the latest and best ideas on Etiquette. Price, $1.00 per Copy.

Social Life is a Book written in Correspondence Style and Explanatory of PRACTICAL ETIQUETTE, and is intended as a Companion Book to "GOOD MANNERS." It contains valuable instructions concerning the customs belonging to polite society, and supplies the most approved forms of Invitations and Replies, etc., etc. Price, $1.00 per Copy.

The Delsarte System of Physical Culture. This Work, by Mrs. Eleanor Georgen, is a Reliable Text-Book, Indispensable in Every School and Home where Physical Training is taught; and the Explanations are supplemented by over Two Hundred and Fifty Illustrations. Price, $1.00 per Copy.

Beauty: Its Attainment and Preservation. The Most Complete and Reliable Work ever offered to Those Who Desire to Be Beautiful in Mind, Manner, Feature and Form. As this Book is more comprehensive in its dealings with the subject of Beauty than any before published, its popularity is a foregone conclusion. Price, $1.00 per Copy.

Needle-Craft: Artistic and Practical. This will be found a Comprehensive and Eminently Useful Volume replete with accurate Engravings of Decorative Needle-Work of every variety, with full instructions for their reproduction, etc. Price, $1.00 per Copy.

The Pattern Cook-Book. A Comprehensive Work on the Culinary Science, Showing How to Cook Well at Small Cost, and embracing The Chemistry of Food, The Furnishing of the Kitchen, How to Choose Good Food, A Choice Collection of Standard Recipes, etc. Every Recipe in THE PATTERN COOK-BOOK has been thoroughly tested. Price, $1.00 per Copy.

Home-Making and House-Keeping. This Book contains full instructions in the Most Economical and Sensible Methods of Home-Making, Furnishing, House-Keeping and Domestic Work generally. Price, $1.00 per Copy.

Needle and Brush: Useful and Decorative. A BOOK OF ORIGINAL, ARTISTIC DESIGNS, AND ONE THAT SHOULD BE SEEN IN EVERY BOUDOIR AND STUDIO. In this Volume will be found innumerable Artistic Designs for the Decoration of a home, all of them to be developed by the Needle or Brush. Price, $1.00 per Copy.

METROPOLITAN ART SERIES.
Sold at the Uniform Price of 50 Cents per Copy.

The Art of Crocheting: Introductory Volume. This Beautiful Work is replete with illustrations of Fancy Stitches, Edgings, Insertions, Garments of Various Kinds and Articles of Usefulness and Ornament, with Instructions for Making Them. Price, 50 Cents per Copy.

Fancy and Practical Crochet-Work (Advanced Studies): A New, Up-to-Date Pamphlet on Crochet-Work. This Pamphlet is one of the largest of this Series, and is filled with New Designs as follows: EDGINGS AND INSERTIONS; SQUARES, HEXAGONS, ROSETTES, STARS, ETC., FOR SCARFS, TIDIES, COUNTERPANES, CUSHIONS, ETC.; DOILEYS, CENTER-PIECES, MATS, ETC.; PRETTY ARTICLES FOR MISSES' AND CHILDREN'S USE; DOLLY'S DOMAIN; BEAD CROCHET AND MOULD CROCHET. Price, 50 Cents.

The Art of Knitting. This Book is complete in its Intention of instructing Beginners and advancing Experts in Knitting, introducing all the rudiments of the work, from the CASTING-ON OF STITCHES to the commencement and development of PLAIN and INTRICATE DESIGNS. Price, 50 Cents per Copy.

The Art of Modern Lace-Making. A Revised and Enlarged Manual of this Fascinating Art, containing over Two Hundred Illustrations of Modern Laces and Designs, together with Full Instructions for the work, from hundreds of PRIMARY STITCHES to the FINAL DETAILS. Price, 50 Cents per Copy.

Wood-Carving and Pyrography or Poker-Work. The largest manual upon Wood-Carving and Pyrography ever prepared for publication. It contains Illustrations for Flat Carving, Intaglio or Sunk Carving, Carving in the Round, and Chip Carving, and also nearly Four Hundred Engravings of Modern, Renaissance, Rococo, German, Norwegian, Swedish and Italian Designs. Price, 50 Cents.

Drawing and Painting. The following List of Chapter Headings indicates the Scope of this Beautiful Work: Pencil Drawing—Tracing and Transfer Papers—Shading—Perspective—How to Sketch Accurately Without a Study of Perspective—Sketching—Water-Colors—Flowers in Water Colors—Oil Colors—Oil Painting on Textiles—Crayon Work in Black and White—Pastel Pictures—Drawing for Decorative Purposes—Painting on Glass—Painting on Plaques—Screens—Lustra Painting—Still Life—Terra Cotta—Lincrusta—Tapestry Painting—China Painting—Golds, Enamels and Bronzes—Royal Worcester. Price, 50 Cents per Copy.

Masquerade and Carnival: Their Customs and Costumes. This Book contains all the Important Points concerning Carnivals and similar festivities, and presents between Two and Three Hundred Illustrations of Historical, Legendary, Shakesperean, National and Original Costumes for Ladies, Gentlemen and Young Folks, with complete Descriptions. Price, 50 Cents per Copy.

The Art of Garment Cutting, Fitting and Making. With the aid of this Book you will need no other teacher in Garment-Making. It contains instructions for Garment-Making at Home, which are to be found in no other work on the subject, are Purely Original with us, and are the Practical Result of Many Experiments Conducted with the Intention of Offering Our Patrons the Best Instructions on the Subject ever Formulated. Price, 50 Cents.

Drawn-Work: Standard and Novel Methods. The most Complete and Artistic Book Ever Published upon this fascinating branch of Needle-Craft. Every step of the Work, from the drawing of the threads to the completion of intricate work, is fully Illustrated and Described. Price, 50 Cents per Copy.

Tatting and Netting. This Pamphlet contains the two varieties of Fancy-Work named in the title, and is the only reliable work combining the two ever issued. Especial effort has been made to provide Rudimentary Instructions for the benefit of the beginner, and at the same time offer the skilled worker Designs of Elaborate Construction. Price, 50 Cents per Copy.

METROPOLITAN PAMPHLET SERIES.
Sold at the Uniform Price of 15 Cents per Copy.

Mother and Babe: Their Comfort and Care. A Pamphlet of 84 pages, devoted to the interest of Young Mothers, illustrated and carefully prepared, with full information concerning the care of infants and the Preparation of their Wardrobes, and also treating of the necessities belonging to the Health and Care of the Expectant Mother. Price, 15 Cents.

Dainty Desserts: Plain and Fancy. Every Housekeeper should possess a copy of "DAINTY DESSERTS: PLAIN AND FANCY," in which she will find directions for the preparation of Dainties adapted to the palate and the means of the epicure or the laborer and to the digestion of the robust or the feeble. Price, 15 Cents per Copy.

Nursing and Nourishment for Invalids. This is a Pamphlet that contains Explicit Instructions and Valuable Advice regarding the Best Methods and Necessary Adjuncts in the Sick Room. CARE, COMFORT AND CONVALESCENCE are fully discussed, and many recipes for the Most Nourishing Foods and Beverages for Invalids are given. Price, 15 Cents per Copy.

BOOKS AND PAMPHLETS.—CONCLUDED.

Tableaux, Charades and Conundrums. This is a New Pamphlet upon this class of Entertainments and Amusements. Charades in all their different varieties, and Tableaux and the details necessary to their Perfect Production are Freely Described and Discussed; and Many Examples of Each are Given. The Conundrums will of themselves provide pleasure for Numberless Hours and Occasions. Price, 15 Cents per Copy.

Fancy Drills. This is a New Pamphlet, containing Directions and Illustrations for the Arrangement and Production of Twelve New Fancy Drills suitable for School, Church, Club, Society and General Evening Entertainments. Among the entertainments offered are the famous Broom and Fan Drills, the New Columbian Drill, the Empire, Doll, Tambourine, Flower and Fancy Dress Drills, etc. Price, 15 Cents per Copy.

Smocking, Fancy Stitches, Cross-Stitch and Darned Net Designs, is the title of our New Pamphlet, which includes all of the Varieties of Needlework mentioned, and also gives a great many Illustrations of each of the different varieties. One of the most important subjects treated in the pamphlet is that of Finishing Seam Ends, Pockets, Pocket-Laps, Collars, Cuffs, etc., by the Tailors' Method. Price, 15 Cents per Copy.

The Correct Art of Candy-Making. A New Illustrated Pamphlet containing simple yet reliable Instructions for Candy Making. It teaches how to make the Finest French as well as the Plainest Domestic Candies, including Cream Candies, Caramels, Bonbons, Nut and Fruit Candies Pastes, Macaroons, Drops, Medicated Lozenges, Comfits, Candied and Dried Fruits, and Candied Flowers and Nuts. Price, 15 Cents per Copy.

The Perfect Art of Modern Dancing. This is the title of a Pamphlet which is provided with Illustrated Instructions for those who wish to Learn to Dance by the Methods Employed by the Best Dancing Masters of the Metropolis, and also How to Dance all of the Popular Square and Round Dances; The German or Cotillon; The Stately Minuet; The Caledonians, and Sir Roger de Coverly. Price, 15 Cents per Copy.

The Perfect Art of Canning and Preserving. This convenient Pamphlet contains full instructions regarding the Canning of Vegetables, including Corn, Beans, Peas, Asparagus, Tomatoes, etc.; the Canning of Fruits of all kinds; the Preparation of Jams, Marmalades, Jellies, Preserves, Pickles, Catsups and Relishes; the Putting up of Brandied Fruits, Spiced Fruits, Fruit Butters, Dried Fruits, Syrups, Home-Made Wines, Vinegars, etc. Price, 15 Cents per Copy.

Extracts and Beverages. In the Preparation of Syrups, Refreshing Beverages, Colognes, Perfumes and Various Toilet Accessories, this pamphlet is invaluable alike to the Belle and the Housekeeper, than whom none know better the marchantability of many of the perfumes and flavoring extracts placed on the market for Toilet and Household use. Price, 15 Cents per Copy.

Birds and Bird-Keeping. A New Pamphlet, illustrated with Numerous Engravings of Cage Birds of Various Kinds, their Cages, and Many Modern Appliances for Cages and Aviaries, are supplied by Full Instructions as to the Care, Food, Management, Breeding and Treatment of the Diseases of Songsters and Feathered Pets in General. Price, 15 Cents per Copy.

A Manual of Lawn Tennis. This Pamphlet is fully illustrated and contains a History of Tennis, the Rules, Details concerning the Development of Play, Descriptions of the Court, Implements, and Serviceable Dress; and a Chapter on Tournaments and How to Conduct Them. Price, 15 Cents per Copy.

Bees and Bee-Keeping. A New Pamphlet, Profusely Illustrated, and treating of the Observances and Details necessary to successful Bee-Keeping. Suggestions are given as to Who Should Keep Bees, How and Where to Buy, Where to Locate and How to Conduct an Apiary and Control Bees; and Brood Rearing, Queen-Rearing, Swarming, Gathering and Extracting Honey, Pasturage and Artificial Food, Transportation, Enemies of Bees, Robbing and Various other Important Matters are fully Discussed. Price, 15 Cents per Copy.

Uses of Crêpe and Tissue Papers. This Pamphlet is Very Fully Illustrated with Designs and Diagrams for Making Paper Flowers and Various Fancy Articles, Christmas, Easter and General Gifts, Novelties for Fairs, A Spring Luncheon, Toilet Furnishings for Gentlemen, Sachets, Cottage Decorations and Dolls, are some of the Lesson Topics included in the Pamphlet. Price, 15 Cents per Copy.

Weddings and Wedding Anniversaries. This is a most Unique and Useful addition to a Practical and Interesting series. It contains the Latest Information and Accepted Etiquette concerning everything relating to the Marriage Ceremony, with descriptions of the Various Anniversaries, from the First year to the Seventy-Fifth, that are directly and suggestively valuable. Price, 15 Cents per Copy.

Child Life. This Pamphlet discusses INFLUENCES ON PRE-NATAL LIFE; BATHING AND CLOTHING FOR INFANTS; FOOD FOR INFANTS; WEANING AND FEEDING CHILDREN AFTER THE FIRST YEAR; DISEASES OF INFANTS AND YOUNG CHILDREN; ERUPTIVE AND OTHER FEVERS; CARE OF CHILDREN'S EYES, EARS AND TEETH; CHILDREN'S AMUSEMENTS; CONVENIENCES FOR THE NURSERY; CHILDREN'S HABITS; PRECOCIOUS AND PERT CHILDREN; HOME INFLUENCES; THE FORMATION OF CHARACTER; THE KINDERGARTEN; THE HOME LIBRARY; CHILDREN'S MONEY; THE DIGNITY OF LABOR; CHILDREN'S PETS; CHILDREN'S ASSOCIATES; SPORTS AND GAMES; TRAINING A BOY FOR BUSINESS; TRAINING GIRLS FOR MATERNITY and THE RITE OF MARRIAGE. Price, 15 Cents per Copy.

METROPOLITAN HANDY SERIES.

Sold at the Uniform Price of 25 Cents per Copy.

Pastimes for Children. This Popular Pamphlet for Children has been Revised and Enlarged, and now contains some of the Best and Most Instructive and Entertaining Amusements for Rainy-Day and other Leisure Hours ever issued. It is suited to the Mental Capacities of Little Ones of all ages, and is filled with Drawing Designs and Games; Instructions for Mechanical Toys, Cutting Out a Menagerie, Making a Circus of Stuffed and Paper Animals, etc., etc. Price, 25 Cents per Copy.

Venetian Iron Work: The Information, Instruction and Designs contained in this handsomely illustrated Manual will be of the utmost value to every one interested in Venetian Iron Work. The details are minute, the Implements fully described, and the Designs so clear and comprehensive that the veriest amateur will have no difficulty in developing the work. Price, 25 Cents per Copy.

Parlor Plants and Window Gardening. The Amateur Florist cannot fail to comprehend the contents of this pamphlet or become expert in the raising of House Plants. It tells all about Necessary Temperatures, Suitable Rooms, the Extermination of Insect Pests, and the General and Special Care of Hundreds of Plants, all of them being Fully Described and Illustrated. Common and Botanical Names of Flowers are Given, Species are Described, and Varieties are Recommended for the Refined Avocation or Diversion of Window Gardening. Price, 25 Cents per Copy.

Artistic Alphabets for Marking and Engrossing. This Book illustrates Fancy Letters of various sizes, the fashionable Script-Initial Alphabet in several sizes, numerous Cross-stitch and Bead-work Alphabets, and a department of RELIGIOUS and SOCIETY EMBLEMS. Price, 25 Cents per Copy.

Social Evening Entertainments. This pamphlet is issued in response to many letters asking for suggestions for Entertainments that are Novel, Original, Amusing and Instructive, and not of the Purely Conventional Types requiring Full Dress, Dancing and Luxurious Refreshments. It meets Every Requirement of our Correspondents, and at the same time offers Pleasing Suggestions to those who desire to vary their Grand Entertainments by an occasional Simpler One. A few of the many Entertainments offered are: A LITERARY CHARADE PARTY, A WITCH PARTY, A GHOST BALL, A HALLOWEEN GERMAN, A NOVEL CARD PARTY, A MIDSUMMER NIGHT'S ENTERTAINMENT, A FLOWER PARTY, A FANCY-DRESS KRIS KRINGLE ENTERTAINMENT, THE BOWERS' CHRISTMAS TREE, A ST. VALENTINE'S MASQUERADE ENTERTAINMENT, etc., etc., all told in conversational style and many of them handsomely illustrated. Just the thing for a Neighborhood Full of Party-Giving, Fun-Loving Young People. Price, 25 Cents per Copy.

THE many worthless imitations of FIBRE CHAMOIS now in the market, make it necessary to call the attention of the public to the fact that for their protection every yard of the genuine material is plainly stamped

FIBRE CHAMOIS

Beware of these imitations and get FIBRE CHAMOIS, or you will be obliged to make your dress over. Dressmakers should examine their bills and see that the material is billed "FIBRE CHAMOIS," otherwise they may get some of the worthless imitations, while paying for the genuine article.

Fashionable Dressmakers everywhere endorse and use Fibre Chamois.

Puffed Sleeves and Skirts supported by Fibre Chamois will not lose their shape. Cheaper, lighter in weight and better than any other stiffening material.

COMES IN THREE WEIGHTS:
No. 10, Light.   No. 20, Medium.   No. 30, Heavy.

COLORS:
Black—Slate—Ecru—Brown—Natural Chamois.

At the Lining Counter of all Dry Goods Stores.

How to Use Fibre Chamois

TO support Puffed Sleeves and Skirts properly, see that you get the correct weights for that purpose, described as follows: **No. 10** for silks and light materials; **No. 20** for heavier goods; **No. 30** for warmth and where canvas is needed.

Always cut the FIBRE CHAMOIS the exact size of the goods, and sew up in the seams with the material; gather or pleat the same as you would the material, and the result will be a stylish garment.

129

FIGURE No. 3.—DECORATION FOR A LADIES' COAT.—(Cut by Pattern No. 8081; 13 sizes; 28 to 46 inches, bust measure; price 1s. 3d. or 30 cents.)

FIGURE No. 1.—LADIES' PROMENADE TOILETTE.—(Cut by Jacket No. 7997; 13 sizes; 28 to 46 inches, bust measure; price 1s. 3d. or 30 cents; and Skirt No. 7902; 9 sizes; 20 to 36 inches, waist measure; price 1s. 3d. or 30 cents.)

FIGURE No. 6.—COMBINATION AND DECORATION FOR A LADIES' COSTUME.—(Cut by Pattern No. 8100; 13 sizes; 28 to 46 inches, bust measure; price 1s. 3d. or 40 cents.)

FIGURE No. 4.—STYLISH COMBINATION FOR A LADIES' BASQUE-WAIST.—(Cut by Pattern No. 8102; 13 sizes; 28 to 46 inches, bust measure; price 1s. 3d. or 30 cents.)

FIGURE No. 2.—COMBINATION AND DECORATION FOR A LADIES' EVENING COSTUME. (Cut by Pattern No. 8075; 13 sizes; 28 to 46 inches, bust measure; price 1s. 3d. or 40 cents.)

FIGURE No. 5.—DECORATION FOR A LADIES' BOX COAT.—(Cut by Pattern No. 8090; 13 sizes; 28 to 46 inches, bust measure; price 1s. 3d. or 30 cents.)

FIGURE No 7.—COMBINATION AND DECORATION FOR A LADIES' COSTUME.—(Cut by Pattern No. 8101; 13 sizes; 28 to 46 inches, bust measure; price 1s. 3d. or 40 cents.)

(For Descriptions see "Dressmaking at Home," on Pages 179 to 181.)

"Recitations and How to Recite"

CONSISTS of a large collection of Famous and Favorite Recitations, both for Adults and Children, and also includes some Novelties in the way of Poems and Monologues sure to meet with the Approval of Everyone Interested in Elocutionary Entertainments.

Valuable and Unique Features of the pamphlet are the General Prefatory Remarks and Suggestions, and those which also precede Each Selection, by which the Reciter is Instructed not only Comprehensively in the Art of Elocution but Specially in whatever Number he Selects for Personal Recitation before an Audience.

The Collection is an Eminently Satisfactory one from which to choose Recitations for the Parlor, for School Exhibitions or Church Entertainments, or for Benefits for Individual or other Charitable Objects.

Every Scholar at School should have a Copy of **"Recitations and How to Recite"**; every Elocutionist, Professional or Amateur, will find it Most Useful; and no Library can Afford to omit it from the list of Up-to-Date Books of Recitations.

Price, 1s. or 25 Cents.

ADDRESS:
THE BUTTERICK PUBLISHING CO. (Limited),
7 to 17 West 13th Street, New York, U. S. A.
171 to 175, Regent Street, London, England.

New Century Busy Work.

TO TEACH THE CHILDREN.

The sets are so arranged that the pupil can use them without aid from the teacher. They are for seat work, for the pupil who is not reciting and who cannot have the direct attention of the teacher. Each set teaches a definite thing and delights the child.

FOR BEGINNERS.	FOR ADVANCED.
1. Numbers 1 to 5, . . . 15c.	1. Numbers 6 to 10, . . 15c.
2. Word Building, . . . 15c.	2. Colors Intermediate
3. Script and Print, . . 15c.	Hues, ... 20c.
4. Colors Spectrum Standards, Black and White, 20c.	3. Colors Intermediate Hues, ... 15c.
5. Colors Spectrum Standards, Black and White, 15c.	4. Birds: Common Birds, 20c.
6. Domestic Animals, . 20c.	9. Hiawatha, Illustrated, 20c.
7. Wild Animals, ... 20c.	10. Pictures for Language Work. . . . . . . 25c.

For sale by all dealers. Sample sets mailed to Superintendents and Teachers of Schools upon receipt of Ten Cents to cover postage.

FAIRY TALE AND FABLE.

Literature and Art for First Year Pupils.

By JOHN G. THOMPSON, Principal State Normal School, Fitchburg, Mass., and THOMAS E. THOMPSON, Superintendent of Schools, Leominster, Author of Fables and Rhymes for Beginners.

The New Century Educational Co.,
BOSTON—113 Devonshire St. NEW YORK—239 Broadway.

FAT FOLKS GET THIN!

BY THE USE OF DR. EDISON'S OBESITY PILLS, SALT AND REDUCING COMPOUND.

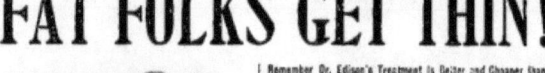

Remember Dr. Edison's Treatment is Better and Cheaper than any other. We have three large stores. Other advertisers of Obesity remedies have no stores, no offices—you can't find them personally.

THESE REMEDIES MAKE GOOD HEALTH AND GOOD FIGURES!

USED BY FAT PHYSICIANS. PRESCRIBED BY ALL PHYSICIANS.

"After long study of Obesity and its cure" writes Ellen Foster Bevins, M. D., "I have come to the conclusion that Dr. Edison's Obesity Remedies more nearly fill the requirements of a thorough cure for this malady than any or all other treatments. These remedies reduce flesh, but do not reduce the system."

Bella Blanchard Bartlett, West Fourth Street, Cincinnati, President of the Cincinnati Woman's Club (for Portland), writes: "Until lately when I was saved by Dr. Edison's Obesity Pills and Salt, I had well to become a chronic sufferer from over-fat. My hips, abdomen and lower limbs became so fleshy as to be both uncomfortable and indecent. I took three bottles for general reduction, and wore an Edison Obesity Band for nine rigid abdominal reduction, losing 11 pounds in seven weeks, and getting far better health and a better figure than I had been mine for years."

Bessie Sterling Van Valkenburg, West End Ave., near 97th St., New York, writes: "I have now taken Dr. Edison's Obesity Pills and Fruit Salt five weeks. They have reduced me 10 pounds on face, neck, bust and shoulders."

Mrs. Julia Leslie Plummerton, Ashland Boulevard, Chicago, writes: "I took four bottles of Dr. Edison's Obesity Pills and wore his Obesity Band five weeks and was brought down from 158 to 138, my old weight."

Laura Davis Benham, Boston, Mass., University Club, writes: "In six weeks Dr. Edison's Pills and Salt reduced me 36 pounds."

Fred. Wm. H. Phipps, Wesley College, Philadelphia, writes: "Dr. Edison's Obesity Band reduced my abdominal measurement 11 inches in four weeks."

PRICES.—Obesity Pills, $1.50 a bottle, three bottles for $4 (enough for one treatment). Obesity Fruit Salt, $1 a bottle. If either Pills or Salt is used, for both, best effects are gained by taking the Pills. Dr. Edison's common Obesity Band is $2.50 up to 50 inches in length, and 10 cents extra for each additional inch. His improved bands are a little more expensive. Send for measuring blanks.

Dr. Edison's Obesity and Supporting Bands should be used by fleshy men and women; his supporting Band by all women in a weak condition.

DR. EDISON'S Obesity Reducing Compound.

"Fat folks who want vegetable remedies in liquid form welcome Dr. Edison's newly Reducing Compound and testify to the rapid and agreeable manner in which it has taken off their superfluous flesh and left them trim and healthy." Dr. Robert Lee Sheridan in the Central Medical Inv.

Lola Mills Drew, West 9th Street, near 8th Ave., New York, writes: "Obesity Reducing Compound took off of me 11 pounds in seven weeks, giving me graceful waist and abdominal lines."

PRICE OF COMPOUND.—Two months' treatment, $6, sent prepaid to all parts of the U. S.

Dr. Edison's PILLS, SALT COMPOUND AND BANDS

Have Made Thousands Thin and Well—What These Remedies Have Done for Others They Will Do for You!

LORING & CO.

THREE STORES:
BOSTON, No. 2 Hamilton Place, Dep. J.; CHICAGO, No. 113 State Street, Dep. No. 144; NEW YORK CITY, No. 40 West 22d Street, Dep. L.

Cut this out and keep it and send for our New 21-Column Paper "How to Cure Obesity." Say you saw this in THE DELINEATOR.

Artistic House Furnishing and Decoration

(For Description see Pages 178 and 179.)

Absolutely Pure-Delicious-Nutritious

The Breakfast Cocoa
MADE BY
WALTER BAKER & CO., Limited,
DORCHESTER, MASS.

Established 1780.

Costs less
than
ONE CENT
a cup.

No
Chemicals.

Always ask your Grocer for
WALTER BAKER & CO.'S, Breakfast Cocoa
Made at
DORCHESTER, MASS.
It bears their Trade Mark, "La Belle Chocolatiere" on every can.
AVOID IMITATIONS.

Cleveland's
Baking Powder

manufactured originally by Cleveland Brothers, Albany, N. Y., now by the Cleveland Baking Powder Co., New York,

has been used by American housewives for twenty-five years, and those who have used it longest praise it most.

It is perfectly pure and wholesome.
Its composition is stated on every can.
It is always uniform and reliable.
It does the most work and the best work.
It is the strongest of all pure cream of tartar powders, as shown by the U. S. and Canadian Govt. Reports.
All the leading teachers of cookery and writers on domestic science use and recommend it.

Have you sent Ten Cents (in Stamps) for a Sample
Package of
Lowney's CHOCOLATE BON-BONS?
"Name on Every Piece."
Perfect Purity. Delicious Quality. Delightful Flavors.

P. S.—If your dealer will not supply you
we will send, on receipt of retail price,
1-lb. box, 60c; 2-lb. box, $1.50; 5-lb. box,
$3.00, delivered FREE in United States.

The Walter M. Lowney Co.
No. 88 Pearl Street,
BOSTON, MASS.

If you want a sure relief for pains in the back, side, chest or limbs, use an

Allcock's
Porous Plaster

BEAR IN MIND—Not one of the host of counterfeits and imitations is as good as the genuine.

133

FIGURE NO. 1.—LADIES' PROMENADE HAT.

FIGURE NO. 5.—YOUNG LADIES' HAT.

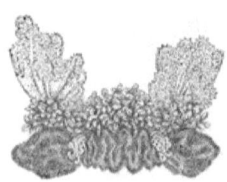

FIGURE NO. 2. LADIES' VIOLET TOQUE.

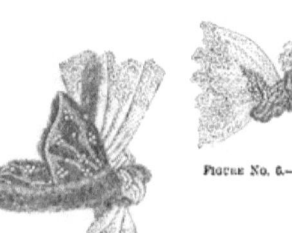

FIGURE NO. 7.—LADIES' VELVET TOQUE.

FIGURE NO. 3.—LADIES' STREET HAT.

FIGURE NO. 6.—LADIES' THEATRE HAT.

FIGURE NO. 8.—LADIES' FELT HAT.

FIGURE NO. 4.—LADIES' HAT.

FIGURE NO. 9.—LADIES' TURBAN.

FASHIONABLE HATS.
(For Descriptions see Page 161.)

FIGURE NO. 10.—LADIES' LARGE HAT.

Figure No. 180 R.—LADIES' EVENING GOWN.—This illustrates Pattern No. 8166 (copyright), price 1s. 8d. or 40 cents.
(For Description see Page 135.)

VOL. XLVII.   February, 1896.   No. 2.

Fashions of To-Day.

Capes fall away from the figure in graceful ripples.
One style of cape is finished with a quaint-looking stole collar; another is rendered picturesque by a hood of the Red Riding-Hood variety.
The absence of darts in some of the new capes brings the outline of the shoulders into prominence.
A double cape without shoulder darts is an acceptable Winter fashion.
One of the new cape-collars springs out in a mass of ripples and ends, plastron-like, in a point just at the waist-line.
Most capes are now provided with storm collars.
A many-pointed sailor-collar with revers-like cuffs, flaring cuffs and a fanciful vest is a smart addition to a jacket-basque.
Either a military or a standing collar may furnish the neck completion for an entirely plain basque.
As in previous seasons, the sailor blouse is accompanied by a deep sailor-collar, which

may have either round or pointed ends.
Characteristics of the picturesque fashions of 1830 are embodied in a long-shouldered basque-waist.
The ever-recurring surplice waist is made with very full and drooping *gigot* sleeves which contribute the desired up-to-date air.
One of the daintiest of modes for evening wear is represented in a low-cut bodice draped with a Marie Antoinette fichu.
The Louis XV. coat basques are long-skirted and made with vests and revers.
Short jacket-fronts and a long, much-rippled back distinguish one style of Louis XV. coat. Another has an added skirt of uniform length.
Pointed effects in revers, cuffs, collars and fronts are in evidence in an exceptionally dressy Louis XV. coat.
A rippled peplum confers a novel air upon a Norfolk basque.
Skirts comprise as many as seven and even nine gores.

FIGURE No. 181 R.—LADIES' MARIE ANTOINETTE EVENING WAIST.—This illustrates Pattern No. 8149 (copyright), price 1s. 3d. or 30 cents.—(For Description see Page 130.)

Entered according to Act of Congress, in the year 1896, by the Butterick Publishing Co. (Limited), in the Office of the Librarian of Congress, at Washington.

THE DELINEATOR.

FIGURE No. 180 R.—LADIES' EVENING GOWN.
(For Illustration see Page 134.)

FIGURE No. 180 R.—This illustrates a Ladies' Princess dress. The pattern, which is No. 8165 and costs 1s. 3d. or 40 cents, is in fourteen sizes for ladies from twenty-eight to forty-six inches, bust measure, and is portrayed in a different development on page 155 of the present number of THE DELINEATOR.

Marie Antoinette brocaded satin, plain satin and Dresden ribbon are here used for the gown, light-green being the prevailing color. The gown is in close-fitting Princess style closed at the left side and falls in handsome flutes in the skirt at the back and sides. It is cut low and square at the top and from the neck falls a deep ripple Bertha of Dresden ribbon shaped to form a point over each sleeve, at the center of the front and in front and back of each sleeve. Over the long double bust darts in each side of the front is applied a strap-like decoration of white satin that is rounded at the lower end and outlined with a frill of white lace edging, a large handsome button ornamenting the lower end. A frill of lace falls from the lower edges of the three-quarter length puff-sleeves, which stand out handsomely and droop from the shoulders. The dress is also arranged for a round or V neck or a high neck and full-length sleeves.

No more appropriate and becoming dinner gown for a matron could be devised than one made like this of black brocaded or plain satin of rich quality, with jewelled trimming. More youthful figures will look graceful in similar gowns of lighter hued silk. Street dresses will be of novelty or standard woollens, with fur or other appropriate trimming.

FIGURE No. 181 R.—LADIES' MARIE ANTOINETTE EVENING WAIST.
(For Illustration see Page 135.)

FIGURE No. 181 R.—This illustrates a Ladies' waist. The pattern, which is No. 8149 and costs 1s. 3d. or 30 cents, is in thirteen sizes for ladies from twenty-eight to forty-six inches, bust measure, and may be seen again on page 154 of this number of THE DELINEATOR.

Figured silk, lustrous satin, white mull and lace edging are here exquisitely united in the waist, which is in the picturesque Marie Antoinette style. The waist is cut low and square at the top and is closed at the left side of a full center-front, which is drawn in pretty, soft puffings below a frill heading. Smooth side-fronts join the smooth side-backs in under-arm and shoulder seams and the center-back

FIGURE No. 182 R.—LADIES' LOUIS XV. TOILETTE.—This consists of Ladies' Jacket-Basque No. 8151 (copyright), price 1s. 3d. or 30 cents; and Three-Piece Skirt No. 8156 (copyright), price 1s. 3d. or 30 cents.—(For Description see Page 137.)

FASHIONS FOR FEBRUARY, 1896.

corresponds in effect with the center-front. Immense elbow puff-sleeves stand out picturesquely and are shirred at the top and bottom, the shirrings at the bottom being spaced to form a small puff above a band that fits the arm closely. The gracefully draped fichu of mull is bordered with a frill of lace edging that is deepest on the shoulders; it is laid in easy folds and is softly knotted at the waistline both front and back, its ends falling over the skirt.

Gauzes, grenadines, plain and shaded *peau de soie* and the chiné weaves of silk that show exquisite floral patterns will be chosen to make a waist of this style and a chiffon, mull or lace fichu will increase its beauty and grace.

An aigrette arranged securely in a bow is effectively adjusted in the hair.

FIGURE No. 182 R.—LADIES' LOUIS XV. TOILETTE.
(For Illustration see Page 136.)

FIGURE No. 182 R.—This consists of a Ladies' jacket-basque and skirt. The jacket-basque pattern, which is No. 8151 and costs 1s. 3d. or 30 cents is in thirteen sizes for ladies from twenty-eight to forty-six inches, bust measure, and may be seen in four views on page 161. The skirt pattern, which is No. 8156 and costs 1s. 3d. or 30 cents, is in nine sizes for ladies from twenty to thirty-six inches, waist measure, and may be seen on page 167 of this number of THE DELINEATOR.

There is a decided air of elegance and refinement in the present development of the toilette, the materials being velvet-striped satin, plain velvet, plain silk and lace edging, with jet for decoration. The fanciful, independent vest is close-fitting and is decorated with jet at the center, and a frill of lace edging arranged in jabots at each side of the center, crosses the front at the neck. The jacket-basque is in Louis XV. style; its dart-fitted fronts are apart all the way down, revealing the vest prettily, and extend deeply on the skirt in sharp points, from which the basque shortens gradually toward the sides, where it is of even depth with the back. Below the waist-line the basque ripples handsomely, the ripples at the back being large and standing out well. Long, double-pointed revers lie smoothly on the fronts and extend well out on the sleeves, which are in the fashionable one-seam leg-o'-mutton style completed by gauntlet cuffs. A pointed rolling collar that flares from the top of a standing collar completes the neck. The pattern provides a wrinkled stock, which is in this instance omitted.

The three-piece skirt ripples stylishly below the hips and the fulness at the back may be gathered or plaited. The side-front seams are covered with jetted passementerie.

Brocaded or plain velvet may be used for the jacket-basque and plain, striped or figured silk, poplin, moiré or broadcloth for the skirt, or one material may be used throughout. Lace and jet or Persian trimming will enter into the decoration of the toilette if it is to have an air of elaboration.

The velvet bonnet is adorned with ribbon, jet and an aigrette.

FIGURE No. 183 R.—LADIES' CALLING COSTUME.
(For Illustration see this Page.)

FIGURE No. 183 R.—This illustrates a Ladies' costume. The

FIGURE No. 183 R.—LADIES' CALLING COSTUME.—This illustrates Pattern No. 8171 (copyright), price 1s. 8d. or 40 cents.
(For Description see this Page.)

pattern, which is No. 8171 and costs 1s. 3d. or 40 cents, is in thirteen sizes for ladies from twenty-eight to forty-six inches, bust measure, and may be seen again on page 153.

This stylish costume is here represented made of blue serge and decorated with black braid and gilt buttons. The waist is provided with a tight-fitting lining, and the fronts are drawn smoothly over the lining, the fulness below the bust being smoothly disposed in a forward-turning plait. A pointed plastron decorated at its side edges with braid imparts a stylish air to the front and is included in the neck, shoulder and arm's-eye seams at the right side and fastened with hooks and loops at the left. The bias French back is made with a center seam. A ripple peplum in two sections lengthens the waist back of the plastron, and triple-pointed epaulettes ripple over the large one-seam *gigot* sleeves, which droop to the elbow. The neck is completed by a standing collar.

The seven-gored skirt is arranged in four side-plaits at the back and ripples stylishly at the sides. A pretty decoration of braid and buttons is arranged back of the side front seams.

The costume will develop well in cloth, which is now extremely fashionable for street and calling costumes, and serge, cheviot, novelty goods, etc., are also commended. Braid, passementerie and fancy buttons will provide attractive ornamentation.

The toque is trimmed with silk, velvet, jet and an aigrette.

FIGURE No. 184 R.—LADIES' EVENING TOILETTE.
(For Illustration see this Page.)

FIGURE No. 184 R.—This consists of a Ladies' basque-waist and seven-gored skirt. The basque-waist pattern, which is No. 8174 and costs 1s. 3d. or 30 cents, is in thirteen sizes for ladies from twenty-eight to forty-six inches, bust measure, and may be seen again on page 163 of this number of THE DELINEATOR. The skirt pattern, which is No. 8154 and costs 1s. 3d. or 30 cents, is in nine sizes for ladies from twenty to thirty-six inches, waist measure, and is also shown on page 168.

Plain and figured satin are combined in this toilette, which is made quite elaborate by the decoration of lace, ribbon, spangles and fancy buttons. The basque-waist, which is in 1830 style, is made with a low, round neck and elbow puff-sleeves that extend to the neck between the full fronts and full back. It is made with a well fitted lining and is shirred all round at the top to form a pretty double puff. The fulness in the lower portion of the waist is drawn well to the center of the front and back. A handsome decoration of

FIGURE No. 184 R.—LADIES' EVENING TOILETTE.—This consists of Ladies' Basque-Waist No. 8174 (copyright), price 1s. 3d. or 30 cents; and Seven-Gored Skirt No. 8154 (copyright), price 1s. 3d. or 30 cents.
(For Description see this Page.)

ribbon all-over embroidered with spangles and caught below the puffs with fancy buttons is arranged on the waist, and deep frills of lace, which are only trimming and not a part of the

Figure No. 185 R.—Ladies' Afternoon Costume.—This illustrates Pattern No. 8132 (copyright), price 1s. 8d. or 40 cents.

(For Description see this Page.)

hips and may be box-plaited or gathered at the back. Lace arranged in jabot style covers the side-front seams of the skirt to within a short distance of the lower edge.

According to the material in which it is fashioned, this toilette may answer for day or evening wear, as it may also be made with a high neck and long sleeves. The beautiful silks, crépons, gauzy tulles and soft chiffons are available if it is intended for ceremonious wear, and novelty goods, cashmere weaves, serge, etc., are appropriate for day wear.

Figure No. 185 R.—LADIES' AFTERNOON COSTUME.

(For Illustration see this Page.)

Figure No. 185 R.—This illustrates a Ladies' costume. The pattern, which is No. 8132 and costs 1s. 8d. or 40 cents, is in thirteen sizes for ladies from twenty-eight to forty-six inches, bust measure, and may be seen again on page 152.

Figured taffeta silk and ribbon were selected for the costume in the present instance, and lace edging, insertion and ribbon decorate it tastefully. The waist is closed along the left shoulder and under-arm seams and displays fulness drawn well to the center. The front is rendered specially attractive by many upright rows of lace edging arranged at regular intervals. Underarm gores separate the front from the seamless back, which is smooth at the top and has fulness at the bottom. A gathered ribbon peplum in two sections with pointed ends adds to the length and dressiness of the waist and a twisted ribbon follows the joining, the ends terminating under ribbon bows. A ribbon stock bowed at the back covers the standing collar, and ribbon bows with long ends are secured at the top of the elbow puff-sleeves, which are banded with ribbon finished in a bow at the front of the arm.

The nine-gored skirt is gathered at the back, where it falls in full, stately folds, and it expands in deep flutes at the sides. A band of ribbon overlaid with lace insertion covers each side-front seam and a ribbon bow is tacked to it near the lower edge.

This costume is not only commended for silks and light woollen goods but for lawns, organdies and sheer fabrics that are now being prepared for wear in Southern climates. Lace edging and insertion will provide effective ornamentation in conjunction with plain or fancy ribbon.

Figure No. 186 R.—LADIES' AFTERNOON TOILETTE.

(For Illustration see Page 140.)

Figure No. 186 R.—This consists of a Ladies' basque-waist and skirt. The waist pattern, which is No. 8169 and costs 1s. 3d. or 30 cents, is in thirteen sizes for ladies from twenty-eight to forty-six inches, bust measure, and may be seen again on page 163 of this number of The Delineator. The skirt pattern, which is No. 8103 and costs 1s. 3d. or 30 cents, is in nine sizes for ladies from twenty to thir-

pattern, droop over the sleeves. A ribbon band encircles the bottom of the waist and ends in a bow in front.

The seven-gored skirt breaks into soft flute folds below the

140   THE DELINEATOR.

ty-six inches, waist measure, and is differently portrayed on its accompanying label.

The toilette is most attractive in style and is developed in velvet-striped Dresden silk and plain silk and velvet. The skirt is five-gored and expands stylishly in deep, rolling flutes at the sides and back.

The basque-waist has short jacket-fronts opening over a full, drooping vest that is formed of a middle section of velvet between two sections of silk. The back of the waist may be seamless and bias or it may be shaped with the conventional basque seams, as preferred. A circular peplum that stands out well in deep ripples lengthens the waist stylishly, its ends being far apart at the front; it is headed by a band of velvet and outlined with a row of spangled trimming. A deep, fancy collar that flares in points at each side of the back and front falls over the waist below a crush stock of the plain silk, the fancy collar being outlined with spangle trimming. Handsome buttons ornament the jacket fronts above the bust, and spangle-trimmed cuff-facings of velvet decorate the sleeves, which are in leg-o'-mutton style with the graceful droop from the shoulders.

Numerous texture and color combinations will at once suggest themselves to the tasteful woman who chooses this mode for a theatre or visiting toilette and handsomely woven woollen

FIGURE No. 186 R.—LADIES' AFTERNOON TOILETTE.—This consists of Ladies' Basque-Waist No. 8169 (copyright), price 1s. 3d. or 30 cents; and Five-Gored Skirt No. 8103 (copyright), price 1s. 3d. or 30 cents.

(For Description see Page 199.)

or silken materials will be enriched with spangled lace, gimp, jewelled trimming or heavy lace insertions.

Silk, jet, ostrich feather and an aigrette are combined in the trimming on the felt hat.

FIGURE No. 187 R.—LADIES' VISITING TOILETTE.
(For Illustration see Page 141.)

FIGURE No. 187 R.—This consists of a Ladies' jacket-basque and skirt. The jacket-basque pattern, which is No. 8142 and costs 1s. 3d. or 30 cents, is in thirteen sizes for ladies from twenty-eight to forty-six inches, bust measure, and may be seen in three views on page 160. The skirt pattern, which is No. 8021 and costs 1s. 3d. or 30 cents, is in nine sizes for ladies from twenty to thirty-six inches, waist measure, and may be seen on its accompanying label.

A deep rich shade of dahlia silk is here combined with ivory-white satin and black lace net. The jacket-basque opens over an independent fancy vest that presents a lace-edged box-plait at the center, soft fulness at each side of the plait and a deep wrinkled belt across the front. The vest is finished with a standing collar that is covered with a softly wrinkled stock closed at the back under a stylish bow. The jacket-basque has dart-fitted fronts and the back and gores are sprung below the waist-line to produce large

FASHIONS FOR FEBRUARY, 1896.

FIGURE No. 187 R.—LADIES' VISITING TOILETTE.—This consists of Ladies' Jacket-Basque No. 8142 (copyright), price 1s. 3d. or 30 cents; and Eleven-Gored Skirt No. 8021 (copyright), price 1s. 3d. or 30 cents.
(For Description see Page 140.)

rippling folds. A fancy sailor-collar overlaid with black lace net and decorated with a row of jet passementerie a short distance from the edge enhances the dressy effect; it lies smoothly on the basque and extends below the waist-line in front. Two large fancy buttons are placed on each front just back of the ends of the collar. The large one-seam leg-o'-mutton sleeves have the stylish droop from the shoulder to the elbow and are finished with upturned pointed cuffs.

Eleven gores are comprised in the skirt, which breaks into natural rippling folds below the hips and displays deeper tubular folds at the back.

This is a becoming style to all figures and may be developed in cloth, silk, velvet and novelty dress goods of various qualities. The decoration should accord with the material. A stylish toilette could be fashioned from Royal-blue faced cloth and white poplin moiré, and jet outlining could trim the sailor collar and cuffs.

The large felt hat is decorated with a fold of ribbon and ostrich feathers.

———•———

FIGURE No. 188 R.—LADIES' TEA-GOWN.
(For Illustration see Page 142.)

FIGURE No. 188 R.—This illustrates a Ladies' tea-gown. The pattern, which is No. 8172 and costs 1s. 8d. or 40 cents, is in thirteen sizes for ladies from twenty-eight to forty-six inches,

bust measure, and may be seen again on page 157 of this number of THE DE LINEATOR.

The tea-gown is in this instance elaborately developed in blue crêpon and pink silk and decorated with lace edging, insertion and lace net. It is made over a close-fitting lining that is of basque depth at the back and extends to the lower edge of the gown in front. The full center-front is gathered at the neck at each side of the closing and a pretty decoration of lace edging is arranged near the lower edge. The smooth side-fronts are fitted by single bust and under-arm darts and side-back gores connect the fronts with the seamless Watteau back, which is laid in a double box-plait at the top, the plait falling unrestrained to the lower edge. The tea-gown may be made in demi-train or round length. A fanciful collar of silk, in two sections, bordered with a deep frill of lace edging and decorated a short distance from the edge with a row of insertion, lies smoothly on the gown and is included in the joining with the standing collar, which is covered with a wrinkled stock. The puff sleeves are sustained by coat-shaped linings that are faced below the puffs with silk overlaid with lace net.

A hostess may preside at an afternoon tea arrayed in this gown, which is calculated to advantageously display plain or fancy silk, lustrous

142   THE DELINEATOR.

poplin and silk-and-wool crépon of delicate, becoming hues. Lace edging and lace insertion will provide appropriate decoration. An attractive tea-gown may be made of old-rose cashmere and flowered white taffeta.

collar, which is in two sections that meet at the center of the front and back and lie smoothly on the cape. The handsome

---

FIGURE No. 189 R.—LADIES' EMPIRE DRESS.

(For Illustration see Page 143.)

FIGURE No. 189 R.—This illustrates a Ladies' Empire dress. The pattern, which is No. 8139 and costs 1s. 8d. or 40 cents, is in thirteen sizes for ladies from twenty-eight to forty-six inches, bust measure, and may be seen again on page 156 of this number of THE DELINEATOR.

Marie Antoinette silk having a delicate apricot ground strewn with garlands is here united with plain velvet and lace edging, and jet passementerie and spangles provide rich decoration. This charming historic gown may be made with a high or low neck, with full-length or elbow puff-sleeves and with a slight train or in round length, as preferred, the pattern providing for the several styles. The short waist, which is here made with a low V neck, is slightly pointed at the center of the front and is fitted by short single bust darts and shoulder and under-arm seams and closed invisibly in front. Four pointed revers ornamented with spangles and jet passementerie stand out stylishly on the large elbow puff-sleeves and from beneath them falls a frill of deep lace edging. The sleeves are completed with pointed cuffs edged with jet passementerie and spangles. The skirt is gathered all round and falls in full soft folds; it is joined to the waist.

The gorgeous silks and velvets that are now displayed are well suited to this historic style and jet and lace insertion and edging will confer that ornamental touch so necessary to richness of effect.

FIGURE No. 190 R.—LADIES' CAPE.

(For Illustration see Page 144.)

FIGURE No. 190 R.—This illustrates a Ladies' cape. The pattern, which is No. 8150 and costs 1s. or 25 cents, is in ten sizes for ladies from twenty-eight to forty-six inches, bust measure, and is again pictured on page 159 of this number of THE DELINEATOR.

The cape is here shown made of faced cloth in a tan shade and consists of two circular capes that are dartless and smooth at the top and ripple deeply all round. At the neck is a storm collar that flares from the throat and rolls becomingly. A band of the cloth stitched on finishes all the edges of the cape stylishly, and another band is set above it along the lower edges of both capes.

The bouclé cloths showing plaids underlying the surface look very well made up into capes of this kind and, besides, are durable. Smooth cloths, will usually be selected for dressy wear.

The large felt hat is trimmed with ribbon and aigrettes.

FIGURE No. 191 R.—LADIES' CAPE, WITH STOLE COLLAR.

(For Illustration see Page 144.)

FIGURE No. 191 R.—This illustrates a Ladies' cape. The pattern, which is No. 8138 and costs 1s. or 25 cents, is in ten sizes for ladies from twenty-eight to forty-six inches, bust measure, and may be seen in two views on page 158.

Black velvet was here chosen for the cape, and feather trimming and jet ornament it elaborately. The cape, which is very elegant in effect, is in circular style and falls in graceful ripples below the shoulders, a plait laid at each side of the center seam producing additional and pleasing fulness at the back. A pretty feature is the stole

FIGURE No. 188 R.—LADIES' TEA-GOWN.—This illustrates Pattern No. 8172 (copyright), price 1s. 8d. or 40 cents.

(For Description, see Page 141.)

storm collar shapes a series of points and rolls over deeply. A cape of this kind is exceedingly chic and its construction is so simple that the mode will enjoy extended popularity. Cloth,

FASHIONS FOR FEBRUARY, 1896. 143

FIGURE No. 192 R.—LADIES'
LOUIS XV. COAT.

(For Illustration see Page 145.)

FIGURE No. 192 R.—This illustrates a Ladies' basque. The pattern, which is No. 8131 and costs 1s. 3d. or 30 cents, is in thirteen sizes for ladies from twenty-eight to forty-six inches, bust measure, and may be seen again on page 162.

This stylish Louis XV. coat is here pictured made of plain and brocaded silk, plain velvet and chiffon and decorated with lace edging and fancy buttons. The jacket fronts of brocaded silk open over a full, drooping vest of chiffon, upon which lap ornamental pieces of plain velvet that are lined with the brocade, edged with lace and reversed in tiny lapels at the top to give the effect of an under jacket or open waistcoat. A frill of lace edging drooping from the neck adds to the artistic effect, and the neck is completed by a standing collar covered with a softly wrinkled stock of plain silk. Broad, pointed revers of velvet adorned with flatly applied lace edging give a stylish effect to the jacket fronts, which are ornamented with large fancy buttons below the revers. At the back and sides the coat is closely adjusted, and a ripple peplum in two sections lengthens it becomingly, the peplum ending at the front edges of the jacket fronts. Large, one-seam *gigot* sleeves fit the forearm closely and flare decidedly above the elbow.

Fancy or plain velvet may be chosen for a basque of this kind, and so may plain and brocaded silk and combinations of velvet, silk and chiffon, with lace edging for decoration.

The hat is stylishly adorned with ribbon and feathers.

FIGURE No. 193 R.—LADIES'
EVENING WRAP.

(For Illustration see Page 145.)

FIGURE No. 193 R.—This represents a Ladies' cape. The pattern, which is No. 8176 and costs 1s. or 25 cents, is in ten sizes for ladies from twenty-eight to forty-six inches, bust measure, and is again illustrated on page 158 of this number of THE DELINEATOR.

A handsome evening wrap is shown at this figure made of a rich silk-and-wool bouclé cloth, with a becoming storm collar of Thibet fur. The cape is in circular style, hangs in ripples all round and its front edges are trimmed with a band of Thibet fur. An attractive feature is the hood, which is in Red Riding-Hood

FIGURE No. 189 R.—LADIES' EMPIRE DRESS.—This illustrates Pattern No. 8139 (copyright), price 1s. 3d. or 40 cents.
(For Description see Page 142.)

velvet, plush, silk and fancy cloakings may be employed, and such garniture will be chosen as is in harmony with the goods.

The felt hat is trimmed with satin ribbon and ostrich feathers.

style and is adjusted over the head to spread widely at the sides. It is lined with silk and shirred near its outer edge to form a frill.

Velvet, brocade, llama wool, plain silk and cloth of fine quality are used for evening wraps, while for day wear kersey, bouclé and plain heavy cloth, Astrakhan, etc., will be chosen.

FIGURE No. 194 R.—LADIES' AFTERNOON TOILETTE.
(For Illustration see Page 146.)

FIGURE No. 194 R.—This consists of a Ladies' surplice waist and skirt. The waist pattern, which is No. 8162 and costs 1s. or 25 cents, is in fourteen sizes for ladies from twenty-eight to forty-eight inches, bust measure, and is differently represented on page 164 of this magazine. The skirt pattern, which is No. 8103 and costs 1s. 3d. or 30 cents, is in nine sizes for ladies from twenty to thirty-six inches, waist measure, and is shown on its accompanying label.

The simple air of the toilette is extremely pleasing. Persian silk was used for the waist, which is in surplice style with plaited fulness in the lower part of the back. The fronts are laid in plaits and crossed in the regular way over the fitted lining on which is applied a lace-covered facing that shows above the crossing of the fronts in a becoming V. A double frill of cream lace arranged on the waist back of the plaits gives the effect of a fichu; and a black ribbon is folded about the edge of the waist and tied in a ribbon bow at the left side of the front. A bias piece of the silk is made into a stock

FIGURE No. 191 R.—LADIES' CAPE, WITH STOLE COLLAR.—This illustrates Pattern No. 8139 (copyright), price 1s. or 25 cents.
(For Description see Page 142.)

FIGURE No. 190 R.—LADIES' CAPE.—This illustrates Pattern No. 8150 (copyright), price 1s. or 25 cents.—(For Description see Page 142.)

with a large bow at the back, to cover the standing collar. Soft frills of lace drooping over the hands from the wrists of the fashionable mutton-leg sleeves complete the artistic effect.

The graceful skirt is of fancy black crépon. It consists of five gores and shows the distended effect and deep flutes of prevailing styles, and may be gathered or plaited at the back.

If a toilette of one material is preferred, camel's-hair, novelty goods, such as illuminated cheviot or serge, silk-and-wool mixtures, or fancy silk, may be chosen. Waists of light silk are tasteful with black silk, cloth, crépon or satin skirts. Spangled ribbon, gimp, lace or less elaborate trimmings may be added.

FIGURE No. 195 R.—LADIES' LOUIS XV. TOILETTE.
(For Illustration see Page 147.)

FIGURE No. 195 R.—This consists of a Ladies' jacket-basque and skirt. The basque pattern, which is No. 8136 and costs 1s. 3d. or 30 cents, is in thirteen sizes for ladies from twenty-eight to forty-six inches, bust measure, and may be seen again on page 100 of this magazine. The skirt pattern, which is No. 8154 and costs 1s.

FASHIONS FOR FEBRUARY, 1896.

opportunity as it does for rare and beautiful combinations of colors and textures. Cloths and many of the new woollens will also make up very satisfactorily in union with pretty and rich fabrics.

The hat is a jet capote trimmed with fur, ribbon and merle wings.

FIGURE NO. 196 R.—LADIES' TAILOR-MADE COSTUME.

(For Illustration see Page 148.)

FIGURE NO. 196 R.—This illustrates a Ladies' costume. The pattern, which is No. 8158 and costs 1s. 8d. or 40 cents, is in fourteen sizes for ladies from twenty-eight to forty-eight inches, bust measure, and may be seen again on page 154.

Novelty wool goods and velvet were here selected for the costume, and the dart seams are strapped and fur and buttons provide the decoration. The close-fitting Eton basque shapes a short point at the center of the front and back and is closed with button-holes and buttons below small round-cornered lapels that flare slightly from the rounding ends of a rolling coat-collar. The removable chemisette of velvet is topped

FIGURE NO. 192 R.—LADIES' LOUIS XV. COAT.—This illustrates Pattern No. 8131 (copyright), price 1s. 3d. or 30 cents.

(For Description see Page 143.)

3d. or 30 cents, is in nine sizes for ladies from twenty to thirty-six inches, waist measure, and is differently illustrated on page 168 of this number.

Black velvet, white satin overlaid with guipure lace and spangled chiffon are combined in this elegant toilette for matinées, visiting, etc., a lining of figured silk and garnitures of mink fur and jet giving an exquisite touch to the whole. The jacket-basque is in Louis XV. style and is closely fitted at the back and sides, where it extends far below the waist-line in deep outstanding flutes. Its short, pointed jacket-fronts are folded back in handsome large revers, the upper edges of which are overlapped by a deep, round collar that crosses the back. A full vest droops softly between the jacket fronts and is crossed by a plaited belt, and at the neck is a standing collar with a flaring ripple ruffle at its upper edge. The immense leg-o'-mutton sleeves are finished with large flaring cuffs.

The skirt comprises seven gores and flares and ripples in most graceful fashion. Its fulness may be collected at the back in box-plaits or gathers, as best suits the figure or the material.

Rich materials, such as brocades, satins, velvets and crépons, have a most stately and graceful effect in a toilette of this style, affording

FIGURE NO. 193 R.—LADIES' EVENING WRAP.—This illustrates Pattern No. 8176 (copyright), price 1s. or 25 cents.— (For Description see Page 143.)

by a standing collar and is closed at the left side. The one-seam *gigot* sleeves droop stylishly above the elbow and are completed by round cuff-facings of velvet outlined at the top and bottom with fur. All the edges of the basque are bordered with fur.

The five-gored skirt is arranged in four closely lapped side-plaits at the back. The side-front seams are covered with fur and three fancy buttons are placed forward of each side-front seam near the lower edge.

Broadcloth, covert cloth, cheviot, mohair and novelty goods will make up in this manner with stylish effect, and the decoration will accord with the dress goods.

FIGURE No. 194 R.—LADIES' AFTERNOON TOILETTE.—This consists of Ladies' Surplice Waist No. 8162 (copyright), price 1s. or 25 cents; and Five-Gored Skirt No. 8105 (copyright), price 1s. 3d. or 30 cents.—(For Description see Page 144.)

FIGURE No. 197 R.—LADIES' TOILETTE.

(For Illustration see Page 149.)

FIGURE No. 197 R.—This consists of a Norfolk basque and skirt. The basque pattern, which is No. 8152 and costs 1s. 3d. or 30 cents, is in thirteen sizes for ladies from twenty-eight to forty-six inches, bust measure, and is differently represented on page 161 of this magazine. The skirt pattern, which is No. 8156 and costs 1s. 3d. or 30 cents, is in nine sizes for ladies from twenty to thirty-six inches, waist measure, and may be seen again on page 167.

This toilette is especially suited for promenade, calling or church wear. It is here shown made of tweed suiting. The three-piece skirt consists of a smooth front-gore and two circular portions that ripple at the sides and meet in a seam at the center of the back; and the fulness at the back may be collected in gathers or in two box-plaits. Straps of velvet ribbon decorate the lower part of the side-front seams and just below their pointed upper ends is set a row of five small buttons.

The Norfolk basque is closely fitted and has three plaits laid on the front and two on the back, the middle plait on the front being over the closing. It is stylishly lengthened by a ripple peplum; and a belt having pointed ends is fastened at the front with a gilt buckle. Straps of velvet ribbon with gilt buttons ornamenting their pointed lower ends are placed above the bust between and back of the plaits, and the standing collar is lapped to the left side, its overlapping end being pointed. The wrists of the leg-o'-mutton sleeves are uniquely decorated with three pointed straps of velvet ribbon in graduated lengths, a button being placed in each point.

Fine plain cloth, the heather mixtures and illuminated cheviot, zibeline and covert cloth are appropriate for the mode, and fancy braid, fur binding and buttons may be used for decoration or the finish may be given by machine-stitching.

An English walking-hat trimmed with a velvet band and quills completes the toilette.

FIGURE No. 198 R.—LADIES' BLOUSE.

(For Illustration see Page 150.)

FIGURE No. 198 R.—This illustrates a Ladies' blouse. The pattern, which is No. 8144 and costs 1s. or 25 cents, is in eleven sizes for ladies from twenty-eight to forty-two inches, bust measure, and may be seen again on page 165 of this number of THE DELINEATOR.

A nautical air pervades this blouse, which is here pictured made of blue flannel. The blouse is shaped by shoulder and under-arm seams and closed at the center of the front under a box-plait that is ornamented above the bust with three large buttons. An elastic inserted in a hem at the lower edge draws the edge in closely about the waist, and the blouse droops in sailor-blouse style. The full sleeves display a box-plait at the outside of the arm and are gathered at the top and bottom and completed by round cuffs. A deep sailor-collar is at the neck, its ends flaring widely from the throat. The edges of the collar and the wrist edges of the cuffs are finished with three rows of machine-stitching done with coarse white silk.

Blouse-waists of this style are commended for cycling, rowing and various athletic exercises, as well as for general wear, and are most frequently made of serge, mohair, flannel and silk. A stylish blouse of this kind may be made of maroon cashmere and white flannel, the latter material being used for the collar and belt.

The felt alpine hat is trimmed with a velvet band and a quill.

FIGURE No. 199 R.—LADIES' PLAIN ROUND BASQUE.
(For Illustration see Page 150.)

FIGURE No. 199 R.—This illustrates a Ladies' basque. The pattern, which is No. 8143 and costs 1s. or 25 cents, is in thirteen sizes for ladies from twenty-eight to forty-six inches, bust measure, and may be seen again on page 162.

This is a style of basque that is universally becoming and is here pictured made of beige faced cloth and velvet and decorated with small fancy buttons. It is adjusted by double bust darts and the usual seams and fits closely both above and below the waist-line. Small fancy buttons are arranged in groups of five at each side of the invisible closing, which is made at the center of the front. The neck is finished with a turn-down military collar of velvet, and the one-seam *gigot* sleeves present the fashionable droop from the shoulder to the elbow and are completed with round cuff-facings of velvet. The pattern is arranged for three different lengths, the deepest being here shown.

There is a refreshing simplicity about the mode which will commend it for tailor suitings, broadcloth, cheviot, wool or mohair, serge or diagonal, camel's-hair, etc. The basque may fittingly accompany any of the new skirts, which will preferably be cut from

FIGURE No. 195 R.—LADIES' LOUIS XV. TOILETTE.—This consists of Ladies' Jacket-Basque No. 8136 (copyright), price 1s. 3d. or 30 cents; and Seven-Gored Skirt No. 8154 (copyright), price 1s. 3d. or 30 cents.—(For Description see Page 146.)

the same material, and requires no decoration, its symmetry and neat adjustment being its special charm.

FIGURE No. 200 R.—LADIES' THEATRE TOILETTE.
(For Illustration see Page 151.)

FIGURE No. 200 R.—This consists of a Ladies' cape and skirt. The cape pattern, which is No. 8153 and costs 1s. or 25 cents, is in eleven sizes for ladies from twenty-eight to forty-eight inches, bust measure, and may be seen differently depicted on page 159. The skirt pattern, which is No. 8154 and costs 1s. 3d. or 30 cents, is in nine sizes for ladies from twenty to thirty-six inches, waist measure, and may be seen again on page 168.

The cape is here pictured made of faced cloth and decorated with llama fur, and the skirt is developed in lustrous black satin. The cape, which is circular in style, is smooth and dartless at the top and may be made with or without a center seam. It breaks into deep, rippling folds below the shoulders and is closed invisibly at the center of the front. The collar is in Medici style and its edges and the edges of the cape are richly bordered with fur.

Seven gores are comprised in the skirt, which may be gathered or box-plaited at the back. The skirt expands fashionably and ripples at the sides.

The cape is a favorite garment for wear with various skirts or to complete a costume of wool for street or travelling use. For evening uses, light-colored cloths of becoming hue are chosen for its development.

The hat is trimmed with ribbon and jet.

LADIES' COSTUME (CLOSED AT THE LEFT SIDE), WITH NINE-GORED SKIRT GATHERED AT THE BACK. (TO BE MADE WITH FULL-LENGTH OR ELBOW PUFF-SLEEVES.) SUITABLE FOR LAWNS, ORGANDIES, SUMMER SILKS, ETC.
(For Illustrations see Page 152.)

No. 8132.—At figure No. 185 R in this number of THE DELINEATOR this costume is represented made of figured silk and ribbon, with lace edging and insertion and ribbon for trimming.

FIGURE No. 196 R.—LADIES' TAILOR-MADE COSTUME.—This illustrates Pattern No. 8158 (copyright), price 1s. 3d. or 40 cents.
(For Description see Page 145.)

This is a charming mode for lawn, organdy, etc., as well as for heavier goods; it is here shown made of crépon, embroidered batiste and ribbon and decorated with ribbon. The lining over which the waist is arranged is fitted by double bust darts and the usual seams and closed at the center of the front. The full front, which is supported by a lining fitted by double bust darts, is gathered at the neck and lower edge, the fulness being drawn well to the center; and the waist is closed along the left shoulder and under-arm seams with hooks and loops. Under-arm gores give a smooth trim appearance at the sides and connect the front with the seamless back, which is smooth across the shoulders and has fulness drawn in gathers at the lower edge. The large balloon-puff sleeves may be in full length or in elbow length, as preferred; the puffs are gathered at the top and bottom and stand out prettily, and a band of ribbon ending in a bow at the outside of the arm finishes the lower edge of the elbow sleeve. A generous ribbon bow is tacked on the shoulder; and the standing collar, which closes at the left side, is encircled by a wrinkled stock of ribbon bowed gracefully at the back. A ribbon peplum in two sections having pointed ends that are wide apart at the front and back lengthens the waist; the sections are gathered at their upper edges and joined to the waist, a twisted ribbon that follows the lower edge of the waist concealing the joining, and a bow with a long end is tucked over each upper back corner of the peplum.

The nine-gored skirt is smooth and dartless at the front and sides, breaking into rippling folds below the hips; and the gores at the back are gathered at the top and expand in graceful folds to the bottom, where the skirt measures about five yards and a half round in the medium sizes. The fulness is held well to the back by a strap tacked across the back-gores underneath. The placket is finished above the center seam and the top of the skirt is completed by a belt.

This is an admirable mode by which to develop the light

FASHIONS FOR FEBRUARY, 1896.

fabrics that are to do service for the South, or for the mild days North; and while it is highly commended for silk and sheer washable goods, it is also an excellent mode for light woollen goods and may be trimmed simply or profusely.

We have pattern No. 8132 in thirteen sizes for ladies from twenty-eight to forty-six inches, bust measure. To make the costume for a lady of medium size, will require seven yards and a half of crépon forty-four inches wide, with a yard and an eighth of embroidered batiste twenty-seven inches wide, and a yard and three-fourths of ribbon five inches wide. Of one fabric, it needs fourteen yards and a half twenty-two inches wide, or twelve yards and five-eighths thirty inches wide, or ten yards and a fourth thirty-six inches wide, or eight yards forty four inches wide, or seven yards and a fourth fifty inches wide. Price of pattern, 1s. 8d. or 40 cents.

LADIES' COSTUME, WITH SEVEN-GORED SKIRT ARRANGED IN FOUR SIDE-PLAITS AT THE BACK.

(For Illustrations see Page 153.)

No. 8171.— At figure No. 183 R in this number of THE DELINEATOR this costume is pictured made of blue serge and handsomely decorated with black braid and gilt buttons.

The costume is here shown made of illuminated serge and Persian velvet. The stylish waist is provided with a lining

fitted by double bust darts and the usual seams and is closed at the center of the front. It has slight fulness that is disposed in a forward-turning plait in each front to produce a perfectly smooth effect, the plait being widest at the lower edge and tapering to nothing at the bust. The fronts are joined in shoulder and under-arm seams to a bias French back that is made with a center seam, and upon them is a fancifully shaped plastron that is included in the shoulder and arm's-eye seams at the right side and fastened with hooks and loops at the left side. The plastron tapers to a point at the lower edge and is decorated at each side with a fur-bordered facing of Persian velvet and three large fancy buttons. The standing collar is of the Persian velvet bordered at each side with fur. Large one-seam leg-o'-mutton sleeves are supported by coat-shaped linings; they are gathered at the top and completed by round cuff-facings of the Persian velvet bordered with fur. Drooping stylishly over the sleeves and included smoothly in the arms'-eyes are triple-pointed epaulettes that ripple stylishly. A peplum in two sections lengthens the waist back of the plastron and its circular shaping causes it to stand out most prominently at the sides and back in ripples. The skirt has a smooth front-gore, a smooth gore at each side, and four back-gores that are arranged in two backward-turning plaits at each side of the center seam. The

FIGURE No. 197 R.—LADIES' TOILETTE.—This consists of Ladies' Basque No. 8152 (copyright), price 1s. 3d. or 30 cents; and Three-Piece Skirt No. 8156 (copyright), price 1s. 3d. or 30 cents.

(For Description see Page 146.)

The costume, which is highly commendable for general day wear, is here pictured made of dark-blue novelty suiting. The lower edge of the basque is pointed at the center both back and front in Eton style and the smooth adjustment is accomplished by a center seam, side-back and under-arm gores and double bust darts. The fronts are reversed in small, round-cornered lapels that form notches with a rolling collar having rounding corners to correspond, and in the opening appears a removable chemisette made with a shallow cape-back and a standing collar. The chemisette is closed on the left shoulder and the basque is closed with button-holes and buttons at the center of the front. The sleeves are in one-seam leg-o'-mutton style, with coat-shaped linings; they are gathered at the top and stand out fashionably above the elbow. The edges of the darts and seams are turned to one side and double-stitched flatly in welt style. A double row of stitching also finishes all the edges of the basque.

The five-gored skirt is noticeably graceful and flares fashionably toward the lower edge, where it measures five yards round in the medium sizes. The front-gore is quite smooth, while the side-gores, though smooth over the hips, break into deep flutes below; and the back-gores are each laid in two backward-turning plaits that flare broadly toward the foot. A placket is finished above the center seam and a belt completes the skirt.

Costumes like this are preferably made of serge, plain or broken-check cheviot, mohair and bouclé, although more expensive materials may be used, if

FIGURE No. 198 R.—LADIES' BLOUSE.—This illustrates Pattern No. 8144 (copyright), price 1s. or 25 cents.
(For Description see Page 146.)

shaping of the skirt produces slight ripples below the hips and the deeper flute-like folds at the back; it expands gradually toward the lower edge, where the skirt measures about five yards and an eighth round in the medium sizes. The fulness is held well to the back by a tape tacked across the plaits on the under side.

The attractive features of this costume may be brought out in crêpon, silk, cheviot and novelty goods, and the decoration will be in harmony with the material.

We have pattern No. 8171 in thirteen sizes for ladies from twenty-eight to forty-six inches, bust measure. For a lady of medium size, the costume needs eight yards and a half of dress goods forty inches wide, with three-eighths of a yard of Persian velvet twenty inches wide. Of one material, it requires fourteen yards and five-eighths twenty-two inches wide, or ten yards and five-eighths thirty inches wide, or nine yards and three-eighths thirty-six inches wide, or seven yards and a fourth forty-four inches wide, or six yards and seven-eighths fifty inches wide. Price of pattern, 1s. 8d. or 40 cents.

LADIES' COSTUME, CONSISTING OF AN ETON BASQUE WITH REMOVABLE CHEMISETTE, AND A FIVE-GORED SKIRT ARRANGED IN FOUR CLOSELY LAPPED SIDE-PLAITS AT THE BACK.
(For Illustrations see Page 151.)

No. 8158.—A stylish combination of novelty dress goods and velvet is shown in this costume at figure No. 196 R. fur, buttons and straps of the dress goods providing pleasing decoration.

FIGURE No. 199 R.—LADIES' PLAIN ROUND BASQUE.—This illustrates Pattern No. 8143 (copyright), price 1s. or 25 cents.
(For Description see Page 147.)

desired. The seams may be either strapped or machine-stitched.
We have pattern No. 8158 in fourteen sizes for ladies from

FASHIONS FOR FEBRUARY, 1896.

twenty-eight to forty-eight inches, bust measure. For a lady of medium size, the costume needs twelve yards and seven-eighths of material twenty-two inches wide, or nine yards and five-eighths thirty inches wide, or eight yards and an eighth thirty-six inches wide, or seven yards and an eighth forty-four inches wide, or six yards and three-eighths fifty inches wide. Price of pattern, 1s. 8d. or 40 cents.

LADIES' PRINCESS DRESS, CLOSED AT THE LEFT SIDE.
(TO BE MADE WITH A HIGH NECK OR WITH A ROUND, V OR SQUARE NECK AND WITH FULL-LENGTH OR THREE-QUARTER LENGTH PUFF-SLEEVES.)

(For Illustrations see Page 155.)

No. 8165.—Marie Antoinette brocaded satin, plain satin and Dresden ribbon form the handsome combination in this dress at figure No. 180 R in this magazine, lace and fancy buttons supplying the trimming.

The graceful Princess dress is here shown made of camel's-hair and a fancy striped ribbon and decorated with ribbon and passementerie. The mode is appropriate for wear on ordinary or ceremonious occasions, as it may be made with a round, square or V neck. It has well fitted fronts of lining that reach to basque depth only and are closed at the center; and the Princess front is closed invisibly at the left side along the shoulder, arm's-eye and under-arm seams. The dress is conformed to the figure by double bust darts, under-arm and side-back gores and a curving center seam, the skilful shaping of the parts below the waist-line producing flute-like folds at the sides and back that expand gracefully toward the lower edge, where the dress measures about five yards and a half round in the medium sizes. A ribbon Bertha is arranged on the dress in square outline and is headed by a band of passementerie; it shapes a deep point at the center of the front, on each sleeve and in front and back of each sleeve and ripples prettily. The standing collar, which closes at the left side, is covered with a wrinkled stock of the striped ribbon bowed broadly at the back. The sleeves may be made in full length or in three-quarter length, as preferred; they are large flaring puffs arranged on coat-shaped linings, which, in the full-length sleeves, are finished to have the effect of deep, close cuffs. A wrinkled ribbon is arranged about each sleeve at the bottom of the puff and disposed in a pretty bow at the front of the arm.

Crépon in new weaves, soft zibeline or cashmere and inexpen-

FIGURE No. 290 R.—LADIES' THEATRE TOILETTE.—This illustrates Ladies' Circular Cape No. 8153 (copyright), price 1s. or 25 cents; and Seven-Gored Skirt No. 8154 (copyright), price 1s. 3d. or 30 cents.

(For Description see Page 148.)

sive silks may be selected for the development of the dress, and if intended for ceremonious wear, silk of fine quality or silk crépon will be effective with a little lace, ribbon or passementerie.

We have pattern No. 8165 in fourteen sizes for ladies from twenty-eight to forty-six inches, bust measure. For a lady of medium size, it needs nine yards and a half of dress goods forty inches wide, with three yards and a fourth of fancy ribbon five inches and a fourth wide. Of one material, it needs seventeen pointed revers of velvet, arranged on the waist in yoke outline, stand out stylishly over a Bertha frill of lace that is narrowest at the ends and at the back and droops gracefully over the sleeves, where it is deepest. The full skirt, which measures about four yards round at the bottom in the medium sizes, may be made with a slight train or in round length; it is gathered at the top and sewed to the waist, falling in soft folds at the front and sides and in stately rolling folds at the back.

Attractive combinations of silk-and-wool goods with velvet will be arranged after this mode.

We have pattern No. 8139 in thirteen sizes for ladies from twenty-eight to forty-six inches, bust measure. To make the dress for a lady of medium size, calls for fifteen yards and three-eighths of silk with a yard and three-fourths of Persian velvet and seven-eighths of a yard of plain velvet each twenty inches wide, and six yards and a half of lace flouncing twelve inches and three-fourths wide. Of one fabric, it requires eighteen yards and three-fourths twenty-two inches wide, or thirteen yards and three-eighths thirty inches wide, or eleven yards and three-eighths thirty-six inches wide, or nine yards and three-eighths forty-four inches wide. Price of pattern, 1s. 8d. or 40 cents.

LADIES' TEA-GOWN OR WRAPPER. (TO BE MADE WITH A DEMI-TRAIN OR IN ROUND LENGTH AND WITH FULL-LENGTH OR THREE-QUARTER LENGTH PUFF-SLEEVES.)

(For Illustrations see Page 157.)

No. 8172.—By referring to figure No. 188 R in this

8132
Front View.

LADIES' COSTUME (CLOSED AT THE LEFT SIDE), WITH NINE-GORED SKIRT GATHERED AT THE BACK. (TO BE MADE WITH FULL-LENGTH OR ELBOW PUFF-SLEEVES.) SUITABLE FOR LAWNS, ORGANDIES, SUMMER SILKS, ETC. (COPYRIGHT.)

(For Description see Page 156.)

yards and an eighth twenty-two inches wide, or thirteen yards and five-eighths thirty inches wide, or twelve yards thirty-six inches wide, or ten yards and an eighth forty-four inches wide, or nine yards and an eighth fifty inches wide. Price of pattern, 1s. 8d. or 40 cents.

LADIES' EMPIRE DRESS. (TO BE MADE WITH A SLIGHT TRAIN OR IN ROUND LENGTH AND WITH A HIGH OR LOW NECK AND FULL-LENGTH OR ELBOW PUFF-SLEEVES.)

(For Illustrations see Page 156.)

No. 8139.—Silk, velvet and lace edging form the combination in this dress at figure No. 189 R in this magazine, jet passementerie and spangles providing the ornamentation.

The dress is here pictured made of silk, plain and brocaded velvet and lace edging. The fronts of the short Empire waist are pointed at the center and are fitted by short darts and closed invisibly; they join the smooth, seamless back in shoulder and under-arm seams. The pattern provides for a high or low neck and for full-length or elbow puff-sleeves. The high neck is completed with a standing collar; and the large balloon puffs are arranged over coat-shaped sleeves that extend to the wrists in the full-length sleeves. The elbow sleeves are completed with pointed rolling cuffs and a deep frill of lace edging. Four

8132
Back View.

number of THE DELINEATOR, this tea-gown may be seen made of crépon, silk, lace net and lace edging, with lace insertion for garniture.

The gown is here pictured made of rose cashmere and shaded

FASHIONS FOR FEBRUARY, 1896.

green silk and decorated with lace insertion and ribbon. It is provided with a lining, which extends to the bottom of the gown at the front and only to basque depth at the back, the lining being closely adjusted by double bust darts, single under-arm darts, side-back gores and a curving center seam; its fronts are closed to a desirable depth at the center and lapped and tacked below. The full center-front of silk is gathered at the neck at each side of a long slash, which is finished for a closing. The smooth side-fronts are fitted by single bust and long under-arm darts taken up with the corresponding darts in the lining. Side-back gores separate the front from the back, which is in Watteau style and is arranged in a double box-plait at the top, the fulness expanding gradually toward the lower edge of the gown. The gown may be made with a demi-train or in round length, as pictured. A deep fancy collar, in two sections that fall in points at each side of the Watteau and in narrow tabs at the front, is included in the seam with the standing collar and lies

8171
Front View.

smoothly on the gown; it is bordered with a row of insertion, and the standing collar is encircled with a ribbon stock bowed prettily at the back. The puff sleeves are gathered at the top and bottom and arranged on coat-shaped linings, which in the full-length sleeves are finished to have the effect of deep, round cuffs that are decorated with three encircling rows of insertion.
The assortment of fabrics suitable for this mode are numerous, and cheviot, serge, faced cloth and novelty goods are some of the textures that will make up most effectively. The gown will answer for either practical or dressy purposes, according to the

8171
Side-Back View.

LADIES' COSTUME, WITH SEVEN-GORED SKIRT ARRANGED IN FOUR SIDE-PLAITS AT THE BACK. (COPYRIGHT.)
(For Description see Page 149.)

materials employed in its construction. Silk, silk-faced crêpon and cashmere associated with silk will be frequently chosen for its development, and ribbon and lace will provide the decoration.
We have pattern No. 8172 in thirteen sizes for ladies from twenty-eight to forty-six inches, bust measure. For a lady of medium size, the garment requires eight yards and an eighth of cashmere forty inches wide, with three yards and three-eighths of silk twenty inches wide. Of one material, it needs fifteen yards and a fourth twenty-two inches wide, or eleven yards and a fourth thirty or thirty-six inches wide, or eight yards and seven-eighths forty-four inches wide. Price of pattern, 1s. 8d. or 40 cents.

LADIES' CAPE, WITH STOLE COLLAR.
(For Illustrations see Page 158.)

No. 8138.—Black velvet is shown in this cape at figure No. 191 R in this magazine, ostrich feather trimming and jet providing the garniture.
The stole collar is a stylish adjunct of the cape, which is here pictured made of plain and brocaded velvet and decorated with feather trimming. The cape, which is in circular style, falls in graceful rippling folds and is shaped by a center seam at each side of which a backward-turning plait is laid. The stole collar is in two sections that lie smoothly on the cape and fall

THE DELINEATOR.

8158
Front View.

8158

LADIES' COSTUME, CONSISTING OF AN EVEN BASQUE WITH REMOVABLE CHEMISETTE, AND A FIVE-GORED SKIRT ARRANGED IN FOUR CLOSELY LAPPED SIDE-PLAITS AT THE BACK. (COPYRIGHT.)

(For Description see Page 159.)

8158
Back View.

LADIES' CIRCULAR, RIPPLE CAPE, WITH HOOD IN RED RIDING-HOOD STYLE (COMMENDABLE FOR DAY OR EVENING WEAR).

(For Illustrations see Page 158.)

No. 8176.—At figure No. 193 R in this magazine this cape is pictured developed for evening wear in bouclé cloth, with Thibet fur for decoration and silk for the hood lining.

The hood, which is in Red Riding-Hood style, is a picturesque and practical adjunct of the cape, which is here shown made of blue eider-down cloth, the hood being lined with silk of the same color. The cape is of fashionable depth and of circular shape, with a center seam, and falls in soft, rippling folds about the figure. The high collar, which is in Medici style, is shaped by a center seam and rolls deeply in front and slightly at the back; its edges and the front edges of the cape are bordered with feather trimming. The hood, which is included in the seam with the collar, is gathered at the neck, and the lining and outside are sewed together a short distance from the outer edge to form a casing for an elastic, which draws the hood up attractively and forms an edge frill.

Bright fancy cloaking, soft to the touch and attractive to the eye, owing to the mixture of silk-and-wool, rich silk, eider-down flannel or delicate hues of cashmere, appropriately lined, will make charming evening wraps to wear at the opera, theatre or at entertainments that may occur at any season of the year.

We have pattern No. 8176 in ten sizes for ladies from twenty-eight to forty-six inches, bust measure. To make the cape for a lady of medium size, will require five yards and three-eighths of material twenty-two inches wide, or three yards and seven-eighths thirty inches wide, or three yards and a half thirty-six inches wide, or three yards and a fourth forty-four inches wide, or two yards and seven-eighths fifty-four inches wide.

deep and square at the front and back; it is included in the seam with the high flaring collar, which is fancifully shaped in four effective points and deeply rolled. Both collars are bordered with feather trimming.

The cape will be made up in smooth or rough surfaced cloth, fancy cloakings that show pretty blendings of color, velvet, plush, etc., and the decoration will harmonize with the material. A stylish cape may be developed in velours du nord and richly trimmed with jet passementerie.

We have pattern No. 8138 in ten sizes for ladies from twenty-eight to forty-six inches, bust measure. For a lady of medium size, the cape calls for four yards of plain cloaking velvet thirty inches wide, with a yard and seven-eighths of brocaded velvet twenty inches wide. Of one fabric, it calls for six yards and five-eighths twenty-two inches wide, or four yards and five-eighths thirty inches wide, or five yards and three-eighths thirty-six inches wide, or three yards and a fourth forty-four inches wide, or two yards and three-fourths fifty-four inches wide. Price of pattern, 1s. or 25 cents.

In each instance five yards and five-eighths of silk twenty inches wide will be needed to line. Price of pattern, 1s. or 25 cents.

LADIES' CIRCULAR CAPE, WITHOUT DARTS
ON THE SHOULDER. (To be Made
Single or Double.)
(For Illustrations see Page 159.)

No. 8150.—At figure No. 190 R in this number of The Delineator this cape is pictured developed in light cloth and trimmed with straps of the material.

The cape is in this instance shown made of plum-colored cloth and finished with machine-stitching. It may be made single or double and is in circular style, both capes having a center seam. The adjustment on the shoulders is smooth and dartless and the capes fall in soft ripples about the figure. The storm collar, which is high and protective, rolls slightly at the back and deeply in front. The collar and capes are closed invisibly.

The utility of a garment of this kind is obvious, since its weight can be lessened by the omission of one cape. It is suitable for all the smooth and rough surfaced cloths now fashionable.

We have pattern No. 8150 in ten sizes for ladies from twenty-eight to forty-six inches bust measure. For a lady of medium size, the double cape needs seven yards and five-eighths of material twenty-two inches wide, or five yards and three-eighths thirty inches wide, or four yards and seven-eighths thirty-six inches wide, or four yards forty-four inches wide, or three yards and an eighth fifty-four inches wide. The single long cape calls for five yards and three-fourths twenty-two inches wide, or four yards and an eighth thirty inches wide, or three yards and

8165
Back View.

8165
Front View.

8165

8165

LADIES' PRINCESS DRESS, CLOSED AT THE LEFT SIDE. (TO BE
MADE WITH A HIGH NECK OR WITH A ROUND, V OR SQUARE
NECK AND WITH FULL-LENGTH OR THREE-QUARTER
LENGTH PUFF-SLEEVES.) (COPYRIGHT.)
(For Description see Page 154.)

a fourth thirty-six inches wide, or two yards and seven-eighths forty-four inches wide, or two yards and five-eighths fifty-four

inches wide. The single short cape needs three yards twenty-two inches wide, or two yards and three-eighths thirty inches wide, or two yards and an eighth thirty-six inches wide, or a yard and five-eighths forty-four inches wide, or a yard and three-eighths fifty-four inches wide. Price of pattern, 1s. or 25 cents.

LADIES' CIRCULAR CAPE, WITHOUT DARTS. (To be Made With or Without a Center Seam.)
(For Illustrations see Page 129.)

No. 8153.—By referring to figure No. 209 R in this number of THE DELINEATOR, this cape may be seen made of cloth and trimmed with llama fur.

This graceful cape is here shown made of dark-blue cloth and velvet, and is shaped in full circular style, which causes it to fit smoothly about the neck and over the shoulders and fall in graceful flute folds below. It is fashionably long, extending to quite a distance below the waist-line and may be made with or without a center seam. At the neck is a high storm collar of dark-blue velvet rolled in Medici fashion, its ends flaring widely. The cape may be lined with a pretty changeable silk.

A beautiful evening wrap could be fashioned by this mode from light-colored brocade in stripes or floral design, with a lining of white fur, the collar being of ermine. Figured or plain velvet, Astrakhan, seal-plush, broadcloth and diagonal are suitable materials for this mode.

We have pattern No. 8153 in eleven sizes for ladies from twenty-eight to forty-eight inches, bust measure. For a lady of medium size, the cape needs three yards of cloth fifty-four inches wide, with three-eighths of a yard of velvet twenty inches wide. Of one material, it requires six yards and an eighth twenty-two inches wide, or four yards and five-eighths thirty inches wide, or three yards and seven-eighths thirty-six inches wide, or three yards and five-eighths forty-four inches wide, or three yards fifty-four inches wide. Price of pattern, 1s. or 25 cents.

LADIES' JACKET-BASQUE, WITH FANCY SAILOR-COLLAR AND SEPARATE VEST.
(For Illustrations see Page 160.)

No. 8142.—Silk, satin and lace net are combined in this jacket-basque at figure No. 187 R in this magazine, jet and buttons providing handsome decoration.

The jacket-basque is here shown made in a combination of velvet, chiffon and lace net with lace edging, gimp and a velvet

8139
Front View.

8139
Back View.

8139

8139
Back View.

LADIES' EMPIRE DRESS. (To be Made with a Slight Train or in Round Length and with a High or Low Neck and Full-Length or Elbow Puff-Sleeves.) (Copyright.)
(For Description see Page 152.)

bow for decoration. Its fronts open over an independent vest that has a plain back fitted with a center seam, and full fronts arranged on dart-fitted lining-fronts, the full fronts ending under a deep wrinkled belt of velvet that is gathered at each end. The full fronts are gathered at the top and bottom and a box-plait laid in the right front conceals the closing and is bordered with lace edging. The neck of the vest is completed with a standing collar covered with a softly wrinkled stock of velvet fastened at the back under a velvet bow. The jacket-basque is fitted by single bust darts and the usual seams, the parts being sprung below the waist-line at the sides and back to produce pretty ripples that roll backward and stand out with stylish effect. The one-seam *gigot* sleeves are supported by coat-shaped linings and have fulness at the top disposed in two rows of shirring; they droop gracefully from the shoulder to the elbow and are completed by upturned cuffs of velvet overlaid with lace net and edged with gimp. A fancy sailor-collar of velvet overlaid with lace net and bordered with gimp is a noticeably dressy feature of the basque; it lies smoothly on the basque and its long, tapering ends extend to within a short distance of the lower edge of the fronts.

The mode is appropriate for cloth, serge and various woollen textures and will develop handsomely in velvet or silk. The vest will be effective made of chiffon, silk or mull and decorated with lace edging. Black velvet and cream chiffon may be tastefully combined in a jacket-basque of this description, and three-fourths of velvet twenty inches wide, with half a yard of chiffon forty-five inches wide, and one yard of lace net twenty-

8172
Back View.

8172
Front View.

8172

8172

LADIES' TEA-GOWN OR WRAPPER. (TO BE MADE WITH A DEMI-TRAIN OR IN ROUND LENGTH AND WITH FULL-LENGTH OR THREE-QUARTER LENGTH PUFF-SLEEVES.) (COPYRIGHT.)
(For Description see Page 152.)

with it may be worn a black or colored cloth or crépon skirt.

We have pattern No. 8142 in thirteen sizes for ladies from twenty-eight to forty-six inches, bust measure. To make the garment for a lady of medium size, requires seven yards and seven-eighths twenty-two inches wide, or six yards and an eighth thirty inches wide, or five yards and a fourth thirty-six inches wide, or four yards and a fourth forty-four inches wide, or

158　　　　　　　THE DELINEATOR.

8138
Front View.
LADIES' CAPE, WITH STOLE COLLAR. (COPYRIGHT.)
(For Description see Page 154.)

8138
Back View.

over a softly folded belt of brown ribbon. The shapely jacket-fronts are turned back above the bust in broad, pointed revers that extend well out on the sleeves and are edged with feather trimming and decorated with buttons. Under-arm and side-back gores and a curving center seam give a close adjustment at the sides and back, where the basque is very much deeper than in front, and the parts are sprung below the waist-line to form deep, rolling flutes or ripples that are held together by a tape

three yards and three-fourths fifty inches wide. Price of pattern, 1s. 3d. or 30 cents.

LADIES' JACKET-BASQUE. (KNOWN AS THE LOUIS XV. COAT.)
(For Illustrations see Page 160.)

No. 8136.—A pretty combination of velvet, spangled chiffon, satin and lace net is pictured in this stylish jacket-basque at figure No. 195 R in this magazine, jet and fur ornamenting it handsomely.

This jacket-basque, which is fashionably known as the Louis

8176
Front View.
LADIES' CIRCULAR RIPPLE CAPE, WITH HOOD IN RED RIDING-HOOD STYLE. (COMMENDABLE FOR DAY OR EVENING WEAR.) (COPYRIGHT.)
(For Description see Page 154.)

tacked underneath. Large one-seam leg-o'-mutton sleeves supported by coat-shaped linings display the fashionable droop above the elbow and a close adjustment below, and are finished with upturned pointed cuffs of velvet edged with feather trimming. The neck is completed by a high standing collar to which is attached a becoming ripple ruffle having rounding front corners, and a deep, flat collar having a rounding lower outline is included in the seam with the standing collar at the back, its ends lapping prettily over on the revers. A ribbon sash-bow may be tacked to the jacket-basque over

8176
Back View.

XV. coat, is here shown made of golden-brown velvet, white chiffon, white satin and brown ribbon and decorated with feather trimming and buttons. The jacket fronts open over a full vest of chiffon arranged on lining fronts that are fitted by single bust darts and closed at the center. The vest is gathered at the top and bottom at each side of the closing and droops slightly

FASHIONS FOR FEBRUARY, 1896.

the left under-arm seam, as shown in the small engraving; it consists of two uneven ends of wide ribbon shirred in loops at the top.

Plain and fancy velvets, rich *peau de soie*, plain and lustrous or with Louis XVI. designs, will be selected for jacket-basques of this kind, and chiffon, lace or mull may

medium size, the garment requires eight yards and an eighth of velvet and three-eighths of a yard of satin each twenty inches wide, five-eighths of a yard

8150
Front View.

8150
Back View.

LADIES' CIRCULAR CAPE, WITHOUT DARTS ON THE SHOULDER. (TO BE MADE SINGLE OR DOUBLE.) (COPYRIGHT.)
(For Description see Page 156.)

be associated with them, while such decoration as jewelled buttons, feather trimming, etc., will enhance their grace and stylishness. Jacket-basques of this kind may appropriately be worn with skirts of contrasting material and plain finish.

We have pattern No. 8136 in thirteen sizes for ladies from twenty-eight to forty-six inches, bust measure. For a lady of

8153

8153
Back View.

LADIES' CIRCULAR CAPE, WITHOUT DARTS. (TO BE MADE WITH OR WITHOUT A CENTER SEAM.) (COPYRIGHT.)
(For Description see Page 156.)

8153
Front View.

of chiffon forty-five inches wide, two yards and an eighth of ribbon eight inches wide, and a half yard of ribbon six inches wide. Of one material, it calls for nine yards and a half twenty-two inches wide, or seven yards thirty inches wide, or five yards and seven-eighths thirty-six inches wide, or five yards and a fourth forty-four inches wide, or four yards and three-eighths fifty inches wide. Price of pattern, 1s. 3d. or 30 cents.

LADIES' BASQUE, WITH PLAITS LAID ON AND RIPPLE PEPLUM. (KNOWN AS THE NORFOLK BASQUE.)

(For Illustrations see Page 161.)

No. 8152.—By referring to figure No. 197 R in this number of The Delineator, this basque may be seen made of tweed and decorated with velvet ribbon and brass buttons.

One of the most effective styles in Norfolk basques is here shown made of cheviot, with a tailor finish of machine-stitching. The basque is closely fitted by single bust darts, underarm gores, side-back gores reaching to the shoulder and a center seam. A box-plait is applied on the back over each side-back seam and three similar plaits are applied on the front, the middle plait on the front concealing the closing. The basque reaches just to the waist-line and is lengthened by a ripple peplum in two sections that meet at the center of the back and front; and the waist is encircled by a belt having pointed ends. At the neck is a standing collar having a pointed, overlapping end closed at the left side. The one-seam sleeves, which are in the fashionable drooping leg-of-mutton style, are gathered at the top and made over coat-shaped linings.

The plain and fancy varieties of cheviot, plaid goods and covert cloth are liked for basques like this, which are also effective when plain goods are used for the box-plaits and plaid for the remainder. Braid and buttons may furnish the decoration.

We have pattern No. 8152 in thirteen sizes for ladies from twenty-eight to forty-six inches, bust measure. For a lady of medium size, the basque needs six yards and three-eighths of material twenty-two inches wide, or four yards thirty-six inches wide, or three yards and a fourth forty-four inches wide, or three yards fifty inches wide. Price of pattern, 1s. 3d. or 30 cents.

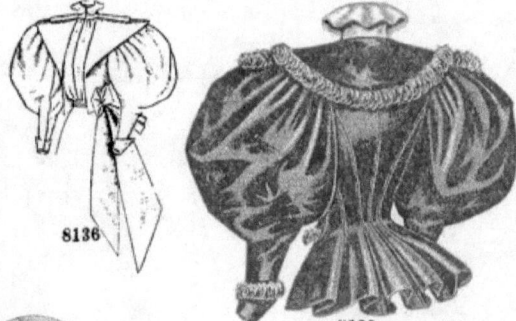

8142
8142
Front View.
8142
Back View.

LADIES' JACKET-BASQUE, WITH FANCY SAILOR-COLLAR AND SEPARATE VEST. (COPYRIGHT.)

(For Description see Page 135.)

8136
8136
Back View.
8136
Front View.

LADIES' JACKET-BASQUE. (KNOWN AS THE LOUIS XV. COAT) (COPYRIGHT.)

(For Description see Page 158.)

LADIES' JACKET-BASQUE, WITH FANCY OR PLAIN SEPARATE VEST. (KNOWN AS THE LOUIS XV. COAT.)

(For Illustrations see Page 161.)

No. 8151.—This fashionable jacket-basque is shown differently made up and trimmed at figure No. 189 R in this number of The Delineator.

The Louis XV. coat in a pleasingly modified form is here shown handsomely developed in velvet, chiffon and lace edging, with lace points, insertion and fancy buttons for garniture. A special feature of the mode is the independent vest, on which is arranged a plastron that may be omitted when greater simplicity is desired. The vest is closely fitted by single darts in the front and back and describes a point at the lower edge, the closing being made at the center of the front; the plastron of chiffon is arranged in a group of forward-turning tucks at each side of a band of insertion applied at the center. A frill of lace edging at the neck is continued in jabot style down each side of the plastron, and the neck is completed by a fancifully pointed turn-over collar in two sections attached to a high standing collar that is encircled with a wrinkled stock having frill ends fastened

FASHIONS FOR FEBRUARY, 1896

at the back. The fronts of the jacket-basque, which open all the way over the vest, shape long points below the waist-line and are fitted by single bust darts. Under-arm and side-back gores and a curving center seam adjust the basque at the sides and

LADIES' BASQUE, WITH RIPPLE PEPLUM SEWED ON.
(KNOWN AS THE LOUIS XV. COAT.)
(For Illustrations see Page 162.)

No. 8131.—Velvet, chiffon and plain and brocaded silk achieve an effective combination in this stylish basque at figure No. 192 It in this number of THE DELINEATOR, fur, lace edging and handsome buttons supplying the artistic decoration.

The basque is a charming Louis XV. mode, now very popular. A handsome combination of black satin, old-gold brocade and cream chiffon was here effected in the basque. Under-arm and side-back gores and a curving center seam perform the close adjustment at the sides and back, and lining fronts fitted by double bust darts are included in the shoulder and under-arm seams. Drooping vest-portions arranged on the lining fronts are gathered at the top and bottom and are overlapped at the sides

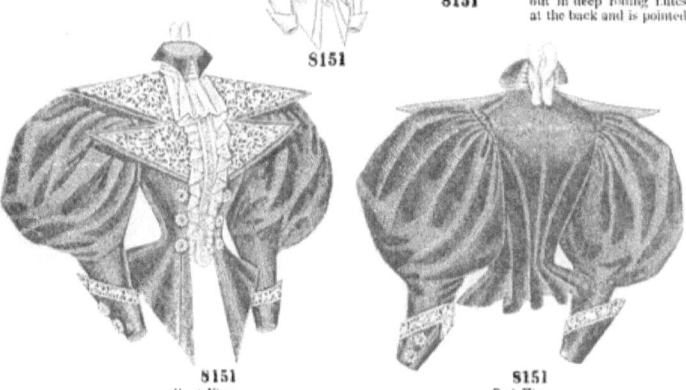

8152
8153 *Front View.*
8152 *Back View.*
LADIES' BASQUE, WITH PLAITS LAID ON AND RIPPLE PEPLUM. (KNOWN AS THE NORFOLK BASQUE.) (COPYRIGHT.)
(For Description see Page 162.)

8151
8151 *Front View.*
8151 *Back View.*
LADIES' JACKET-BASQUE, WITH FANCY OR PLAIN SEPARATE VEST. (KNOWN AS THE LOUIS XV. COAT.) (COPYRIGHT.)
(For Description see Page 163.)

back and the parts are sprung to produce fashionably outstanding ripples in the short skirt. The one-seam *gigot* sleeves are subdued by coat-shaped linings; they are shirred twice at the top and deep pointed cuffs complete them. Large revers shaped in two sharp points give a stylish finish to the jacket fronts and project well out on the sleeves; they are overlaid with lace points.

Velvet jacket-basques in Louis XV. style are worn with silk skirts at day receptions, weddings and at many brilliant social functions, and chiffon, lace and jewelled buttons are favorite decorations.

We have pattern No. 8151 in thirteen sizes for ladies from twenty-eight to forty-six inches, bust measure. For a lady of medium size, the garment needs seven yards and three-eighths of velvet twenty inches wide, with five-eighths of a yard of chiffon forty-five inches wide, and two yards and a fourth of edging six inches wide. Of one material, it calls for seven yards and three-fourths twenty-two inches wide, or five yards and three-fourths thirty inches wide, or four yards and three-fourths thirty-six inches wide, or three yards and seven-eighths forty-four inches wide, or three yards and a half fifty inches wide. Price of pattern, 1s. 3d. or 30 cents.

by longer ornamental pieces that are lined with the brocade and reversed at the top in small lapels and give the effect of an under jacket or open waistcoat. Short, loose jacket-fronts that are open all the way reveal the fanciful arrangement of the vest attractively; they are lengthened by a deep ripple peplum in two sections that flare but slightly at the center of the back. The peplum stands out in deep rolling flutes at the back and is pointed at the front ends. Large revers joined to the front edges of the jacket fronts project in points well over on the sleeves. The sleeves are in leg-o'-mutton style mounted on coat-shaped linings and present the fashionable droop. The standing collar is covered with a wide, wrinkled ribbon bowed at the back, and narrower ribbon is folded over the joining of the peplum to the basque. Feather trimming edges the revers and two large buttons are set on the jacket fronts near the lower edge, with stylish effect.

effect below as well as above the waist-line and giving a long, slender waist. The pattern provides for three different lengths, as illustrated, and the closing is made invisibly at the center of the front. The neck may be finished with a standing or turn-down military collar, both being equally stylish. The one-seam mutton-leg sleeves have the fashionable droop over the elbow, and are mounted on coat-shaped linings.

The basque is one of the standard designs that will make up satisfactorily in any material and permits elaboration in the form of fancy collars, bretelles, yokes, etc., or a decoration of passementerie, gimp, lace, ribbon or any other garniture in vogue. We have pattern No. 8131 in thirteen sizes for ladies from twenty-eight to forty-six inches, bust measure. For a lady of medium size, the basque needs five yards and three-eighths of material twenty-two inches wide, or four yards and an eighth thirty inches wide, or three yards and three-eighths thirty-six inches wide, or two yards and three-fourths forty-four inches wide, or two yards and five-eighths fifty inches wide. Price of pattern, 1s. or 25 cents.

8131
Front View.

8131
Back View.

LADIES' BASQUE, WITH RIPPLE PEPLUM SEWED ON. (KNOWN AS THE LOUIS XV. COAT) (COPYRIGHT.)
(For Description see Page 161.)

Spangled or jewelled trimmings, fancy buttons, lace and ribbon of the most elaborate description are used as garniture on basques of this style. The materials for such basques are chosen from among the richest novelty goods, and fancy or plain silk and velvet is also largely used. A fanciful basque of this type made of velvet or rich silk, or a combination of both, may supplement a skirt of black cloth or crêpon.

We have pattern No. 8131 in thirteen sizes for ladies from twenty-eight to forty-six inches, bust measure. For a lady of medium size, the basque needs six yards of plain with five-eighths of a yard of brocaded satin each twenty inches wide, and five-eighths of a yard of chiffon forty-five inches wide. Of one material, it calls for six yards and a fourth twenty-two inches wide, or four yards and five-eighths thirty inches wide, or four yards thirty-six inches wide, or three yards and a fourth forty-four inches wide, or three yards fifty inches wide. Price of pattern, 1s. 3d. or 30 cents.

LADIES' BASQUE-WAIST, WITH RIPPLE PEPLUM SEWED ON. (TO BE MADE WITH A BIAS WHOLE BACK OR A CONVENTIONAL BASQUE BACK.)
(For Illustrations see Page 163.)
No. 8169.—Velvet-striped

8143

LADIES' PLAIN ROUND BASQUE, WITH ONE-SEAM LEG-O'-MUTTON SLEEVES. (TO BE MADE WITH A STANDING OR TURN-DOWN MILITARY COLLAR AND IN ONE OF THREE DIFFERENT LENGTHS.)
(For Illustrations see this Page.)

No. 8143.—Cloth and velvet are associated in this basque at figure No. 199 R in this number of THE DELINEATOR, with small buttons for decoration.

This handsomely shaped basque is here shown made of novelty woollen goods. The usual double bust darts, under-arm and side-back gores and curving center seam are used in fitting the basque, the shaping producing a smooth

8143
Front View.

8143
Back View.

LADIES' PLAIN ROUND BASQUE, WITH ONE-SEAM LEG-O'-MUTTON SLEEVES. (TO BE MADE WITH A STANDING OR TURN-DOWN MILITARY COLLAR AND IN ONE OF THREE DIFFERENT LENGTHS.) (COPYRIGHT.)
(For Description see this Page.)

dress goods, and plain silk and velvet are shown united in this basque-waist at figure No. 186 R in this magazine, but-

FASHIONS FOR FEBRUARY, 1896.

tons and spangled passementerie providing the decoration. The waist is here shown made of camel's-hair, silk and velvet and decorated with fur and buttons. The lining over which the waist is arranged is closely adjusted by double bust darts and the usual seams and closed at the center of the front. The Eton jacket-fronts open over a full vest of silk that is formed of a narrow center-section of velvet between two full portions of silk that are gathered at the neck and lower edges and lapped over the sides of the center section, the overlapping edges being trimmed with fur. Hooks and loops close the vest at the left side of the center section and the vest is included in the shoulder and under-arm seams of the waist, which may be made with a broad, seamless bias back or with a conventional basque-back, as preferred. Large one-seam gigot sleeves, sustained by coat-shaped linings, fit the forearm closely and are bouffant above the elbow, the fulness being collected in gathers at the top. The standing collar is encircled with a softly wrinkled stock of velvet fastened at the back under a dainty bow, and a fancy collar in two sections bordered with fur is included in the seam with the standing collar and lies smoothly on the waist. The waist is lengthened by a ripple peplum in two sections that are wide apart at the front; and over the joining of the peplum is arranged a

by combining different materials. A dainty touch will be given by the introduction of a vest of silk, chiffon, etc., when velvet, silk, novelty goods, cloth and goods of light or heavy weight are used for the waist.

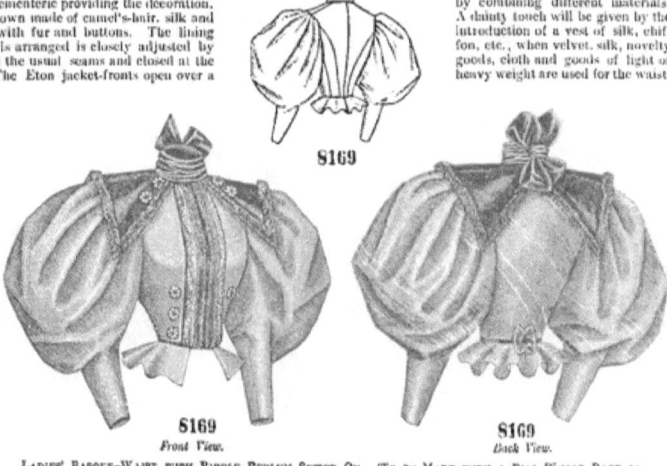

8169
Front View.

8169
Back View.

LADIES' BASQUE-WAIST, WITH RIPPLE PEPLUM SEWED ON. (TO BE MADE WITH A BIAS WHOLE-BACK OR A CONVENTIONAL BASQUE-BACK.) (COPYRIGHT.)

(For Description see Page 162.)

We have pattern No. 8169 in thirteen sizes for ladies from twenty-eight to forty-six inches, bust measure. For a lady of medium size, the basque-waist needs three yards and an eighth of dress goods forty inches wide, with one yard of velvet and a yard and a fourth of silk twenty inches wide. Of one material, it calls for six yards and seven-eighths twenty-two inches wide, or four yards and three-eighths thirty-six inches wide, or three yards and

8174

8174
Front View.

8174

8174
Back View.

LADIES' BASQUE-WAIST, IN 1830 STYLE. (TO BE MADE WITH A HIGH OR ROUND NECK AND WITH FULL-LENGTH OR ELBOW PUFF-SLEEVES.) (COPYRIGHT.)

(For Description see Page 164.)

soft band of velvet that ends under a bow at the center of the back. The attractive features in this waist may be best brought out

three-fourths forty-four inches wide, or three yards and three-eighths fifty inches wide. Price of pattern, 1s. 3d. or 30 cents.

LADIES' BASQUE-WAIST, IN 1830 STYLE. (TO BE MADE WITH A HIGH OR ROUND NECK AND WITH FULL-LENGTH OR ELBOW PUFF-SLEEVES.)

(For Illustrations see Page 163.)

No. 8174.—This waist forms part of the beautiful evening toilette shown at figure No. 184 R in this magazine, made of plain and figured satin, with an elaborate garniture of lace, ribbon, spangles and buttons.

The waist has a charmingly quaint effect, the sleeves making it distinctly of the 1830 style. It may be made with a high or low neck and with full-length or elbow puff-sleeves.

Bronze shaded silk was here used for the waist, which has a high-necked lining closely fitted by the usual seams and double bust darts. The full back and fronts are shaped in low, round outline at the top and are separated on the shoulders by the large puff-sleeves, which extend to their upper edges. The top of the fronts, back and sleeves are drawn by three rows of shirring spaced to form two pretty puffs, and the fulness at the lower edge of the waist is drawn to the center of the front and back. In the high-necked waist the lining is faced above the full portions with silk overlaid with cream lace net, and the neck is finished with a standing collar, from which, at the top, a ripple ruffle in two sections stands out prettily. A wrinkled ribbon is adjusted about the collar and fastened under an upright bow at the back. A strap extends over the closing from the collar to the lower edge of the waist and is decorated with lace rosettes. A row of insertion follows the lower edge of the waist, and a standing frill of edging rises above the full portions.

Spangled or jewelled trimming will be lovely on waists made like this of silk patterned in any of the numerous dainty designs seen this season for wear with black satin or crêpon skirts. For ordinary uses cheviot, novelty goods, serge, etc., will make up well in this way. A stylish waist may be made of cream taffeta strewn with pink roses, and pearl passementerie may follow the neck edge.

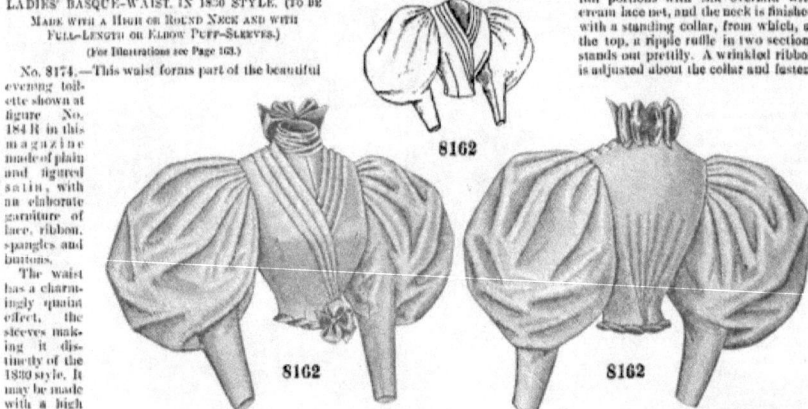

8162

LADIES' SURPLICE WAIST. (TO BE MADE WITH A HIGH NECK OR WITH A NECK LOW IN FRONT.) (COPYRIGHT.)
(For Description see Page 165.)
Front View.   8162   Back View.

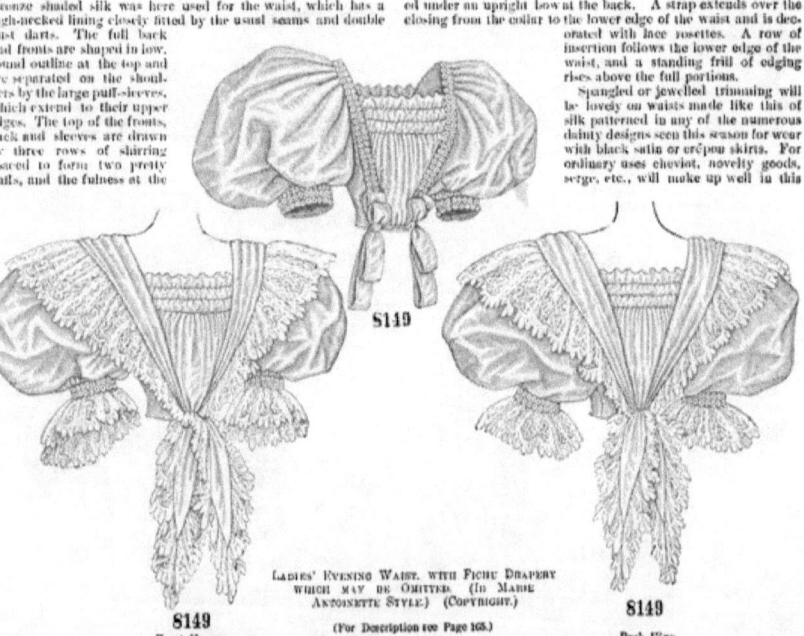

LADIES' EVENING WAIST, WITH FICHU DRAPERY WHICH MAY BE OMITTED. (IN MARIE ANTOINETTE STYLE.) (COPYRIGHT.)
(For Description see Page 165.)
8149 Front View.   8149 Back View.

FASHIONS FOR FEBRUARY, 1896.

We have pattern No. 8174 in thirteen sizes for ladies from twenty-eight to forty-six inches, bust measure. To make the garment for a lady of medium size, requires six yards and an eighth of material twenty-two inches wide, or four yards and three-eighths thirty inches wide, or three yards and three-fourths thirty-six inches wide, or three yards and an eighth forty-four inches wide. Price of pattern, 1s. 3d. or 30 cents.

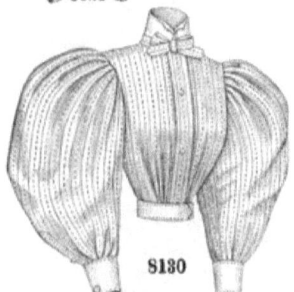

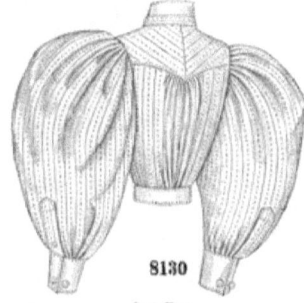

8130
Front View.
8130
Back View.

LADIES' SHIRT-WAIST. (TO BE MADE WITH PERMANENT OR REMOVABLE STANDING OR TURN-DOWN COLLAR.)
(COPYRIGHT.)
(For Description see Page 166.)

back. The one-seam leg-o'-mutton sleeves, which are made over coat-shaped linings, are gathered at the top and show a puff-like droop over the elbow. A twisted ribbon follows the lower edge of the waist and ends under a rosette bow at the front.

All materials that drape prettily, whether of woollen or silken texture, plain or fancy, are suitable for waists of this style, which is so fanciful in itself that but little decoration is required.

We have pattern No. 8162 in fourteen sizes for ladies from twenty-eight to forty-eight inches, bust measure. For a lady of medium size, the waist needs five yards and a half of material twenty-two inches wide, or three yards and seven-eighths thirty inches wide, or three yards and three-fourths thirty-six inches wide, or three yards and an eighth forty-four inches wide, or three yards fifty inches wide. Price of pattern, 1s. or 25 cents.

LADIES' EVENING WAIST, WITH FICHU DRAPERY WHICH MAY BE OMITTED. (IN MARIE ANTOINETTE STYLE.)
(For Illustrations see Page 164.)

No. 8149.— At figure No. 181 R in this magazine this waist is shown daintily developed in a combination of Marie Antoinette brocaded silk, plain satin, mull and lace edging. The waist is in Marie Antoinette style and is graceful made either with or without the fichu drapery, as illustrated in the engravings. With the drapery it is shown made of silk and lace edging, while without the drapery it is made entirely of silk. The waist is made over a lining fitted in the usual way and closed at the center of the front, and the neck is in low, square outline. The full center-front and full

LADIES' SURPLICE WAIST. (TO BE MADE WITH A HIGH NECK OR WITH A NECK LOW IN FRONT.)
(For Illustrations see Page 164.)

No. 8162.— At figure No. 194 R in this magazine this waist is pictured made of Persian silk and prettily decorated with lace edging, lace net and ribbon. The waist is in the always admired surplice style and is here shown made of camel's-hair. The fronts are rendered smooth-fitting at the sides by darts taken up with the second bust darts in the well fitted lining with which the waist is provided; and their becoming fulness is laid in deep, forward-turning plaits that lap closely at the bottom and spread toward the shoulder edges. They cross in surplice fashion, revealing the lining in a V at the top, and are separated by under-arm gores from the back, which is smooth at the top but has fulness collected in backward-turning, overlapping plaits at the bottom, the plaits flaring upward. The lining will be cut away above the fronts if a neck low in front be desired. The high-necked waist shows the lining faced and the neck finished with a standing collar that is covered with a wrinkled ribbon arranged in a bow of four outstanding loops and two ends at the

8144
Front View.
8144
Back View.

LADIES' BLOUSE, WITH SAILOR COLLAR THAT MAY BE MADE WITH SQUARE OR ROUNDING LOWER FRONT CORNERS. (COPYRIGHT.)
(For Description see Page 167.)

center-back are shirred at the top to form two puffs and a frill and are also shirred at the bottom, the fulness being drawn in soft, pretty folds. The side-fronts and side-backs are perfectly smooth and meet in seams on the shoulders and under the arms and the waist is closed at the left side of the center-front. The short sleeves are large, full puffs mounted on fitted linings; they are gathered twice at the bottom to form a small puff above the narrow bands which complete them and are also gathered at the top and prettily draped by tackings to the lining; passementerie covers the bands, and lace frills may be added, if desired. The fichu drapery, which combines the silk and lace, is in two parts and is widest on the shoulders; it extends in soft

LADIES' SHIRT-WAIST. (TO BE MADE WITH PERMANENT OR REMOVABLE STANDING OR TURN-DOWN COLLAR.)

(For Illustrations see Page 165.)

No. 8130.—Fancy striped percale was used for this stylish shirt-waist, with white linen for the collars and cuffs. The back has fulness at the center collected in gathers at the upper edge, which is joined to the lower edge of a pointed bias yoke shaped with a center seam. The fronts are smooth at the top and are closed at the center with button-holes and buttons or

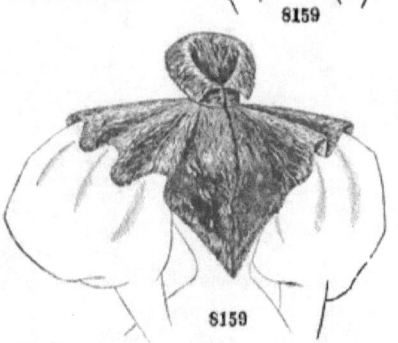

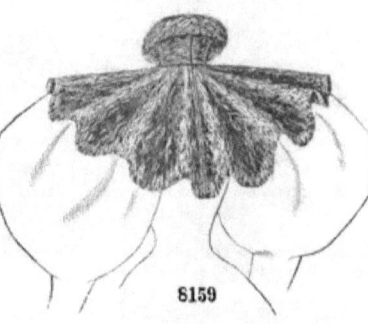

Front View. *Back View.*

LADIES' CAPE-COLLAR. (TO BE MADE WITH ROUND OR POINTED STORM COLLAR. (COPYRIGHT.)

(For Description see Page 167.)

folds down each side of the front and back and is tied at the bottom of the waist, the ends hanging below the waist in long points. Passementerie and ribbon form a pleasing decoration for the waist when the drapery is omitted.

Chiffon or gauze tissues over silk are extremely effective when made up into waists like this, and lace, ribbon, jewelled or spangled trimming, etc., are handsome for garniture. An admirable evening toilette may combine a full, flaring skirt of cream-white moiré poplin with a waist of this kind made of white chiffon bearing printed roses and plain white chiffon. The latter will be used for the fichu and the frills may be of point appliqué lace.

We have pattern No. 8149 in thirteen sizes for ladies from twenty-eight to forty-six inches, bust measure. For a lady of medium size, the waist needs five yards and five-eighths of silk twenty inches wide, with two yards and an eighth of lace edging five inches and a fourth wide. Of one material, it requires six yards twenty-two inches wide, or four yards and three-eighths thirty inches wide, or three yards and five-eighths thirty-six inches wide, or three yards and a fourth forty-four inches wide. The fichu drapery calls for a yard and a fourth of silk twenty inches wide with twelve yards of lace edging seven inches and a fourth wide.

Of one material, it calls for four yards twenty-two inches wide, or two yards and a half thirty-six inches wide, or two yards forty-five inches wide. Price of pattern, 1s. 3d. or 30 cents.

1025

LADIES' DRAWERS, EXTRA WIDE IN THE LEG. (KNOWN AS THE UMBRELLA DRAWERS.) (COPYRIGHT.)

(For Description see Page 167.)

studs through a box-plait formed at the front edge of the right front. Tapes inserted in a casing at the back are tied over the fronts to regulate the fulness at the waist. The large mutton-leg shirt sleeves, which are gathered closely at the top and slightly at the lower edge, are slashed at the back, the edges of the slashes being finished with underlaps and pointed overlaps; they are completed with straight cuffs that are closed with link buttons, and the laps are closed with a button and button-hole. The pattern provides for a standing and a turn-down collar, either of which may be made permanent or removable, as preferred. When the collar is removable, the neck is finished with a fitted band to which the collar is buttoned. The corners of the standing collar are bent back slightly and the turn-down collar is mounted on a high standing band. A belt encircles the waist and a string tie with pointed ends is tied in a bow at the throat.

Both cotton and silken textures of light weight and usually in light colors are used for shirt-waists and patterns showing small figures are preferred. The finish of stitching illustrated is seldom varied, although pipings are sometimes seen.

We have pattern No. 8130 in thirteen sizes for ladies from twenty-eight to forty-six inches, bust measure. For a lady of medium size, the shirt-waist requires three yards and a fourth of striped percale with ⅜ of a yard of linen each thirty-six inches wide. Of one material, it needs five yards twenty-two inches wide, or four yards and a

FASHIONS FOR FEBRUARY, 1896. 167

fourth twenty-seven inches wide, or three yards and a fourth thirty-six inches wide. Price of pattern, 1s. or 25 cents.

LADIES' BLOUSE, WITH SAILOR COLLAR THAT MAY BE MADE WITH SQUARE OR ROUNDING LOWER FRONT CORNERS.

(For Illustrations see Page 165.)

No. 8144.—By referring to figure No. 198 R in this magazine,

LADIES' CAPE-COLLAR. (TO BE MADE WITH ROUND OR POINTED STORM COLLAR.)

(For Illustrations see Page 166.)

No. 8159.—This cape-collar is pictured made of fur. It is shaped by a center seam and has a rounding lower outline at the back, while in front it extends to the waist-line in a deep point. It is closed invisibly and its circular shaping causes it to ripple on the shoulders and at the back. It may be completed by a rounding storm collar or by a pointed storm collar shaping a point at each side, both styles being shown in the engraving.

Velvet, plush, plain or fancy cloaking and fur will make up stylishly in this manner.

We have pattern No. 8159 in three sizes, small, medium and large. In the medium size, the cape-collar will need two yards and a fourth of material twenty-two inches wide, or a yard and three-fourths thirty inches wide, or a yard and a half thirty-six inches wide, or a yard and a fourth forty-four inches wide, or seven-

8156
Side-Front View.

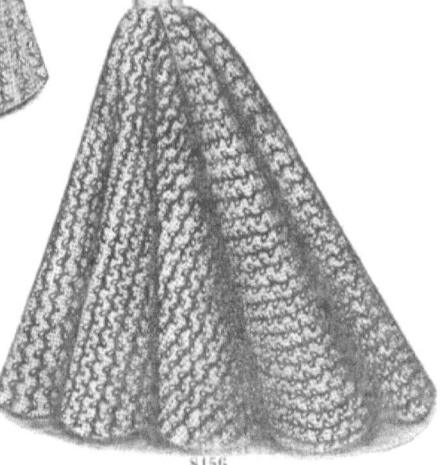

8156
Side-Back View.

LADIES' THREE-PIECE SKIRT. (TO BE GATHERED OR LAID IN TWO BOX-PLAITS AT THE BACK.) (COPYRIGHT.)
(For Description see Page 168.)

this blouse may be seen made of dark flannel and trimmed with buttons and stitching.

This style of blouse is most satisfactory and convenient for physical culture exercises and all sorts of athletic sports. It is here illustrated made of navy-blue illuminated serge and white flannel. It closes invisibly at the center of the front under a wide box-plait which is formed in the right front. The seamless back is joined to the fronts in under-arm and shoulder seams and the lower edge of the blouse is turned under for a hem, through which an elastic or tape is passed to draw the edge in close about the waist, the blouse drooping in regular sailor-blouse style. The deep and extremely wide sailor-collar may be made with square or rounding lower front corners; its ends meet at the throat and flare widely below. The full sleeve has a box-plait extending its entire length at the outside of the arm; it is gathered at the top at each side of and under the box-plait, and is also gathered at the bottom and completed with a round cuff.

French flannel, serge, cashmere, camel's-hair and outing flannel are appropriate materials for making blouse-waists of this description, and Hercules or soutache braid or machine-stitching may be employed if trimming be desired. The blouse may contrast with or match the skirt with which it is worn, according to taste.

We have pattern No. 8144 in eleven sizes for ladies from twenty-eight to forty-two inches, bust measure. To make the blouse for a lady of medium size, needs three yards and three-eighths of dark with five-eighths of a yard of light dress goods forty inches wide. Of one material, it requires five yards and a half twenty-two inches wide, or four yards and five-eighths thirty inches wide, or four yards thirty-six inches wide, or three yards and five-eighths forty-four inches wide, or three yards and a half fifty inches wide. Price of pattern, 1s. or 25 cents.

eighths of a yard fifty-four inches wide. Price of pattern, 7d. or 15 cents.

LADIES' DRAWERS, EXTRA WIDE IN THE LEG. (KNOWN AS THE UMBRELLA DRAWERS.)

(For Illustration see Page 166.)

No. 1025.—These drawers are of great width in the leg and are shown made of cambric and trimmed with a deep frill of embroidered edging below two groups of fine tucks. They are shaped with short leg-seams and widely lapped in front, and are gathered at the top across the sides and back and joined to a yoke that is round and smooth at the front and straight at the back, where it is shirred on tapes.

Fine nainsook, cambric, muslin, dimity or China silk may be selected to make the drawers, and lace or embroidery will be used as decoration.

We have pattern No. 1025 in nine sizes for ladies from twenty to thirty-six inches, waist measure. To make the garment for a lady of medium size, needs two yards and an eighth of material thirty-six inches wide. Price of pattern, 10d. or 20 cents.

LADIES' THREE-PIECE SKIRT. (To be Gathered or Laid in Two Box-Plaits at the Back.)

(For Illustrations see Page 167.)

No. 8156.—Other views of this skirt may be obtained by referring to figures Nos. 182 R and 197 R in this magazine.

The skirt is here pictured made of golden-brown novelty crépon. It is a new three-piece mode of dignified lines and fashionable width, measuring about six yards round at the bottom in the medium sizes. The front-gore is smooth and dartless, and the two very wide circular portions are smooth across the hips and have bias back edges meeting in a seam at the center of the back. The shaping causes handsome flute-like folds to fall out below the hips and the fulness at the back may be gathered or laid in a box-plait at each side of the seam, a strap tacked underneath holding the fulness in position. The placket is finished above the center seam and the top of the skirt is completed by a belt.

Fashionable dress goods of silk, silk-and-wool and all-wool are adaptable to the mode, as are also many washable fabrics. Black broadcloth may be used for a skirt of this kind, which is destined to accompany a fancy waist of silk or a Louis XV. coat-basque of velvet or some other rich material.

We have pattern No. 8156 in nine sizes for ladies from twenty to thirty-six inches, waist measure. For a lady of medium size, the skirt needs eight yards of material twenty-two inches wide, or six yards and seven-eighths thirty inches wide, or five yards and a half thirty-six inches wide, or four yards and seven-eighths forty-four or fifty inches wide. Price of pattern, 1s. 3d. or 30 cents.

LADIES' SEVEN-GORED SKIRT. (To be Box-Plaited or Gathered at the Back.)

(For Illustrations see this Page.)

No. 8154.—This skirt is shown differently made up at figures Nos. 184 R, 195 R and 200 R in this number of The Delineator.

This is an exceptionally handsome skirt and is here represented made of rich *peau de soie*. Seven gores are comprised in the skirt—a smooth front-gore, two gores at each side that are dartless and smooth across the hips but break into natural folds below, and two back-gores which may be gathered or laid in two box-plaits at the top, as preferred. Deep flute-like folds sweep out toward the lower edge, where the skirt measures about five yards and a quarter in the medium sizes, and are obtained by either plaits or gathers. A tape tacked across the back on the inside holds the folds in position. A placket is finished above the center seam and the top of the skirt is completed with a belt.

Plain or figured silk, satin, Gismonda moiré and many fashionable woollen dress goods may be developed by this mode, the graceful lines being calculated to satisfy the most exacting taste.

We have pattern No. 8154 in nine sizes for ladies from twenty to thirty-six inches, waist measure. For a lady of medium size, the skirt needs nine yards and an eighth of material twenty-two inches wide, or seven yards and seven-eighths thirty inches wide, or seven yards and a fourth thirty-six inches wide, or six yards and three-eighths forty-four inches wide, or five yards and three-eighths fifty inches wide. Price of pattern, 1s. 3d. or 30 cents.

8154
Side-Front View.

8154

8154
Side-Back View.

LADIES' SEVEN-GORED SKIRT. (To be Box-Plaited or Gathered at the Back.) (Copyright.)

(For Description see this Page.)

FASHIONS FOR FEBRUARY, 1896.

Styles for Misses and Girls.

FIGURE No. 201 R.—MISSES' OUTDOOR TOILETTE.

(For Illustration see this Page.)

FIGURE No. 201 R.—This consists of a Misses' jacket and skirt. The jacket pattern, which is No. 8137 and costs 1s. or 25 cents, is in seven sizes for misses from ten to sixteen years of age, and may be seen again on page 179 of this number of THE DELINEATOR. The skirt pattern, which is No. 8116 and costs 1s. or 25 cents, is in seven sizes for misses from ten to sixteen years of age, and is again pictured on its accompanying label.

The jacket is here shown made of gray-faced cloth and Astrakhan and decorated with Astrakhan and a handsome button. It has an extremely jaunty air and its loose double-breasted fronts are widely lapped at the top and round gracefully at the lower corners. A trim adjustment at the back and sides is due to under-arm and side-back gores and a curving center seam, the parts being sprung below the waist-line to produce pretty ripples. Stylish gored sleeves in three sections flare above the elbow and fit the arm closely below. A turn-down military collar attached to a high standing collar completes the neck. A machine-stitched welt finishes the opening to a breast pocket in the right front.

The four-gored skirt is made of striped bouclé suiting. It has a straight-back breadth gathered at the top and ripples slightly below the hips. A ribbon falls from the belt over each side-front seam and terminates in a huge rosette a short distance from the lower edge.

The skirt may be made of any stylish dress goods and the jacket of plain or fancy coatings of seasonable weight, and machine-stitching or a velvet collar will give a very dressy touch.

The poke hat is decorated with ribbon, feathers and aigrettes.

FIGURE No. 201 R.—MISSES' OUTDOOR TOILETTE.—This consists of Misses' Jacket No. 8137 (copyright), price 1s. or 25 cents; and Four-Gored Skirt No. 8116 (copyright), price 1s. or 25 cents.

(For Description see this Page.)

pattern, which is No. 8146 and costs 1s. 3d. or 30 cents, is in nine sizes for misses from eight to sixteen years of age, and is shown differently made up on page 176 of this magazine.

The dress is here pictured developed in résèda crêpon and dark-green silk and decorated with ribbon, buttons and simulated button-holes. The five-gored skirt, which is joined to the waist, ripples and flares prettily, and the fulness at the back is collected in two box-plaits that spread toward the lower edge.

Three box-plaits are laid on the front and back of the closely fitted waist. A stylish turn-down collar in two sections mounted on a high standing collar finishes the neck. About the waist is a wrinkled belt from which, at each side of the front, loops and ends of ribbon hang quite low over the skirt. The gored leg-o'-mutton sleeves are each in three sections and stand out stylishly above the elbows.

Woollen goods and velvet or plain and plaid goods may be effectively united in this dress and in its decoration the fancy for buttons may be freely indulged. Passementerie or insertion will also be attractive as a trimming.

FIGURE No. 203 R.—MISSES' AFTERNOON COSTUME.

(For Illustration see Page 171.)

FIGURE No. 203 R.—This illustrates a Misses' costume. The pattern, which is No. 8168 and costs 1s. 6d. or 35 cents, is in seven sizes for misses from ten to sixteen years of age, and may be seen again on page 173.

Fancy striped silk, plain velvet and lace net are here stylishly united in the costume. The full front and full back, which are in low round outline, are arranged on a well fitted lining that is faced above the full portions with silk overlaid with lace net to give the effect of a round yoke. A velvet Bertha, which follows the yoke outline, is bordered with a frill of lace below a band of passementerie and gathered up closely at the ends and at the center of the front under a pretty ribbon bow. A ribbon stock bowed at the back encircles the standing collar, and full puffs cover the coat-

FIGURE No. 202 R.—MISSES' DRESS.

(For Illustration see Page 170.)

FIGURE No. 202 R.—This illustrates a Misses' dress. The
A

shaped sleeves to the elbow, a decoration of lace edging giving a round cuff effect at the wrist. The waist is closed at the back and a ribbon belt terminates in long loops and ends at the closing. The pattern also provides for a low round neck and elbow puff-sleeves.

The four-gored skirt falls in stylish ripples below the hips and its straight back-breadth is gathered compactly at the top.

Some very stylish costumes are made up like this of plain or illuminated serge, fancy or plain mohair and many novelty goods; for evening or party wear fancy silk, pale tints of cashmere, gauze over silk and crêpon make up charmingly and are enhanced by such decoration as lace, passementerie and ribbon.

FIGURE NO. 204 R.—MISSES' BLOUSE.
(For Illustration see Page 171.)

FIGURE NO. 204 R.—This illustrates a Misses' blouse. The pattern, which is No. 8145 and costs 10d. or 20 cents, is in seven sizes for misses from ten to sixteen years of age, and may be seen again on page 180.

Blue and white serge were here chosen to make the blouse and Hercules braid decorates it effectively. The blouse is shaped by shoulder and under-arm seams and closed at the center of the front under a broad box-plait that is formed in the right front. The lower edge is drawn closely about the waist by a tape inserted in a casing and the blouse droops in the usual manner. The ends of the deep sailor-collar flare stylishly from the throat at each side of the plait. The full sleeves display a box-plait on the outside extending from the shoulder to the wrist and are completed by round cuffs.

A blouse of this style is serviceable for general or special wear and may be made of flannel, serge, silk or cashmere and decorated with braid or finished with machine-stitching.

FIGURE NO. 205 R.—GIRLS' DRESS.
(For Illustration see Page 172.)

FIGURE NO. 205 R.—This illustrates a Girls' dress. The pattern, which is No. 8166 and costs 1s. or 25 cents, is in eight sizes for girls from five to twelve years of age, and may be seen again on page 177.

This stylish dress is very attractive in its present development of sage-green and cream-white cashmere, with a tasteful decoration of ribbon and gilt buttons. The front and back of the waist have fulness drawn well to the center by gathers at the top and bottom and are arranged over a well fitted lining. Ripple bretelles of white cashmere are arranged at round yoke depth on the waist at each side of the fulness and fall in triple points over the sleeves, the ends tapering to points at the bottom of the waist. The neck is finished with a standing collar and the coat-shaped sleeves are covered with bouffant puffs above the elbow. The straight, full skirt is decorated with ribbon above the hem; it is gathered at the top and joined to the waist.

Cashmere, Henrietta, serge and various novelty goods will be made up in this manner and velvet or satin ribbon will contribute appropriate decoration.

FIGURE NO. 206 R.—GIRLS' DRESS.
(For Illustration see Page 172.)

FIGURE NO. 206 R.—This illustrates a Girls' dress. The pattern, which is No. 8170 and costs 1s. or 25 cents, is in seven sizes for girls from three to nine years old, and may be seen in three views on page 177.

Figured challis and plain velvet are combined in the dress in this instance and velvet ribbon is most attractively arranged for decoration. The full front of the waist droops becomingly at the center, the fulness spreading prettily toward the bottom, and the back has gathered fulness at each side of the closing. A well adjusted lining supports the waist. Large puffs droop over coat-shaped sleeves to below the elbow, and a standing collar is at the neck. The dress may be made with three-quarter length puff-sleeves and with a frill at the neck, if preferred. The deeply hemmed skirt falls in soft folds from the waist.

For any of the pretty cashmeres, crêpons and novelty goods that girls may wear this is an extremely becoming mode and it will also be appropriate for many washable fabrics. Ribbon, lace or embroidery are available for decoration.

FIGURE NO. 207 R.—GIRLS' APRON.
(For Illustration see Page 172.)

FIGURE NO. 207 R.—This illustrates a Girls' apron. The pat-

FIGURE NO. 202 R.—MISSES' DRESS.—This illustrates Pattern No. 8146 (copyright), price 1s. 3d. or 30 cents.
(For Description see Page 169.)

tern, which is No. 8147 and costs 10d. or 20 cents, is in eight sizes for girls from five to twelve years of age, and may be seen again on page 181.

Good style as well as protectiveness distinguish the apron here shown made of fine white lawn and embroidered edging. A frill-bordered Bertha fichu is a dressy adjunct; it follows the low neck of the short round waist, over which it is crossed in fichu style at the front and is closed at the back. To the waist, which is closed at the back, is joined a full skirt that is deeply

FASHIONS FOR FEBRUARY, 1896.

hemmed at the bottom. A dainty bow of satin ribbon is tacked on each shoulder.

The dress, which is fully shown on page 177, is made of plaid mohair and velvet, and is fashioned by pattern No. 8170, price 1s. or 25 cents.

The apron will answer for best wear if made of fine nainsook, cambric or lawn, and for school or ordinary use chambray in delicate shades of pink, blue, buff, lavender, etc., will be pretty

FIGURE NO. 204 R.—MISSES' BLOUSE.—This illustrates Pattern No. 8145 (copyright), price 10d. or 20 cents.
(For Description see Page 173.)

sizes for girls from three to nine years of age, and may be seen in three views on page 178 of this number of THE DELINEATOR.

The attractive little dress is here shown made up in a combination of plaid bouclé and velvet of a harmonizing shade. The full, gathered skirt is joined with a cording of velvet to the waist, which has a round yoke above full portions, the fulness in the front being laid in box-plaits and side-plaits at the top and gathered at the lower edge and drooping in French style. A turn-down collar mounted on a standing collar gives a stylish finish to the neck, and below it is a deep fancy collar that is round at the back and extends in pointed tabs on the sleeves and at each side of the front. Small gold buttons ornament the tabs effectively. The sleeves are of the one-seam leg-o'-mutton order.

Although combinations are best suited to this mode, a single material will be perfectly satisfactory if braid, ribbon or other trimming is judiciously added.

FIGURE NO. 209 R.—GIRLS' DANCING DRESS.
(For Illustration see Page 174.)

FIGURE NO. 209 R.—This illustrates a Girls' dress. The pattern, which is No. 8167, price 10d. or 20 cents, is in nine sizes for girls from two to ten years of age, and may be seen again on page 178.

Flowered silk showing an artistic chiné effect is here pictured in the dress and lace edging and ribbon contribute appropriate decoration. The dress may be worn with or without a guimpe and has a short, square-necked waist shaped by shoulder and under-arm seams and closed at the back. The full skirt is joined to the lower edge of the waist at the sides and extends to the top of the waist at the center of the front and back, where it is finished to form a frill for the neck; it hangs in full, soft folds to the lower edge, which is deeply hemmed, and long loops and ends of ribbon fall over the skirt at each side. The puff sleeves are shirred to form a frill, from under which falls a Vandyke lace frill, and Vandyke lace edging is arranged in epaulette style over the tops of the puffs.

Plain and fancy silk, chiffon over silk, pale tints of cashmere, crépon and Henrietta will make up stylishly in this manner, and flowered challis or cashmere will also develop prettily by the mode. Lace and ribbon are the most appropriate garnitures.

FIGURE NO. 203 R.—MISSES' AFTERNOON COSTUME.—This illustrates Pattern No. 8168 (copyright), price 1s. 6d. or 35 cents.
(For Description see Page 169.)

and serviceable. Lace or embroidered edging will provide effective decoration on all the materials named.

FIGURE NO. 208 R.—GIRLS' DRESS.
(For Illustration see Page 173.)

FIGURE NO. 208 R.—This represents a Girls' dress. The pattern, which is No. 8157 and costs 10d. or 20 cents, is in seven

FIGURE No. 210 R.—GIRLS' SHORT COAT.
(For Illustration see Page 174.)

FIGURE No. 210 R.—This illustrates a Girls' coat. The pat-

FIGURE No. 211 R.—GIRLS' CIRCULAR CAPE.
(For Illustration see Page 174.)

FIGURE No. 211 R.—This illustrates a Girls' cape. The pattern, which is No. 8175 and costs 10d. or 20 cents, is in ten sizes for girls from one-half to nine years of age, and may be again seen on page 179 of this number of THE DELINEATOR.
The cape is here pictured made of blue faced cloth, lined with gay plaid silk and decorated with pointed straps and gilt buttons. It is circular in shape, fitting smooth at the top and falling in large rippling folds about the figure. The hood, which is in Red Riding-Hood style, is an attractive accessory; it is shirred to form a frill at the edge and is included in the seam with the standing collar. The cape is closed at the front.
Serviceable and stylish capes of this kind are made of cloth, cheviot, heavy wool suitings and fancy cloakings, and a plain, striped or changeable silk lining is admired.
The hat is of blue felt trimmed with ostrich feathers.

MISSES' COSTUME, WITH FOUR-GORED SKIRT HAVING A STRAIGHT BACK-BREADTH. (To be Made with a High or Round Neck and with Full-Length or Elbow Puff-Sleeves.)
(For Illustrations see Page 175.)

No. 8168.—Another view of this costume, showing it made of striped silk, plain velvet and lace net, may be obtained at figure No. 203 R in this magazine, and lace, ribbon and passementerie provide the decoration.

FIGURE No. 205 R.—GIRLS' DRESS.—This illustrates Pattern No. 8166 (copyright), price 1s. or 25 cents.
(For Description see Page 179.)

tern, which is No. 8173 and costs 10d. or 20 cents, is in eight sizes for girls from five to twelve years of age, and may be seen again on page 180.
Tan broadcloth, lace net and velvet are here combined in the coat, and lace, Astrakhan, machine-stitching and buttons contribute effective decoration. The coat is closely adjusted by under-arm and side-back gores and a curving center seam, the parts being sprung below the waist-line to produce graceful ripples. The loose fronts are reversed above the closing in pointed lapels that are faced with velvet and adorned with gilt buttons. The gored leg-o'-mutton sleeves, which are each in three sections, flare above the elbow and fit closely below. The large sailor-collar is slashed at the front and back and is overlaid with lace and bordered with Astrakhan. A high standing collar is at the neck and pockets are inserted in the fronts.
Cheviot, tweed, whipcord and fancy coating may be developed in this manner and a simple finish of machine-stitching will be in good taste, although for dressy purposes some pretty garniture is commended. A stylish little coat may be fashioned from tan melton and dark-brown velvet and trimmed with steel buttons and rows of black soutache braid.
The pretty hat is stylishly trimmed with velvet and ribbon.

This charmingly simple gown is here represented made of Dresden silk, with a pretty decoration of lace and ribbon. It is appropriate for day or evening wear, as it may be made with high or low neck and with long or elbow sleeves. The waist is provided with a lining fitted by single bust darts and the usual seams and the closing is made invisibly at the back. The full front and full backs are low and round and the lining is faced above them to have the effect of a round yoke; they are gathered at the top and at the waist-line, the fulness being drawn well to the center. A draped Bertha bordered with a frill of lace falls over the waist and sleeves and is

FIGURE No. 206 R.—GIRLS' DRESS.—This illustrates Pattern No. 8170 (copyright), price 1s. or 25 cents.
(For Description see Page 179.)

draped by gathers under a ribbon rosette at the center of the front and back. The standing collar is covered with a wrinkled

FASHIONS FOR FEBRUARY, 1896. 173

stock of ribbon closed at the back under four outstanding loops. The coat-shaped sleeves are covered to the elbow with stylish puffs that are gathered at the top and bottom. A wide ribbon drawn softly about the waist is tied at the back in two loops and two long ends.

The four-gored skirt has a straight back-breadth that is closely gathered at the top, and a gore at each side and a front-gore that are dartless and smooth at the top and falls in large ripples below the hips. It expands toward the lower edge, where it measures about three yards and three-quarters round in the middle sizes. The placket is finished at the center of the back breadth and the top of the skirt is completed with a belt. The small engraving shows the effect of a low neck and sleeves of elbow length.

Silk in gay colorings, flowered and figured French cashmere, silk-faced crépon and novelty goods are materials that present possibilities for artistic effect and individuality when made up by this mode, and lace and ribbon when decoratively applied will have an improving effect.

We have pattern No. 8168 in seven sizes for misses from ten to sixteen years of age. To make the costume for a miss of twelve years, requires nine yards and a half of material twenty-two inches wide, or seven yards thirty inches wide, or five yards and three-eighths thirty-six inches wide, or four yards and seven-eighths forty-four inches wide. Price of pattern, 1s. 6d. or 35 cents.

MISSES' DRESS, CONSISTING OF A WAIST HAVING PLAITS LAID ON, AND GORED SLEEVES IN THREE SECTIONS, AND A FIVE-GORED SKIRT LAID IN TWO BOX-PLAITS AT THE BACK.

(For Illustrations see Page 176.)

No. 8146.—Crépon and silk are associated in this dress at figure No. 202 R in this number of THE DELINEATOR, ribbon, buttons and simulated button-holes providing the decoration.

The dress presents new and pretty features and is here shown made of checked bouclé suiting. The waist is fitted by single bust darts, side-back gores reaching to the shoulders and the usual under-arm gores. The darts are concealed by applied box-plaits that are widest at the top, where they pass into the shoulder seams, and narrow gradually to the waist-line, and a similar box-plait is applied at the center of the

FIGURE No. 207 R.—GIRLS' APRON.—This illustrates Pattern No. 8147 (copyright), price 10d. or 20 cents.
(For Description see Page 176.)

FIGURE No. 208 R.—GIRLS' DRESS.—This illustrates Pattern No. 8157 (copyright), price 10d. or 20 cents.
(For Description see Page 171.)

front. Three box-plaits are applied on the back to correspond with those in front, the center plait concealing the closing. The neck is completed by a standing collar to the top of which is attached a rolling collar in two sections that flare slightly at the center of the front and back, the lower front corners being prettily rounded. The gored sleeves, which are each in three sections and made over coat-shaped linings, are gathered at the top, the shaping producing a bouffant effect above the elbow and a close adjustment below.

The five-gored skirt has a front-gore and a gore at each side that are smooth at the top, and two back-gores that are laid in a box-plait at the top at each side of the placket, which is made above the center seam. The sides break into natural folds below the hips and the back expands gradually to the lower edge, where the skirt measures about three yards and a quarter in the middle sizes. The skirt is joined to the waist, which is encircled by a softly wrinkled belt of the material fastened at the back under a dainty bow.

This attractive mode is as suitable for silk, challies and goods of light weight as for cashmere, serge, cheviot and goods of similar weave.

We have pattern No. 8146 in nine sizes for misses from eight to sixteen years of age. To make the dress for a miss of twelve

striped gingham. The graceful little waist is made over a lining fitted by single bust darts and under-arm and side-back gores, and the closing is made invisibly at the center of the back. The fulness in the front and back is drawn to the center in gathers at the neck and lower edge and droops slightly in front. The standing collar is overlaid with a wrinkled satin ribbon, which is bowed stylishly at the back. Full puffs that are gathered at the top and bottom cover the coat-shaped sleeves, to the elbow, where they flare decidedly, and over them graceful triple-pointed bretelles fall in pretty ripples. The bretelles are bordered with a frill of edging and a row of insertion and sewed smoothly to the waist across the shoulders and at each side of the fulness in the front and back under twisted ribbons that are caught at the upper and lower corners of the bretelles with pretty bows. The straight, full skirt is deeply hemmed at the bottom, gathered at the top and joined to the waist.

Cashmere, Henrietta, crêpon or any pretty wool goods is appropriate to this mode, with lace, ribbon or braid for trimming.

We have pattern No. 8166 in eight sizes for girls from five to twelve years of age. To make the dress for a girl of eight years, requires seven yards of material twenty-two inches wide, or five yards and an eighth thirty inches wide, or four yards and a fourth thirty-six inches wide, or three yards and three-fourths forty-four inches wide. Price of pattern, 1s. or 25 cents.

———◆———

GIRLS' DRESS. (To be Made with Full-Length or Three-Quarter-Length Puff-Sleeves and with a Collar or a Frill at the Neck.)
(For Illustrations see Page 177.)

No. 8179.—This dress is shown made of flowered challis and velvet and trimmed with velvet ribbon at figure No. 206 R in this magazine.

This is a very pretty mode for cotton as well as woollen goods and will be acceptable to mothers who make up their little daughters' Summer wardrobes early. Striped gingham was here used for the dress, which has a full, gathered skirt depending from a round waist. A deep hem finishes the bottom of the skirt. The waist is adjusted over a lining fitted by under-arm and side-back gores, and its front and back are joined in shoulder and under-arm seams and gathered at the neck and lower edges, the front being long enough to droop prettily. The closing is made at the back. The neck may be finished with a standing collar or with a gathered lace-edged frill, as preferred.

Figure No. 209 R.—Girls' Dancing Dress.—This illustrates Pattern No. 8167 (copyright), price 10d. or 20 cents.
(For Description see Page 171.)

years, requires eight yards and a half of material twenty-two inches wide, or six yards and seven-eighths thirty inches wide, or five yards and three-eighths thirty-six inches wide, or four yards and three-eighths forty-four inches wide, or four yards and an eighth fifty inches wide. Price of pattern, 1s. 3d. or 30 cents.

———◆———

GIRLS' DRESS.
(For Illustrations see Page 177.)

No. 8166.—Green and white cashmere are pictured in this dress at figure No. 205 R in this magazine, with ribbon and buttons for decoration. The dress is here shown made of fancy

Figure No. 210 R.   Figure No. 211 R.

Figure No. 210 R.—Girls' Short Coat.—This illustrates Pattern No. 8173 (copyright), price 10d. or 20 cents.
Figure No. 211 R.—Girls' Circular Cape.—This illustrates Pattern No. 8175 (copyright), price 10d. or 20 cents.—(For Descriptions see Page 172.)

FASHIONS FOR FEBRUARY, 1896.

Large puffs arranged on the coat-shaped sleeves extend to below the elbows, and the sleeves will be cut off at the puff and finished with a lace-edged frill when elbow sleeves are desired.

Soft, full dresses like this can be made to look very dainty by the use of ribbon, lace and insertion when the dress is of silk, cashmere or other soft woollen or any cotton fabric.

We have pattern No. 8170 in seven sizes for girls from three to nine years of age. To make the dress for a girl of eight years, requires seven yards and an eighth of material twenty-two inches wide, or five yards and an eighth thirty inches wide, or four yards and a half thirty-six inches wide, or three yards and three-fourths forty-four inches wide. Price of pattern, 1s. or 25 cents.

GIRLS' DRESS, WITH FANCY COLLAR.
(For Illustrations see Page 178.)

No. 8157.—At figure No. 208 R in this number of THE DELINEATOR this dress is shown in a combination of bouclé cloth and velvet, with buttons for trimming.

Réséda shot suiting is here combined with dark-green velvet, hemmed at the bottom, gathered at the top and sewed to the waist with a cording of velvet. A velvet ribbon rosette is tacked to the bottom of the waist at each side of the fulness in the front and at the center of the back. Two rows of narrow silk braid follow the free edges of the collars. The small engraving portrays the dress with the fancy and turn-down collars omitted.

Camel's-hair, Henrietta, crépon, French flannel, cashmere and other pretty woollens may be chosen for this dress, and velvet or satin ribbon, gimp, braid, spangle trimming, etc., will make a pretty decoration.

We have pattern No. 8157 in seven sizes for girls from three to nine years of age. To make the dress for a girl of eight years, requires three yards and five-eighths of dress goods forty inches wide, with five-eighths of a yard of velvet twenty inches wide. Of one material, it needs six yards and an eighth twenty-

two inches wide, or four yards and three fourths thirty inches wide, or four yards and a fourth thirty-six inches wide, or three yards and five-eighths forty-four inches wide. Price of pattern, 10d. or 20 cents.

GIRLS' DRESS. (TO BE WORN WITH OR WITHOUT A GUIMPE.)
(For Illustrations see Page 178.)

No. 8167.—At figure No. 209 R in this magazine this charming little dress is shown made of flowered silk, with a pretty decoration of lace and ribbon.

The dress is here pictured made of Dresden silk and decorated with ribbon. The short, low-necked body is shaped by short shoulder and under-arm

8168
Front View.

8168
Back View.

MISSES' COSTUME WITH FOUR-GORED SKIRT HAVING A STRAIGHT BACK-BREADTH. (TO BE MADE WITH A HIGH OR ROUND NECK AND WITH FULL-LENGTH OR ELBOW PUFF-SLEEVES.) (COPYRIGHT.)

(For Description see Page 172.)

The waist is arranged over a lining that is closely adjusted by single bust darts and under-arm and side-back gores, and the closing is made with buttons and button-holes at the back. The upper part of the waist consists of a round yoke to which are joined the full front and full backs. The front is laid in three box-plaits separated by two forward-turning plaits at the top and is gathered at the bottom and droops in blouse fashion at the center. The back is gathered at the top and bottom, the fulness being drawn well to the center. The sleeves are of the one-seam leg-o'-mutton style, gathered at the top and made over coat-shaped linings; they droop and flare stylishly above the elbow. A deep fancy collar of velvet, shaped to form a pointed tab over each sleeve and at each side of the front, is a stylish addition to the dress. A standing collar, to the upper edge of which is joined a turn-down velvet collar in two sections, finishes the neck, the front ends of the turn-down portions being rounding and the back ends square. The full skirt is deeply

seams and the skirt extends over the body to the neck at the center of the front and back and joins the lower edge of the body at the sides after being gathered. The skirt is turned under and gathered to form a frill heading at the neck and is deeply hemmed at the bottom. The short, puff sleeves are sustained by linings and are gathered at the top and a short distance from the lower edge to form a frill. The dress is intended to be worn with or without a guimpe.

Pretty home and school dresses will be made up in this manner of various washable fabrics, like chambray, Scotch gingham, dimity, lawn, etc., and cashmere, serge or Henrietta cloth in becoming tints will be employed for serviceable dresses to wear the year round with guimpes of lawn or of taffeta or China silk.

We have pattern No. 8167 in nine sizes for girls from two to ten years of age. To make the dress for a girl of eight years, requires seven yards and seven-eighths of material twenty-two inches wide, or six yards and a half twenty-seven inches wide, or five yards and an-eighth thirty-six inches wide, or four yards and a fourth forty-four inches wide. Price of pattern, 10d. or 20 cents.

GIRLS' CIRCULAR RIPPLE CAPE, WITH HOOD IN RED RIDING-HOOD STYLE.
(For Illustrations see Page 179.)

No. 8175.—Another view of this cape, showing it made of cloth and lined with plaid silk, is given at figure No. 211 R in this number of The Delineator, pointed straps of the cloth and small buttons contributing stylish decoration.

Cloth in a warm shade of green was here selected for the cape, which has a pretty hood in Red Riding-Hood style. The cape is perfectly smooth and dartless at the top, but, being of circular shaping, hangs about the figure below the shoulders in rippling folds. A double row of machine stitching finishes the free edges of the cape and also the edges of the collar, which is in standing style with rounding ends. The hood, which is lined with silk, is included in the joining of the collar: it has gathered fulness at the neck and is drawn in far enough from the edge to form a frill. The small view shows the cape made up without the hood.

Bouclé cloths look very well made up into simple capes like this and a fur trimming at the edges is a seasonable as well as an attractive decoration. The cape and hood should be lined with bright plaid silk. If desired, the cape may be made up to match the costume, if the latter be developed in cloth or heavy serge. If the material is of unseasonable weight, an interlining may be added.

We have pattern No. 8175 in ten sizes for girls from one-half to nine years of age. To make the cape for a girl of eight years, requires two yards and five-eighths of material twenty-two inches wide, or two yards thirty inches wide, or a yard and five-eighths thirty-six inches wide, or a yard and five-eighths forty-four or fifty-four inches wide, each with two yards and three-fourths of silk to line. Price of pattern, 10d. or 20 cents.

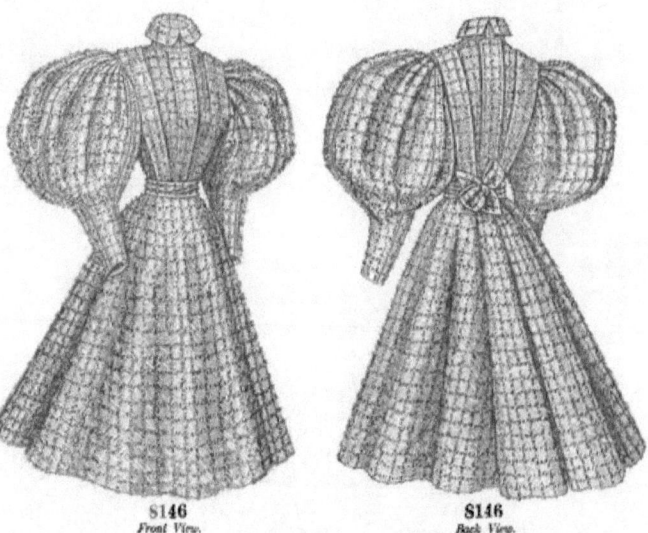

8146
Front View.

8146
Back View.

MISSES' DRESS, CONSISTING OF A WAIST HAVING PLAITS LAID ON AND GORED SLEEVES IN THREE SECTIONS, AND A FIVE-GORED SKIRT LAID IN TWO BOX-PLAITS AT THE BACK. (COPYRIGHT.)

(For Description see Page 173.)

close-fitting standing collar that closes at the throat. A breast pocket finished with a welt is inserted in the right front. The gored sleeves are each in three sections, and the fulness at the top is laid in two side-plaits at each side of two box-plaits so arranged that a seam, which is pressed open and stitched, comes at the center of each box-plait. Two rows of machine-stitching make a stylish finish for the free edges of the jacket.

Stylish coats may be made by this mode from tailor cloth, broadcloth, or from any of the plain and fancy coatings now in vogue. A pretty mode of finishing the collar would be to inlay it with a darker shade of velvet when the coat is made of light cloth. A coat of tan melton would be improved by a collar inlaid with golden-brown velvet and machine-stitching done with brown silk.

We have pattern No. 8137 in seven sizes for misses from ten to sixteen years of age. To make the jacket for a miss of twelve years, will require five yards and three-fourths of goods twenty-two inches wide, or four yards and three-eighths thirty inches wide, or three yards and five-eighths thirty-six inches wide, or two yards and seven-eighths forty-four inches wide, or two yards and a half fifty-four inches wide. Price of pattern, 1s. or 25 cents.

GIRLS' COAT, WITH LEG-O'-MUTTON SLEEVES IN THREE SECTIONS. (TO BE MADE WITH OR WITHOUT A SAILOR COLLAR THAT MAY BE PLAIN OR SLASHED.)
(For Illustrations see Page 180.)

No. 8173.—A stylish combination of cloth, velvet and lace net is shown in this coat at figure No. 210 R in this magazine, the trimming consisting of Astrakhan and buttons.

The stylish coat is here pictured made of dark-green cloth. The back and sides are nicely fitted by a center seam and under-arm and side-back gores, the shaping giving in effect a long, slender waist and producing ripples in the skirt. The loose fronts are reversed in lapels, although they close to the throat, the closing being made with hooks and loops along the lapels and with buttons and button-holes in a fly below the lapels. The lapels extend in points on a deep sailor-collar that ripples

MISSES' JACKET, WITH GORED SLEEVE IN THREE SECTIONS.
(For Illustrations see Page 179.)

No. 8137.—This jacket forms part of an outdoor toilette at figure No. 201 R in this number of The Delineator, cloth and Astrakhan being shown in its development.

Light gray box-cloth was chosen for this jaunty jacket, the loose fronts of which are lapped diagonally and closed with buttons and button-holes in a fly, a large smoked-pearl button being decoratively placed in the upper corner of the overlapping front. The lower front corners of the jacket are rounding, and at the sides and back the jacket is nicely conformed to the figure by side-back and under-arm gores and a curving center seam, the parts being sprung below the waist-line to form stylish flutes. The turn-down military rolling collar is mounted on a

FASHIONS FOR FEBRUARY, 1896.

at the center of the back and may be plain or slashed, as preferred. A standing collar is at the neck. The leg-o'-mutton sleeves are each in three sections and flare in the prevailing style across the back; its ends meet at the neck and flare widely below. The full sleeves are on the bishop order, with a box-plait arranged the entire length at the outside of the arm; they are gathered at the top and bottom and finished with round cuffs.

Blouses of this kind will make up nicely in serge, camel's-hair, cashmere and flannel, and, if desired, a decoration of Hercules or soutache braid may be added.

We have pattern No. 8145 in seven sizes for misses from ten to sixteen years of age. To make the blouse for a miss of twelve years, requires two yards and seven-eighths of dark with five-eighths of a yard of light dress goods each forty inches wide. Of one material, it needs five yards and a fourth twenty-two inches wide, or four yards thirty inches wide, or four yards thirty-six inches wide, or three yards and an eighth forty-four inches wide, or three yards fifty inches wide. Price of pattern, 10d. or 20 cents.

8166
Front View.

8166
Back View.

GIRLS' DRESS. (COPYRIGHT.)
(For Description see Page 174.)

style above the elbow; the fulness at the top is collected in two downward-turning side-plaits at each side of two box-plaits arranged so that a seam, which is stitched in tailor style, comes at the center of each box-plait. Stitching also outlines the fly and the lower edge of the jacket and black Hercules braid and soutache braid effectively edge the collars and lapels and outline curved openings to inserted side-pockets.

In coats of this kind made of plain or fancy cloth the lapels may be overlaid with fur, or fur binding may trim the coat effectively. Silk facings and trimmings of braid will also be attractive.

We have pattern No. 8173 in eight sizes for girls from five to twelve years of age. To make the coat for a girl of eight years, requires five yards and an eighth of material twenty-two inches wide, or three yards and an eighth thirty-six inches wide, or two yards and a half forty-four inches wide, or two yards fifty-four inches wide. Price of pattern, 10d. or 20 cents.

MISSES' BLOUSE, WITH SAILOR COLLAR THAT MAY BE MADE WITH SQUARE OR ROUNDING LOWER FRONT CORNERS.
(For Illustrations see Page 169.)

No. 8145.—A combination of blue and white serge is pictured in this blouse at figure No. 204 R in this magazine, with blue braid for garniture.

The blouse, which allows perfect freedom of the arms and is consequently particularly adapted to bowling and all gymnastic exercises, is here illustrated made of green serge and tan flannel. The front and back are joined in under-arm and shoulder seams and the lower edge is turned under to form a hem, in which an elastic or tape is inserted to hold the edge in closely about the waist, the blouse drooping in sailor-blouse style. The blouse closes at the front under a wide box-plait that is formed in the right front. The sailor collar, which may be made with square or rounding lower front corners, falls deep and square and is unusually wide

apron may be seen differently made up. Nainsook and embroidered edging are here united in the apron, which is thoroughly protective. The skirt is hemmed at its lower and back edges and its upper edge is gathered and joined to the short, round waist, which is shaped by shoulder and under-arm seams and closed at the back with button-holes and buttons. The apron is given its dressy air by a fichu Bertha in two sections bordered by a frill of edging. The Bertha follows the round,

GIRLS' APRON, WITH FICHU BERTHA.
(For Illustrations see Page 181.)

No. 8147.—By referring to figure No. 207 R in this number of the DELINEATOR, this dainty

8170

low neck of the waist and is crossed in surplice or fichu fashion at the front and carried about the waist to close at the back

8170
Front View.

8170
Back View.

GIRLS' DRESS. (TO BE MADE WITH FULL-LENGTH OR THREE-QUARTER LENGTH PUFF-SLEEVES AND WITH A COLLAR OR A FRILL AT THE NECK.) (COPYRIGHT.)
(For Description see Page 174.)

8157

under a full ribbon bow, the frill and bow falling prettily over the skirt.

Lawn, dotted Swiss and fine cambric are dainty for little aprons like this, and small or Swiss embroidery are pretty for trimming. White dimity will prettily develop such an apron and Irish point embroidery and ribbon may furnish the trimming.

We have pattern No. 8147 in eight sizes for girls from five to twelve years of age. To make the apron for a girl of eight years, requires two yards and a fourth of nainsook thirty-six inches wide, with four yards and a half of edging five inches and three-fourths wide. Of one material, it needs four yards and one-fourth twenty-seven inches wide, or two yards and seven-eighths thirty-six inches wide. Price of pattern, 10d. or 20 cents.

GIRLS' YOKE APRON, WITH ROUND BERTHA.

(For Illustrations see Page 182.)

No. 8160.—Aprons like this are dressy-looking as well as protective. Fine lawn is the material pictured in this apron. The upper part of the apron is a square yoke that is low and round at the top; it is shaped by shoulder seams and closed at the back, and from the yoke the skirt falls in pretty folds, being gathered at the top where it joins the yoke. The skirt is hemmed at its lower and back edges. Gathered sleeve frills, that narrow gradually under the arms where their ends are joined, are edged with narrow lace and form a pretty finish for the arms'-eyes. The yoke is entirely concealed by a smooth, round Bertha that is joined to its upper edge and bordered at the lower edge with a frill of the material edged with narrow lace. The plaited ends of sash-ties are attached to the sides of the apron at the waist-line; the ties are deeply hemmed at the loose ends and are prettily bowed at the back.

White materials of inexpensive or fine quality may be chosen for the development of this apron. Nainsook, cambric, cross-barred muslin, Swiss and India lawn are suitable for it, and lace or embroidery will provide a pretty decoration. A dainty apron was made of nainsook and the Bertha was cut from all-over embroidery and trimmed with frills of nainsook embroidered edging, the frills at the arms'-eyes being made of similar edging.

We have pattern No. 8160 in ten sizes for girls from three to twelve years of age. To make the apron for a girl of eight years, requires three yards and three-fourths of material twenty-seven inches wide, or three yards thirty-six inches wide. Price of pattern, 13d. or 20 cents.

ARTISTIC HOUSE FURNISHING AND DECORATION.

(For Illustrations see Page 181.)

An interior which lacks the element of comfort, be its appointments ever so sumptuous, repels rather than invites. Especially should the apartment in which the members of the family oftenest assemble have an atmosphere of home-like cosiness that will appeal at once to those who enter it. The architecture of some rooms almost forbids pretty effects in furnishing, yet the artistic instinct of the home-maker will suggest ways and means by which happy results may be attained. Formality is no longer the rule in the choice of furniture. All sorts of odd pieces may be brought together, though harmony must be preserved in the general effect.

A graceful hanging for a broad doorway in a hall is suggested in the first picture shown on page 181. From a pole fastened across the top are simply hung portières of figured velours —gold on a dark-green ground—which fall in rich folds to the floor. Over the top is festooned a short drapery of the velours. It is caught through the grille above the doorway and fastened at each end, where a jabot is formed, gold cord and tassels being ornamentally adjusted over the ends. A deep dado of stencilled burlap borders a plain wall paper. Before the portières, on the floor, lies a mat.

In the second view is pictured a sitting-room of homelike aspect. The floor is cov-

8157
Front View.

8157
Back View.

GIRLS' DRESS, WITH FANCY COLLAR. (COPYRIGHT.)

(For Description see Page 175.)

8167

8167
Front View.

8167
Back View.

GIRLS' DRESS. (TO BE WORN WITH OR WITHOUT A GUIMPE.) (COPYRIGHT.)

(For Description see Page 175.)

ered with red velvet filling, which is at once cheerful and effective. The wall paper is a deep cream figured with green and gold. The frieze is a scroll combining the two colors and the dado shows a figure of a darker green than that on the paper above on a ground of yet another shade of the same hue. The fire-place is tiled with white, and the cabinet mantel above is of cherry, its broad mirror reflecting the ornaments upon its shelves.

FASHIONS FOR FEBRUARY, 1896. 179

DRESSMAKING AT HOME.
(For Illustrations see Page 129.)

The handsome and dignified lines of the recent designs in gowns and jackets call into requisition the richest and most elab-

8175

The fender and trimmings of the fire-place are of brass, which lights up cheerily when the fire glows in the grate. A large sofa of red corduroy with a generous complement of cushions is placed at the right of the fire-place, and before it lies a black bearskin rug, which looks well upon the glowing carpet. A tall draught screen of fancy figured silk stands protectingly near the sofa. A round table for a lamp and books is conveniently placed, and at a little distance from it is an easy chair covered like the sofa. The tufted foot-rest is of red plush. The portières are of red velours figured with green, one hanging in straight folds and the other being simply held back with a red cord and tassel. A stand with a growing plant, near the doorway, adds a pretty note of color. A number of pictures are hung on the walls, the paper furnishing a favorable background for them. A plain brass chandelier with an elaborate center-piece is suspended from the ceiling.

The third illustration shows a tastefully furnished bed-room entpened with white and Delft-blue Brussels. The walls are covered with white paper figured with blue and upon them are hung engravings and water-color pictures. The bed of white channelled iron fitted with brass balls, and at the head is arranged a canopy of blue Liberty silk trimmed with blue silk gimp and tassels. A valance of silk is disposed round the bottom of the bed, upon which is spread a white Marseilles coverlet and embroidered linen pillow-shams. A stand near the bed supports books and a lamp. The doorway is hung with a portière of blue-and-white figured Liberty silk. The dressing-table is of cherry and stands in front of a window draped with point d'esprit curtains, a sash curtain of plain mull covering the lower sash. A wall-pocket for magazines is fixed near the dressing-table. The fire-place is laid with cream encaustic tiles and the grate and trimmings are of wrought iron. The cabinet mantel is of oak and on its shelf are pretty ornaments, which are duplicated in effect by the pretty oblong mirror behind them. An oriental rug lies before the fire-place. Near it is a large sofa upholstered in dark-blue denim, and upon it are a number of easy pillows. An easy chair matching the sofa, two fancy chairs and a denim-

8175
Front View.

8175
Back View.

GIRLS' CIRCULAR RIPPLE CAPE, WITH HOOD IN RED RIDING-HOOD STYLE. (COPYRIGHT.)
(For Description see Page 176.)

orate weaves. Nor are superb materials sufficient to gratify the present extravagant taste. Trimmings studded with spangles or mock jewels, or both, are lavishly used on these fabrics, which, though in themselves highly decorative, take kindly to this treatment. Buttons also continue to hold a prominent place among garnitures, and in their various handsome varieties—cut-steel, carved ivory or bone, pearl, Rhinestone and miniatures surrounded by Rhinestones or other mock jewels—they are truly worthy of a place on the stateliest gowns.

Sleeves have still abundant fulness above the elbow, but are shown in a host of pretty designs in which original and attractive methods of disposing the fulness are introduced. Some sleeves have a broadening effect, while in others the tendency is to give a quaint slope-shoulder appearance.

Skirts show the graceful ripples that display handsome dress materials to the fullest advantage and their fulness is disposed in a variety of ways.

Designs for jackets are almost as numerous as the jackets themselves, and the finish is usually strapped or stitched seams and edges.

FIGURE No. 1.—LADIES' PROMENADE TOILETTE.— Black satin was used for the skirt, and krimmer for the jacket of this toilette, which is dignified and in perfect taste. The jacket is in double-breasted Eton style and the fronts are reversed above the closing in wide lapels by a collar that is as wide as the lapels at the ends and may be worn standing like a storm collar. The sleeves are in three sections, with their abundant fulness arranged in box-plaits at the top. The skirt is a peculiarly graceful mode, being in two circular sections seamed at the sides and without any fulness at the top, the shaping alone producing ripples that deepen toward the back. The jacket

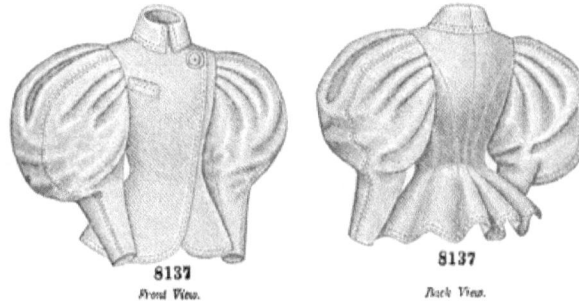

8137
Front View.

8137
Back View.

MISSES' JACKET, WITH GORED SLEEVE IN THREE SECTIONS. (COPYRIGHT.)
(For Description see Page 176.)

covered foot-rest complete the furnishings. The chandelier is of brass. The bed might be hidden by a screen covered with denim embroidered with white cotton in chain stitch, and the room might thus be made to perform the double duty of bed-room and boudoir. A bed room could be daintily furnished in printed or plain denim of any preferred color. The material could be used for furniture and hangings.

pattern is No. 7997, and the skirt is No. 7902, each costing 1s. 3d. or 30 cents.

FIGURE No. 2.—COMBINATION AND DECORATION FOR A LADIES' EVENING COSTUME.—The tasteful combination represented in this costume embraces Marie Antoinette brocade and pale-green satin, the brocade repeating the green tone with a charming commingling of rose and yellow in numerous delicate tints.

The skirt is made with nine gores and is of great width at the lower edge, hanging in straight folds at the back and rippling at the sides. A frill of point appliqué lace is headed with smilax and sprays of blossoms. A Marie Antoinette fichu gives a picturesque air to the bodice; it outlines the round neck at the back and frames gathered fulness at the front, where the neck is in Pompadour outline followed by smilax. The ends of the fichu are fastened over a deep, wrinkled girdle under nosegays, from which sprays of smilax droop upon the skirt. The back has slight fulness in the lower part. Long Suède gloves meet the short puff-sleeves, which are the only portions of the waist cut from brocade. This exquisite toilette may be duplicated by pattern No. 8075, price 1s. 3d. or 40 cents.

FIGURE No. 3.—DECORATION FOR A LADIES' COAT.—The ornamentation of buttons and machine-stitched straps shown on this coat is very jaunty. The coat was made of dark-green covert cloth, the pattern used being No. 8081, price 1s. 3d. or 30 cents. The back is seamless at the center and fulness below the waist-line of each side-back seam is underfolded in a box-plait, while the skirt ripples at the sides. The fronts lap diagonally from the shoulder and the closing is fashionably made at the top and below the waist-line, buttons being placed at the center and right side to correspond with the upper closing button. The sleeves extend to the neck over the shoulders and pointed straps ornamented with buttons and covered with stitching are arranged on them. Straps to match finish the edges of the coat and collar. The collar is in turn-down military style (though it may be of the standing order) and has a pointed strap over its ends.

FIGURE No. 4.—STYLISH COMBINATION FOR A LADIES' BASQUE-WAIST.—This waist was made by pattern No. 8102, which costs 1s. 3d. or 30 cents, and it is known as the Valkyrie waist. It may have a bias whole back or a regular basque-fitted back, the lower part of the back being concealed by a broad bias girdle closed with two large buttons and button-holes at the left of the front. The front is very fanciful, having smooth side-fronts and a full vest drooping very slightly over the girdle. The vest is framed by the tapering ends of a fancy collar that passes round the back at round-yoke depth and extends in points at the front and back on the

pleasing, black satin and plaid silk being effectively united.

FIGURE No. 5.—DECORATION FOR A LADIES' BOX-COAT.—The stylish coat here shown was made of mode faced cloth by pattern No. 8099, price 1s. 3d. or 30 cents. The back is half-fitting instead of in the usual loose and less becoming box style, and the

8173   8173

8173
Front View.   Back View.

GIRLS' COAT, WITH LEG-O'-MUTTON SLEEVES IN THREE SECTIONS. (TO BE MADE WITH OR WITHOUT A SAILOR COLLAR THAT MAY BE PLAIN OR SLASHED.) (COPYRIGHT.)

(For Description see Page 176.)

fronts, though loose, are skilfully shaped to reveal the curves of the figure. Above the bust the fronts are reversed in notched lapels by a rolling collar and they are closed with button-holes and large pearl buttons placed just below the bust and waist-line. Side pockets are inserted, square-cornered laps concealing the openings to them. The fulness at the top of the gored sleeves is collected in downward-turning plaits in front and back of the shoulders and their seams are covered with wide straps stitched on at both edges. All the edges of the jacket are strapped to correspond.

FIGURE No. 6.—COMBINATION AND DECORATION FOR A LADIES' COSTUME.—A combination of brown faille, black velvet and black satin overlaid with white lace is seen in this stylish costume. The back has plaited fulness in the lower part, but is smooth at the top. Side-fronts plaited at the lower edge and decorated with buttons above the bust are at each side of surplice sections of velvet which are also ornamented with buttons. Between the surplice sections is revealed a chemisette and standing collar of the satin overlaid with lace; and a collar that falls in a square tab at the back and is pointed at the ends rolls over the waist below. The sleeves are plaited at the top, a ribbon decoration emphasizing the slope-shouldered effect thus produced. Fanciful cuff-facings and a band outlining the pointed lower edge of the waist are of satin overlaid with lace. The great fulness and broad effect of the skirt is due to its shaping and to groups of tuck-plaits at the hips, a group of similar plaits being made at the center of a white box-plait formed at the back. The number of the pattern used for this costume is 8100, price 1s. 8d. or 40 cents.

8145

FIGURE No. 7.—COMBINATION AND DECORATION FOR A LADIES' COSTUME.—The rich combination of black satin and heavy white lace over black satin here pictured is peculiarly suited to this simple, graceful costume, which was cut according to pattern No. 8101, price 1s. 8d. or 40 cents. The

8145   8145
Front View.   Back View.

MISSES' BLOUSE, WITH SAILOR COLLAR (THAT MAY BE MADE WITH SQUARE OR ROUNDING LOWER FRONT CORNERS). (COPYRIGHT.)

(For Description see Page 177.)

huge *gigot* sleeves. Paquin points fall over the wrinkled stock at each side of the front. The development of the waist is very

FASHIONS FOR FEBRUARY, 1896.

admirable shaping of the skirt, which consists of five gores, causes it to hang in the ripples now fashionable and fulness at the top of the back is laid in backward-turning plaits. The waist has a wide back with only a center seam, and the front is perfectly smooth at the top but has plaited fulness below the bust. The rounding lower outline of the waist and the V-shaped upper edge are followed by a band of white satin overlaid with spangled trimming, the lining above the front and back

S147 Front View. S147 Back View.
GIRLS' APRON, WITH FICHU BERTHA. (COPYRIGHT.)
(For Description see Page 177.)

being faced with black satin overlaid with white lace. The overlaid satin is also used for round cuffs, that are turned up over the lower edges of the full Paquin sleeves. At the neck is a wrinkled stock with frill ends closed at the back. A costume of similar style could be fashioned from wood-brown crêpon and Persian silk. The latter material could fill the V-shaped openings, which could be outlined with narrow brown spangle trimming. The silk may be used for the stock collar.

FASHIONABLE HATS.
(For Illustrations see Page 188.)

The demi-saison reveals but few novelties in millinery, as preparations are now making for the early Spring styles that introduce buds, blossoms and foliage. Modifications of existing styles, a deft touch here and there, a new bow, buckle, rosette or plume arranged in a new position or adorning an improved shape, include the novelties in millinery this month.

FIGURE NO. 1.—LADIES' PROMENADE HAT.—This fine brown felt is adorned with plain and fancy ribbon artistically arranged about the crown, three long ostrich feathers drooping majestically at the back. The brim projects over the face, but is caught up at the back, where a garland of full-blown roses, buds and leaves peep prettily from underneath.

FIGURE NO. 2.—LADIES' VIOLET TOQUE.—Green velvet forms the foundation of this toque and violets are closely massed back of the fluted brim in front. Aigrettes of lace stand high at each side above a foreground of violets and an outspread velvet loop upon which sparkles a steel ornament.

FIGURE NO. 3.—LADIES' STREET HAT.—A young lady may wear this hat with a certainty of its becomingness and the decoration may be easily copied. In the front is a wide Dresden ribbon that is formed in a broad loop and end at each side and in soft puffs at the center, and back of this bow are willowy ostrich feathers and a spreading aigrette.

FIGURE NO. 4.—LADIES' HAT.—This hat is of gray chenille braid and has a low crown and brim rolled evenly all round. Black satin ribbon is arranged in dainty bows against the brim at the back and against the crown at each side of the front. A black ostrich plume that mingles with the ribbon droops over the brim at each side, with charming grace.

FIGURE NO. 5.—YOUNG LADIES' HAT.—A most artistic arrangement of satin ribbon is disposed at the back of this black felt hat and a long Rhinestone buckle extends across the front and conceals the ends of an ostrich tip that droops with coquettish grace at each side.

FIGURE NO. 6.—LADIES' THEATRE HAT.—Transparency and airiness of effect distinguish this dainty creation, which is given height by a tall aigrette rising at the left side, and acquires width from fan-plaits of appliqué lace placed at each side of soft green velvet puffs, a jet wing being adjusted at each side of the puffs. A jewelled ornament sparkles just forward of the aigrette, and pink roses decorate the crown.

FIGURE NO. 7.—LADIES' VELVET TOQUE.—Golden-brown velvet covered with iridescent spangles is used for the crown and loops at the back of this toque and black marten fur forms the narrow brim, a tail rising above the velvet loop. Cream-white lace is arranged at the back to form an aigrette. An end of the lace falls on the hair and is apparently held in place with a steel buckle.

FIGURE NO. 8.—LADIES' FELT HAT.—This hat has a black felt brim and a TAM O' SHANTER crown of black velvet encircled with soft folds of Spanish-yellow velvet. A tasteful trimming of velvet, feathers and a tall aigrette rises above the crown at the back, and pink roses peep from underneath the brim.

FIGURE NO. 9.—LADIES' TURBAN.—The upturned brim of this smart turban is narrow at the center of the front and back and deep at the sides, and the low crown is encircled by Dresden ribbon, which is arranged to form a compact background for a large blackbird at each side, the tall black quills that rise back of the birds giving becoming height.

FIGURE NO. 10.—LADIES' LARGE HAT.—This shape suggests the LOUIS XI mode and is made of black velvet with an edge border of upright chenille points and graceful plumes nodding over the sides

8160

S160 Front View. S160 Back View.
GIRLS' YOKE APRON, WITH ROUND BERTHA. (COPYRIGHT.)
(For Description see Page 178.)

a single plume towering high and drooping in front. A steel buckle is stylishly fastened directly in front against the crown

Styles for Little Folks.

FIGURE NO. 212 R.—LITTLE GIRLS' WRAPPER.
(For Illustration see this Page.)

FIGURE NO. 212 R.—This illustrates a Little Girls' wrapper. The pattern, which is No. 8161 and costs 10d. or 20 cents, is in nine sizes for little girls from one-half to eight years of age, and may be seen again on page 184.

The wrapper is here pictured made of French flannel showing a fancy pink stripe on a blue ground. It is shaped by shoulder and under-arm seams and has fulness at the top laid in tucks that are held by feather-

A delicate shade of pink flannel was here selected to make this dainty little sack, which has a simple decoration of satin ribbon. The sack is shaped by center, shoulder and under-arm seams. The one-seam leg-o'-mutton sleeves have fulness at the top collected in gathers and flare prettily. A pretty turn-down collar finishes the neck and ribbon tie-strings secure the sack at the throat. Ribbon decorates the collar, sleeves and free edges of the sack.

Sacks of flannel are necessary in a child's wardrobe for wear with white dresses of nainsook or cambric to give sufficient warmth and insure comfort when changes of weather demand weightier clothing. Feather-stitching, embroidery and ribbon are the decorations most frequently employed on little garments of this kind.

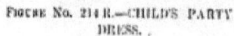

FIGURE NO. 214 R.—CHILD'S PARTY DRESS.
(For Illustration see this Page.)

FIGURE NO. 214 R.—This illustrates a Child's dress. The pattern, which is No. 8164 and costs 10d. or 20 cents, is in

FIGURE NO. 212 R.

FIGURE NO. 213 R.

FIGURE NO. 214 R.

FIGURE NO. 215 R.

stitching in both the back and front, the fulness falling freely below. The closing is made under ribbon bows at the center of the front, and the deep facing at the lower edge and the hems at the front edges are secured with feather-stitching. The full sleeves are completed with wristbands, and the rolling collar has square, flaring ends; the wristbands and collar are decorated with feather-stitching.

Flannel, cashmere, serge, flannelette or eider-down may be chosen for this wrapper, with stitching and ribbon for trimming.

FIGURE NO. 213 R.—CHILD'S HOUSE-SACK.
(For Illustration see this Page.)

FIGURE NO. 213 R.—This illustrates a Child's house-sack. The pattern, which is No. 8163 and costs 5d. or 10 cents, is in seven sizes for children from one-half to six years of age, and may be seen again on page 186 of this number of THE DELINEATOR.

FIGURE NO. 212 R.—LITTLE GIRLS' WRAPPER.—This illustrates Pattern No. 8161 (copyright), price 10d. or 20 cents. FIGURE NO. 213 R.—CHILD'S HOUSE-SACK.—This illustrates Pattern No. 8163 (copyright), price 5d. or 10 cents. FIGURE NO. 214 R.—CHILD'S PARTY DRESS.—This illustrates Pattern No. 8164 (copyright), price 10d. or 20 cents. FIGURE NO. 215 R.—LITTLE GIRLS' DRESS.—This illustrates Pattern No. 8148 (copyright), price 10d. or 20 cents.

(For Descriptions see Pages 183 and 183.)

seven sizes for children from one-half to six years of age, and is shown again on page 183 of this number of THE DELINEATOR.

The simple little dress is here pictured in a combination of India silk, lace net and lace insertion. The upper part of the

FASHIONS FOR FEBRUARY, 1896.

dress is a pointed yoke overlaid with lace net and trimmed at the lower edge with a frill of edging set on under a fancy-stitched band. The skirt is plain at the sides and gathered across the front and back where it joins the yoke. A band of insertion and a frill of lace edging decorate the neck, and ribbon arranged in rosettes on the shoulders and at the corners of the yoke gives a pretty touch to the dress. The full sleeves are completed with wristbands of insertion trimmed with a frill of edging.

Light-colored silk, crépon or cashmere may be selected for party dresses like this, and for ordinary wear serge, cheviot, silk-and-wool mixtures or other soft goods will look well. Velvet ribbon, buttons and braid will provide pretty trimming.

FIGURE No. 215 R.—LITTLE GIRLS' DRESS.
(For Illustration see Page 182.)

FIGURE No. 215 R.—This illustrates a Little Girls' dress. The pattern, which is No. 8148 and costs 10d. or 20 cents, is in nine sizes for little girls from one-half to eight years of age, and is shown made up differently on page 183 of this magazine.

A neat little dress for every-day wear is here pictured made of mixed cheviot and plain red cloth. It has a full, gathered skirt depending from a plain waist that is closed at the back. A band of plain cloth trimmed with white braid decorates the skirt above the hem. Round cuffs of red cloth finish the full, bishop sleeves and the red material is also used for the rolling collar, which is in two sections that flare in points at the front and back. The edges of the cuffs and collar are followed by a row of white braid.

The dress is well suited to all inexpensive woollen goods, as well as to more dressy weaves, and ribbon, lace, narrow silk gimp and braid, which are always pretty trimmings for children's dresses, may make it quite fanciful. It is also a specially pretty style for wash goods.

FIGURE No. 216 R.—CHILD'S LONG COAT.—This illustrates Pattern No. 8155 (copyright), price 10d. or 20 cents.
(For Description see this Page.)

FIGURE No. 216 R.—CHILD'S LONG COAT.
(For Illustration see this Page.)

FIGURE No. 216 R.—This illustrates a Child's long coat. The pattern, which is No. 8155 and costs 10d. or 20 cents, is in eight sizes for children from two to nine years of age, and is given a different portrayal on page 185.

This picturesque top-garment for little folks is here shown

8164 8164
Front View. Back View.
CHILD'S DRESS, HAVING A POINTED YOKE AND A SKIRT WITH STRAIGHT LOWER EDGE FOR HEMSTITCHING. (COPYRIGHT.)
(For Description see this Page.)

of velvet edged with beaver fur gives a close neck finish, and a large sailor-collar to match falls below, its ends passing under the plait in front. The sleeves are great puffs finished with deep velvet cuffs that are trimmed at the wrists with fur.

Fancy coatings of all kinds will combine effectively with velvet or Bengaline in this little coat.

The velvet hat is trimmed with ostrich tips, a fancy pin and fur.

FIGURE No. 217 R.—BABY'S FIRST SHORT DRESS.
(For Illustration see Page 184.)

FIGURE No. 217 R.—This illustrates a Baby's first short dress. The pattern, which is No. 8133 and also includes a cambric and a flannel skirt, costs 1s. 3d. or 30 cents, is in one size—for one-half year—only, and is illustrated in full on page 180.

The garment is simple and dainty for a baby's first short dress, and is here pictured made of white China silk. For the square yoke the silk is laid in fine plaits. The skirt is seamless and is gathered where it joins the yoke; feather-stitching done with pink silk fastens its hem to position. Feather-stitching decorates the free edges of gathered epaulettes that stand out prettily over the sleeves, which are in full puff style with wristbands also ornamented with feather-stitching.

Lawn, nainsook and soft silk-and-wool weaves are selected for these little dresses and dainty trimmings of lace, baby ribbon and fancy stitching are added.

CHILD'S DRESS, HAVING A POINTED YOKE AND A SKIRT WITH STRAIGHT LOWER EDGE FOR HEMSTITCHING.
(For Illustrations see this Page.)

No. 8164.—A pretty combination of white silk, lace insertion

made up in a combination of brown-and-green bouclé cloth and green velvet. A box-plait that widens toward the lower edge is applied on the front edge of the right front and conceals the closing, and a similar plait is inserted at the back in Watteau fashion. A rolling collar

8148 8148
Front View. Back View.
LITTLE GIRLS' DRESS. (TO BE MADE WITH STANDING OR ROLLING COLLAR.) (COPYRIGHT.)
(For Description see Page 184.)

and lace net is shown in this dress at figure No. 214 R in this magazine, ribbon and lace edging supplying the decoration.

Lawn and fancy tucking are here combined in the dress, which is simple and dainty in appearance. The pointed yoke is fitted by shoulder seams and closed at the back with button-holes and small pearl buttons. From the lower edge of the yoke hangs a full, straight skirt, which is gathered at the top, where it joins the yoke, and is deeply hemmed at the bottom, the hem being held with a row of feather-stitching. The bishop sleeves are gathered at the top and bottom and are completed with wristbands that are ornamented with a narrow lace frill headed by a feather-stitched band. A similar frill of edging headed by a feather-stitched band follows the lower edges of the yoke, and at the neck is an upright frill set on under a feather-stitched band.

Fine nainsook, lawn, dimity, mull and cambric, with all-over embroidery, Hamburg or lace edging and insertion for trimming, will be especially appropriate for this mode.

We have pattern No. 8164 in seven sizes for children from one-half to six years of age. To make the dress for a child of four years, requires two yards and seven-eighths of lawn thirty-six inches wide, with a fourth of a yard of fancy tucking twenty-seven inches wide. Of one material, it needs four yards and an eighth twenty-two inches wide, or three yards and an eighth thirty inches wide, or two yards and seven-eighths thirty-six inches wide, or two yards and a fourth forty-four inches wide. Price of pattern, 10d. or 20 cents.

LITTLE GIRLS' DRESS. (TO BE MADE WITH STANDING OR ROLLING COLLAR.)

(For Illustrations see Page 185.)

No. 8148.—Plain cloth is combined with cheviot in this dress at figure No. 215 R in this number of THE DELINEATOR, and bands of the cloth and braid supply the decoration.

This simple dress is here pictured made of lawn and all-over embroidery and consists of a round waist and a straight, full skirt. The front of the waist joins the back in shoulder and under-arm seams and the closing is made at the back with button-holes and pearl buttons. The skirt, which is deeply hemmed at the bottom, is gathered at the top and sewed to the waist. The full, bishop sleeves are gathered at the top and bottom and completed with round cuffs trimmed at their lower edges with a narrow frill of embroidered edging. Either a standing collar or a rolling collar in two sections, the ends of which flare prettily, may finish the neck, both styles being illustrated in the engravings. The rolling collar is decorated at its free edges with a frill of edging.

The dress will be very pretty made of cashmere, camel's-hair, serge, cheviot and also of washable materials.

We have pattern No. 8148 in nine sizes for little girls from one-half to eight years of age. To make the dress for a girl of five years, requires two yards and three-eighths of lawn thirty-six inches wide, with a fourth of a yard of all-over embroidery twenty-seven inches wide. Of one material, it needs four yards twenty-two inches wide, or three yards and three-eighths twenty-seven inches wide, or two yards and three-eighths thirty-six inches wide, or two yards and an eighth forty-four inches wide. Price of pattern, 10d. or 20 cents.

LITTLE GIRLS' WRAPPER.

(For Illustrations see this Page.)

No. 8161.—Fancy-striped flannel is shown in this wrapper at figure No. 212 R in this magazine, ribbon bows and fancy stitching contributing the garniture.

This attractive wrapper is here pictured made of flannel in a delicate shade of pink. It is shaped by shoulder and under-arm seams, and in the upper part of each front, just back of the hemmed front edges, are laid three forward-turning tucks which are sewed to yoke-depth below the neck. Three backward-turning tucks are made at each side of the center of the seamless back and are sewed to the same depth as those in the fronts. The hems and tucks are feather-stitched to position. Below the tucks the fulness resulting from them falls in a free graceful way and the bottom of the wrapper is finished with a deep hem-facing feather-stitched to position at the top. The rolling collar has square ends that flare prettily in front, and its ends and lower edge are decorated with a row of feather-stitching. The full bishop sleeves are gathered top and bottom, and finished with wristbands that are ornamented at the top and bottom with a row of feather-stitching. Three pretty ribbon bows placed over the closing in the front give a dressy touch to the wrapper.

French flannel, cashmere, Henrietta, outing flannel and eider-down are adapted to this mode, and although feather-stitching is the most approved decoration, narrow velvet and satin ribbon, silk braid and lace would also be appropriate trimmings.

We have pattern No. 8161 in nine sizes for little girls from one-half to eight years of age. To make the wrapper for a girl of five years, requires five yards of goods twenty-two inches wide, or three yards and seven-eighths twenty-seven inches wide, or three yards and five-eighths thirty-six inches wide, or three yards forty-four inches wide. Price of pattern, 10d. or 20 cents.

8161
Front View.

8161
Back View.

LITTLE GIRLS' WRAPPER. (COPYRIGHT.)

(For Description see this Page.)

CHILD'S LONG COAT.

(For Illustrations see Page 185.)

No. 8155.—Bouclé cloth and velvet are united in this quaint little coat at figure No. 216 R in this number of THE DELINEATOR, and decoration is provided by beaver fur.

The coat is here shown handsomely made of cloth. The loose fronts join the backs in shoulder and under-arm seams and the closing is concealed by an applied box-plait that is

FASHIONS FOR FEBRUARY, 1896.

narrow at the top and widens gradually toward the lower edge, the plait being joined to the front edge of the right front. A similar plait is inserted in Watteau fashion at the center of the back, its side edges being joined separately to the back edges of the backs below the waist-line so as to contribute additional fulness to the skirt. A deep broad sailor-collar gives a particularly stylish air to the coat; it is included in the seam with a high rolling collar having pointed flaring ends and its front edges are secured underneath the plait on the front. The full puff sleeves are gathered at the top and bottom and completed by deep round cuffs; they stand out well from the arm and are supported by a lining that is composed of a coat-shaped under-portion, extending to the lower edge of the cuff, and a full upper-portion that is in two sections, the lower portion being smooth and only of the depth of the cuff, while the upper section is large and gathered at the top and bottom, this shaping of the sleeve lining providing for an easy adjustment over large dress sleeves.

Coats of this kind will be made of faced cloth, whipcord, fancy coatings and cheviots and will be most generally finished with machine-stitching or several rows of mohair, silk or soutache braid. Dressy coats will have collars and cuffs of velvet or Bengaline.

We have pattern No. 8155 in eight sizes for children from two to nine years of age. To make the coat for a child of four years, requires five yards and a half of material twenty-two inches wide, or three yards and five-eighths thirty-six inches wide, or three yards forty-four inches wide, or two yards and three-eighths fifty-four inches wide. Price of pattern, 10d. or 20 cents.

SET OF BABY'S FIRST SHORT CLOTHES, COMPRISING A DRESS, CAMBRIC SKIRT AND FLANNEL SKIRT.

(For Illustrations see this Page.)

No. 8133.—The dress in this Set is shown differently developed at figure No. 217 R in this number of THE DELINEATOR. A pretty little set of first short clothes, the undergarments of which are constructed on hygienic principles, allowing the weight of the garments to fall on the shoulders, is here illustrated. The dress is made of nainsook and embroidered edging and has a square yoke shaped with shoulder seams and a full skirt that is gathered where it joins the yoke and falls in pretty folds. The skirt is straight at the lower edge, where it is finished with a hemstitched hem. The yoke closes at the back with button-holes and buttons and is ornamented with alternate upright rows of feather-stitching and hemstitching, the lower edge being outlined with a feather-stitched band. The full sleeves, which are gathered at the top and bottom, stand out with a pretty flare above narrow wrist-bands that are trimmed with a frill of lace. Over the sleeves lace-edged epaulette frills of embroidered edging stand out prettily and give a stylish air to the little garment. A frill of edging finishes the neck. The small engraving shows the dress without the epaulette frills.

Fine cambric was used for one petticoat, which has a low-necked body, made double and shaped by shoulder and under-arm seams and closed at the back with buttons and button-holes. The full round skirt is gathered at the top and joined to the body; it is hemmed at the lower edge and decorated with a cluster of three tucks above a ruffle of embroidered edging.

For the other petticoat flannel was selected, the low-necked body being made double of cambric and shaped with under-arm seams. The body is closed at the back and also on the shoulders with buttons and button-holes, the overlapping shoulder edges being pointed. The closing on the shoulders will be found of great convenience as it permits slipping the skirt off and on when a fresh flannel petticoat is needed without removing the other garments. The lower edge of the flannel skirt is embroidered.

Nainsook, lawn or any soft goods may be used for the dress, with trimmings of fine lace. One petticoat may be of cambric, muslin, nainsook, etc. and the other of white or tinted flannel.

Pattern No. 8133 is in one size only—fitted for one-half year. The dress requires a yard and seven-eighths of nainsook thirty-six inches wide, with a yard and a fourth of embroidered edging three inches wide. Of one material, it needs two yards thirty-six inches wide. The cambric skirt, calls for a yard and three-eighths of material thirty-six inches wide. The flannel skirt, needs three-

8155
Front View.
8155
Back View.

CHILD'S LONG COAT. (COPYRIGHT.)
(For Description see Page 184.)

8133
Front View.
8133
Back View.

8133
Front View.
8133
Back View.
8133
Front View.
8133
Back View.

SET OF BABY'S FIRST CLOTHES, COMPRISING A DRESS, CAMBRIC SKIRT AND FLANNEL SKIRT.
(COPYRIGHT.)
(For Description see this Page.)

fourths of a yard of flannel twenty-seven inches wide, or three-fourths of a yard of flannel thirty-six inches wide, each with half a yard of muslin thirty-six inches wide. Price of pattern, 1s. 3d. or 30 cents.

INFANTS' LONG CAPE, WITH HOOD, CIRCULAR YOKE AND RIPPLE CAPE-COLLAR.

(For Illustrations see this Page.)

No. 8141.—This pretty cloak is made of cream flannel. The upper part of the cloak is a shallow round yoke having a center seam, and from the lower edge of the yoke depends a long cape portion that is gathered at its upper edge and hangs in graceful folds. Over the cape falls a circular, ripple cape-collar, and included in the seam with it is a round, seamless hood lined with cream silk and drawn up prettily to have a frill effect at the edge by elastic run in between the lining and outside. The edges of the cape, hood and collar are ornamented with scallops worked with silk, and a row of Valenciennes lace is also added with dainty effect to the edge of the hood. A full rosette of cream satin baby-ribbon is placed on the hood at the center of the back and the cape is fastened at the neck with cream ribbon ties bowed prettily. The cape may be made more simple by omitting the collar as shown in the small view.

White surah or heavily corded silk, cashmere, Henrietta, flannel and camel's-hair will be suitable for an infants' cape of this style and an effective decoration may be supplied by lace edging, ribbon and feather-stitching.

Pattern No. 8141 is in one size only. To make the cape will require three yards and a-half of material twenty-two inches wide, or two yards and three-eighths twenty-seven inches wide, or a yard and five-eighths thirty-six inches wide, or a yard and five-eighths forty-four inches wide, or a yard and a fourth fifty-four inches wide. Price of pattern, 10d. or 20 cents.

INFANTS' HOUSE-SACK, WITH STOLE SAILOR-COLLAR.

(For Illustrations see this Page.)

No. 8140.—Cream flannel was selected for this dainty little sack, which is shaped by center, shoulder and under-arm seams, the center and under-arm seams being terminated a short distance above the lower edge to form the back in two square tabs. The stole sailor-collar is of uniform depth at the front and back and slopes gracefully over the shoulders. The full sleeves are gathered at the top and narrowly hemmed at the bottom, and laid in forward and backward-turning plaits far enough above the lower edge to give a frill effect at the wrist. The plaits in the lower part of the sleeves are ornamented with two rows of feather-stitching made with light blue silk, and similar stitching

decorates the center and under-arm seams. A shell edge in light-blue silk is crocheted around the edges of the collar, jacket and sleeve, forming a very effective trimming. Baby-blue ribbon ties are bowed prettily at the throat.

Little garments of this style may be made of French flannel and cashmere in delicate tints suited for infants, and fancy stitching, lace edging and baby ribbon are the most appropriate decorations. An exceptionally dainty sack was of pale-blue merino, with two rows of velvet baby ribbon at all the edges.

Pattern No. 8140 is in one size only and will require a yard and three-eighths of material twenty-two inches wide, or a yard and an eighth twenty-seven inches wide, or a yard thirty-six inches wide. Price of pattern, 5d. or 10 cents.

8141
Front View.

8141
Back View.

INFANTS' LONG CAPE WITH HOOD, CIRCULAR YOKE AND RIPPLE CAPE-COLLAR. (COPYRIGHT.)
(For Description see this Page.)

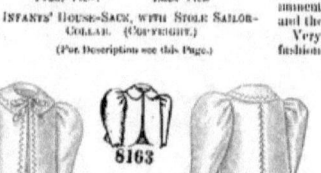

8140
Front View.

8140
Back View.

INFANTS' HOUSE-SACK, WITH STOLE SAILOR-COLLAR. (COPYRIGHT.)
(For Description see this Page.)

8163
Front View.

8163

8163
Back View.

CHILD'S HOUSE-SACK. (TO BE MADE WITH SQUARE OR ROUNDING CORNERS.) (COPYRIGHT.)
(For Description see this Page.)

CHILD'S HOUSE-SACK. (TO BE MADE WITH SQUARE OR ROUNDING CORNERS.)

(For Illustrations see this Page.)

No. 8163.—At figure No. 213 it in this magazine this dainty little sack is shown developed in pale-pink flannel and trimmed with satin ribbon.

A very useful adjunct to a child's wardrobe is this house-sack, which is here illustrated made of grey flannel. The sack is shaped by center, shoulder and under-arm seams and may have square or rounding lower front corners, as shown in the engravings. A rolling collar, which may have square or rounding lower corners, finishes the neck, and light-blue ribbons close the sack at the throat. The one-seam leg-o'-mutton sleeves are gathered at the top and hemmed at the bottom, a row of feather-stitching done in light-blue silk securing the hem. A row of similar stitching ornaments the center and under-arm seams, and the edges of the sack and collar.

Very pretty sacks of this style may be fashioned from dotted, striped or plain flannel, cashmere, Henrietta and eider-down, and narrow velvet or satin ribbon, narrow silk braid and lace may be used for trimming, although feather-stitching forms the most approved decoration for these little sacks.

We have pattern No. 8163 in seven sizes for children from one-half to six years of age. To make the sack for a child of five years, requires two yards and three-eighths of material twenty-two inches wide, or two yards twenty-seven inches wide, or a yard forty-four inches wide. Price of pattern, 5d. or 10 cents.

SET OF INFANTS' OUTDOOR CLOTHES, COMPRISING A DRESS, COAT, CAP AND SHOE.

(For Illustrations see Page 187.)

No. 8134.—This is a pretty little outfit for an infant to wear when it takes its daily outing in the baby carriage or in nurse's

FASHIONS FOR FEBRUARY, 1896.

arms. The dress is made of nainsook and fancy tucking, and decoration is contributed by tucks and lace edging and insertion. It has a full skirt of the proper length, deeply hemmed at the bottom and gathered at the top, where it is joined to the lower edge of a yoke that is square at the back and fancifully pointed in front. The yoke is closed at the back with button- and button-holes, and its lower edge is outlined with a frill of lace edging, an upright frill of lace edging also finishing the neck. The full sleeves are gathered at the top and bottom and are trimmed at the wrist with a lace frill set on under a narrow band of nainsook. The bottom of the skirt is ornamented above the hem with two tucks between two rows of lace insertion. Allowance for the tucks must be made when cutting out, as they are not considered in the pattern.

The pretty little coat is made of white serge and decorated with ribbon. The upper part of the coat is a square yoke, shaped by shoulder seams and closed at the front with button-holes and buttons. From the lower edge of the yoke depends a full skirt which is hemmed at the lower and front edges and gathered at the upper edge where it joins the yoke. The full puff sleeves are arranged over coat-shaped linings which are finished below the sleeves to have the effect of close cuffs. The circular cape falls in pretty ripples and is included in the seam with a round hood, which is in Red Riding-Hood style. The hood is shirred to form a dainty frill at the outer edge and its ends are reversed. Both cape and hood are lined throughout with white silk.

For the cap white corded silk was chosen and lace, ribbon and fur decorate it prettily. The cap has a smooth front that extends to the center of the back, where its ends are joined in a seam. The front is laid in small plaits along its back edge and sewed to a circular center. A puff of the silk is arranged at the front edge of the cap and a gathered curtain is attached to the lower edge. Ribbon ties are sewed to the lower front corners of the cap.

The little shoe, which is made of silk and decorated with fancy-stitching, consists of a sole and an upper. The upper is shaped by a seam at the center of the back and a short seam at the lower part of the front, the closing being made above the front seam with silk lacings through eyelets.

The dress will make up daintily in Swiss, lawn, mull and fine cambric and the garniture may consist of embroidered edging, feather-stitched bands, etc. The cap may be developed in surah, Bengaline and cashmere, with a silk lining. The shoes may be of kid or cider-down.

Pattern No. 8134 is in one size only. The dress will require two yards and seven-eighths of nainsook thirty-six inches wide, with a fourth of a yard of fancy tucking twenty-seven inches wide. Of one fabric, it needs two yards and seven-eighths thirty-six inches wide. The coat calls for five yards and a half of goods twenty-two inches wide, or four yards and seven-eighths thirty inches wide, or three yards and seven-eighths thirty-six inches wide, or three yards and a fourth forty-four inches wide. The cap calls for seven-eighths of a yard of material twenty inches wide, or five-eighths of a yard twenty-seven or more inches wide, with a yard and three-fourths of ribbon an inch and three-fourths wide for the ties, etc. A pair of shoes will need a fourth of a yard of goods twenty or more inches wide, or a piece of kid measuring seven inches and a half by nine inches and a half. Price of pattern, 1s. 8d. or 40 cents.

8134

8134 Front View.

8134 Back View.

8134 Front View.

8134 Back View.

SET OF INFANTS' OUTDOOR CLOTHES, COMPRISING A DRESS, COAT, CAP AND SHOE. (COPYRIGHT.)
(For Description see Page 186.)

Styles for Men and Boys.

FIGURE NO. 218 R.—BOYS' SUIT.
(For Illustration see Page 188.)

FIGURE No. 218 R.—This consists of a Boys' box-plaited jacket, knee trousers and cap. The jacket pattern, which is No. 8127 and costs 10d. or 20 cents, is in fourteen sizes for boys from three to sixteen years of age and is also shown on page 190. The trousers pattern, which is No. 3783 and costs 7d. or 15 cents, is in twelve sizes for boys from five to sixteen years old, and is pictured again on its accompanying label. The cap pattern, which is No. 3033 and costs 5d. or 10 cents, is in seven sizes from six to six and three-fourths, cap sizes, or from nineteen inches and a fourth to twenty-one inches and a half, head measures, and is also shown on its label.

A serviceable suit for general wear is here shown made of broken-checked cheviot. The knee trousers fit nicely and are closed with a fly. They are plainly finished.

The shapely jacket, which is known as the golf or Norfolk jacket, shows a box-plait at each side of the front and similar plaits are formed in the back. The fronts are closed with buttons and button-holes at the center, and are reversed above the closing in notched lapels by a rolling collar. A belt is buttoned about the waist and the coat sleeves are comfortable. Bone buttons and stitching afford the neat completion.

The hat is in Tam-O'Shanter style, with a band that fits the head closely.

Tweed, worsted, vicuna, homespun cheviot and other materials of good wearing qualities are best adapted to suits of this style and stitching will provide the finish unless a braid binding is preferred.

FIGURE NO. 218 R.—BOYS' SUIT.—This consists of Boys' Box-Plaited Jacket No. 8127, price 10d. or 20 cents; Knee Trousers No. 3783, price 7d. or 15 cents; and Cap No. 3033, price 5d. or 10 cents.

(For Description see Page 187.)

FIGURE NO. 219 R.—LITTLE BOYS' SAILOR SUIT.

(For Illustration see this Page.)

FIGURE NO. 219 R.—This illustrates a Little Boys' suit. The pattern, which is No. 8128 and costs 1s. or 25 cents, is in seven sizes for little boys from two to eight years of age, and is differently illustrated on page 189 of this number of THE DELINEATOR.

Blue and white cloth were appropriately combined in this natty little sailor suit. The blouse droops in the regular way and is turned back above the closing in lapels that are ornamented with gilt buttons. The ends of a large, removable sailor collar of white cloth decorated with blue braid overlap the lapels and between them appears a chemisette ornamented with an emblem. A whistle attached to a lanyard is thrust in a patch pocket on the left front. White, braid-trimmed cuffs complete the sleeves, which display a box-plait down the outside of the arm. The close-fitting knee trousers close at the sides and are ornamented at the lower part of the outside seams with three gilt buttons and closed below the buttons with short straps.

No prettier or more suitable development than this could be devised for the little suit, but red-and-blue or blue alone will also be found satisfactory.

FIGURE NO. 220 R.—LITTLE BOYS' DRESS.

(For Illustration see this Page.)

FIGURE NO. 220 R.—This illustrates a Little Boys' dress. The pattern, which is No. 8129 and costs 10d. or 20 cents, is in six sizes for little boys from two to seven years of age, and is shown differently made up and decorated on page 189 of this magazine.

The dress is here pictured made up in a combination of brown and white serge. The skirt is box-plaited and depends from a body that is plain at the back and separates in front to reveal in V shape a vest trimmed at the top with curving rows of white braid. The long ends of a large sailor-collar of white serge trimmed with brown braid frame the vest attractively, and a belt of the white material outlined with the braid covers the joining of the skirt and waist, its pointed overlapping end being ornamented with a strap. The full sleeves show a box-plait at the outside of the arm and side-plaits turning from the box-plait at the wrist, where the box-plait is ornamented with pearl buttons.

Very handsome dresses for small boys may be made after this design of velvet, corduroy or fine cloth, with silk soutache or Hercules braid or pipings of a contrasting color for decoration. Tweed, cheviot, serge, etc., will be selected for ordinary wear.

FIGURE NO. 221 R.—LITTLE BOYS' APRON.

(For Illustration see this Page.)

FIGURE NO. 221 R.—This represents a Little Boys' apron. The pattern, which is No. 8135 and costs 10d. or 20 cents, is in six sizes for little boys from one to six years old, and is pictured again on page 189 of this number of THE DELINEATOR.

The apron is thoroughly protective and is pretty enough to serve as a dress. It is here shown made of gray linen. The front shows a box-plait down the center and is extended to form a back-yoke from which full backs depend. The backs are held in at the waist by belt-straps starting from the under-arm seams and secured with buttons and button-holes over the closing, which is also made with buttons and button-holes. The rolling collar is in two sections and is prettily trimmed with red linen braid, and a patch pocket on each front and the wristbands completing the full bishop sleeves are also decorated with braid.

Percale, chambray and gingham are also used for aprons like this and pipings of contrasting goods, washable braid or tiny frills of the material or colored edging may provide decoration.

FIGURE NO. 219 R.—LITTLE BOYS' SAILOR SUIT.—This illustrates Pattern No. 8128, price 1s. or 25 cents.

(For Description see this Page.)

FIGURE NO. 220 R. FIGURE NO. 221 R.

FIGURE NO. 220 R.—LITTLE BOYS' DRESS.—This illustrates Pattern No. 8129, price 10d. or 20 cents. FIGURE NO. 221 R.—LITTLE BOYS' APRON.—This illustrates Pattern No. 8135, price 10d. or 20 cents.

(For Descriptions see this Page.)

A neat apron was made of brown linen and trimmed with frills of edging embroidered in red.

FASHIONS FOR FEBRUARY, 1896.

LITTLE BOYS' SAILOR SUIT, HAVING KNEE TROUSERS WITHOUT A FLY.
(For Illustrations see this Page.)

No. 8128.—A stylish combination of dark-blue and white cloth is represented in this suit at figure No. 219 R in this number of THE DELINEATOR, blue braid and gilt buttons providing a neat decoration.

Blue serge was used for the suit in this instance. The trousers are shaped by inside and outside leg-seams, a center seam and hip darts and are closed at the sides. The outside leg-seams are bound with braid and are terminated a little above the lower edge, straps on which slides are slipped being joined be-low the seams to the front and buttoned over on the back. A row of three buttons is placed on the front above the strap. Side pockets and a right hip pocket are inserted, and the trousers are finished with under waistbands in which the usual button-holes are made for attaching the trousers to an underwaist.

The blouse is made with shoulder and under-arm seams and an elastic is inserted in the hem at the lower edge to draw the edge closely about the waist, the blouse drooping in true sailor-blouse fashion. The fronts are closed at the center with buttons and button-holes and are reversed above the closing in lapels that are trimmed with cross-rows of white soutache braid and overlapped by the ends of a deep sailor-collar that is buttoned underneath to the blouse. A chemisette is also buttoned in and both of these accessories are decorated with rows of black braid crossed in basket fashion at the center of the chemisette and in the back corners of the collar. The edges of the collar and lapels and the front edges of the blouse are also bound with braid; and a patch pocket in which a whistle attached to a lanyard is thrust is also bound and trimmed with black braid to correspond with the chemisette. The sleeves display a box-plait down the outside of the arm and are finished with round, braid-trimmed cuffs.

The suit is among the most attractive of the many sailor suits and offers exceptional opportunities for combinations of cloth in two colors or of silk and cloth. Braid is the favorite trimming.

We have pattern No. 8128 in seven sizes for little boys from two to eight years of age. For a boy of five years, the suit requires three yards and a half of goods twenty-seven inches wide, or a yard and three-fourths fifty-four inches wide. Price of pattern, 1s. or 25 cents.

8128
Front View.

8128
Back View.

LITTLE BOYS' SAILOR SUIT, HAVING KNEE TROUSERS WITHOUT A FLY.
(For Description see this Page.)

LITTLE BOYS' DRESS, WITH BOX-PLAITED SKIRT AND SAILOR COLLAR.
(For Illustrations see this Page.)

No. 8129.—Brown and white serge form the stylish combination shown in this little dress at figure No. 220 R in this number of THE DELINEATOR, decoration being contributed by buttons, braid and stitching.

The dress is here pictured made of blue and white flannel and decorated with braid and buttons. The skirt, which is deeply hemmed at the bottom, is laid in box-plaits all round and depends from a long waisted body that is simply shaped by shoulder and under-arm seams and a seam at the center of the back. The fronts of the body flare broadly toward the shoulders over a vest that is sewed permanently at the right side and fastened with buttons and button-holes at the left side. The sailor collar is deep and broad at the back and has long tapering ends that join the front edges of the fronts. The one-seam sleeve is comfortably wide and has a box-plait extending from the shoulder to the wrist, where two side-plaits are made at each side of the box-plait; all the plaits are stitched at their outer folds from the wrist to a short distance above, and small buttons decorate the box-plait. A shaped belt in two sections, joined in a seam at the back, follows the joining of the skirt and waist and its pointed overlapping end is passed through a slide-strap of the material.

Serge, flannel and such washable fabrics as piqué, chambray, gingham, etc., are made up in this manner and trimmed with braid or finished with stitching. A combination of two colors or materials, although not essential to produce a good effect, is desirable.

We have pattern No. 8129 in six sizes for little boys from two to seven years of age. For a boy of four years, the dress will require three yards and an eighth of white with seven-eighths of a yard of blue flannel, each twenty-seven inches wide. Of one fabric, it needs four yards twenty-seven inches wide, or three yards and an eighth thirty-six inches wide. Price of pattern, 10d. or 20 cents.

8129
Front View.

8129
Back View.

LITTLE BOYS' DRESS, WITH BOX-PLAITED SKIRT AND SAILOR COLLAR.
(For Description see this Page.)

LITTLE BOYS' APRON.
(For Illustrations see this Page.)

No. 8135.—Another view of this apron may be had by referring to figure No. 224 R in this magazine, where it is pictured made of gray linen and decorated with red linen braid.

The protective little apron is here shown made of blue checked gingham. The front is formed at the center in a broad box-plait that is stitched along its under folds all the way; it is extended to form a square back-yoke to which the gathered upper edges of the full backs are joined. Included in the under-arm seams at the waist-line are belt straps having pointed ends that are crossed at the center of the back where they are buttoned together over the closing, which is made with buttons and button-holes. At the neck is a rolling collar in two sections that flare at the front and back and are edged with embroidered edging. Similar edging trims the belt-straps, the upper edges of pointed patch pockets on the fronts, and the lower edges of wristbands finishing the full bishop sleeves, which are gathered at the top and bottom.

The small boy cannot have too many aprons and this one is

8135
Front View.

8135
Back View.

LITTLE BOYS' APRON.
(For Description see this Page.)

a particularly practical design. Cotton cheviot, gingham and calico are durable materials for them and colored embroidery or ruffles of the material are good trimmings.

We have pattern No. 8135 in six sizes for little boys from one to six years of age. For a boy of four years, the apron requires two yards and three-

8127
Front View.

8127
Back View.

BOYS' BOX-PLAITED JACKET, WITH THE PLAITS LAID IN THE FRONT AND BACK. (KNOWN AS THE GOLF OR NORFOLK JACKET.)

(For Description see this Page.)

8126
BOYS' SAILOR COLLARS AND CUFFS.
(For Description see this Page.)

fourths of goods twenty-seven inches wide, or two yards thirty-six inches wide. Price of pattern, 10d. or 20 cents.

BOYS' BOX-PLAITED JACKET, WITH THE PLAITS LAID IN THE FRONT AND BACK. (KNOWN AS THE GOLF OR NORFOLK JACKET.)

(For Illustrations see this Page.)

No. 8127.—At figure No. 218 R in this number of THE DELINEATOR this jacket is shown made of broken-checked cheviot and finished with stitching and buttons.

The jacket is the fashionable golf or Norfolk jacket and is here shown made of cheviot. The seamless back is formed in a box-plait at each side of the center and is joined in side and shoulder seams to the fronts, which are each laid in a box-plait from the shoulder to the lower edge and are closed at the center with buttons and button-holes. Above the closing the fronts are reversed in small, notched lapels by a rolling coat-collar. A belt having rounding ends buttoned in front is worn and below it a patch pocket is stitched on each front. One row of stitching finishes the edges of the jacket, collar, lapels and belt and two rows outline cuffs on the coat sleeves, which are ornamented below the stitching with two buttons.

Tweed, worsted, mixed and checked cheviot, homespun and similar durable materials in mixtures in which brown tones are most prominent, are best liked for such jackets. The jackets are worn with ordinary close-fitting trousers for general wear and with knickerbockers for golf and other sports, leggings or golf stockings meeting the lower edges of the knickerbockers.

We have pattern No. 8127 in fourteen sizes for boys from three to sixteen years of age. To make the jacket for a boy of eleven years, will require three yards and three-eighths of goods twenty-seven inches wide, or a yard and five-eighths fifty-four inches wide. Price of pattern, 10d. or 20 cents.

BOYS' SAILOR COLLARS AND CUFFS.
(For Illustrations see this Page.)

No. 8126.—These stylish collars and cuffs are pictured made of serge and decorated with braid. One style of collar is perfectly plain and is turned down over a neck-band that closes at the throat; it is deep and very broad at the back and its stole-like ends flare prettily from the throat. The cuff accompanying this collar is plain also and rolls up on the sleeve over a narrow band that is slipped under the sleeve.

The other collar is just as deep and broad at the back but its ends meet on the breast and are slashed to have the effect of notched lapels. This collar is also slashed at the center of the back, and a small section fitted in at the neck gives a good roll to the collar and fits the collar easily to the neck of the garment with which it is worn. The cuff belonging to the collar is finished with a band and adjusted exactly like the plain cuff, but has a slash at the back to correspond with the slash in the back of the collar.

These accessories will match or contrast with the suit they accompany and serge, Galatea, piqué, duck, etc., are suitable materials.

We have pattern No. 8126 in six sizes for boys from two to twelve years of age. To make the notched collar and cuffs for a boy of six years, will require seven-eighths of a yard of goods twenty-seven inches wide, or five-eighths of a yard fifty-four inches wide. The plain collar and cuffs will need five-eighths of a yard twenty-seven inches wide, or half a yard fifty-four inches wide. Price of pattern, 5d. or 10 cents.

MEN'S LOUNGING OR HOUSE JACKET.
(For Illustrations see this Page.)

No. 8125.—This comfortable lounging-jacket is pictured made of military-blue cloth and decorated in military style with black braid. It is nicely conformed to the figure by side-back gores and a curving center seam and the fronts open all the way down and have neatly rounded lower corners. The coat sleeves are of comfortable width, and the neck is finished with a rolling collar. Side-pockets and a left breast pocket are inserted in the fronts.

Cloth, flannel and serge in such colors as gray, blue, brown, dark-red or blue will be used for jackets of this style and braid will provide appropriate decoration.

We have pattern No. 8125 in ten sizes for men from thirty-two to fifty inches, breast measure. To make the jacket for a

8125
Front View.

8125
Back View.

MEN'S LOUNGING OR HOUSE JACKET.
(For Description see this Page.)

man of medium size, requires three yards and a fourth of material twenty-seven inches wide, or a yard and five-eighths fifty-four inches wide. Price of pattern, 1s. 3d. or 30 cents.

ILLUSTRATED MISCELLANY.

STYLISH LINGERIE.

(For Illustrations see Pages 191 and 192.)

Popular favor is about equally divided among stock collars,

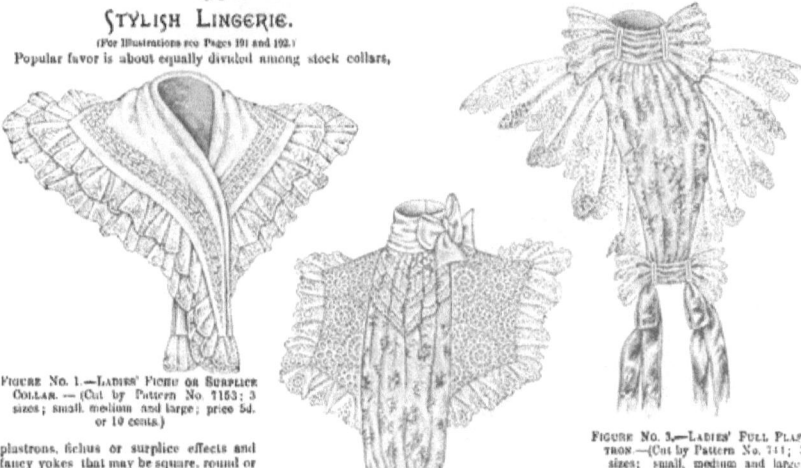

FIGURE NO. 1.—LADIES' FICHU OR SURPLICE COLLAR. — (Cut by Pattern No. 7153; 3 sizes; small, medium and large; price 5d. or 10 cents.)

plastrons, fichus or surplice effects and fancy yokes that may be square, round or pointed. A collar and plastron are combined to give a dressy touch to a plain basque or waist, the transforming effect being remarkable. If creamy lace chiffon or *mousseline de soie* enter into the construction of these dainty accessories, a softening and beautifying result is invariably attained.

FIGURE NO. 1.—LADIES' FICHU OR SURPLICE COLLAR.—White silk mull was selected to make this accessory and lace insertion

and edging provide appropriate decoration. The collar is shaped by pattern No. 7153, price 5d. or 10 cents. The sheer nature of the material adapts it charmingly to this mode, in which the material is

FIGURE NO. 2.—LADIES' FANCY COLLAR, WITH FRENCH FRONT.—(Cut by Pattern No. 933; 3 sizes; small, medium and large; price 5d. or 10 cents.

FIGURE NO. 3.—LADIES' FULL PLASTRON.—(Cut by Pattern No. 741; 3 sizes; small, medium and large; price 10d. or 20 cents.)

doubled and shaped by a center seam, a point being formed below each shoulder. Upturning plaits produce soft wrinkles and the ends

FIGURE NO. 5.

(For Descriptions of Figures Nos. 1, 2, 3, 4 and 5, see "Stylish Lingerie," on Pages 191 and 192.)

FIGURES NOS. 4 AND 5.—LADIES' FANCY COLLARS.—(Cut by Pattern No. 918; 3 sizes; small, medium and large; price 5d. or 10 cents.)

cross in surplice fashion below the bust, the free edges being adorned with frills of lace edging below insertion.

FIGURE NO. 3.—LADIES' FANCY COLLAR, WITH FRENCH FRONT. —Severely plain bodices will be greatly improved by the use of a fancy collar and front of this style. An exquisite combination of Dresden silk, white satin, guipure lace and lace edging with satin ribbon is illustrated in this instance. The Dresden silk front is decorated with narrow lace edging and the revers are bordered with a frill of lace, the wrinkled ribbon stock being fastened at the side under a pretty bow. The pattern employed is No. 933, price 5d. or 10 cents.

FIGURE No. 3.—LADIES' FULL PLASTRON.—Dresden

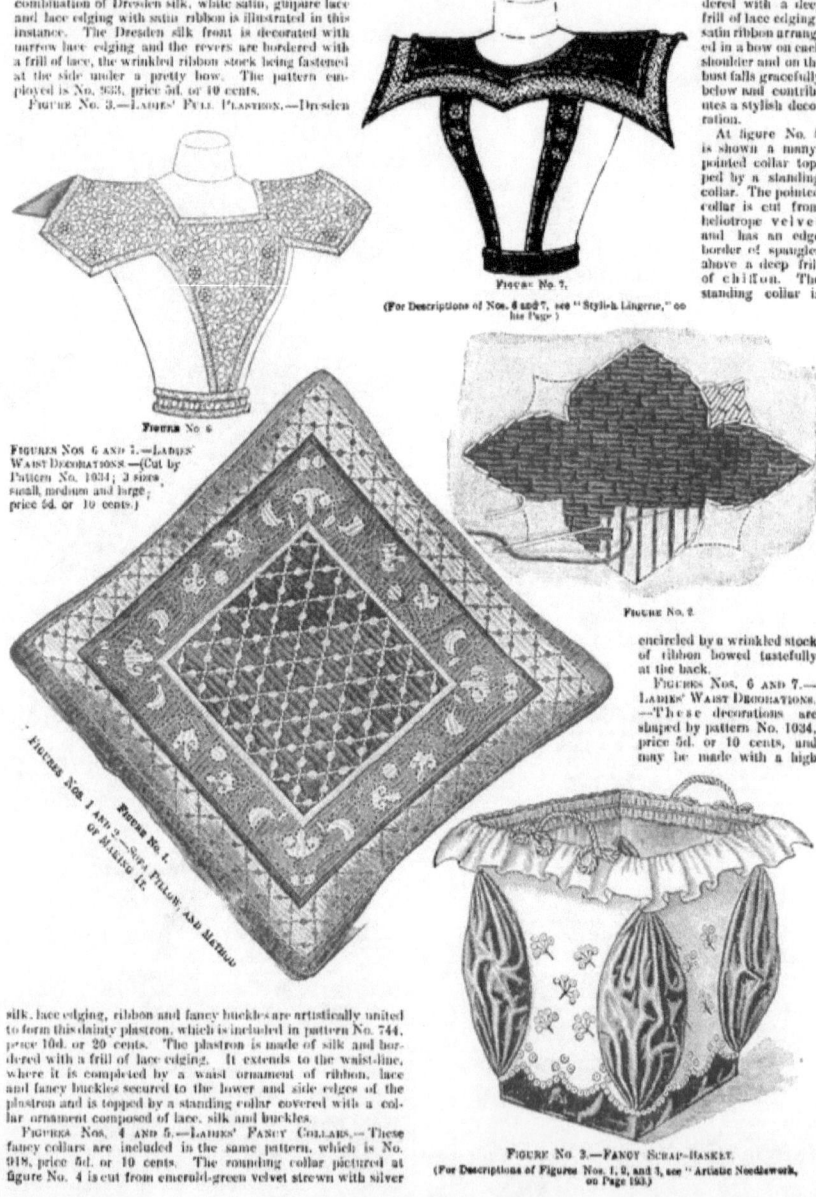

(For Descriptions of Nos. 6 and 7, see "Stylish Lingerie," on his Page.)

FIGURES NOS. 6 AND 7.—LADIES' WAIST DECORATIONS.—(Cut by Pattern No. 1034; 3 sizes, small, medium and large; price 5d. or 10 cents.)

spangles and bordered with a deep frill of lace edging; satin ribbon arranged in a bow on each shoulder and on the bust falls gracefully below and contributes a stylish decoration.

At figure No. 5 is shown a many-pointed collar topped by a standing collar. The pointed collar is cut from heliotrope velvet and has an edge border of spangles above a deep frill of chiffon. The standing collar is encircled by a wrinkled stock of ribbon bowed tastefully at the back.

FIGURES NOS. 6 AND 7.—LADIES' WAIST DECORATIONS.—These decorations are shaped by pattern No. 1034, price 5d. or 10 cents, and may be made with a high

silk, lace edging, ribbon and fancy buckles are artistically united to form this dainty plastron, which is included in pattern No. 744, price 10d. or 20 cents. The plastron is made of silk and bordered with a frill of lace edging. It extends to the waist-line, where it is completed by a waist ornament of ribbon, lace and fancy buckles secured to the lower and side edges of the plastron and is topped by a standing collar covered with a collar ornament composed of lace, silk and buckles.

FIGURES NOS. 4 AND 5.—LADIES' FANCY COLLARS.—These fancy collars are included in the same pattern, which is No. 918, price 5d. or 10 cents. The rounding collar pictured at figure No. 4 is cut from emerald-green velvet strewn with silver

FIGURE NO. 3.—FANCY SCRAP-BASKET.

(For Descriptions of Figures Nos. 1, 2, and 3, see "Artistic Needlework," on Page 193.)

or low neck. The Pompadour decoration pictured at figure No. 6 is developed in white satin overlaid with lace, bordered with fur and decorated with jewelled buttons. It answers the purpose of epaulettes, plastron and belt.

At figure No. 7 is shown a differently shaped though equally dressy decoration made of sapphire-blue velvet and trimmed with fur, lace and fancy buttons. A standing collar is provided for use when the neck of this decoration is made high. Both decorations are closed invisibly on the left shoulder.

FIGURE NO. 4.—STOOL CUSHION.
(For Description see "Artistic Needlework," on this Page.)

top. The outside is bordered with black velvet cut out in scollops at the top and outlined with gilt spangles, and above it smoothly applied pale-green silk embroidered in a simple device with spangles. At the corners old-rose silk is fulled on, with pretty effect. From the upper edge falls a plain frill of green silk. The handles are wound with old-rose silk cord. If desired, simpler fabrics could be used.

FIGURE NO. 4.—STOOL CUSHION.—A plaid effect is uniquely carried out with colored wools in this oblong cushion, designed for a piano stool. Shaded red and white wools are used in the work, which is done on canvas in the same stitch as that shown at figure No. 1. The back of the pillow is covered with red silk corresponding with one of the shades of the wool, and the edges are finished with heavy white silk cord, a pair of full tassels to match depending from each corner, with rich effect. Any of the clan plaids seen in dress goods may be copied in work of this kind, with satisfactory results. If desired, threads of silk may be effectively introduced among the woollen stitches.

THE WORK-TABLE.
(For Illustrations see Pages 193 and 194.)

FIGURES NOS. 1 AND 2.—DRESSING-TABLE.—An eminently

ARTISTIC NEEDLEWORK.
(For Illustrations see Pages 192 and 193.)

FIGURES NOS. 1 AND 2.—SOFA-PILLOW, AND METHOD OF MAKING IT.—At figure No. 1 is pictured a handsomely embroidered sofa-pillow. The embroidery is done on canvas with colored wools in the manner shown at figure No. 2. Dark-green wool is used for the plain border round the pillow and inside it Nile-green wool is used, the lattice design upon it matching the border. A conventionalized floral design is then wrought on a dark-green ground with Nile-green and old-rose wools and the lattice design in the center is done with Nile-green, which stands out well from the dark green ground. The color scheme is simple and pretty. Any tasteful mingling of colors may be introduced, and the design may be varied to suit individual fancy. The back of the pillow may be covered with silk of any desired tone.

FIGURE NO. 3.—FANCY SCRAP-BASKET.—A basket of this kind may be conveniently placed in library or sitting-room to receive scraps of any kind. The basket—a cheap willow one—is lined with old-rose China silk arranged in several rows of shirring at the

FIGURE NO. 2.

FIGURES NOS. 1 AND 2.—DRESSING-TABLE.
(For Descriptions of Figures Nos. 1 and 2 see "The Work-Table," on Pages 193 and 194.)

FIGURE NO. 1.

useful article for a bedroom in which space is limited is here suggested. The frame-work may be made by a carpenter or by anyone skilful with tools.

At figure No. 1 is shown the upper drawer extended and held by means of chains and pulleys. The upper ends of the chains are fastened to the mirror support; the chains are then drawn through the pulleys, which are attached to the sides of the stand, and the lower ends are secured to the front corners of the drawer. In the drawer openings are made for wash bowl, pitcher, soap-dish and mug, which when not in use may be placed underneath and concealed by a curtain that depends from the upper drawer. The lower drawer may be used for clothing. Both drawers have brass handles. A small support placed high up on one side holds a fancy pitcher. Dry-goods boxes are available for tables of this kind.

At figure No. 2 is given a complete view of the dressing-table. Around the top runs a narrow spindle border and below it in front hangs a short curtain of flowered cretonne. The sides are similarly curtained, and against them may be hung towels, sponges, wash-cloths and the like, while the curtains conceal from view. An oval mirror is supported at the back and on the stand are placed a lace cover and toilet articles.

FIGURE NO. 3.—SHOE-AND-SLIPPER BAG.—Shoes and slippers have a habit of straying from their mates if not kept together in a receptacle of this character. This bag is made of tan linen canvas and bound at the edges with tan worsted braid. A row of braid is applied across the center and three vertical rows are stitched to separate the pockets, of which there are two sets. A box-plait

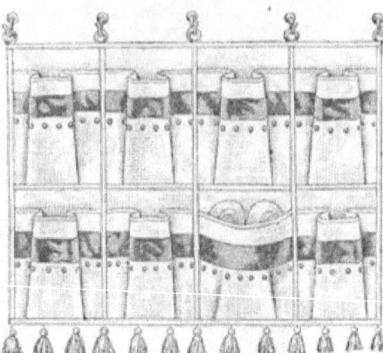

FIGURE NO. 3.—SHOE AND SLIPPER BAG.—(Cut by Pattern No. 4857, price 5d. or 10 cents.)

(For Description see "The Work-Table," on this Page.)

underneath is a row of red buttons. Red worsted tassel fringe depends from the bottom and at the top brass rings are adjusted for slipping over hooks placed in a closet or in any other out-of-the-way place. Cretonne or burlap may be similarly made up. The pattern used in making the bag is No. 4857, price 5d. or 10 cents.

CHILDREN'S CORNER.

(For Illustrations see Pages 194 and 195.)

The doll-house that good Kris Kringle brought in his pack has a beautiful exterior, but within it is bare of furniture. The windows are curtained and it looks cosy to the passer-by, but for all that it is a forlorn place. You are a practical little home-maker and I will tell you how to produce a suite of furniture which will just suit the doll folks, even if it is home-made. Excellent models for a chair, table and rocker are here suggested, and you may make any number of them.

At figure No. 1 is shown the table. Thin cardboard or heavy paper may be used for it and you may have a white table for your drawing-room and paint the others any color you think will suit the rooms they are to be placed in. The lower part of the table is cut from one piece of paper, as pictured at figure No. 2. Cut out the paper precisely like the diagram, which you may first trace upon tracing paper and then transfer to stiff paper. After it has been drawn, cut it out and fold it according to the dotted lines,

FIGURE NO. 1.—TABLE.

FIGURE NO. 3.—DIAGRAM FOR TOP OF TABLE.

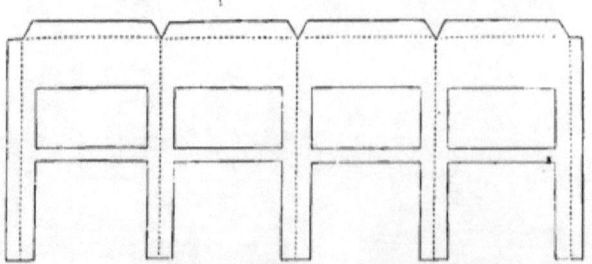

FIGURE NO. 2.—DIAGRAM FOR LOWER PART OF TABLE.

(For Descriptions of Figures Nos. 1, 2, 3 and 4, see "Children's Corner," Pages 194 and 195.)

FIGURE NO. 4.—CHAIR.

is folded in each pocket, the folds of the plaits being secured only at the bottom and the top being spread open. Wide red braid is disposed along the top of each row of pockets and

pasting the projecting ends beyond the dotted lines at each end together. Then bend over the tops above the dotted lines and upon them paste the top of the table shown at figure

No. 3, and you will have a table which will stand as securely as if made of wood.

Now for the chair, shown at figure No. 4. As before, trace and transfer the diagram, pictured at figure No. 5, to stiff paper and cut it out and fold according to the dotted lines. The back of the chair is represented in the first section of the diagram, while the second shows one side, which should be bent round at the dotted line. The third section portrays the seat and front legs. The seat is covered with flowered paper to imitate furniture covering and bent over into place. Then the fourth section, which represents the other side, is brought into position, the narrow end beyond the dotted line being pasted to the seat which meets it. It isn't at all difficult, is it? You may use different colored papers for the chairs, for you know it is quite fashionable to have all sorts of furniture in one room.

The rocker is pictured at figure No. 6, and is made in exactly the same way as the other pieces of furniture. The diagram for the rocker is shown at figure No. 7. It, of course, requires some patience and deftness of fingers to put these little things together, but then your Kindergarten training has fitted you for such work, which is interesting as well as instructive. I am sure you will be pleased with the result.

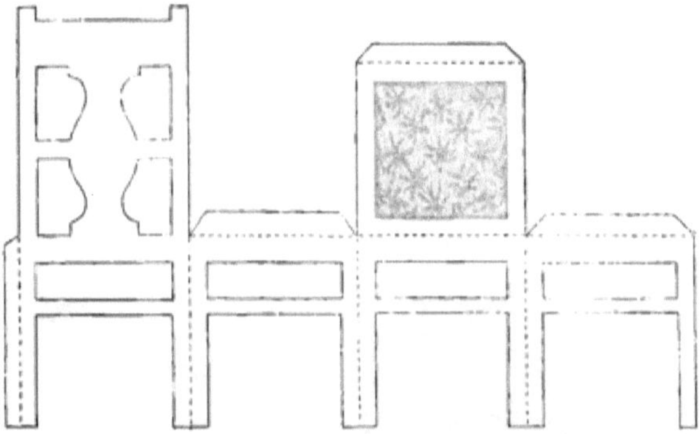

STYLES FOR GENTLEMEN.

(For Illustrations see Page 196.)

The illustrations in this department for this month include two knot and four puff scarfs and two tubular ties.

FIGURE No. 1.—GENTLEMEN'S KNOT

FIGURE No. 5.—DIAGRAM FOR CHAIR.

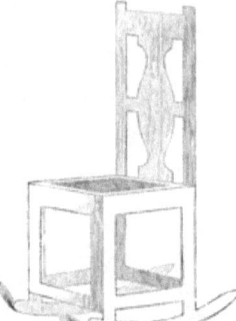

FIGURE No. 6.—ROCKER.

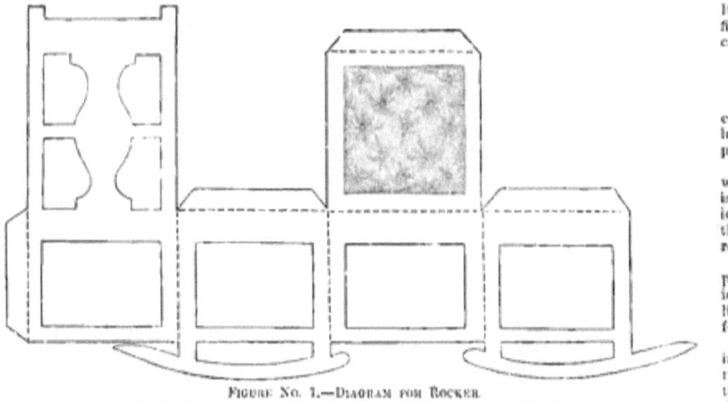

FIGURE No. 1.—DIAGRAM FOR ROCKER.
(For Descriptions of Figures Nos. 5, 6 and 7, see "Children's Corner," this Page.)

SCARF.—This shape is known as The Trilby and has widely flaring ends. It is made of black, fancifully-woven cotton goods showing small squares with a red figure in the center.

FIGURE No. 2.—GENTLEMEN'S KNOT SCARF.—Black satin figured in light-blue and gold was chosen for the manufacture of this scarf, which is called The Seneca.

FIGURE No. 3.—GENTLEMEN'S TUBULAR TIES.—The manner in which they are constructed accounts for the name given these ties, which are made of blue silk figured in white.

FIGURE No. 4.—GENTLEMEN'S PUFF SCARF.—This shape is called The Calyx and is preferably developed in black silk figured in green.

FIGURE No. 5.—GENTLEMEN'S PUFF SCARF.—The handsome scarf here pictured is made of black satin showing unique figures in blue and gold. The shape is known as the Fronteuac.

FIGURE No. 6.—GENTLEMEN'S PUFF SCARF.—This shape is called The Clifford. It is made of black satin figured in red and is a favorite with all good dressers.

FIGURE No. 7.—GENTLEMEN'S PUFF SCARF.—A puff scarf in long, slender outline is here pictured. It is made of green satin figured in red and has been christened The Holbein.

A fanciful short-waisted basque is admirably lengthened by a fluted peplum.

The yoke-back shirt-waist—which, by-the-bye, is abiding—is conveniently made with collars that may be removed and replaced by ribbon stocks.

Three-piece skirts are popular and are convenient fashions for remodelling circular skirts of a former season.

The Eton basque forming part of a costume of the formal type gains its title from the short point described at the front and back, this being a prominent feature of the Eton college garment.

Gathers and side and box plaits vary the backs of fashionable skirts and in all these styles the ripple effect is maintained.

A closing at the left side is an advantage in the basque of a costume, since it permits the fulness to remain undisturbed across the front.

Revers near the shoulders, short puff-sleeves and a very short though close-fitting waist render the fashionable Empire gown a very complete copy of its prototype of nearly a century ago.

A becoming severity is attained in the waist of a very stylish costume by edges or capes of another, and some are only bordered with a contrasting variety. The mode has especial attraction for economical women who possess garments of two kinds neither of which is presentable by itself or capable of being remodelled alone.

Chinchilla edgings, collars and even large capes

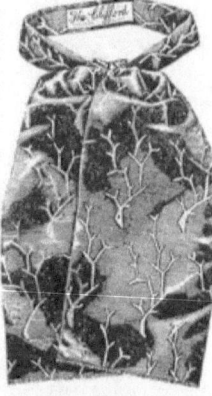

FIGURE NO. 6.—GENTLEMEN'S PUFF SCARF.

are in high favor, as this fur is always sure to be whenever laces and velvets are fashionable. It is one of the most agreeable of furs to wear and it blends well with everything, but it is both costly and fragile. Only women who can afford new furs every year should select Chinchilla for every-day wear.

Tippets and boas of long-

FIGURE NO. 1.—GENTLEMEN'S KNOT SCARF.

FIGURE NO. 4.—GENTLEMEN'S PUFF SCARF.

FIGURE NO. 3.—GENTLEMEN'S TUBULAR TIES.

a perfectly smooth back and a plastron front. Pointed epaulettes and a frilled peplum are interesting accessories of the same costume.

A fanciful Bertha detracts from the severity of a Princess gown, which flows below the waist-line in a series of ripples.

Mixed furs were never so popular as this season. Fashionably shaped collars, capes and muffs are made up with alternating gores of a different fur. Some garments have yokes of one fur and standing collars and rippled outer

FIGURE NO. 2.—GENTLEMEN'S KNOT SCARF.

FIGURE NO. 5.—GENTLEMEN'S PUFF SCARF.

FIGURE NO. 7.—GENTLEMEN'S PUFF SCARF.

(For Descriptions of Figures Nos. 1, 2, 3, 4, 5, 6, and 7, see "Styles for Gentlemen," on Page 195.)

haired furs rival in popularity the same throat ornaments made of long ostrich plumes and stripped feathers wired upon cord.

TATTING.—No. 41.

ABBREVIATIONS USED IN MAKING TATTING.

d. s.—Double-stitch or the two halves forming one stitch.   p.—Picot.   *.—Indicates a repetition as directed wherever a * is seen.

TATTED DOILY.

FIGURE NO. 1.—Begin with one thread and make a ring thus: 2 d. s., then 9 p. each separated by 2 d. s.; close the ring, tie

FIGURE NO. 1.—TATTED DOILY.

tightly and neatly, and cut the threads off as closely as possible. Still using one thread make a ring of 6 d. s., join to a p. of center ring, 6 d. s. and close, turn and make a large ring of 4 d. s., 1 p., 3 d. s., then 4 p. each separated by 3 d. s., 4 d. s. and close. Turn and make another tiny ring and join as before to the center ring, then a large ring joined to the side picot of the last large ring, and continue in this way until there are 9 large and 9 small rings, but in the 9th large ring instead of making the last p., join to side p. of large ring first made; tie neatly and cut the threads.

* Next, work with 2 threads. With one thread make a ring of 6 d. s., join to a middle picot of a ring in wheel just made, 6 d. s. and close. Next, make a ch. with 2 threads of 7 d. s., 3 p. each separated by 4 d. s., then turn and with one thread make a ring of 3 d. s., 5 p. each separated by 3 d. s., 3 d. s. and close; this ring falls inside the ch. turn and finish the ch. thus: 4 d. s., 2 p. each separated by 4 d. s., then 7 d. s. Repeat from * for all the circles.

Next round.—* Make 7 d. s. with one thread, join to center p. in a ch. around circle, 7 d. s., close. Make a chain of 7 d. s., 4 p. each separated by 4 d. s., then a ring of 3 d. s., 6 p. each separated by 3 d. s., 3 d. s. and close; let the ring turn inside the chain same as in last round, finish the ch. thus: 4 d. s., 3 p. each separated by 4 d. s., then 7 d. s. Repeat from *; at the end of round tie the threads neatly.

This doily may be made as much larger as desired by adding more rounds like the last, but the chains must be increased in length in each round so as to make the latter lie flatly, and the rings at the center of each ch. must also be made larger.

TATTED EDGING.

FIGURE No. 2.—For the heading use one thread. Make a ring of 4 d. s., 1 p., 4 d. s., 1 p., 4 d. s., 1 p., 4 d. s., draw up,

turn and a short distance from the last ring, * make a ring of 5 d. s., 1 p., 5 d. s., 1 long p. using a measure three-eighths of an inch wide, 5 d. s., 1 p., 5 d. s., close; turn and make a ring of 5 d. s., join to p. of small ring, 5 d. s., 1 p., 5 d. s., 1 p., 5 d. s., close; turn, and make a ring of 4 d. s., join to picot of opposite ring, 4 d. s., 1 long three-eighths-in. p., 4 d. s., 1 p., 3 d. s., close; turn make a ring like the last except that you omit the long p. by making it of the ordinary length, and repeat from *.

* Next, with one thread make a small ring of 4 d. s., 1 p., 4 d. s., 1 long three-eighths-in. p., 4 d. s., 1 p., 4 d. s., close. With 2 threads make a ch. of 5 d. s., then 5 p. each separated by 3 d. s., then 5 d. s. With one thread make a ring of 5 d. s., join to opposite ring, 5 d. s., 1 long p., 5 d. s., 1 p., 5 d. s., close. With 2 threads make another ch. the same as before, and repeat from *. Join the two pieces together by their long p. the same as in hair-pin work. Baby ribbon can be drawn through the space if desired.

TATTED EDGING.

FIGURE No. 3.—With one thread make 5 d. s., 1 p., then 4 p. each separated by 3 d. s., 5 d. s. Make 3 more rings like the last except that instead of making the first picot you join it to the 1st p. in ring just made, and in the last ring join to corresponding p. of opposite ring instead of making last p. Tie the center threads neatly and cut as closely as possible.

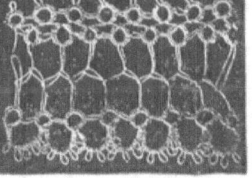

FIGURE No. 2.—TATTED EDGING.

Next use 2 threads, leave 1 p. free, next make a joining and tie in the next. * Make a ch. of 5 d. s.; with one thread make a tiny ring of 2 d. s., 3 p. each separated by 2 d. s., 3 d. s. and close; with 2 threads make another ch. of 5 d. s. and fasten in next p.; repeat 5 times more from *, tie neatly and firmly. In making the next scollop join to last one as shown in the picture.

For the Heading.—Fasten the thread in the p. where the last ch. was fastened. Make 7 ch. * 1 d. c. in the next p., 5 ch., skip joinings, p., 1 d. c. in the next p., 2 ch., 1 d. c. in the next, 4 ch., 1 d. c. in the next, 2 ch., 1 d. c. in the next, 4 ch., 1 d. c. in the next, 2 ch. and repeat from *.

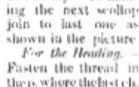

FIGURE No. 3.—TATTED EDGING.

Next row.—1 d. c. with 3 ch. between in every long space and in every d. c. underneath. Baby-ribbon may be run in the heading.

FANCY STITCHES AND EMBROIDERIES.

BY EMMA HAYWOOD.

EMBROIDERED PHOTOGRAPH-FRAMES.

Very charming are the novelties for embroidered photograph-frames, and so great is the variety that it seems difficult to make a choice. One idea, however, is common to all, and that is to

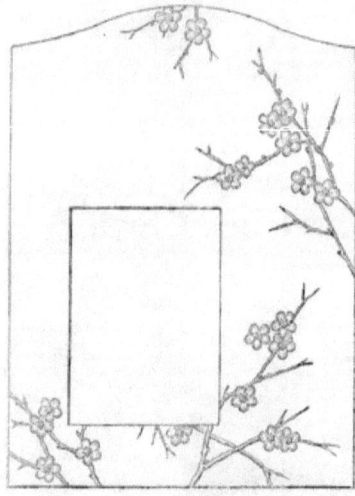

ILLUSTRATION No. 1.

cover not only the photograph but the entire frame with glass; this makes the frame practically an embroidered mat for the picture. Doubtless the idea originated in the fact that a handsomely embroidered frame, especially if delicate in coloring, soon becomes soiled if not protected from exposure to dust and handling. This led to the embroidered frame being framed with a more or less elaborate gilt moulding. In many cases this was considered somewhat too expensive a method.

Now, however, thanks to the demand for such a frame, there are on sale at the leading fancy-work stores a beautiful assortment of frames ready for mounting at home and costing but a very reasonable sum. These frames are accompanied by a piece of linen of the required size and shape stamped ready for working. Moreover, these stamped designs are remarkably good and up to date in style. These mounts are to be found square, round, oval, heart-shaped, in the form of a palette, octagonal and in other odd shapes suited to Renaissance embroidery designs. All these frames are made for a cabinet-sized photograph, with a good margin for the needlework. They are well finished at the back and may be placed on a table or hung, at pleasure. For hanging they would look well backed with plush or velvet showing a margin around the outer edge of the frame. The back is affixed to the glass by a simple patented invention consisting of teeth that can be bent over the edge of the glass, holding it firmly and forming a brass or gilt beading around the embroidery. The cheaper frames are square and held together only at the corners, like a blotting pad, by means of triangular metal clips.

Illustration No. 1 shows a charming little design in Japanese style that decorates a space in the most satisfying manner without filling it. There is very little work in this design, which closely resembles one stamped upon linen in a frame exactly like that shown in the drawing. This frame may be had at small cost. I mention these details in order that readers at a distance from large cities may know exactly what is obtainable, for such frames are likely to be very popular, forming as they do charming presents for friends of both sexes. The other designs here given are a little more elaborate than those solid with the frames, but they likewise exactly represent shapes obtainable. The design in the first illustration represents the dainty almond blossom, always in bloom in advance of the foliage. It should be worked with filo floss. The silks colored with Asiatic dyes are very lasting and particularly glossy. Filo floss consists of six strands, any number of which can be used, according to the quality of the work. For small designs, such as those under consideration, one strand is sufficient. Delicate shades of pink should be employed for the blossoms, with soft golden-brown for the stems.

The design in Illustration No. 2 can be worked in two ways, either in solid embroidery or by working the ribbon in embroidery and the berries and leaves in spangles. Treated in the latter way on a ground of cream or delicate colored satin, the effect

ILLUSTRATION No. 2.

is exquisite. Spangle work is quickly done, but it is at present a novelty, because of the difficulty in obtaining spangles sufficiently small for dainty work. They are to be had, though not at all likely to become common. On this account work of this kind brings quite a good price and is only to be found at high-class shops. If carried out in embroidery only, the berries and leaves should be solid, while the ribbon may be outlined and filled in with an open lace stitch. A silk or satin ground in either case looks richer than the linen.

Illustration No. 3 shows a very handsome and decorative design in a style that, while it obviously owes its origin to a primer of ornament, is so far modified as to be practically adapted for needle-work. The richness of this pattern certainly calls for a silk or satin ground. The scrolls that fill in the spaces between the forms about the opening are outlined first with outlining silk and then, outside of that, with fine Japanese gold thread of the kind that does not tarnish. The fillings are likewise put in with silk, either with bars, as shown in the drawing, or with any open-work lace stitch that may be preferred. The rest is worked in solid satin stitch, except the dots, which are represented by French knots. In working the satin stitch care should be taken to follow the curves exactly as indicated by the shading. This requires some little skill and experience, but the art of following such curves is essential to all good embroidery. When the forms are small, as in this case, no shading should be attempted beyond putting in the more prominent parts with a paler tone, to bring them out well. Either one or two colors may be used with good effect. Thus, the flower-like forms might be put in with pale pink, blue or heliotrope; the leafy scrolls would look well in soft gold or green, while the larger scroll should be outlined in a light burnt-sienna shade and filled in with gold color to match as nearly as possible the Japanese thread.

In mounting such embroideries it is a great improvement to place a sheet of cotton batting between the work and the cardboard, taking care to have it very even in thickness and exact as to shape. The opening must be cut out with a neat curve and snipped close to the embroidery. The linen or silk can be affixed at the back with fish glue and then nothing remains to be done but to place the cardboard thus covered between the glass and the back board, insert the picture, turn over and press down the teeth, and the framing will be complete. It may interest those who decorate in water colors rather than in embroidery to know that the cardboard supplied for the mounting is of such a quality that it may be readily painted upon in water colors.

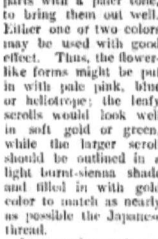

ILLUSTRATION No. 3.

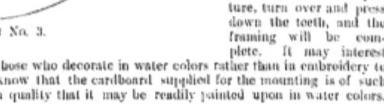

SEASONABLE DRESS GOODS.

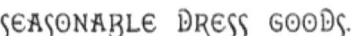

Broadcloth is just now in high favor as a dress fabric. In lustre it vies with satin and in elegance it has no rival among woollen fabrics. A broadcloth gown is an eminently practical choice for the present season, since it may conveniently be worn much later than many other of the Winter materials. For reception wear broadcloth gowns are made up with velvet of the richest silks, which usually form a part. If not the whole, of the bodice. For the promenade, however, the broadcloth is frequently developed alone. While all the fashionable colors are represented in this material, royal-blue may be singled out oftenest from among the array of broadcloth gowns seen on well-dressed women. Black broadcloth skirts are now accounted as elegant as crépon for wear with fanciful silk waists, and from afar they look very like a heavy silk or satin, so deceptive is their high lustre.

A toilette combining royal-blue and white broadcloth and black velvet was recently made up for visiting wear by a very attractive mode. The skirt, which was cut from the blue cloth, was in eleven gores, fell in ripples below the hips and was boxplaited at the back. The basque was of the Louis XV. order. The back was much rippled below the waist-line and the fronts opened over a vest of white cloth folded in a box-plait at the center and crossed at the bottom by a full girdle-section of velvet. A deep fanciful sailor-collar of velvet defined points at the back, on the shoulders and below the shoulders, the ends of the collar tapering to the waist-line after the fashion of lapels. A wrinkled stock of velvet with a great bow at the back was the neck finish, and flaring cuffs, also of velvet, completed the gigot sleeves. A stylish soft-crowned hat of black velvet trimmed with black feathers and pink roses and glacé gloves matching the blue cloth supplemented this toilette.

Another happy choice for the late Winter season is mohair, which will certainly be among the leading fabrics for Spring, when a greater variety than ever in this material is promised. The serge and diagonal weaves in solid colors and two tones are great favorites and look well when made up by some simple mode. There is a basket weave of mohair that appears both in black and in colors. The black is in high vogue, though very few gowns are made up entirely of the colorless material. Usually a becoming color is united with black in the bodice of a gown, the color being preferably brought next the face. This will be recognized as a thoroughly practical fashion. Most of the bodice necessaries are adjustable and several sets of differing colors may be supplied and thus a pleasing variety afforded with only one gown. Armure mohair, figured mohair bearing silky-looking dots and other devices and striped mohair in a herring-bone pattern are all acceptable in black and they never lose the gloss which is such a fascinating feature. A tailor-made costume of the black herring-bone striped mohair could have a vest of leather or of chamois-colored cloth in its bodice and might be further brightened with gilt buttons. The Sicilienne brilliantines, the most familiar of mohair weaves, have not lost prestige, though the family of mohairs has grown so extensively. Every class of colored mohair is reproduced in the hueless tone as well. Black mohair crépons with glistening silk stripes, flowers, arabesques and other devices are rich fabrics that are much sought and will no doubt be much worn during the early Spring. This material is so decorative in itself that little applied garniture is required. For morning wear on the street black camel's-hair, plain or with the surface varied by bouclés or silky-looking hairs, is well liked.

Checked goods have a very large following. In some the colors are neutral and the checks are broken or only suggested; in others the checks are large and of two or more colors, and again the checks are decided and show white in conjunction with navy-blue, dark-red, black or brown, after the manner of shepherd's checks. A favorite way to make up checked goods, especially of the last named class, is to combine with them a solid-hued serge agreeing with the color in the check. Thus, a skirt may be modelled by some fashionable style in a brown-and-white checked material, its associate being a Norfolk jacket of brown serge or diagonal clasped about the waist by a narrow belt of leather or gold ribbon. This will make a smart and generally becoming morning toilette.

For travelling, whether by land or sea, there is no more durable and stylish fabric than Irish frieze, which is a rough mixed material and shows natural browns and grays (the latter in several shades) intermingled with white. These are preferably made up without ornament and by simple modes, those embodying a skirt and short coat being very popular.

Cheviots are close kin to Irish frieze and are shown in a diversity of color mixtures, subdued tones, of course, prevailing. A stylish specimen is woven to suggest checks in steel-blue, black and brown, with here and there a tuft of white, and over the surface is a haze of soft white hairs. In another specimen the color mixture is old-blue, black and gray. In-visible-blue and bronze-brown grounds are illuminated with red and green silk threads, and tiny ringlets of the color of the ground lie lightly upon it. Another specimen presents a Persian color scheme and a surface made rugged with knots and bouclés in black. Yet another recalls men's trouserings in its mixtures of brown-and-white or gray, black and white. Invisible plaids, too, are offered in cheviots in stylish color mixtures. An exceptionally dressy fabric is shown with a silk-mixed ground of navy-blue marked off in hollow squares with broad black stripes woven with basket effect. Another has a slightly waved dark-brown ground against which a floral device in Cashmere colors appears, with artistic effect. Either of these patterns may be made up with Louis XV. coats fashioned partially from velvet. Mixed suitings showing smooth surfaces give satisfaction. Red-and-blue, brown-and-blue, brown-and-green and olive-and-black are among the combinations shown in these fabrics. A novelty which will not look amiss even when Winter is on the wane is a corded fabric in seal-brown, the cords being raised and woven sufficiently far apart to reveal threads of gold silk imbedded in the spaces. Ultra and conservative tastes alike will be impressed with the beauty and elegance of this material.

Among the dainty evening fabrics for very young women's gowns are white *mousseline de soie* embroidered with leaves in shaded green silk and gold threads, and white *mousseline* embroidered with a tracery design in pink and green and a vermicelli pattern in fine gold thread. There are printed chiffons bearing floriations in all evening tints, that require the aid of a solid color to "fix" the design. Both plain and changeable *chiffonettes* are made up with the graceful, airy effect so essential to evening gowns that are desired for youthful wearers. A silk-and-wool material that is often chosen for party wear belongs to the crépon type. It is a gauzy texture in cream, yellow, blue, pink, green, heliotrope or white, marked with crinkled narrow satin lines that are white in every instance. In another gauzy crépon the white ground is favorable to the silk arabesques in pink, cream and other tints, which diversify it.

Without the warning which Fashion often gives, *moiré* has been revived. It is a ribbed silk like poplin, and, like that material, is part wool and part silk, presenting a velvety effect; hence its name *moiré velours*, though it is also known as moiré poplin and *moiré croquelé*. It is shown in black, white and solid colors, and also flowered in chiné effects. A sumptuous ball gown was made for a fashionable matron of this exquisite material in cream figured with roses in the clouded warp printing. With it was used cream *point appliqué* lace. The gown is a Princess cut with a low, round neck and falling below the line of the waist in stately ripples. The sleeves are great puffs that reach just to the elbows, and over them from the neck falls a Bertha of the lace that is formed in plaits and falls in points on the shoulders and in front. A narrow row of pearl trimming heads the lace and helps to adorn the rich gown. Printed *moiré velours* may be combined with the plain moiré or with any of the fashionable silken goods. Gismonda moiré continues in favor. It is of the miroir type and is smooth like satin. This may be had in plain or chameleon colors and with *imprimé* figures.

A handsome dinner gown may be made of black satin figured with pink roses clustered in nosegays, in chiné effect. In most silks the patterns are vaguely defined, far more artistic results being thus attainable than by distinct printing or weaving. A blue shaded *poult de soie* is beautifully decorated with serpentine garlands of chiné roses.

Taffetas having shaded grounds and floral decorations printed upon the warp are still in request and are made up in gowns having portions of the waist of velvet. They are also used for fanciful waists, which—notwithstanding whisperings to the contrary—are as much in vogue as ever for wear with skirts of black cloth, crépon, satin or *moiré velours*. Such combinations possess too many charming possibilities to be soon abandoned.

Simple, girlish-looking waists may be made up for evening wear of *frou-frou*, a thin, gauzy silk like the Liberty weave, slightly crinkled and traversed vertically and horizontally with white bars. All the evening tints are shown in this silk, the bars, however, invariably being colorless. Fluffy styles may be developed in this material, with happy results.

In selecting evening colors the effect upon the complexion should be carefully studied under artificial light, which produces material changes. Thus, a brunette finds pink impossible under the glare of the sun, while in the softer glow of gas it is decidedly becoming. Her blonde sister has a like experience in the use of yellow. In most of the shops provision is made for viewing by gaslight the goods offered for evening wear.

FASHIONABLE GARNITURES.

Upon nearly every style of gown trimming abounds and even with the so-called tailor-made dress a simple adornment is admissible. Braiding is again in vogue and may decorate the vest, sailor collar or yoke of a cloth gown. Soutache braid is the usual choice for such a purpose, and a scroll design is often selected. Upon the basque, which is fashioned with utter plainness, braid frogs with their complement of olive buttons are often applied and impart a smart military air. The same severe style will admit of a decoration of small gilt or silver buttons in groups to yoke depth, below the waist-line on the seams, or in any other way that taste may suggest. Colored trimmings prevail, though black has its advocates.

Leather bands are also among the new garnitures and considerable variation is shown in them. Plain leather in the natural color may be purchased in the piece and from it may be cut vests, peplums, belts and collars for gowns of navy-blue, green or brown cloth or camel's-hair. Leather appliqué bands are very attractive. The centers are colored green or tan in a dull Suède finish and the edges are in the natural color. A design cut from the natural leather is appliquéed upon the center and the edges are outlined with silk cord in Persian colors. In some varieties spangles are introduced with beautiful effect. A very light and charming leather trimming is offered in bands of various widths consisting of a succession of interlinked rings. The trimming is double and may be sewed invisibly to position. A street toilette of dark-green broadcloth and old-rose and green shaded taffeta is elaborated with leather trimming of this description in medium width. The gored skirt is made with a box-plaited back, the material lending itself gracefully to the ripples, which fall naturally in the skirt. A Louis are slightly reversed at the top and produce the effect of an open waistcoat. The reversed portions are overlaid with trimming. Broad lapels are added to the jacket fronts and these, too, are adorned with the leather band. The coat is lengthened by a peplum which ripples across the back and over its joining to the basque is applied a band of the trimming, which likewise encircles the wrists of the *gigot* sleeves. The full collar is cut from silk and is finished with a spread bow at the back. A dark-green velvet hat trimmed with black ostrich tips and steel buttons, and glacé kid gloves complete a very striking and stylish *ensemble*.

A fine kid band trimming for evening or even very dressy daytime gowns is beautifully colored with gold and light tints that suggest a rainbow effect and upon it is wrought a tinsel and spangle embroidery which intensifies the glittering effect. Then there is a gold galloon bearing feather appliqués seeded with iridescent beads. Great favor is shown gold trimmings in this period of gay dressing and the variety is unusually large. Heavy gold military galloons are employed to strap the seams of waists, but broader gold bands are used more reservedly. The inch-wide belt of gold galloon occupies a very prominent place among trimmings, and is, for the most part, worn upon waists with added basques or peplums. Odd buckles provide the means of closing. Then there is a soft gold ribbon for the neck which is treated like any other ribbon stock, its flexibility rendering this possible. A *fleur-de-lis* device is woven in one gold galloon and a Greek design in another, the effect in both being very attractive. Dark woollen fabrics admit of these showy trimmings.

There are also gold galloons embroidered with gold spangles or jet cabochons or with both, jet materially lessening the garish effect. A fine gold gauze spread over cloth printed in Persian colors gives an artistic effect to a band trimming which is further ornamented by jet beads and an embroidery of Persian silk cord. Persian combinations in colored beads on gold galloons are also seen. In one specimen a lattice effect is produced on a gold gauze galloon. Jewels and colored spangles also glisten upon gold foundations. When white is the combination color used with a dark material, as is often the case, any gold trimming used is applied on the white, to which it takes kindly.

An expensive gold cloth is shown for vests or yokes, or for the front and back of bodices. When devoted to the last named purpose, its brightness is veiled with some white diaphanous textile, such as chiffon, either plain or embroidered. A charming effect is thus attained. There are also gold appliqué trimmings in varying widths and possessing various degrees of resemblance to lace. Heavy gold medallions may be effectively placed upon vests or yokes of white cloth, though their use is not limited to such purposes. Modistes employ them variously. Galloons of white cloth, satin or taffeta are embroidered with fine gold thread in vermicelli patterns as well as with silks in small flowers and Dresden colorings. Silk and satin bands of this sort are particularly dainty and are employed upon gowns of white satin, silk and *moiré velours*.

Conventionalized palms and geometrical figures are cut out in shaded taffeta and mounted upon net bands studded with beads. This trimming is offered in many colors and is applicable to silk or fine woollen gowns. Appliqué effects are very popular in a variety of garnitures. Fanciful collars embodying a square back, square epaulettes and pointed revers are among the novelties in appliqué decorations. One is of white cloth cut out in conventional flowers and adjusted in a gold net, the flowers being outlined with Persian silk cord. Another is of printed cloth outlined with a gold film and embroidered with jet cabochons. In a third the appliqué figures are of black velvet, some being constructed of tiny gold spangles and outlined with Persian silk. There are also net collars of the same character,

brilliant with colored spangles, and collars of black *mousseline de soie* with white *mousseline* appliqué figures embroidered at the edges with white or black silk. These collars are very decorative and may do duty upon plain bodices.

Yokes, shoulder straps, epaulettes, bodices, Berthas and like decorations are made of net, gold gauze or gold passementerie and heavily embroidered with spangles and mock jewels, for the bodices of evening gowns. A specially attractive garniture for the neck of a Pompadour waist is of black net all ablaze with jewels and beads, and one for a V-shaped bodice is similarly embellished.

Pearl trimmings in bands, in passementerie and in drapery effects are largely used for evening dresses and are shown in white with colors to produce Dresden effects. When made upon net foundations, silver or gold beads and tinted spangles of the most variety are effectively scattered among the pearls. Bands of pearl trimming, combining white, pale-pink and green pearls and cream appliqué lace edging, were used upon an evening toilette of white satin and chiffon. The satin skirt had seven gores and fell in undulating folds about the figure. Upon each side-front seam was applied a band of passementerie, the gleaming satin ground greatly enhancing its good effect. The low, round-necked bodice was full. The smooth-fitting foundation was of satin, which shone through a shirred back and fronts of chiffon. Bands of trimming were disposed vertically on the back and front, starting just below the shirring at the top and ending at the waist-line, where a belt of the trimming was arranged. The huge puff sleeves fell to the elbows and were shirred at the top like the waist, a frill of lace flowing over each below the shirring. White Suède gloves with narrow white stitching met the sleeves.

While laces are extensively used upon evening gowns, they are usually combined with other trimming. Real appliqué and Renaissance laces are oftenest employed. There are also Renaissance appliqué laces made on La Tosca nets in cream and white, and appliqué duchesse, which is also made on net but is only shown in pure white. Edgings only are shown in these last two varieties of lace. In the real appliqué, however, both insertions and edgings are displayed.

Chiffon and *mousseline* bands embroidered with silk, gold threads or spangles are quite as much in favor as ever and skilful modistes adapt them to many purposes. Fanciful cape or sailor collars are cut from chiffon and trimmed richly with lace. These are conveniently worn over silk theatre waists. Straps of lace insertion or embroidered chiffon are applied vertically upon silk and other dressy waists and fastened down at or below the bust with pearl ornaments set in a ring of Rhinestones. These ornaments suggest buttons, but are much lighter in weight, being made upon net instead of metal foundations and are, therefore, entirely appropriate to arrangements of lace and kindred trimmings.

Ribbon straps are used upon bodices and are fastened down at their lower ends beneath fancy buttons.

These fancy buttons are in high vogue. They are brought into requisition especially upon coats of the Louis XV. order and are usually chosen to harmonize with the remainder of the trimming, this being easily possible since the variety is so great. Ribbon stocks are as popular as ever. Cream satin ribbon is now greatly in demand and when not applied full and arranged in loops or a bow at the back, it is carried twice round the neck, like the stocks which our grandfathers wore, and arranged in a bow at the back. Ribbon belts are frequently chosen to correspond with the neck dressing and are simply disposed in a bow at the back. Ribbons of the Persian variety are still accorded favor, the soft coloring and uncertain designs being artistic and well suited to adorn most of the fashionable fabrics.

GARMENT - MAKING EXPLAINED AND SIMPLIFIED.—"The Art of Garment Cutting, Fitting and Making," just published by us, will yield a complete education in the science of making feminine garments to all who give it intelligent study. It treats the subject in an original manner, nearly all the methods described being the result of experiments made to determine the simplest, most economical and most artistic system of dressmaking, and the instructions being clear and complete and supplemented by full illustrations. The tailor mode of developing women's garments is fully explained, and a separate chapter is devoted to renovation and "making over," giving the book a special value to home dressmakers who, from either necessity or choice, desire to practise economy. The scientific principles which govern the construction of our patterns have been used in this work, which will give useful hints to the most skilful dressmakers and ladies' tailors, as well as valuable instruction to the amateur who sews for herself and family. Price, 2s. (by post, 2s. 3d.) or 50 cents.

OF INTEREST TO YOUNG MOTHERS.—We have lately published another edition of the valuable pamphlet entitled "Mother and Babe: Their Comfort and Care." This work is by a well known authority on such matters and contains instructions for the inexperienced regarding the proper clothing and nourishment of expectant mothers and of infants, and how to treat small children in health and sickness, together with full information regarding layettes and their making. Price, 6d. (by post, 7½d.) or 15 cents.

MIDWINTER MILLINERY.

Gorgeous effects are sought in millinery as in dress trimmings and they are found in glittering spangle and bead embroideries, sparkling Rhinestone, and steel ornaments and bright-colored flowers and ribbons. Lace, especially of the appliqué variety, is extensively used, generally in combination with other trimmings, and it always contributes a dainty, refined effect.

Soft crowns are very fashionable. They are especially picturesque when coupled with narrow brims. Pure-white satin crowns of this type under deep-cream appliqué lace embody a new idea in fashions the success of which is well exemplified in a hat upon which the satin gleams richly through the yellowish appliqué lace covering the crown. A band of pearl-and-Rhinestone trimming encircles the crown. The brim is of rose-colored velvet faced with gilt spangled net, which is shown to advantage at the back, where the brim is turned up. At the left side two rosettes of velvet sustain two small black tips and a white aigrette—for aigrettes are ubiquitous.

Another hat of the same character has a draped crown of white satin veiled with cream appliqué lace and a brim of gilt spangled *point de Gène* lace also draped with appliqué lace and bent after the manner of a Napoleon shape. In front at the left side are three small pink tips and an aigrette. The back is upturned and against the brim at one side rests a bunch of violets, while at the other side is a fan of lace. These hats are usually worn in the evening or while driving.

Brocaded velvet in a Dresden color scheme is tastefully associated with black velvet in a charming street hat of the Louis XVI. order. The soft crown is of the fancy velvet and the rather broad brim is formed of a puffing of black velvet caught up at the left side under a bunch of black tips and a white aigrette. A bunch of violets falls upon the hair at the back.

A black velvet cap of the "Angelo" style may becomingly crown a youthful head covered with fluffy tresses. The cap has a soft crown which droops over the band supporting it. Loops of cream appliqué lace and a bunch of violets are disposed at the left side and at the right side a small black tip falls upon the hair.

A unique-looking toque is of accordion side-plaited black velvet overlaid with steel spangled net. At the center of the back is fixed a butterfly bow of turquoise satin ribbon between two black tips that fall on the hair, and around the brim is adjusted a realistic-looking serpent composed of black scale spangles. At one side of the front the head stands erect and at the other side is a coil into which the serpent is adroitly twisted. This contributes a brilliant trimming.

A veritable picture hat, very dressy in effect, has a large, soft crown of rose-colored velvet shirred at the bottom and a rather broad brim of black felt edged with felt braid. The brim is rolled upward at the left side and under it is fixed a Rhinestone buckle that sparkles prettily when it rests upon dark locks. Over its edge fall three black plumes.

Very Frenchy is a hat of light-gray felt the brim of which is draped with dark-gray velvet under cream lace sown with small steel spangles. At the left side is a bow of gray velvet which supports a white feather aigrette. The back is built up with white chrysanthemums among which is a bit of foliage to break up the massed whiteness of the flowers. The style of this hat is exceptionally jaunty and its neutral coloring renders it adaptable to a gown of almost any hue.

Black hair lace with appliques of cream lace is very stylish as a brim trimming. It is effectively used over a broad chenille-covered wire brim on a hat having a soft crown of light-blue miroir velvet. At the left side are two black tips and a white aigrette and at the right side is a single tip. On a twist of blue velvet under the crown toward the back is a white silk rosette.

Hair lace is also used in a toque having a soft crown of green velvet embroidered with jet beads and tiny gold spangles, and a brim made of the lace and adjusted like the brim of a Napoleon hat. At the left side a black tip and a white aigrette are upheld by a rosette of green velvet.

The black-and-white combination is as fashionable in millinery as in gowns. It is carried out effectively in a broad-brimmed hat of white felt. At the left side is disposed a fan of white lace and against it are set four black tips which fall away from each other and their common center. At the right side is a large black satin bow and another is arranged under the brim where it rolls from the face at the left side.

A most attractive combination hat has a soft crown of green velvet and a brim of black felt braid slightly fluted. In front velvet is spread in fans and between them is an enamelled ornament, while back of the fans are green merle wings that extend toward the back. Under the brim at each side white chiffon is arranged in a knot in front and in an end at the back, cream Valenciennes lace being sewed at the edge.

A simple hat for every-day wear and one that may be easily reproduced is a broad-brimmed brown felt. At the front and back are arranged broad bows of Persian ribbon in which a rosedagreen tone predominates, and from the center of the front bow rises a full white aigrette which completes the trimming.

A fitting complement to a brown cloth gown is a hat having a brown velvet crown and a brim of brown satin veiled with black accordion-plaited chiffon. At the left side rise two brown tips and an aigrette and at each side of the back under the brim are clustered brown velvet roses with yellow centers.

A brown chenille-dotted veil should be worn with a hat of this kind. Brown veils are especially flattering to the complexion, unless it be very sallow, when a fine-meshed black veil with widely separated chenille dots is recommended. Navy-blue veils are pretty and stylish, but they not only reveal but emphasize every complexional blemish. The blue veil should, therefore, be cautiously chosen.

For travelling and shopping the favorite hat, and the one which is most easily put on, is the felt Alpine. It is shown in navy-blue, brown and black, and in light-gray with a black silk-bound brim and a band of the same round the crown. When the severity which characterizes an untrimmed Alpine hat is unbecoming, one or two quills may be thrust into the band at the left side. The gray Alpine hats are at present especially smart. A veil is always worn with a hat of this kind, one of tissue or chiffon being preferable to net, which is more in keeping with a dressy hat.

Black chenille braid adorns a very stylish hat. Black satin ribbon is folded about the crown and fastened in front with a cut-steel buckle. At the left side black tips and an aigrette are supported by a rosette of black crimped satin and at the right is a rosette of plain satin. Color is given the hat by bunches of American Beauty roses with foliage adjusted at each side of the back under the brim, which is reversed in the approved way.

A tasteful union of colors is carried out in a small hat of the toque order. The crown is of green taffeta in a réséda shade and over it is softly draped black net embroidered with jet beads and spangles. The brim is of hair lace wrought with black chenille and formed in flutes all round. At the left side is a rosette of green miroir velvet, above which towers a green aigrette of much lighter hue, and at the right is a bunch of violets. Violets are also clustered at each side of the back under the brim. This hat is exceptionally dressy and equally appropriate for day or evening wear.

Turbans are trim and jaunty and seem to belong to tailor-made walking suits. A box-shaped turban has a crown of black felt braid and a brim of black velvet edged top and bottom with braid. Black taffeta is twisted round the crown and arranged in a chou at the left side to support two fancy black quills.

A dainty cap-shaped head-dress is of black velvet drawn in soft folds over the crown. A simple band acting as a substitute for the brim. At the left side toward the back is arranged a loop of black velvet, and in front of it is a widely-spreading fan of cream appliqué lace against which rests a bunch of violets, some of the flowers straggling upon the hair.

Shaded purple roses without foliage give color to a stylish hat of black chenille braid, the brim of which is slightly bent in front. Against the crown in front is a black velvet bow, above which stand two black tips and the inevitable aigrette. At each side of the back the brim is turned up under a tuft of roses, which rest easily upon the hair.

Narrow-back sailor-hats are as fashionable as ever and are as generally becoming as the straw sailor which inevitably returns with the Summer. One reason for their popularity is the fact that they are easily trimmed, the broad effect being usually preferred in their adornment. Glacé taffeta in two colors, Persian ribbon, crinkled velvet formed in bows or rosettes and colored wings or quills are the usual decorations, which even an amateur of moderate skill can arrange with satisfaction.

MEXICAN STAMPED LEATHER.

BY M. C. FREDERICK.

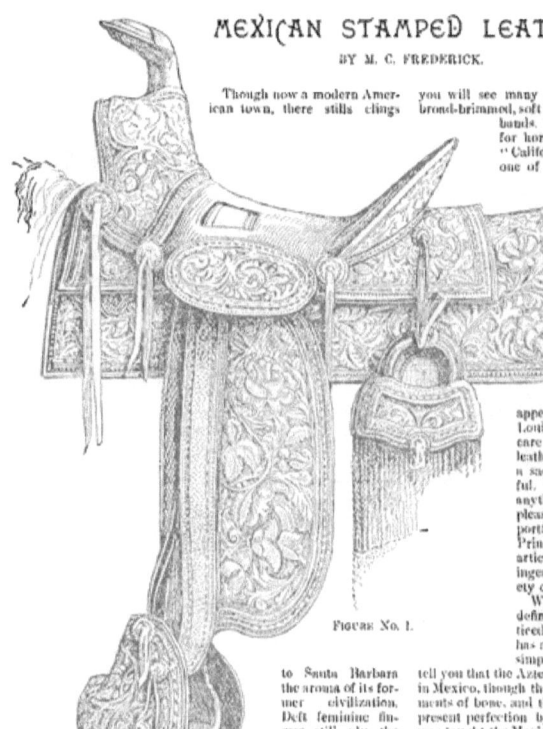

FIGURE NO. 1.

Though now a modern American town, there still clings to Santa Barbara the aroma of its former civilization. Deft feminine fingers still ply the needle on Spanish drawn-work of exquisite fineness and beauty, and still more characteristic of the days when the village was governed by an *alcalde* is the beautiful stamped leather work of the men. This, in the old days when horsemanship was the one great accomplishment of the people and large sums of money were spent on equestrian trappings, was a most important part of saddle making. At that time, however, the chief decoration was rich embroidery done in silver and gold and bright-colored silks, to which the stamping was necessary. Eventually the embroidery disappeared and the entire surface of the huge saddles was covered with the stamping.

Should you, as most tourists do, visit Santa Barbara in Winter, you will see many gentlemen and not a few ladies wearing broad-brimmed, soft felt hats of a light shade, with stamped leather bands. These *sombreros* are especially popular for horseback riding and very picturesque and "Californian" are they. Perhaps you purchase one of them, and then at a shop devoted especially to leather goods seek a band for it. While doing so a variety of other lovely things in the same curiously wrought leather will meet and delight your eye. Had your visit been twelve years earlier, you would have purchased only the hatband, unless, indeed, you had invested in one of the saddles to which the work was at that time almost entirely confined. The Princess Louise came then, and the beauty of the stamped work at once appealed to her artistic sense. But Princess Louise did not want a hat-band, neither did she care for a saddle, yet have a specimen of Mexican leather stamping she must. So she consulted a saddler. He did not know. It was doubtful. The stamping had never been applied to anything but the heaviest of leather, but to please her Highness he would try. Result: a portfolio so completely satisfactory that the Princess ordered several more, besides other articles she suggested. And so, thanks to her ingenious idea, you can now find a great variety of leather goods in this much admired work.

Where did the art originate? It has not been definitely decided. Until recently it was practiced only by the Mexicans, of whom California has a goodly population, transferred to us in fee simple along with the state. Some of them will tell you that the Aztecs thus adorned leather when Cortez landed in Mexico, though their work was very crudely done with instruments of bone, and that the art was improved and brought to its present perfection by the Spanish *conquistadores*. Others say it was taught the Mexicans by the Mission Fathers from old Spain, and if you search farther still you will find reason to believe that it is of Moorish origin and was probably introduced into Spain at the time of the Moorish invasion in the eighth century. Yet it is always called Mexican, never Spanish. It may be well to state that "Mexican stamped leather," "Mexican art leather" and "Mexican carved leather" are one and the same. In some respects it is similar to the stamped leather popular among English ladies for binding their favorite volumes and spoken of as "engraved and tooled calf," or "cut and stamped leather."

FIGURE NO. 2.

but it is very much more elaborate and artistic-looking. You may see a Santa Barbara leather worker any day, with selected, cowhide or saddle skirting for the heavier work and calf-skin for the lighter. Each worker, as a rule, makes his own tools from nails or small steel rods about the thickness of pencils and a trifle longer than the width of the palm, the number and variety depending on his skill and ingenuity. Besides the small variation in thickness, they differ only in the shape of the end that imprints the leather. There is always a bluntly pointed instrument used as a tracer, a few edged tools of different widths—some straight, some curved—used for cutting, and a smoother. All the rest are dies, or punches, the device often being the individual idea of the worker, though many are used in common, among these last being tiny stars, crescents, rays, a series of minute circles, or the ordinary stipple for background work.

The leather is first moistened with a sponge until the surface becomes soft and yielding. With the tracer the worker rapidly draws a group of curves as with a pen. Over these an edged tool is drawn in the same manner. The tracing process is often deemed superfluous by experts, the cutting strokes being made at once, though a false one would spoil the work. The smoother, the end of which is slanting, is held firmly against the leather, its longer ends following the cut. It is driven along by the spoke-mallet, one side of the cut being thereby hammered down, the other remaining untouched, to be ornamented with delicate tracery later on. This tool leaves behind it a smooth, polished depression, which is really a bevel, separating the petals of the flowers and also separating the background from the flowers, stems, fruit and foliage, by throwing the opposite side of the incision into strong relief, effecting in the stamped figure what shading does in drawing. The smoother is likewise used inside the margins of broad petals, with a little space between, the

FIGURE No. 3.

FIGURE No. 4.

the simplest of instruments—a number of small stamps or punches, a spoke from a wagon wheel and a small slab of marble on the table before him—turning out work most artistic in character and finish. He works so easily and so rapidly that you wonder any thing so beautiful should demand so little care, just as Nast, Beard, or Aoki, the Japanese artist, will paint a picture so quickly and in such a tantalizingly nonchalant manner that it looks as though any tyro could do the same thing. It is true that pleasing results may be obtained in stamped leather with comparatively little practice, but the work of which one may feel justly proud only comes from long practice, a steady hand, an accurate eye and genuine artistic perceptions. The very best quality of russet leather, perfectly free from oil, is upward slant toward the center, to give the effect of a curled edge. Much of the richness of the work is due to the use of this simple little instrument.

Then, with marvelous rapidity, the worker takes up tool after tool, and under the light blows of the mallet, falling as regularly as a watch ticks, the more solid work is put in, then the light lines, stamens, etc.

Although a pattern is easily transferred, as in wood carving, the design is usually executed free-hand directly on the leather in the manner described. The design is evolved as the work proceeds, a leaf here, a scroll there, according to the space to be filled and the symmetry of the whole. The stems have the rounded appearance of real stems, and there is an absence of flatness and stiffness in the best work hardly to be expected from the material employed. Notwithstanding the depth of the stamping, no part of the leather is cut away, and when finished, if the work is skilfully done, all trace of the cutting has disappeared. Once completed, the elasticity which admits of such beautiful results does not return to mar the effect, and the saddle that has encountered rain and all kinds of hard usage still retains its ornamentation. The various articles represented in the accompanying illustrations were selected with special reference to showing the boldness and freedom of this decorative work, but it may be as fine and as intricate as the skill and imagination of the artist will permit. The picture of a stamped leather saddle (represented in

Figure No. 5.

Figure No. 6.

detail at figure No. 1) is given to illustrate the purpose for which this artistic work is still extensively employed. There are saddles on which the work is so elaborate, with such exquisite fineness of detail, as to make them very valuable.

The basket border shown on the ends of the music roll (figure No. 2) is another favorite, used both for border and all-over work. A square stamp, properly marked, alternates with a plain space in such a manner as to admirably represent a basket effect.

The bellows (figure No. 3) has for years been a favorite article for decoration in wood carving, burnt work, etc., and it is particularly effective in stamped leather, the brass nozzle and fancy-headed brass tacks giving it just the proper finish and contrast in color.

The portfolio (figure No. 4) exhibits a typical Mexican design. The little border added is very popular on nearly all kinds of work. Its plain Greek pattern is made with a little triangular punch, two sides of which are curved, the imprint being repeated in two rows, with the points alternating.

The design in detail for a card-case (figure No. 5) shows the finished work on the left half, while on the right the outlines have been cut and the heavy tooling done.

In the full-sized drawing of a flower (figure No. 6) the markings of the various tools are clearly shown. The dark margin is not background, as might be inferred, but a part of the figure itself, which is often further ornamented with a border of rays as shown in one part. Indeed, in most cases the design so completely fills in the leather that the background is scarcely apparent and, although depressed, it is ordinarily so slightly marked as to be hardly distinguishable from the plain surface of the leather.

The Mexican leather workers' designs are always in arabesques of a character peculiarly their own. They conventionalize plants or flowers to which they take a fancy, the passion flower used on the tennis belt (figure No. 7) being a favorite and capable of great elaboration. There is a certain characterizing individuality in the work of each artist that renders it readily distinguishable by experts. Imagination alone frequently furnishes the motif of the best designs, but there are always the same flowing lines and grace of composition.

Besides the articles usually found in a stock of leather goods, this decoration is applicable to many other uses. The writer has seen a photograph of a handsome table made in the City of Mexico, the leather top of which was decorated with a stamped depiction of the national sport of bull fighting. A gentleman recently paid a large sum for two stamped leather panels from an old building in Spain. Stamped leather panels might effectively be used in mantels, book-cases and cabinets, and many other uses will suggest themselves to the artistic home-maker. With age this leather becomes dark and exceedingly rich in tone.

Figure No. 7.

its beauty being greatly enhanced. Very small scroll and other tasteful patterns, mounted on mouldings, make handsome frames for large pictures, but as the frames are likely to attract more attention than the picture, they should be used with the greatest discretion. Boxes of every shape, hand satchels, chatelaines, bags, music rolls, purses, fancy photograph and mirror frames (figure No. 8), book and magazine covers, cigar cases, diaries, shawl-straps, trunk tags, table mats, wall pockets and card-cases are some of the articles to which the stamping readily lends itself. To whatever it may be applied, no decorative work is more satisfying, or more richly repays the time and patience spent upon it. Sometimes the ground work is stained a different color, though this is considered in rather questionable taste and is never done by the Mexicans.

However, this process of decoration is adaptable to entirely different modes of treatment, as was seen in the California room of the Woman's Building at the World's Fair, where was shown an entire set of furniture upholstered in leather decorated with a cactus design originated for the purpose. In such work very few tools are required, and the clever wood carver, burnt worker or hammered brass decorator might very readily adapt designs used in those arts to leather stamping, securing some novel and original effects. But it must be admitted that the Mexican manifests his good taste in confining himself to foliated and floriated scrolls, as that style of treatment gives less evenness of surface and more "expression" than any other. Even his largest patterns have no suggestion of coarseness, and in a simple design in which there is very little tooling there is a roundness and finish not seen nor even attainable in machine-pressed leather. Sometimes only a neat border is used. An appropriate frame for a burnt-work etching may be made on the same piece of leather.

Specimens of Mexican stamped leather have found their way to every part of the United States as well as to various European countries, and the approval with which it has everywhere been received shows that as a decorative art it does not depend upon a passing fancy, but becomes more firmly established the better it is known. Any good blacksmith should be able to make a set of experimental tools for essaying this work.

FIGURE NO. 8.

THE HOME.

SIXTEENTH PAPER.—ADULTERATED AND DETERIORATED FOODS.

For the past decade or two there really have been very few food products sold that had concealed in them mischievous adulterations, although rival producers cry out to the public: "Beware of worthless imitations!" "Be sure you get the original article!" "None genuine unless our signature is on the label!" This sort of "wolf" warning deepens distrust and awakens needless anxieties, since in nine cases out of ten one preparation is just as good as its rivals selling for about the same price. Very likely none of them is as excellent as it might be and will be when an alert and instructed public and producers actuated by intelligent self-interest combine to raise the standard of food to a higher level, ultimately, perhaps, to perfection. Writers upon food adulteration have done the public no small service, but they go on and on crying out against adulterations while chemists of ability and unimpeachable honor, employed by the government to look with scientific severity into our food preparations, find little to criticise and less to condemn.

Since 1875 no serious indignation against grocers' goods has been justifiable. Such adulterations as have been discovered have been almost invariably simple dilutions in quality. Food exhibitions have done much toward opening the understanding of our intelligent and influential citizens to the comparative merits of various foods, and we have thereby been taught to exact a high standard of quality in every article purchased from grocers, and, as a rule, we are getting what we demand. A careful testing of the differing brands thus annually exposed in competition has taught the progressive housekeeper that the same food product may differ in strength, flavor and appearance according to the materials and mode of manufacture. The influences set afloat at such expositions happily go back to gardens, farms, vineyards, orchards, and thence to canners, preservers, mills, wine presses, cattle ranches, poultry yards and to private and co-operative dairies. The producer will discover that prosperity comes only from the best products when the housewife learns which is the best and refuses to purchase any other. Even with the superiority of present food preparations there still remain grades of value and attractiveness in many articles, differences that will always be found as long as there are skilled and unskilled producers, the latter perhaps, as conscientious as the former but less capable. To learn which of many brands is best and to require it even though it cost more money than is demanded for less dexterously manufactured foods, is a duty to one's family as well as a satisfaction to the purchaser's sense of justice. It is an unworthy sentimentality to choose the products of incapable persons on the plea that "they must live." Nature's law calls for the survival of the fittest and Nature is both wise and kind.

Of course, there are deteriorated foods which cannot properly be catalogued in a list of adulterations, and to pass upon these belongs largely to the province of the cook. Nor need the intelligence of this functionary be large. Meats that have been kept too long or were unfit for food before the animal was slaughtered bear the marks of inferiority outwardly, and so do fruits and vegetables. Only the direst poverty excuses those who purchase such health-destroying substances.

In France, where the preparation and preservation of food products has been carried nearer perfection than in any other country, the government rigidly inspects the quality of all nourishment sold in its markets, and is now giving attention even to the modes of cooking them. It has during the past year established cooking schools which pay especial attention to the preparation of foods calculated to promote health. The editor of *Le Gourmet*, M. Colombier, has charge and supervision of this instruction. He first takes a class to market and points out the good and bad qualities in foods. When he first began this mode of instruction his comments to his pupils upon the stale articles exposed for sale, meats, fruits, dairy products and vegetables, so angered the market people that his subsequent visits had to be made under police protection. Among the interesting recommendations M. Colombier is urging upon French cooks is the preservation of the natural flavors of each kind of food instead of destroying it by sauces and seasonings, thereby also retarding digestion and assimilation. This is a valuable hint to English and American cooks as well.

From reports furnished by the government of the United States one finds that there are more marked and general adulterations in drinks than in foods, in coffees and teas than in cereals, in jellies than in preserved or canned fruits, the latter not affording opportunities for secreting unworthy adulterations nor for concealing overripe or immature fruit. Of course, this does not apply to small fruits, blackberries, whortleberries, etc., which may have been heedlessly gathered or left too long unpreserved. For these articles the honor of the persons who preserve them must be trusted at first—and experience afterwards.

It has been claimed that poison is generated about and in the solder used to seal the cans and around the rubber rings and corks employed with glass cans and bottles. For the first accusation there is no justification. Whatever danger there may be of lead poisoning is due to changes in the metal after the can is opened and the contents left in it. Every can of fruit, fish, meat or vegetables should be emptied into an earthern dish as soon as opened and every glass jar should have its rubber ring removed from possible contact with the acid. Poison from chemical changes in the rubber is but remotely possible, but it is easy to be on the safe side in this matter.

To know whether a can of beef, fish or, indeed, any food product is preserved properly in tin—that is, while at its highest heat, one has only to notice the top of the can. If this be depressed, even in the least, its contents are in a proper condition. If it be raised or even perfectly level, the article was not sufficiently heated when it was sealed and it is or has been in a more or less fermenting condition. A little careful observation of the tops of cans by the purchaser will prevent a wrong selection or, if the goods have been ordered without inspection, they should be critically examined at once upon receipt and each can that does not show a slight depression should be immediately returned or its shipper notified.

What effect age has upon canned meats, fruits and vegetables no one knows definitely, but experience proves that after they are a year old they are not as good in flavor as when fresher, and very likely they are not as wholesome. The prudent purchaser will demand foods put up within the year. Voyagers to the Arctic or Antarctic regions or those undergoing a siege may have to eat foods canned long ago, but we need not.

To determine whether tea is pure is the province of the expert alone. The consumer has only to suit his taste as to flavor and avoid purchasing a too-cheap product. Black tea—so its importers claim—is the least likely to be adulterated with pulverized soapstone, Prussian-blue or plumbago.

Coffee is often adulterated when it is purchased already ground and put up in packages, but its admixtures are not as injurious to health as to one's temper and taste. It is difficult to adulterate raw coffee, although to those who have not made themselves acquainted with the appearance of the various coffees grown in different countries, all coffees look very nearly alike. But ah, their contrasts in flavor! A coffee importer replied when asked which kind of coffee is the most general favorite: "The kind that is habitually taken." Of roasted unground coffees government experts have found no adulterations; therefore, the purchaser is safe when he has his roasted coffee ground at home or under his own eyes at the store. Of ground coffees nineteen in twenty-one specimens tested were found to be adulterated, but none of the mixtures were harmful to health, consisting as they did of parched wheat, rye, beans, peas, chicory, hominy, caramel, liquorice, etc. To test ground coffee, place a little in water and if pure it will float and stain the water slowly. If of chicory, peas or beans, it sinks. The chicory will also color the water. Another test is to take some of the ground product into the mouth. Coffee crumbles when crushed between the teeth, while chicory is soft and compressible.

Fruit jellies should be purchased of trustworthy makers because of tested specimens most were found to be made of apples flavored with essences and colored with aniline—not unwholesome but one wants what he asks for.

No chocolates or cocoas were found to be adulterated.

Of baking powders nearly a hundred were analyzed and none of them were found to contain harmful adulterations, the least desirable ingredient being alum, not an enemy to health in the small quantities used in baking powders. Flour and starch are said to be essential to them. Ammonia, tartrate of lime and (in eight specimens) a little terra alba were also found. These we know are not essentials, although they are not so mischievous that great anxiety need be felt if one is compelled to use a baking powder containing them. However, when possible, such combinations will be scorned by good housekeepers.

Lard is adulterated, if at all, by water. If it sputters when heated, it is deteriorated in value though not in wholesomeness.

Butter is often mixed with oleomargarine, but the latter is more wholesome if sweet and clean than butter that has not been properly washed or pressed free from soured milk. Its odor, its grain or texture and the business honor of the buttermaker must be trusted in selecting butter. Very little injurious adulteration is possible to it, but it may contain a vicious acid engendered by age; therefore, always avoid what is called "cooking butter." Sweet lard or fresh oleomargarine is safer as well as more agreeable to the taste than stale butter. The quality of rancid butter cannot be concealed by flavoring, nor can any but the most robust digestion safely cope with it.

Milk may be poor because some of its cream has been removed, because water has been added to it or because the cows have been imperfectly nourished. Good brands of condensed milk are preferred to inferior fresh milk, both for health's sake and from the standpoint of economy. In cities the law can usually be depended upon to preserve purchasers from frauds in milk.

Of an immense number of specimens of white sugar gathered from all sources not one was found unadulterated and only a very small number of brown sugars were discovered to be impure, and these had in them only a little glucose, which is not harmful to health though cheaper and not so sweet as cane sugar. Pulverized sugar is often suspected of containing adulterations. Whether it is or not may be readily determined. One has only to dissolve a spoonful or so of it in a glass of water; if it contains flour or gypsum, the adulterating materials will sink to the bottom of the glass because they are not soluble as is the sugar.

Olive oil cannot be cheap if it is genuine. Perhaps no other article we consume is so frequently adulterated. However, the adulterating liquids are usually harmless.

Strained honey is often only a mixture of a little of the real article with much glucose, the latter making it far less sweet, though by some tastes it is preferred. But purchasers prefer to make their own mixtures, and not pay honey prices for a much cheaper substance. The inability of most persons to detect deteriorations when purchasing strained honey would suggest that it is wisest to buy honey in the comb, although it is claimed that there is a clever method of manufacturing wax combs and filling them with honey not from bees.

The housewife who is able to do so without injury to her health or neglect of her children, should cause to be properly made in her own kitchen, bread, pastry, jellies and preserves and have also the canning of fruits and vegetables done for her family's use under her own supervision. She may then sleep peacefully and not dream of having fed her family upon poisoned foods and rejoice when awake over the superior flavor of the preparations thus skilfully made at home. Directions for dexterity in sealing, proportions of seasoning, times of gathering or selecting and purchasing materials for Winter storage are among the interesting studies of many of the best educated women. They like such occupation, because it justifies their pride in the excellence of their tables, and they like the thrift of it and the safety to delicate digestions of such pure aliments.

A. B. LONGSTREET.

PATTERNS BY MAIL.—In ordering patterns by mail, either from this office or from any of our agencies, be careful to give your post-office address in full. When patterns are desired for ladies, the *number* and *size* of each should be carefully stated; when patterns for misses, girls, boys or little folks are needed, the *number*, *size* and *age* should be given in each instance.

CROCHETING.—No. 55.

ABBREVIATIONS USED IN CROCHETING.

l.—Loop.
ch. st.—Chain stitch.
s. c.—Single crochet.
d. c.—Double crochet.
h. d. c.—Half-double crochet.
tr. c.—Treble crochet.
p.—Picot.
sl. st.—Slip stitch.

Repeat.—This means to work designated rows, rounds or portions of the work as many times as directed.

☞ * Stars or asterisks mean, as mentioned wherever they occur, that the details given between them are to be repeated as many times as directed before going on with the details which follow the next *. As an example: * 6 ch., 1 s. c. in the next space and repeat twice more from * (or last *), means that you are to crochet as follows: 6 ch., 1 s. c. in the next space, 6 ch., 1 s. c. in the next space, 6 ch., 1 s. c. in the next space, thus repeating the 6 ch., 1 s. c. in the next space, *twice* more after making it the first time, making it *three* times in all before proceeding with the next part of the direction.

CROCHETED FASCINATOR.

Figure No. 1.—This fascinator is made of Ice wool and Shetland floss. Make a chain of 15 stitches.

First row.—Make 1 s. c. in the 6th st. from the hook, 3 ch., 1 s. c. in the 6th st. from last s. c., 3 ch. skip 3 st., 1 s. c. in the next, 2 ch., skip 3, 1 s. c. in the next, turn.

Second row.—Join on Shetland floss, make a ch. of 3 sts., then 1 d. c. in each of the 3 sts. of the two 3-chs. and 1 in the s. c. between, making 7 in all, but only work off 2 loops of each d. c. until the 7 are picked up, then draw through all on the hook and close the half puff by putting the wool over the hook and drawing through the loop. Make 3 ch., 1 s. c., 3 ch. in the next s. c., then another half puff like the one just made, 3 ch.

Third row.—Make 7 d. c. in the eye of the half-puff working the d. c. off as each is made; complete the second half-puff the same as the first.

Fourth row.—Resume the Ice wool. Make 3 ch., 1 s. c. in the 3rd d. c. of puff, 3 ch., 1 s. c. in the 5th d. c., 4 ch., 1 d. c. over the s. c. in the middle of the first half-puff, also fastening down the second half-puff with this d. c., 4 ch., 1 s. c. in the fourth d. c. of next puff, 3 ch., 1 s. c. between the sixth and seventh d. c., 3 ch., 1 s. c. at the middle of puff, 3 ch., 1 s. c. in the second d. c. of first half of puff, turn. This row has been worked on the wrong side of puffs.

Fifth row.—4 ch., 1 s. c. in s. c. of last row. 3 ch., 1 s. c. in next s. c., 3 ch., 1 s. c. in same s. c. along the side. * 3 ch., 1 s. c. in middle of 3-ch., and repeat 3 times more from *, 3 ch., turn.

Sixth row.—1 s. c. in middle of 3 ch., 2 ch., wind the wool around the tip of the little finger 5 times, pass the hook under the wind-over and fasten with a single crochet, 1 ch., 1 s. c. in the middle of next 3-ch., 3 ch., 1 s. c. in the middle of next 3-ch. and repeat twice more from *, 4 ch., turn.

Seventh row.—* Make 2 s. c. over the wind-overs, 3 ch., 1 s. c. in middle of 3-ch., 4 ch., and repeat twice more from *; fasten the last 4-ch. over the 3-ch., 3 ch., turn.

Eighth row.—1 s. c. over the first ch., and repeat across the row with 3-chs., and s. c.

Ninth row.—Like the last; then 3 puffs in the next row, made as directed for the second row. Continue in this way making 1 extra wind-over and 1 extra puff in each wind-over-and-puff-row for two more rows, then make 2 rows of each until there are 8 puffs in a row, then 1 row of 9 puffs, 1 of 10, 1 of 11, 1 of 12 and 1 of 13; this brings you to the center of fascinator, and after this row there should be 15 wind-over rings; then make 13 puffs and finish to correspond with the first half, decreasing in the same manner as the widenings were made. Around the edges of the fascinator make scollops of 2 long d. c. each, and a picot made thus: 4 ch., 1 s. c. in first st. of ch., 2 d. c., 1 p., 2 d. c., 1 p., 2 d. c. all in the same place, fasten down with a s. c. so that the scollop will lie perfectly flatly.

HAIR-PIN LACE.

Figure No. 2.—Make the hair-pin work about half an inch wide, with 3 s. c. over each wind-over, and of any length desired.

To make the Heading:—*First row.*—1 d. c. in first loop of hair-pin work, * 2 ch., 1 d. c. in next loop, and repeat from * to end of row, turn.

Second row.—3 ch., 1 d. c. in first double underneath, * 2 ch., 1 d. c. in next double and repeat from * to end of row.

To make the Edge:—*First row.*—1 d. c. in first loop of hair-pin work, * 2-ch., 1 d. c. in next loop, and repeat from * to end of row.

Second row.—1 d. c. in first double underneath. * 2 d. c. in next space, 1 d. c. in double underneath, and repeat from *, 6 ch., skip two spaces, 1 d. c. in next double, and repeat from first * to end of row.

Third row.—10 d. c. in space, with 6 ch. between the 5th and 6th doubles to end of row.

Fourth row.—8 d. c. in first space, 8 ch., 8 d. c. in next space, and repeat to end of row.

FIGURE No. 1.—CROCHETED FASCINATOR.

Fifth row.—5 d. c. in first space of 4th row, * 6 ch. and catch it in the 2nd stitch of the 6-ch., repeat twice from *; make 5 d. c. in same space and repeat to end of row.

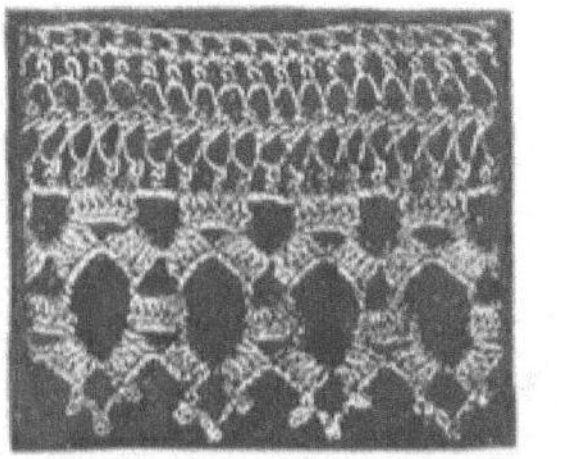

EDGING OF FEATHER-EDGE BRAID AND CROCHET.

FIGURE No. 3.—Crochet on one side of a piece of feather-edge braid as follows:

First row.—*With 1 s. c. fasten together 4 loops to form an angle; then three times alternately 1 ch., 1 s. c. on the next 3 loops; then * 5 ch., 1 s. c. on the same loop on which the last s. c. was worked, twice alternately 1 ch., 1 s. c. on the next 2 loops; repeat 5 times from *, then 1 ch. and repeat from *, but at every repetition, instead of the middle of the first 5-ch. work 1 s. c. on the middle of the last ch. in the preceding figure.

Second row.—On other side of braid * 9 s. c. separated each by 1 ch. on the 9 loops over the angle, then for one figure work 9-ch., 1 sl. st. on the last of these, 11 s. c. on the 9-ch., 1 sl. st. on the st. on which the preceding sl. st. was worked, then 4 s. c. separated each by 1 ch. on next 4 loops, 1 ch., fasten together the following 4 loops with 1 s. c., 1 ch., 4 s. c. separated each by 1 ch. on the next 4 loops, 1 figure as before, but fasten the 5th s. c. to the corresponding st. in the first figure, and repeat from *.

Third row.—Take a second piece of feather-edge braid and on one side work one round like the last worked to complete the four-leaf design, fastening the two figures to the corresponding figures, and joining points of the design with a single crochet as represented.

Fourth row (on the other side of the braid).—Like the second row. (See picture.)

Fifth row or top.—* 1 s. c. on the point in the preceding round, 8 chs. caught with s. c. as represented.

Sixth row.—Treble crochets alternating with 1-chs. in every other stitch of ch. below.

Seventh row.—2 s. c. in every 1-ch. of sixth round.

CROCHETED DESIGN FOR INFANTS' HOODS, SACKS, CAPES, AFGHANS, PURSES, ETC.

FIGURE No. 4.—*First row.*—Make a chain of the desired length, divisible by 16 if possible. If, however, it requires a few more stitches than some multiple of 16, allow one-half of the number at each side.

Second row.—Single crochet the entire length, and turn.

Third row.—(Supposing the number of stitches to be divisible by 16.) 7 s. c., * 6 ch. and fasten in next s. c.; 9 ch. and fasten in same; 6 ch. and fasten in same s. c.; 15 s. c. *. Repeat between the stars to end of row, and turn.

Fourth row.—7 s. c., * 1 ch. and carry it back of ch.-loops of last row, and then make 15 s. c. *. Repeat between the stars to end of row; turn.

Fifth, Sixth, Seventh and Eighth rows.—S. c. entire length, and turn.

Ninth row.—3 s. c., * 3 d. c. in first of chained loops of 3rd row, 1 ch., 3 d. c. in same loop; omit 2 s. c. of last row and make 5 s. c., then 3 d. c. in last of chained loops. (Leave the center loop.) 1 ch., 3 d. c. in same loop, 9 s. c. *. Repeat between the stars to end of row, turn.

Tenth row.—3 s. c., * 2 ch. (Leave the 6 d. c.) 5 s. c., 2 ch., 9 s. c. *. Repeat from * to * to end of row, turn.

Eleventh row.—3 s. c. *; put hook through the loop made by the 1-ch. in cluster of 6 d. c. and through first ch., and draw thread through both thus making it 1 s. c.; 7 s. c., put hook through cluster of 6 d. c. and last ch. st. thus making 1 s. c., 9 s. c. *. Repeat between the stars to end of row, turn.

Twelfth row.—Same as 5th row.

Thirteenth row.—6 s. c., * 3 d. c. in center-loop of 3rd row, 1 ch., 3 d. c. in same loop; omit 3 s. c. of last row, 13 s. c. *. Repeat to end of row, turn.

Fourteenth row.—6 s. c., * 3 ch., 13 s. c. *. Repeat between the stars to end, turn.

Fifteenth row.—7 s. c. *; put hook through loop in last cluster of 6 d. c. and through next s. c. of last row thus making it 1 s. c., 7 s. c., 6 ch. and fasten in next s. c. of last row; 9 ch. and fasten in same st., 6 ch. and fasten in same st., 7 s. c. *. Repeat between the stars, turn.

Sixteenth row.—15 s. c., * 1 ch., 15 s. c. *. Repeat between the stars to end of row, turn.

Seventeenth, Eighteenth, Nineteenth and Twentieth rows.—Same as 5th row.

Twenty-first row.—11 s. c., * 3 d. c. in first loop of 6 ch., 1 ch., 3 d. c. in same loop; omit 2 s. c. of last row, 5 s. c., 3 d. c. in last loop of 6-ch., 1 ch., 6 d. c. in same loop, 12 s. c. *. Repeat between the stars to end of row, turn.

Twenty-second row.—11 s. c., * 2 ch. (behind loops), 5 s. c., 2 ch. (behind loops), 7 s. c. *. Repeat between stars to end of row, turn.

Twenty-third row.—11 s. c. *; put hook through loop of first cluster of 6 d. c. and also through s. c. of last row, thus making it 1 s. c.; 7 s. c., put hook through loop of last cluster and through s. c. and make 1 s. c. *. Repeat between the stars to end of row, turn.

Twenty-fourth row.—Same as 5th row.

Twenty-fifth row.—14 s. c., * 3 d. c. in center loop, 1 ch., 3 d. c. in same loop; omit 3 s. c., make 13 s. c. *. Repeat between the stars to end of row, turn.

Twenty-sixth row.—14 s. c., * 3 ch. (behind loops), 13 s. c. *. Repeat between the stars to end of row, turn.

Twenty-seventh row.—* 7 s. c., 6 ch., fasten in next s. c. of last row; 9 ch., fasten in same st., 6 ch., fasten in same st., 7 s. c.; put hook through loop of last cluster of 6 d. c. and through

FIGURE No. 4.—CROCHETED DESIGN FOR INFANTS' HOODS, SACKS, CAPES, AFGHANS, PURSES, ETC.

s. c. to make 1 s. c. *. Repeat between the stars to end of row. To continue the work repeat from 4th row, inclusive.

THE ART OF KNITTING.—No. 56.

ABBREVIATIONS USED IN KNITTING.

k.—Knit plain.
p.—Purl, or as it is often called, seam.
pl.—Plain knitting.
n.—Narrow.
k 2 to.—knit 2 together. Same as n.
th o or o.—Throw the thread over the needle.
Make one.—Make a stitch thus: Throw the thread in front of the needle and knit the next stitch in the ordinary manner. (In the next row or round this throw-over, or put over as it is frequently called, is used as a stitch.) Or, knit one and purl one out of a stitch.
To Knit Crossed.—Insert needle in the back of the stitch and knit as usual.
sl.—Slip a stitch from the left needle to the right needle without knitting it.
sl and b.—Slip and bind. Slip one stitch, knit the next; pass the slipped stitch over the knit stitch as in binding off work.
To Bind or Cast Off.—Either slip or knit the first stitch; knit the next; pass the first or slipped stitch over the second, and repeat as far as directed.
Row.—Knitting once across the work when but two needles are used.
Round.—Knitting once around the work when four or more needles are used, as in a sock or stocking.
Repeat.—This means to work designated rows, rounds or portions of work as many times as directed.

✱ ✱ Stars or asterisks mean, as mentioned wherever they occur, that the details given between them are to be repeated as many times as directed before going on with those details which follow the next ✱. As an example: ✱ K 2, p 1, th o, and repeat twice more from ✱ for last ✱, means that you are to knit as follows: k 2, p 1, th o; k 2, p 1, th o; k 2, p 1, th o, thus repeating the k 2, p 1, th o, *twice* more after making it the first time, making it *three* times in all before proceeding with the next part of the direction.

BABIES' KNITTED SACK.

FIGURE No. 1.—This little sack is made of pink and white Saxony, and is formed in one section and joined under the arms and along the sleeves. Cast on 67 stitches with the white wool for the lower edge of the back, and knit back and forth until there are 35 ridges. (Two rows of knitting make a ridge.) Now at each side of this center piece cast on 26 sts. and knit until there are 26 more ridges. Now knit back 50 sts. at one side, take another needle and bind off 28 sts. Knit off the remaining sts. on the needle. Knit at each side 5 ridges, then cast on 7 sts. at each side and knit 16 ridges; then bind off 31 sts. for each sleeve. Knit 35 ridges for each front and bind off across the bottom. Pick up the stitches across the bottom of each sleeve, and with the pink knit 6 ridges. Sew up the garment under the arms and along the sleeves.

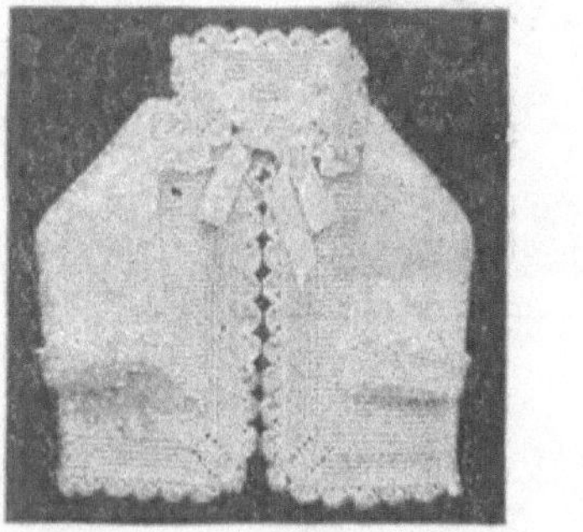

Now with the pink yarn pick up the sts. across the bottom and knit across once. Now knit 2, th o twice, n: then knit plain until within 3 sts. from the end; th o twice, n, k 1. In knitting back knit 3, p 1, then knit plain until within 2 sts. of the end; then p 1, k 1; knit in this way until there are 6 ridges, then bind off. Pick up the sts. along each front beginning at the bottom and knit back plain. Now k 1, th o, n, and knit plain to the top of the sack. Knit back plain to within 2 of the end then p 1, k 1. Knit in this way until there are 6 ridges and overhand the slanting corners of the border together.

Now pick up the sts. across the neck and border and knit one ridge plain, then k 7 sts., th o twice, n, * k 5, th o twice, narrow and repeat from * across the work. In working back drop the last half of every put-over thread. Now knit one more plain ridge, then k 2, th o twice, n: then knit plain to

FIGURE No. 1.—BABIES' KNITTED SACK.

within 3 sts. of the end, th o twice, n, k 1. In knitting back k 3, p 1, and knit plain until within 2 sts. of the end; then p 1, k 1. Knit in this way until there are 6 ridges. Finish the edge of the sack with a crocheted scallop of 1 s. c., * skip 1 st., make a shell of 1 s. c. and 3 d. c. in the next one, 2 c h., skip 2, 1 s. c. in the next, and repeat from * for all the edges of the sack, collar and sleeve. Run ribbon through the holes and tie in a pretty bow.

KNITTED LACE.

FIGURE No. 2.—Use No. 90 linen thread, and steel needles No. 20 for this lace. Cast on 20 stitches and knit across plain.
First row.—Sl 1, k 3, o, n, k 1. o twice, k 6, o, n, k 1, o twice, n, o, n, p 1 in same stitch before slipping it off the needle.
Second row.—N, o, n, k 1, p 1, k 2, o, n, k 6, p 1, k 2, o, n, k 3.
Third row.—Sl 1, k 3, o, narrow 3 times, k 1, o twice, k 4, o, n, k 2, o twice, n, o, n, p 1 in same stitch.
Fourth row.—N, o, n, k 1, p 1, k 3, o, n, k 4, p 1, k 4, o, n, k 3.
Fifth row.—Sl 1, k 3, o, n, k 2, n, n, k 1, o twice, k 2, o, n, k 3, o twice, n, o, n, p 1.
Sixth row.—N, o, n, k 1, p 1, k 4, o, n, k 2, p 1, k 6, o, n, k 3.
Seventh row.—Sl 1, k 3, o, n, k 1, o twice, k 3, n, n, k 1, o, n, k 4, o twice, n, o, n, p 1.
Eighth row.—N, o, n, k 1, p 1, k 5, o, n, k 6, p 1, k 2, o, n, k 3.
Ninth row.—Sl 1, k 3, o, narrow 3 times, k 1, o twice, k 4, o, n, k 5, o twice, n, o, n, p 1.
Tenth row.—N, o, n, k 1, p 1, k 6, o, n, k 4, p 1, k 4, o, n, k 3.
Eleventh row.—Sl 1, k 3, o, n, k 2, n, n, k 1, o twice, k 2, o, n, k 6, o twice, n, o, n, p 1.
Twelfth row.—N, o, n, k 1, p 1, n, pass purled stitch over, n, pass last st. over, n, pass stitch over, k 1, o, n, k 2, p 1, k 6, o, n, k 3.
Thirteenth row.—Sl 1, k 3, o, n, k 1, o twice, k 3, n, n, k 1, o, n, k 1, o, twice, n, o, n, p 1.

Repeat from 2nd row.

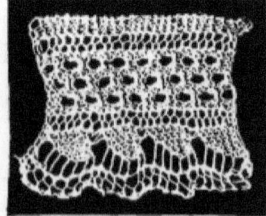

FIGURE No. 2.—KNITTED LACE.

MYRTLE LEAF LACE.

FIGURE No. 3.—Cast on 26 stitches.

First row.—K 2, th o, n, k 1, th o, k 2, sl 1, n, pass slipped stitch over, k 2, th o, k 1, th o, k 2, sl 1, n, pass slipped stitch over, k 2, th o, k 2, th o, n, o twice, k 2,

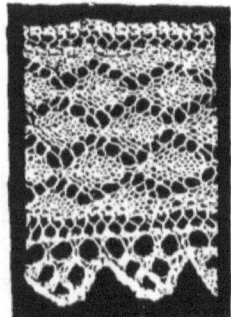

FIGURE NO. 3.—MYRTLE LEAF LACE.

Second row.—K 3, p 1, k 1, th o, n, p 17, k 1, th o, n, k 1.
Third row.—K 2, th o, n, k 2, th o, k 1, sl 1, n, pass slipped stitch over, k 1, th o, k 3, th o, k 1, sl 1, n, pass slipped stitch over, k 1, th o, k 3, th o, n, k 4.
Fourth row.—K 5, th o, n, p 17, k 1, th o, n, k 1.
Fifth row.—K 2, th o, n, k 3, th o, sl 1, n, pass slipped stitch over, th o, k 5, th o, sl 1, n, pass slipped stitch over, th o, k 4, th o, n, o twice, n, o twice, k 2.
Sixth row.—K 3, p 1, k 2, p 1, k 1, th o, n, p 17, k 1, th o, n, k 1.

Seventh row.—K 2, th o, n, n, k 2, th o, k 1, th o, k 2, sl 1, n, pass slipped stitch over, k 2, th o, k 1, th o, k 2, sl 1, k 1, pass slipped stitch over, k 1, th o, n, k 7.
Eighth row.—K 8, th o, n, p 17, k 1, th o, n, k 1.
Ninth row.—K 2, th o, n, n, k 1, th o, k 3, th o, k 1, sl 1, n, pass slipped stitch over, k 1, th o, k 3, th o, k 1, sl 1, k 1, pass slipped stitch over, k 1, th o, n, o twice, n, o twice, n, o twice, n, k 1.
Tenth row.—K 3, p 1, k 2, p 1, k 2, p 1, k 1, th o, n, p 17, k 1, th o, n, k 1.
Eleventh row.—K 2, th o, n, n, th o, k 5, th o, sl 1, n, pass slipped stitch over, th o, k 5, th o, sl 1, k 1, pass slipped stitch over, k 1, th o, n, k 10.
Twelfth row.—Cast off 8 stitches leaving 25 on the left hand needle, k 2, th o, n, p 17, k 1, th o, n, k 1. Repeat.

KNITTED EDGING.

FIGURE NO. 4.—Cast on 10 stitches.
First row.—K 2, thread over twice and n, k remainder plain.
Second row.—K 7, k first loop and p 2nd, k 2.
Third and Fourth rows.—K across plain.
Fifth row.—K 2, thread over twice and narrow, put thread over twice and narrow, k remainder plain.

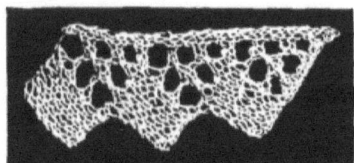

FIGURE NO. 4.—KNITTED EDGING.

Sixth row.—6, k first loop plain and p 2nd, k 1, k first loop plain and p 2nd, k 2.
Seventh and Eighth rows.—K across plain.
Ninth row.—K 2, thread over twice and n, put thread over twice and n, th o twice and n, k remainder plain.

Tenth row.—K 6, k first loop plain and p 2nd, k 1, k 1st loop plain and p 2nd, k 1, k first loop plain and p 2nd, k 2.
Eleventh row.—K across plain.
Twelfth row.—Bind off 6 stitches. Knit remainder plain.

INFANTS' KNITTED SOCK.

FIGURE NO. 5.—This little sock is made of pink and white Saxony. Cast on 80 stitches, turn, and make one rib which consists of 2 rows; in the next rib, widen at each end and also at the center of the work. Make one plain rib without widening; in the next rib widen once at the center of the work or toe, then make 6 ribs without widening. In the next rib k 43 st., then leave the rest on the other needle; join on the white wool and with another needle work back 16 sts., now on these 16 sts., leaving the others unworked, make 3 ribs with the white, then join the pink on and make 2 ribs, then with the white make 3 ribs, then one rib with the pink. Now join these 9 ribs on each edge to 9 sts. on the two needles, sewing them over and over with a needle and wool, and passing through each

FIGURE NO. 5.—INFANTS' KNITTED SOCK.

stitch. Slip each stitch off the needle as sewed. Now pass all the stitches onto one needle and make 4 ribs with the pink. Next, k 2, * th o twice, n, k 2, and repeat 13 times more from *, th o twice, n, k 2, k back plain dropping the second half of the 2 put-overs, make 2 more ribs, then k 2, * purl 3, k 3, and repeat 9 times more from last *; this forms the ankle rib.; work back purling the knitted and knitting the purled stitches; make 13 rows, then knit one row, and p one; now make 1 rib-row then k 2, * th o twice, n, k 2, and repeat 14 times more from *; k back plain dropping the second half of the 2 put-overs; make one more rib-row and bind off.

For the Border around the top of Sock.—Cast on 4 sts.
First row.—K 1, th o twice, n, th o twice, k 1.
Second and Fourth rows.—Knit back plain, dropping the second half of the 2 put-overs.
Third row.—K 2, th o twice, n, th o twice, k 1.
Fifth row.—K 3, th o twice, n, th o twice, k 1.
Sixth row.—Bind off 3, dropping the second half of the 2 put-overs and leaving 3 on the left-hand needle which knit plain. Repeat from first row until the strip is long enough to go across the top of the sock, and sew it on over and over. Sew up the sock at the back. Run a thread across the toe-portion for a short distance, and draw it in to shape the toe. Run very narrow ribbon through the 2 rows of holes and tie in a pretty bow.

A WOMAN'S PAMPHLET.—The value of pure toilet and flavoring extracts can scarcely be overestimated, yet every woman knows that purity is the quality which is most conspicuously lacking in the majority of such articles offered in the shops. To enable those who doubt the reliability of manufactured perfumes and cooking extracts to make them easily and cheaply at home, we have published a valuable little pamphlet entitled "Extracts and Beverages," in which are presented full and explicit instructions for preparing a large assortment of delicious syrups, refreshing beverages, colognes, extracts, etc. All the recipes and directions are of such a nature that they can be followed by any one, with the aid of the implements and utensils which may be found in the average home. Price, 6d. (by post, 7½d.) or 15 cents.

THE CHILDREN'S VALENTINE PARTY.

FIGURE NO. 1.

Mr. and Mrs. Lawson Byers were people of modern ideas who believed in a bright and happy childhood for children, and in providing their own with healthful and innocent amusements they recognized the fact that the calm, prosaic life of the adult does not satisfy the imaginative tendencies and restless mind of the child.

"I sincerely pity the grown person who cannot look back to a happy childhood," said Mrs. Byers on more than one occasion when the subject was under discussion.

"Yes, the keenest enjoyment comes when the mind is fresh and active," acknowledged her husband; "then the impressions are most vivid."

It was not that these two people were foolishly indulgent or too lenient, but they entered heartily into the pastimes of their children, and helped them to enjoy with zest the amusements befitting their age.

Elsie and Herbert had been commendably studious all Winter, standing well in their classes, and had been rather closely confined in the school-room in consequence, but now that Spring was at hand and Nature seemed disposed to throw off her sombre mood and take on a gayer air, Mrs. Byers pleasantly surprised the children by promising them a Valentine Party for the 14th of February.

Elsie, who was quite skilful with brush and water-colors, undertook, with Herbert's aid, to prepare the invitations. They bought from a picture dealer for a trifle a quantity of scraps of pebble-board, such as are used in making mats for pictures, and with the help of a pinking-iron Herbert cut out a quantity of heart-shaped cards, like those shown at figure No. 1. These Elsie decorated with an edge of gold paint put on in splashes, and painted on each one a tiny spray of some Spring blossom, such as the violet, crocus, windflower, primrose or the like (see figures Nos. 2 and 3), while on the reverse side of the card was written an invitation in verse, a product of Mr. Byers' pen, which ran in this wise:

On Valentine's Day,
Your books put away,
And let your hearts gladden with joy.
The school-room forsake,
Your Valentine take,
We'll welcome each girl and each boy.

St. Valentine's Day, Feb. 14th.

Elsie and Herbert Byers.

The verse was written so that it conformed to the shape of the card and Elsie and Herbert took especial pains with the writing, copying the verse in a neat, legible hand.

These hearts were put into square white envelopes and properly addressed. When the invitations were piled up on the table ready to be sent out, they made quite a formidable heap.

After talking the matter over with her husband, Mrs. Byers decided that it would be more convenient to have the party in the afternoon than at night, as some of the children lived at quite a distance from the Byers' residence. Each invitation, therefore, bore the words, "3 to 6 o'clock." As the house was to be darkened and lighted by artificial means,

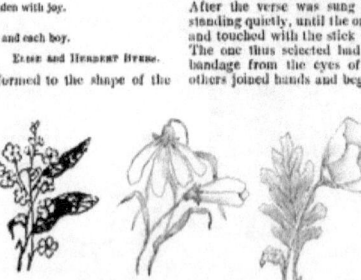

FIGURE NO. 2.

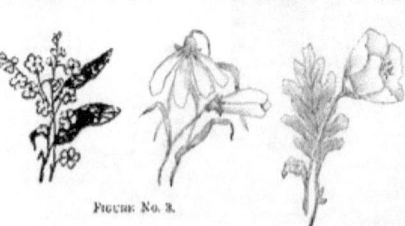

FIGURE NO. 3.

it was concluded that the effect would be quite the same as if the entertainment was given at night.

Numerous pots of gay tulips, fragrant hyacinths and other bright Spring flowers were placed about the rooms, which were made gayer still in decoration by a quantity of hearts cut out of tissue paper of various colors and hung in a long row by colored silken threads from a bamboo rod placed between the double parlors.

The girls were gathered in the back parlor, while the boys were in the front room. At a given signal each boy selected a paper heart and pinned it on his coat, putting that side next his coat on which had been written the name of the girl he was to take to the refreshment table. He had to keep this name a secret, so that each girl was kept in a delightful state of suspense as to which boy was to be her Valentine.

Several games were played by the merry throng, among them a new one called "The Stolen Heart." One of the party was blindfolded and held in his hand a small heart-shaped silken bag of sachet-powder. Several others formed a circle around him, and, joining hands, moved to the measure of the following verse, which they sang:

Alack-a-day! alack-a-day!
Some one has stolen your heart away;
But dry your eyes and calm your grief,
And see if you can catch the thief.

At the conclusion of the verse one of the members of the circle snatched the perfume bag from the person blindfolded and concealed it in the hand held behind him. All the others forming the circle held their hands behind them in like manner. The loser of the heart then raised the bandage from his eyes and looking around the circle tried to guess who had stolen his heart. If he made a wrong guess, he was re-blindfolded and tried it again, but if he guessed rightly, the guilty one exchanged places with him and was blindfolded in turn. This game occasioned much laughter and amusement.

Another game somewhat similar in character was called "St. Valentine." In it the member of the party who was blindfolded was given a stick, and the others circled around him, and sang as they moved:

Around and around with laughter gay,
We circle on St. Valentine's Day,
Come make a choice, good luck be thine,
And now select a Valentine!

After the verse was sung the singers stopped and remained standing quietly, until the one blindfolded stretched out his hand and touched with the stick the one he selected for a Valentine. The one thus selected had to quit the circle and remove the bandage from the eyes of the person blindfolded, while the others joined hands and began to circle around again, singing as they went:

Your choice is made, be kind and true,
To that one who stands next to you!
Forever to us, through rain or shine,
Must this one be your Valentine.

Much laughter followed if a blindfolded boy happened to choose another boy for his Valentine, or if a girl made a like mistake. In such case the one chosen was blindfolded and the game proceeded as before.

Another interesting game was called "The Postman." The company sat around in a circle or in a row and one of the players passed up and down before them holding in his hand a letter. He turned abruptly to some one of the party and said:

"Here's a letter postmarked A (or B or any other letter he might choose to call). Where is it from?" The one of whom the question was asked had to quickly give the name of some city or country beginning with the letter called, or else take the Postman's place. For instance, if the Postman said: "It is marked R. Where is it from?" The one he asks must at once answer: "It is from Rochester (or Rome, Ravenna, Rheims, Richmond, Russia, Red Sea or any other place beginning with an R). "Who is it for?" next asked the Postman of some one else, and that one had to give the name of some member of the party beginning with an R, or, if there was no one among the players having such an initial, the person asked was required to give some name in history or fiction beginning with the required letter. If this letter was R, he was allowed to answer with Rebecca, Rowena, Rachel, Robin Hood, Ruth, Richard the Lion-hearted or Robinson Crusoe. When anyone failed to give a prompt response as to the post-mark or name of the person to whom the letter might belong, that one was obliged to exchange places with the Postman and proceed to deliver the letter to some one else. This game was found to quicken the wits and aid in a review of one's knowledge of geography, history and fiction.

Yet another game played was called "The Marketman." The leader of this game said to the person next to him: "I'm on my way to market; what have you to sell?" "Guess what?" the other replied, imitating some animal or bird. The leader guessed as to the creature represented and then turned to the next player and repeated the sentence: "I'm on my way to market; what have you to sell?" The one interrogated imitated, in turn, some animal or bird. Here were some of the sounds heard: "Bow-wow!" "Moo-o-o!" "Miouw!" "Baa-a!" "Pretty Poll; Polly want a cracker?" "Caw-caw-caw!" "Bob White! Bob White!" "Quack! quack! quack!" "Cluck! cluck! cluck!" "Cock-a-doodle-do-o-o!" "Gobble! gobble! gobble!" "Pot-rack-pot-rack!" "Queake! queake! queake!" "Whoo! whoo!" When the various players had given imitations of what they had to sell, the leader walked around the circle, and said: "Sheep (or hens, geese, cows, &c.) are bringing a good price in the market, and now is the time to take them there." When he thus called the name of some creature that had been imitated, the one who had given the imitation was required to get up and follow the leader, repeating the call or cry. The leader continued his journey to market until all the players were following him around in a circle, bleating, baa-a-ing, clucking, &c., each one according to the creature represented. Of course, the effect was highly ludicrous, and everybody finally broke into hearty laughter.

Figure No. 4.

When the children had played games for an hour or more, the boys were told to hunt up their Valentines according to the names written on the tissue-paper hearts, and as the young couples were thus paired off they went into the refreshment room, where Mrs. Byers and two or three of her married friends, assisted by two servants, saw that they were served to the simple refreshments that had been prepared. There were two prettily decorated tables, one at each end of the room. At one table meat sandwiches, stalks of celery, chicken salad, beaten biscuit and small cups of cocoa were served; at the other table were fancy cakes and fruits. In the hall, at a pretty stand, lemonade in which pieces of pineapple, banana and conserved cherries floated, was handed around in small glass cups throughout the afternoon. This drink was both pretty and refreshing, a wholesome beverage to which the children did full justice.

After the refreshments had been disposed of, a young lady engaged by Mrs. Byers sat down at the piano in the parlor and played dance music for the merry youngsters until it was time for them to depart. When they were getting ready to leave, a large covered basket was brought into the hall and each child reached into it and drew out a pretty little fancy bag containing candy and nuts. These bags were made out of tarlatan in different colors, cut in the form of hearts, edged with cheap lace, gathered at the top with a cord, and on each one was pasted a pretty flower of the sort to be had in sheets for scrap books (see figure No. 4). These fancy bags made very dainty souvenirs for the children to take home with them and many were kept as pleasant reminders of the Valentine party given by Elsie and Herbert.

HENRY C. WOOD.

SEASONABLE COOKERY.

IN THE MARKETS.—CANNED GOODS.—WAYS TO COOK TOMATOES, CORN, LOBSTER, APRICOTS, ETC.

The first suspicion of the approach of Spring arises this month from the presence in the large city markets of the North of early fruits and vegetables, though at prices beyond the reach of any but the favored few. Among these luxuries are cucumbers, tomatoes, new Bermuda potatoes and string beans and (by the middle of the month) asparagus may also be had. Egg-plant, mushrooms, salsify, sweet potatoes and parsnips are all procurable to add variety to the tables of those who can afford them. Tiny baskets of strawberries are for those to whom money is not a question to be considered. The market list also includes the following:

Fish—White fish, salmon, smelts, herring, shad, haddock, codfish, bass, flounders, oysters, crabs, clams, scallops, terrapin and mussels.

Meats—Beef, pork, mutton, veal, poultry, geese, turkeys, chickens, ducks and squabs.

Game—Reed birds, pheasants and wild ducks (both mallard and red-head), hares, wild turkeys and canvas-back ducks.

Vegetables—Onions, turnips, spinach, celery, cabbage, beets, cranberries and radishes.

Fruits—Oranges, mandarins, pineapples, bananas, apples, shaddocks, lemons and Malaga grapes.

CANNED FOODS, AND HOW TO COOK THEM.

The average housewife relies principally upon canned vegetables and fruits during this month and the next. By this means the modern table really knows no season. Corn, peas, beans, tomatoes and asparagus are to be had, excellent in quality and reasonable in cost, during the Winter months. Soups of many kinds for the first course at dinner, pumpkin, rhubarb, huckleberries, apples and peaches for the making of tarts and puddings, salmon, lobster and shrimp for salads, oysters, clams, mussels, all come in canned form. The variety of articles put up in tin and glass for table use increases each year. By a process of sealing that is comparatively new the tin cans are soldered entirely on the outside, thus avoiding any danger that might arise from the acids of fruits and vegetables coming in contact with an alloy of lead. Illness caused by the use of canned goods usually results from the food becoming tainted after the cans are opened. Left in the tin for any considerable time after opening the food is likely to become dangerous for use. Vegetables if removed from the tin and set in a cool place may be safely kept for twenty-four hours. The flavor of canned goods will be improved if exposed to the air at least an hour before being used. Of canned goods the common vegetables are most largely consumed, the tomato easily leading the list as an all-round-the-year favorite. There are many ways of using this delicious vegetable beside the ordinary stewing usually practiced. A few of these are here given:

SCALLOPED TOMATOES.—Place a layer of canned tomato in a baking dish, season with pepper, salt and bits of butter, then add a layer of bread crumbs, then tomato again, with the seasoning until the tomato is all used. Have the crumb for the top layer. Bake for twenty minutes in a hot oven, and just before removing cover the top with grated cheese. Instead of the crumb, boiled rice may be used; it should be seasoned with salt, pepper and curry powder.

TOMATO PIE.—This is a particularly good way to utilize left-over pieces of beef and lamb. Chop fine a quantity of beef or lamb. Line a baking dish with cracker crumbs, then add a layer of the beef, season with pepper, salt and butter and add a layer of tomato stewed and seasoned as for the table. Begin again with the crumb and make ready another layer, ending with the crackers. Add any gravy that may be at hand, or a slight sprinkling of milk to moisten. The pie should be quite as moist as scalloped oysters.

TOMATO SAUCE.—Boil one canful of tomatoes for twenty minutes in a porcelain-lined saucepan, adding one tea-spoonful of salt; then strain through a coarse sieve to remove the seeds, forcing through the sieve all of the substance of the vegetable. Season with a half tea-spoonful of Worcestershire sauce or a tea-spoonful of mushroom catsup. This sauce may be used in many ways, three of which are here given:

1. STEWED TRIPE.—Cut one pound of beef tripe into small pieces, stew gently for twenty minutes, drain and add one pint of the tomato sauce. When boiling, serve.

2. ROAST MEAT IN TOMATO.—Make one quart of the sauce as directed. Slice roast beef or lamb thin as for the table and just before serving place it in the boiling sauce. Cook just long enough to heat the meat, and serve. The secret of making an inviting dish of already cooked meat is in not forgetting that it is cooked enough. It should be only heated through.

3. BOILED FISH.—Tie up in a piece of cheese cloth a pound and a half of fresh codfish and cook for half an hour in boiling salted water with just sufficient heat to keep at the boiling point. Take out, drain on a plate, remove the cloth, lay on a heated platter and pour over the fish one pint of the tomato sauce.

TOMATO CREAM SOUP.—

1 quart of tomato.
½ cupful of rice.
1 quart of water.
1 pint of milk.
1 salt-spoonful of pepper.
2 tea-spoonfuls of salt.
1 table-spoonful of butter.
2 table-spoonfuls of flour.
1 salt-spoonful of soda.

Place the rice, tomato, water, salt and pepper together in a granite pan, and cook until the rice is tender but not broken. Rub the butter and flour together and stir into the above mixture. When it thickens and has cooked for three or four minutes add the soda dissolved in a little cold water, then the milk, which has been heated to the boiling point in a separate saucepan. Serve at once without more heating, as if boiled with the tomato there is always a danger of the milk breaking.

ASPARAGUS WITH CREAM SAUCE.—Drain the liquor from a can of asparagus and place it in a long saucepan on the fire; carefully lay the asparagus in a square of cheese cloth, gather together the cloth, tie its ends together and lay the package in the saucepan with the liquor. Add a half table-spoonful of salt and enough boiling water to cover and gently bring to a boil. After cooking for three or four minutes lift it from the water, drain well, then turn from the cloth, laying the vegetable on a heated dish with a foundation of squares of toasted bread. Pour over it this sauce:

1 table-spoonful of butter.   1 table-spoonful of flour.
3 cupfuls of cream or milk.

Melt the butter, add the flour and mix until smooth. Then add the milk, stir until it thickens, seasoning with salt if needed.

SUCCOTASH.—Drain the water from one can of Lima beans and add one can of corn. Place in a double boiler, stir into the vegetables two cupfuls of milk and cook until tender. Season with butter, salt and pepper.

CORN FRITTERS.—

1 can of corn.
1 egg.
½ cupful of milk.
1 tea-spoonful of salt.
2 cupfuls of flour.
1 tea-spoonful of butter (melted).
1 tea-spoonful of baking powder.
½ tea-spoonful of pepper.

Chop the corn very fine in a chopping bowl, add the salt and pepper, then the egg beaten well, then the butter, milk and flour. When smooth add the baking powder and fry by the spoonful in a frying pan in plenty of boiling hot fat. The fat should be quite ready to use before the baking powder is added. This will make eighteen fritters almost equal to those made from the fresh corn.

TO COOK STRING BEANS.—The beans should be turned into a colander and rinsed with cold water, then placed in a saucepan with boiling water and one tea-spoonful of salt. They should be cooked gently until tender and then drained. Milk is added and when boiling it is thickened to a cream with a little cornstarch dissolved in some of the milk, then seasoned with butter. Salt and pepper are added after the dishing. Pepper is never stirred into a cream or milk dressing of any kind, as it is unsightly. If milk is not used, melted butter is poured over the beans and salt and pepper are added.

TO COOK PEAS.—Drain the peas in a colander, pouring cold water over them to rinse them. Place in a saucepan and add just enough water to keep them from burning. Add butter, salt and pepper, and serve them thoroughly heated.

CREAMED MUSHROOMS.—Drain off the liquor from the mushrooms and place it in a bowl to be used for the sauce. Place on the fire in a granite pan one table-spoonful of butter, heat slowly and add one table-spoonful of flour; stir until they are blended but not in sufficient heat to brown and gradually add the liquor from the mushrooms and enough cream to make a thin sauce; into this turn the mushrooms, season with salt and when thoroughly hot serve on squares of toast.

CANNED FISH.—Canned lobster is served in a variety of ways. The can should be opened some little time before it is wanted, to restore the flavor. These two recipes make favorite dishes for company luncheons:

LOBSTER À LA NEWBURG.—

1 can of lobster.
1 table-spoonful of butter.
3 hard boiled eggs.
1 cupful of cream.
½ cupful of sherry wine.
1 table-spoonful of flour.

Press the hard boiled whites of the eggs through a sieve and mash the yolks finely with a little of the cream. Heat the butter to melting, add the flour and when smooth (but not hot enough to brown either flour or butter) add the lobster cut into small pieces with a silver knife, also the whites and yolks of the eggs and the remainder of the cream. When quite hot add the wine. Season and serve.

DEVILLED LOBSTER.—

1 can of lobster.
1 cupful of breadcrumbs.
2 hard boiled eggs.
½ a lemon.
1 pint of cream sauce.
Seasoning.

Cook the lobster for ten minutes in a little water, then drain, and when cold cut into dice with a silver knife. Add the breadcrumb, the egg chopped very fine and the juice of the lemon. For seasoning use salt, cayenne pepper and a grating of nutmeg, seasoning quite high. Add enough of the cream sauce—a recipe for which is given in this paper—to make a paste. Fill scallop shells with the mixture, smooth the tops, sprinkle with breadcrumbs and brown in a very hot oven.

SALMON.—Drain off part of the oil from a can of salmon, heat the fish in the oil remaining, adding a quarter of a cupful of water. When hot season with salt and pepper, lay on slices of toasted bread, and over all pour a pint of cream sauce.

CREAMED SALMON.—Drain off all the oil from the salmon, place the fish in a granite pan, add enough milk to nearly cover it and cook very gently for five minutes. Thicken to a cream with cornstarch thinned in cold milk. Add butter and salt and serve at once, with a sprinkling of pepper over the fish when quite ready for the table.

APRICOT PUDDING.—The canning of apricots has made it possible for a variety of desserts to be made from this delicious fruit. Soak one half pint of granulated tapioca over night in enough cold water to cover it. In the morning drain the juice from a can of apricots, stir it into the tapioca, and add half a cupful of sugar and enough water to make it rather thin. Let this boil until clear. Cover the bottom of a pudding dish with the fruit, sprinkle with sugar and pour on the tapioca. Bake for half an hour and serve cold with a cream or milk sauce.

APRICOT CREAM PUDDING.—

1 pint of milk.
½ cup of sugar.
2 table-spoonfuls of corn starch.
½ table-spoonful of butter.
2 eggs.
½ tea-spoonful of salt.

Dissolve the cornstarch in half a cupful of the milk and place the remainder on the fire in a double boiler. Add the sugar, and when boiling stir in the cornstarch. When about as thick as cream add the butter and salt and the well beaten whites of the eggs. Cook for two minutes, turn into a serving dish and cover with the fruit. Make a sauce of the juice of the apricots and two cupfuls of sugar, boiling steadily for ten minutes. Serve both sauce and pudding cold.

BLAIR.

DRAWN-WORK.

JAPANESE DRAWN-WORK DOILY.

FIGURE No. 1.—This doily is made of Japanese silk or pongee

CORNER OF HANDKERCHIEF IN DRAWN-WORK.

FIGURE No. 2.—This engraving shows a very pretty corner for a handkerchief of linen lawn. The design is so clearly illustrated that no directions are necessary for its development. Each corner of the handkerchief may be decorated by this design, or the corners may differ in design.
In the book on Drawn-Work mentioned are a number of designs suitable for handkerchiefs, with details. The method of properly hemstitching a handkerchief is also given and will prove invaluable even though the worker does not care to add drawn-work to the article she is working upon. In making handkerchiefs, India linen lawn is considered the best material to select. It is fine and sheer, and the threads are more easily drawn than in other fabrics. Besides, the texture is sufficiently strong to undergo renovation without detriment to appearances. For the information concerning Japanese drawn-work thanks are due Mrs. S. E. Criss-Wise, 399 5th Av., New York.

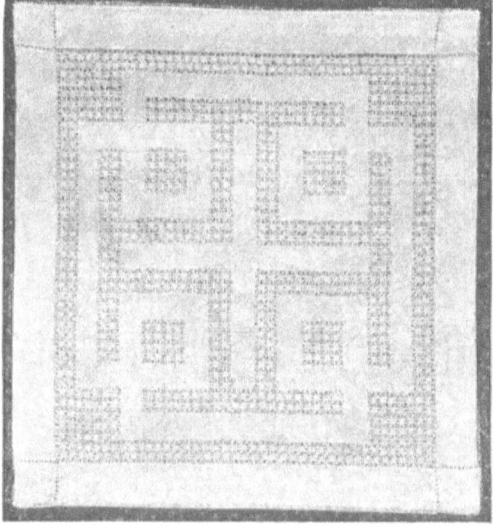

FIGURE No. 1.—JAPANESE DRAWN-WORK DOILY.

of a delicate écru tint. It is about five inches square, but may be made as much larger as desired. The engraving represents it in a size pretty for finger-bowl or tumbler doileys. After the threads are drawn in the manner indicated, they may be knotted in any design preferred. In our book The Art of Drawn-Work, price 50 cents or 2s., are numberless pretty designs, given in full size, and with explicit instructions. Any of these designs could be adapted to Japanese doileys. The design shown at figure No. 2 could be used for the doily shown at figure No. 1. Japanese silk could also be used for a handkerchief and the corners could be decorated with drawn-work the same as in linen.

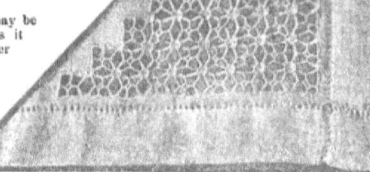

FIGURE No. 2.—CORNER OF HANDKERCHIEF IN DRAWN-WORK.

NOTICE TO SUBSCRIBERS.—It is the aim of the Publishers to issue the DELINEATOR each month so that it will be in the hands of subscribers in the various parts of the country about the same time and simultaneously with the placing of the patterns on sale by our agents. Owing, however, to the difficulty of handling such an enormous edition, and to the large number of extra orders which come in for certain issues, it has not always been possible to do this and unavoidable delay has ensued in distributing the magazine. Increased facilities for printing, binding and circulating have now been secured, and subscribers can rely on receiving their copies about a uniform date hereafter.—THE BUTTERICK PUBLISHING CO. (LIMITED).

TO CORRESPONDENTS.—We wish to state that it is impossible for us to answer questions in the number of the magazine subsequent to that already in the hands of correspondents. The enormous edition of THE DELINEATOR compels an early going to press, and questions to which answers are desired in a certain magazine should reach us not later than the fifth of the second month preceding the month specified. For instance, letters to be answered in THE DELINEATOR for December should reach us before the fifth of October. Letters for the correspondents' column of the magazine, addressed to the firm, will find their way into the proper channel. Correspondents who desire answers by mail must enclose stamp for postage.

A FAN WITH A HISTORY.

A beautiful fan with an interesting and romantic history is illustrated at figure No. 1. It is in the handsomest style of Rococo embroidery, and the maker was one of the brightest ornaments of the brilliant but ill-starred court of Louis XVI. It was while residing at Versailles that Gertrude, Countess Latour, member of one of the oldest of the noble families of France, occupied her leisure hours by perfecting herself in the dainty and elaborate art of embroidery which was afterwards to stand her in good stead. Beauty, wealth and homage were hers, but then came the Revolution and Reign of Terror and swiftly misfortune fell upon her noble house. One by one its members laid down their lives for their king until finally the Countess alone survived. Thus bereft, stripped of her possessions, her suitors dead, herself in the power of the enemies of her order, her lot seemed indeed a sorrowful one. Just when she was herself expecting a summons to the guillotine an Austrian officer fell in love with and rescued her from the *sans culottes*, and to him as a recompense she plighted her troth. But he was poor, and the woman who had hitherto lived but for pleasure was confronted by the serious problem of how she should maintain herself. For the first time she thought of putting her skill with the needle to account, and as she really had a gift for this work her nimble fingers earned for her a modest living until her warrior lover came into his inheritance and was able to claim her for his own.

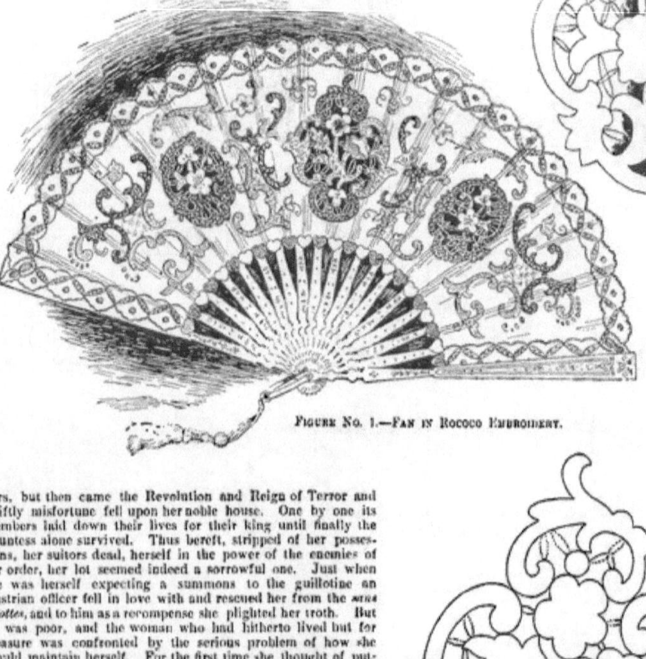

Of all the mementoes of this noble lady now in the possession of her descendants the one most treasured is the fan which forms the subject of this article, worked by her own hands during the dark hours of her adversity. Her great-granddaughter, inheriting from her illustrious ancestress both fondness and gift for embroidery, resolved to make an exact copy of this fan. Though a labor of love, her task was by no means an easy one and many times she failed before she finally secured a duplicate which in the stitches employed, the design followed and the dainty color blendings secured could not be distinguished from the original. This fac-simile she brought to America and it is from this copy that our illustrations are made.

Rococo embroidery is distinctive in character. Both in design and color harmonies is it unlike the ornamentation of any other period. What first strikes the eye in this design is the medallions in relief, the cutting out of which constitutes a difficult part of the work. They are peculiar to the Rococo period. The border is distinctive also in its graceful outlines. Another peculiarity is the absence of the large patterns so prevalent in work of the Renaissance period.

For those of our readers who would like to attempt a copy of this *chef d'œuvre* of embroidery, a detailed de-

FIGURE No. 1.—FAN IN ROCOCO EMBROIDERY.

FIGURE No. 2.—DETAIL OF SIDE MEDALLION.

FIGURE No. 3.—DETAIL OF CENTRAL MEDALLION.

scription of its construction is given. The foundation is of gauze, so that when the silk is cut away from within the three medallions after the embroidery is finished the transparent background will show with fine effect. The entire design may be carefully transferred to the silk in outline by means of colored transfer paper. Red paper would serve best on the pale-green silk of which the model is made. It will be noted that the medallion and other ornaments on the right of the central medallion are simply reversed in the designs used on the left. The work is executed with a single strand of filo floss embellished here and there with gold passing, the thread being passed through the material instead of being couched on to it. The colors employed are shades of pink, olive-green and gold shading to brown. All the flower forms are put in with solid embroidery in tints of pink, as is also the heart-shaped border that comes next to the fan sticks. The flower centers of the medallions (see figures Nos. 2 and 3) may be put in with French knots or an appropriate lace stitch filling. The outlines of the entire design in each medallion are accentuated with the gold thread held down by button-hole stitches matching the filling used throughout the design, these stitches being done in filo floss. The heart border is outlined in the same way, as are also the scollops on the outer edge. The outside border (see figure No. 4) is embroidered with the darker shades of pink and the ovals within the scollops are filled with an open lace stitch. All the scroll-work (see figures Nos. 5 and 6), so distinctively characteristic of Rococo embroidery, is put in with the olive-green and golden-brown tints alternating. Except for the portions already described, the outlining is in stem stitch, omitting the gold threads. All the forms are filled in with open stitches, varied as much as possible. Straight and standing bars, coral stitch, cross stitch and others of a similar nature are brought into requisition, the great variety contributing to the fine effect. The central fillings of the forms between the medallions and outside of them are composed of crossed lines held down by stars and are put in with gold thread.

The finished effect is very rich and well repays the trouble of working. Portions of the design might be utilized in other ways or substitutions made. For instance, the medallions with the flower forms omitted would make charming settings for little Watteau subjects, hand-painted either on the gauze or upon silk. Watteau subjects on fans are always popular and are particularly well suited to accompany Rococo ornamentation.

FIGURE No. 4.—DETAIL OF OUTSIDE BORDER.

FIGURE No. 5.—DETAIL OF ORNAMENTS AT EXTREME LEFT AND RIGHT.

FIGURE No. 6.—DETAIL OF ORNAMENTS BETWEEN MEDALLIONS.

A TEXT-BOOK OF DRAWING AND PAINTING.—"Drawing and Painting" is the title of a book published by us that should be within easy reach of everyone who possesses or aims at acquiring skill with the pencil or brush. It treats comprehensively, yet not too technically to suit the ordinary reader, of pencil drawing and sketching, of painting with both oil and water colors on all sorts of materials, and of the uses of gilds, enamels and bronzes. The chapters entitled "Oil Painting on Textiles," "Painting on Glass," "Painting on Plaques," "Screens," "Lustra Painting," "Kensington Painting," "Tapestry Painting," "Fancy Work for the Brush," and "China Painting" will be of especial interest to women; and every branch of the decorative art is entered into with a thoroughness that renders the book one of the most complete art works ever published. Price, 2s. (by post, 2s. 3d.) or 50 cents.

TO PARENTS OF SMALL CHILDREN.—Under the title of "Pastimes for Children" we have published an attractive little pamphlet treating of all manner of entertaining and instructive amusements for children, among which may be mentioned games of all kinds, slate-drawing, the making of toys and toy animals, the dressing of dolls, puzzles, riddles, and much other matter of interest to children. The book is very handsome in appearance, being bound in ornamental but durable paper; and it is copiously illustrated with attractive and appropriate engravings. Price, 1s. (by post, 1s. 2d.) or 25 cents.

ECCLESIASTICAL EMBROIDERY.—No. I.

BY EMMA HAYWOOD.

Embroidery for ecclesiastical purposes is a branch of the art differing radically from what is commonly known as skilled needlework. It is true that one occasionally sees vestments decorated in a manner better suited to a white-and-gold parlor than to religious purposes, but this is generally more the result of ignorance on the part of the worker than of a wilful misuse of the materials at command.

First in importance comes the question of design. Here let me remark that the ordinary designer, however clever in producing patterns specially suited for needlework, is not qualified to design church work unless possessed of a knowledge of the significance of each individual vestment and of the full meaning of each color called for in the round of the church seasons, combined with exact information as to the emblems and symbols employed since the foundation of the Christian Church. Mere prettiness or harmony of outline is not the first consideration, although the beautiful should at all times be aimed at. The basis of every ecclesiastical design is to give it all the meaning possible in relation to the use to which it is dedicated.

The special designs for this article comprise a

No. 1.—THE WHITE STOLE.

No. 2.—THE RED STOLE.

No. 3.—THE PURPLE STOLE.

No. 4.—THE GREEN STOLE.

set of stoles for Church seasons intended for use in preaching or administering any of the sacraments of the Protestant Episcopal Church except the Holy Communion. For this last sacrament the stole called for is of somewhat different make; it should be longer and wider than the ordinary stole and should accord exactly in style with the whole set of vestments properly belonging to the Eucharistic service. While full canonical vestments are not found throughout the Church, the stole is everywhere in use by Churchmen; therefore, the many busy workers ready and willing to offer their time and talents in the service of their religion will find the suggestions given helpful. The designs of working size, with small color sketches or patterns of the silks to be employed, can be had, if desired.

A preaching stole should reach the knee; therefore, to be correct, it varies in length according to the height of the wearer. It narrows considerably towards the neck, in the center of which it measures only a trifle over two inches. At this point it is decorated by a small cross (illustration No. 5) that accords in style with the embroidered ends. These measure about four inches and a quarter wide. A piece of real lace or very fine hemstitched lawn about twelve inches long and an inch and a quarter deep is tacked into the neck and renewed from time to time as it becomes soiled. This preserves the stole, keeping it pure and clean throughout. Each end is finished with a fringe, usually made to match the coloring of the needlework; it should be of silk, doubled twice or thrice to make it rich and heavy. It is best to have this fringe made by a house accustomed to manufacture for ecclesiastical work. From three inches to three inches and a half is a good depth for it. The slope of the stole is usually cut on one side only and commences from just about where the embroidery leaves off, unless, as is sometimes the case, the embroidery is carried up very high, when the slope must be gradual on both sides. Stoles are usually made of brocaded silk and lined with soft silk of a color harmonizing with the embroidery. A figured lining wears better than a plain one, because it does not so readily show marks. There must be an interlining of some strong, firm material that is not too harsh; coarse butcher's linen answers the purpose admirably. No finish is required at the edges, a very neat slip-stitch being employed and the brocade allowed to slightly overlap the lining.

The accompanying illustrations show designs to be worked in the four liturgical colors: White for festivals appertaining to our Lord, the Virgin Mary and the Saints and Angels; red, emblem of fire and blood, for Whitsuntide and the festivals of the Apostles and Martyrs; purple or violet for seasons of penitence, of which Lent is the chief; green, the symbol of hope and peace, for ordinary days, of which the Trinity season includes the greater part.

To begin with the white stole, either the rose or lily or both are most frequently introduced on festival vestments, the lily being essentially the emblem of purity. Conventional or semi-conventional designs alone are in good taste. Illustration No. 1 shows a lily backed by a suggestion of the rose form as the central object. This gives opportunity for beautiful and effective coloring. The scroll work is in the *vesica piscis* form, representing Christ himself. This is surmounted by a lily, half open, in turn surmounted by a crown evolved from the lily stamens. The train of ideas thus presented to the mind needs no further comment. For coloring, delicate shades of blue, pink, green and gold could be used to advantage, but more than one scheme of color is available. In every instance the entire design is outlined with untarnishable Japanese gold thread couched down with fine silk to match.

The red stole (illustration No. 2) need not be of the old-fashioned crimson color, but rather of a rich terra-cotta shade. The colors for working on red must be very carefully selected. Here

ILLUSTRATION NO. 5.—VARIOUS FORMS OF CROSSES.

we have the pomegranate, with its seeds bursting forth, emblematic of the seed sown by the blood of the martyrs and also of the abundant fruits of the Holy Ghost. Again, we have the seven gifts of the Holy Spirit in the seven seeds surmounting the blossom of the pomegranate. The triple form of the flower symbolizes the Godhead.

The Lenten stole (illustration No. 3) is also full of suggestion. Here again we have the *vesica piscis* enclosing a Greek cross. The nails represent the Passion leading to the crown above, behind which shine forth rays of glory.

The color for penitential seasons, purple or violet, so-called, is really rather a shade of rich dark-blue. Only one color should be used for the embroidery in this instance. Either terra-cotta red or old-gold will look well on the blue. The gold outline accentuates the design sufficiently.

The green selected for the fourth stole (illustration No. 4) need not be of the violent, decided hue sometimes employed. There is no reason why we should not avail ourselves of the artistic shades now at command for religious purposes, provided we keep within certain limits. The design has for its motive the clover leaf, always recognized as an emblem of the Trinity. The triple emblem is repeated again and again in the leaves themselves, in their arrangement at the upper part of the design, which also suggests the *vesica* form, in the three small circles and in the method of displaying the scrolls on either side. The central tier likewise gives the initial of the Sacred Name, so every line of the design is replete with meaning. Effective and varied coloring can be introduced into this design.

For working all these designs solid embroidery is, of course, preferable and most appropriate because so rich. At the same time a little modification is permissible if time or expense be an object, but such modification should be directed by an experienced worker or the just balance and proportion of the design may be lost.

A black stole is only required on Good Friday and for funerals. With regard to the materials for working I find none better than the Asiatic-dyed filo silks; the colors are beautiful and the sheen of the silk is unsurpassed.

WOMEN IN THE PROFESSIONS.

MEDICINE.—By AIMÉE RAYMOND SCHROEDER, M.D.

At the present day the question which so sorely perplexed many people thirty or forty years ago, "Shall women be permitted to study medicine?" is no longer pertinent, since they do study it in constantly increasing numbers, in colleges of their own as well as in some of the men's colleges the doors of which have been opened to them. Since, in great measure, demand regulates supply, we may infer that women physicians are wanted. Some have attained eminence either as private practitioners or as writers upon medical topics; many more are leading lives of usefulness among their patients and supporting themselves in comfort while not attaining, nor likely to attain, fame. The same may be said of men physicians—it is only the few who reach the heights, while the majority live quietly, honestly, serviceably, in the valleys.

I do not intend to make a comparison of the sexes in the profession. Both are established in it; both are needed; the best of both will survive, the poorest of both, we all trust, will in time be eliminated. No comparison could be perfectly just, since the men have been so much longer in the field and are so immensely in the majority that the advantages given by wealth, large and firmly established colleges, laboratories, hospitals and clinics must tip the statistical balance in their favor. Besides, the fact that what women accomplish has been done—and, to a certain extent, is still done—under disadvantages, should be taken into account.

To be sure, in these days a woman does not have to storm at the door of a medical college to gain reluctantly accorded admittance, and is not obliged to endure coldness or incivility from professors and classmates. She can choose from among several medical colleges devoted to the instruction of women only, the curricula of which are on a par with the best in the land and vastly superior to the average. One of the number was the first to introduce the prolonged term of study and the preliminary examination in general branches of study now demanded by the State, as well as a graded course, and the constant quizes which, as a rule, have to be sought outside the college gates at additional expense. To be sure, too, the medical libraries are open to women as well as to men, and they can work in various laboratories under the same conditions accorded their brethren.

It is in hospital and clinical work that women find the lack of equality in training. Her own hospitals, excellent though they may be, are few in number when compared with those of the men and offer but few positions to internes. The largest and best hospitals in the country do not admit women as internes. To fit herself for practice by practical experience, a woman has to pay for admission to clinics or go without the knowledge until private practice brings it to her. Many men have to do the same, but some men obtain the position of clerks or assistants at clinics free of charge, and this women, with rare exceptions, do not.

Although it is superfluous in these days to ask whether women shall practice medicine, it is a legitimate question for a woman to ask herself whether she personally shall or shall not do so. To assist her in reaching a decision, it is well that she should know the conditions of success.

In the first place, what is success, medically speaking? Popularity? Financial prosperity? Profound erudition and deep study? None of these alone. Some quacks and charlatans are notoriously richer than the wealthiest physicians, and many deep students of medicine are incapable of treating patients or of earning a competence. As the average woman who is considering the adoption of medicine as a profession wishes both to stand well in the sight of her conscience and her fellow practitioners, and also to insure herself an income, it is evident that success rated mean a measure of each of these things in fair and due proportion. To attain such success some of the conditions are as follows:

In the first place, no allowance should be expected on the score of sex. *Professionally* there is no sex. Scientific attainments and requirements are the same for men and women, and a woman who enters the profession should expect and wish to be judged by the same standards which are applied to men. It is absurd to say: "Medicine is for me a legitimate sphere, and I can be very useful in it, but you must show consideration for me because I have only a woman's brain, a woman's education and a woman's strength." Nevertheless the attitude of some women students during their college course shows that this absurdity is sometimes, perhaps unwittingly, committed. Happily such are few in number; happily, also, there is a sifting and eliminating process known as Examination whereby the profession is saved from chaff.

An essential qualification for success is good health and a strong nervous system. It is not denied that some women of delicate constitution have rendered excellent service, are practising with profit to their patients and to themselves, yet they are, and must be, the exceptions. The ideal physician is of robust constitution, able to endure hard work, vigils, mental strain and responsibility. Much that is unpleasant and repulsive is to be encountered. It may be said by way of encouragement that the nervous system can be *trained*, and that sights and experiences which at first cause a feeling of disgust become endurable, and this without any hardening of the sensibilities. It is a popular opinion that doctors become hardened to the sufferings of others. Perhaps some do, but I believe that, as a rule, they simply acquire self-control, and learn that the subordination of their emotions to the necessities of their work shows truer sympathy than the waste of working force in expressions of compassion. "Used to pain" in a certain sense they must become, in order to save their own strength and to help their patients. A doctor who broke down over every case would be but a feeble dependence in the hour of need. Yet the truest sympathy of heart and manner is compatible with this self-command. Women physicians occasionally err by assuming a hardness of manner which they do not feel.

Good mental endowments are essential to success. True it is that occasionally weak sisters (and brothers) manage in some mysterious manner to skim through the examinations, but this is yearly becoming more difficult owing to the higher standards adopted by the schools. Moreover the ambition to merely pass an examination is scarcely enough for the woman of high ideals. Irrespective of the moral question involved in attempting to handle human lives without the necessary knowledge, pride should rebel at the small satisfaction to be derived from such low aspirations. As one of the most eminent of women physicians has often said, "Every case in practice is an examination of the fitness of the physician." For these severe and constant tests the sort of cramming which sometimes enables a superficial student to pass examinations is of no avail. Only a sound foundation of actual knowledge supplemented by daily additions from study and practical experience will suffice.

A good general education and good breeding are essential to ideal success, though, perhaps, not to financial success. I can call to mind several women (and men) who despite lack of training in even elementary English branches, have by reason of a dogged persistency acquired a fair amount of medical knowledge and have good and lucrative practices. Their success is, however, in spite of and certainly not because of their deficiencies. If education is ever good and desirable, it is doubly, triply so to the physician, who must lead a life of study on the one hand, and on the other, must meet and understand human beings with all their complexities, varied temperaments, traits, trainings, experiences, sympathies and idiosyncrasies. Persons of culture and refinement are repelled by its lack in others, and many a physician, without, perhaps, realizing why, has lost desirable patients because of his or her lack of general education and *savoir faire*. Hypersensitive patients are apt to be unjust and often reject a good doctor of rough manner for a poor one of pleasing address.

The woman physician should especially cultivate womanliness in manner, looks and attire, and this notwithstanding the fact that some exceedingly unwomanly women have made great successes. When the supply of women physicians was more limited, those desiring their services were necessarily less critical; as the number increases only the fittest will survive.

The choice of a good college is a most important consideration. It is a poor economy to choose a school because it will graduate the student in less time than will other institutions. Rather, if possible, choose the one having the most exacting requirements, the one with the most extended and thoroughly taught curriculum, the one conferring a diploma which will represent honest, hard, masterly work, and carry respect wherever it is shown.

Money is a very desirable thing for the medical student, and this I say in spite of the fact that many, very many, women have acquired their medical knowledge under the most adverse financial circumstances, have endured manifold privations and have even joined in arduous study the work necessary for self support in teaching, nursing, typewriting, and even sewing. Noble and worthy of honor are such efforts, and a lesson to those who fold their hands and say, "Fate is too strong; I can do nothing." But I may be permitted to observe that theirs was not the best way of working; that with minds and bodies free to devote to their studies they would have attained even greater success; that many who have been obliged to study under such difficulties or not at all have impaired health from the double strain, and have thereby allowed non-sympathizing on-lookers to say, "You see, a woman cannot study without breaking down," whereas the woman thus criticised was simply incapable of doing the work of two persons.

The books and apparatus needed in the study of medicine are expensive. The college fees are moderate, but they amount to a considerable sum in the aggregate. The room of a student should be comfortable, her food abundant and of good quality, and her clothing warm. After graduation, too, there will always come a period of expenditure without income, when living has to be paid for, an office hired and, perhaps, furnished, a fair outside show maintained, and patients waited for. It is better, I think, to work and accumulate the necessary funds before beginning the study of medicine, than to undertake it hampered with the necessity for acquiring both money and knowledge at the same time.

There is among recent graduates a longing to settle in the large cities, comprehensible enough when one considers the advantages of clinics, consultants, medical libraries and meetings, and the "attraction of mass." Yet in the cities is found also the sharpest competion, not only with the multitude of reputable physicians, but also with mental healers, quacks, prescribing drug clerks and free dispensaries. Experience shows that those settling in smaller towns become self-supporting much sooner than those who begin in the large cities, owing partly, perhaps, to the facts that living is cheaper in the smaller places and that the payment of the doctor's bills is not so often avoided.

Aside from the actual practice of medicine, there is a vast field for physicians. In foreign countries—especially in Germany, that land of science—the physician who after graduation perhaps never treats a patient, but devotes himself to some special branch of research, to original investigation in some congenial direction, is held to be as worthy of honor and to render services to medicine as truly as those who practice the healing art. It is not possible to make as much money in this way as in active practice, nevertheless some income can be thus derived. Women who possess means of their own can profitably devote themselves to some special branch of science. The case is fresh in mind of a young woman who has been appointed to a position on the Board of Health for the study of diphtheritic serum. Another young and gifted woman physician has renounced the practice of medicine in order to devote her time to histology, pathology and bacteriology, is instructor in one of these branches in a medical college and does excellent work in the others. Chemistry and medical botany also afford employment to those qualified to accept it. Good workers, men or women, are rare in these fields. Americans should aspire to have their country take its place at the front in scientific research, as it already has in the practice of medicine.

Kindergarten Papers.

No. 18.

BY MRS. SARA MILLER KIRBY.

[MRS. KIRBY WILL BE GLAD TO ADVISE AS TO TRAINING SCHOOLS, MOTHERS' CLUBS OR THE ESTABLISHING OF KINDERGARTENS. LETTERS TO HER SHOULD BE ADDRESSED CARE OF THE EDITOR OF THE DELINEATOR, AND BE ACCOMPANIED BY A STAMP FOR REPLY BY MAIL.]

SUGGESTIONS FOR HOME KINDERGARTEN WORK.

While it is hardly possible to conduct the conventional Kindergarten in the home, still there is much the mother can do if she has the Kindergarten spirit. Every thing that helps the child to a better physical growth, every thing that cultivates obedience, truthfulness, self-reliance, every thing that trains in punctuality and observation, is in reality Kindergarten training. The Kindergarten supplies what the home is sometimes unable to supply, either from lack of play room, the multiplied duties of the mother or the want of associates of the child's own age.

There are many things to be said for and some against the Kindergarten. I am a firm believer in it, but when it develops self-consciousness, tends to a restless desire for constant change of amusement or is in charge of a Kindergartner who is not both naturally fitted and thoroughly trained for the work, then the Kindergarten does more harm than good. Mothers who were formerly well-known Kindergartners do not always send their children to the outside Kindergarten, but often prefer to gather the children of a few friends about them and give the work in their own home nursery.

On the other hand, the outside Kindergarten is often a better preparation for the school life which follows, as it provides a more gradual transition from the free home life to the strict discipline of the primary school. Then, too, mothers cannot devote all their time to their children. They must be companionable to their husbands; they must attend to household, social and religious duties and give some attention to mental and spiritual cultivation. Besides, to do the other duties well, they must have time for relaxation, rest and recreation. The wife and mother must not think of her husband and children for to-day alone, she must do everything she can to be fresh and companionable for them and herself, ten or more years ahead. The only way to accomplish this is to decide between essentials and non-essentials. Every mother must decide for herself how much of these things she is able to do. In cities it is generally wise to send children to the Kindergarten, but in small towns which are without a Kindergarten and in the country my advice would be to the mothers to make their children's lives as wholesome and healthy as possible and leave the rest to Providence. If there comes an opening for Kindergarten work, take advantage of it.

Now as to things to work with, it is not absolutely necessary to have the exact Kindergarten material in order to develop the child according to the Kindergarten method. To understand this it may be well to restate some Kindergarten principles. The Kindergarten gifts and occupations are only a means to an end, the tools used suited to the child's age and strength, for the development of character. Character should be the aim of all education—a fitting, as said so many times before, of the human being to live rightly with God, Nature and his fellow man. It goes without saying that for this right living the individual succeeds best who is sound physically, mentally and morally. Then, as we cannot divide life into distinct periods and tell just when and how each development begins, Froebel would have us begin at the beginning. So, as all early development comes through the senses, he arranged material which he personally proved, if rightly used, would meet these requirements and allow the child to educate himself by his own activity at the child's age called "play." The Kindergartner and mother watch his development by his manifestations and supply new and more difficult material to meet, direct and stimulate its increasing growth. They stand to the child as the careful gardener stands to the plant, ever ready to water, to prune, to give sun, shade or any condition necessary to induce this particular plant to reach its highest perfection of growth, flower and fruit. Sometimes the gardener with the simplest contrivances is able to accomplish as much and more than the man with every convenience at hand. In like manner we often see mothers in the humblest homes, bringing up children who are worthy of the honor and esteem of all who know them, because the mothers have been able to make the most and best use of every-day things and to find beauty and goodness in all.

FRAU SCHRODER'S WORK.

Froebel himself would have been able to conduct a Kindergarten in a desert, for even there he would still have had the sand and sky. This use of every-day material is one great point that Frau Schroder, Director of the Pestalozzi-Froebel Haus, Berlin, is said to insist upon to her training class. In Germany many Kindergartners take service as governesses, and I believe the training classes there require their graduates to do one year's work in a family before beginning as teachers in the schools.

Mrs. Susan F. Harriman, in a paper read before the educational association last Summer, tells what she saw of this simple home work when visiting Frau Schroder's establishment. The school, as is usual in all schools, is divided into classes according to age and development. At stated periods a child is taken from each of these classes to help form a group the members of which are of different ages, this group corresponding to the home circle. Some young woman is put in charge of this group whose business it is to keep the children busy and happy, mentally helpful to each other, and to use some simple home duty or occupation as a means of educational training. The group Mrs. Harriman describes was engaged with an ordinary home work-basket and through it occupation was found for each of the group. One child wound and fastened the spools; another sorted and arranged the needles; a third used the emery, one girl made a dress for her doll from a piece of silk found in the basket; another did some mending; an older boy was given a pencil and paper on which to write a letter or do a bit of drawing. Mrs. Harriman, in commenting upon this method, says: "The value of this work as a means of developing the power of adaptability, of enabling a girl to turn everything to use and make it serve her purpose, cannot be overestimated. 'Eyes and they see not, ears and hear not,' describes the condition of most of us. We are looking for more favorable circumstances and better materials to work with when every day finds us surrounded with a wealth of opportunity that we overlook because it is so near at hand. Making the most and best of opportunities that are near by has been the foundation of many a successful career."

Mrs. Harriman, speaking of the practical work of Frau Schroder's school, says that though situated in the heart of a great city, it has beautiful flower and vegetable gardens. In the care of these the children help as much as they are able, removing dead leaves, planting seed and picking flowers and fruit. Many of the German schools have valuable gardens where the pupils have practical work in horticulture and forestry combined with the ordinary school studies. Mrs. Harriman describes a small class at Frau Schroder's school, the members of which picked currants, stemmed them, pressed out the juice and made it into jelly for their own use at luncheon and to carry to sick friends.

A mother of my acquaintance who believes in interesting her children in household occupations often places a chair by her baking table in which sits a small observer who rolls and pats a small piece of dough almost as well as mama. An older child delights in making a genuine small cake when her mother bakes a large one, following the recipe but using spoonfuls where her mother uses larger quantities.

MOTHERS' CLUBS.

Most of the prominent Kindergarten training classes now offer a course of study to mothers. At the Teacher's College, New York City, the course is a short one of eight weeks, including with each lesson a lecture on Froebel's theory, the learning of songs and the practice of games selected for home use.

At Pratt Institute, Brooklyn, the course extends over two years. The class meets once a week for forty weeks, each session being of two hours' duration. The gifts and occupations suitable for home use are studied and lessons are given in each. Songs and games are practised and applied to occupation and gift. The *Mother-play* and *Education of Man* are studied with the view of making their lessons applicable to such subjects as obedience, truthfulness and punishments. Experiences are exchanged and discussions take place on hygiene, food, clothing and other allied topics. The art of story telling is studied, and lists of the best books and playthings for children are made. Mothers may also have the advantage of the many lectures offered there on educational subjects and topics of the day.

At the Chicago Kindergarten College the course is extended over a period of three years. Its catalogue has this to say regarding the "Mothers' Classes:"

The first year's course will include practical work with such gifts and occupations as can best be used in the Nursery; study of Froebel's *Mutter und Kose Lieder*, which will enable the mother to grasp the principle of the system and to reapply them on the innumerable occasions which arise in the home life; also discussions and the answering of questions concerning the study and experiment of the week previous.

The second year includes work with gifts and occupations, science work for little children, the study of Froebel's *Mutter und Kose Lieder*, discussions and the answering of questions.

The third year the lessons include advanced work with all the gifts and occupations, games and stories of the Kindergarten, the study of Froebel's *Mutter und Kose Lieder* and *Education of Man*. All mothers belonging to this department, who request it, are furnished with courses of collateral reading and are assisted in other ways to enlarge their knowledge and insight in this direction.

The lessons in all three of the institutions mentioned are open to any woman interested in Kindergarten work but of course, there are no certificates or diplomas given for these courses of study.

The Chicago Kindergarten College also offers to assist classes or clubs formed in towns and villages at a distance from Chicago. These clubs are called "Local Unions" and as far as possible are given the same course of study as that carried on at the College. For this purpose the College has a special Secretary of the Mothers' Department, who will organize classes, arrange and superintend their work, conduct the correspondence with the classes, and give information to all interested in this department of work. Further information, constitutions and plans of organization will be furnished any one upon application to the college authorities."

I have given the above for the information of mothers, including those to whom I have written personally explaining as fully as possible in a letter the advantages offered them by three prominent Kindergarten training schools. Better satisfaction is obtained by following such a plan and seeking aid from such a source, where the work is systematic and is in charge of specialists. However, if it is not possible to follow this plan, a home club may be formed among a group of friends somewhat as follows: Decide to meet at the house of each member in turn once a week, or once every other week, for from one to two hours. Take up each time one of the *Mother-play* songs to read and talk about. Try to recall familiar songs, stories and experiences with children that bring out the same thought, studying with the *Mother-play* and the Baroness Marenholtz-Bülow's book, *Child and Child-nature*. Let each mother make notes during the week of perplexities and happy experiences with her children to relate for discussion and mutual helpfulness. Let a record be kept of these discussions for additional light upon future child study. Learn songs, games and stories, mothers also giving the ones they have used. Select subjects and, using THE DELINEATOR "Kindergarten Papers" as a guide, decide what use can be made of the gifts, occupations, songs, games and stories to illustrate those subjects. Programmes of work for the week or month would thus be formed. These could be tested with the children and afterwards discussed and criticised from the standpoint of actual practice. If found unsuccessful, learn why. Family excursions or familiar stories may be worked out in this way. Froebel's "Farmyard Gate" would be an interesting subject for a country child's actual Winter observation, or for the city child recalling his Summer visit in the country, and might include learning the names of the animals in the farmyard, cutting out and mounting their pictures, building houses like the ones they are kept in, finding out the food and care they need, what they do for people, etc., etc. There may be found plenty of material for stories, songs, games, gift lessons, sewing, weaving, paper folding and cutting and drawing.

HOUSEHOLD WORK.

Household experiences may also be used to good advantage. For instance, in THE DELINEATOR for March, 1895, some illustrations were given of how the subject of baking and the baker could be developed. Commence with the germination of seeds as there directed. Select finger plays and songs such as, "This is the Way the Rain Comes Down," "Shower and Flower," "Wake, Says the Sunshine," "The Farmer," "The Mill Wheels are Turning" and others. The "Baker Sequence" in the paper referred to shows how to use a gift in illustrating a subject. Decide what other gifts and what occupations could be used. Make lists of the tools used. Collect as many pictures as possible that will show any phase of the subject from the first preparation of the field for sowing to the completed loaf of bread. To carry out Froebel's law of unity, show first the grain, then the loaf of bread and connect them by the steps between. Take only the main points; too much detail is tiresome to the child and renders the subject confusing. Show all the grains used for bread-making and let the children learn to know and be able to sort them.

The general rule for either the mother or the professional Kindergartner is to first get full information herself concerning the subject and processes. Select the main points that are instructive, helpful and interesting, keeping in mind the age and characteristics of the child. As the subject is presented, encourage the child to invent new uses of the gift and occupation illustrating the subject, to turn everyday materials to account, to look for pictures and suggest songs. This will show the child's line of associations and classifications, indicate his individuality and aid in correcting wrong ideas.

The children might be allowed to accompany the mothers to meetings of the mothers' club. Devote the first half of the allotted time to them and then send them out of doors to play while The *Mother-play* is read, experiences exchanged and other meetings planned. The programme for the children would admit of great variety. At one time they could learn songs and finger plays and at another, games, marches or dances. (See THE DELINEATOR for September, 1895, for an illustration of the Kindergarten ring); the work could be divided among the mothers present, one telling a story, another showing pictures illustrating a gift, and a third giving an occupation lesson. After many songs, games and finger plays had been learned a certain number of children might be asked to bring pictures, and one at a time rise in the ring, show these pictures, tell what they were and give some explanation or a short description of them. Then another child might be asked to name a song, game or finger play suggested by the picture in which all could join.

There are many games for testing the senses that might be used with profit at such meetings. For sight there are: first, the naming of the various visible objects; second, the sending of several children each to a different window for a short time to tell upon their return what has been seen; third, sending a child into another room to name upon return the furniture, etc., seen; fourth, having a child walk past a table with a variety of objects upon it and recall as many as possible; fifth, distinguishing between fresh and dried fruits. Insist upon good language being used. When a child learns to write the result may be written instead of being given orally. If the child has been accustomed to recount his experiences, he will take great delight in putting his little stories upon paper. Be careful to have him omit personal details. The color top will be useful in this connection.

Similar exercises may be applied to smell, taste, touch and hearing. With hearing the child may be taught to name the object by sound and also to locate the direction from which the sound comes, trying different parts of the room and also sounds in other rooms. With these sound exercises the musical scale may be practiced, first as "do, re, mi, fa, sol, la, te, do," then sing to "la" or "ah" and finally give ear tests on different notes, singing them to "la" or "ah." The Tonic Sol-Fa music system accomplishes much in this direction, its adherents claiming that most children can learn to sing if training for the ear and vocal organs is commenced early. This system also has a series of simple hand signs to aid in the teaching. Books of first steps and directions for this system can be obtained from most music dealers.

BOOKS FOR MOTHERS

For a mother's club the following books may be recommended as comprehensive and not too technical:

teacher, when it would be necessary to keep the children in one group. Here is the list:

FIRST GIFT.—Six soft balls, standards of the six colors, to be made at home by directions given in THE DELINEATOR for October, 1894.
SECOND GIFT.—If for several children, obtain in bulk.
THIRD GIFT.—If for several children, obtain in bulk.
FOURTH GIFT.—If for several children, obtain in bulk.
FIFTH AND SIXTH GIFTS.—Omit unless there are children six years old. Do not give until most positions possible for the third and fourth gifts as mentioned in THE DELINEATOR papers on these gifts have been given.
SEVENTH GIFT.—Use all forms for the older children, but only circles and squares for the younger ones. Use the circles with the first and second gifts, the squares with the third and fourth and half squares with the fifth gift.
PARQUETRY PAPERS.—These are used to repeat the work of the seventh Gift by pasting the designs upon paper. Select ungummed, coated, Assortment No. 6-1 in each of the forms. For later use get what is known as Ungummed coated Assortment No. 6-b in each form. For small quantities buy Ungummed Coated Parquetry Papers in small envelopes. These contain 100, 200 and 500 pieces, as desired.
MOUNTING SHEETS FOR PARQUETRY.—Style No. 2, 12 leaves 7x9 white Bristol.
EIGHTH GIFT.—Paper box with 1000 sticks assorted from 1 inch to 5 inches. This is sufficient for a good sized class. Colored sticks may be purchased if desired, but they are not necessary.
NINTH GIFT.—Soldered rings. A double order is required for any but small classes.
DRAWING PAPER.—Dotted sheets 7x9.
PAPER CUTTING.—Papers 4x4, ruled and coated, beginning with "Assortment A." Blunt pointed scissors.
SEWING.—Use at first the simplest patterns in "Design Cards" 4x3¼ inches, or square white Bristol, and draw and prick them at home. Miss Arnold's "Natural History Sewing Card" may be used for older children. Sew in the natural colors. Moderately fine embroidery silks are preferred, and may be bought at home stores. Cultivate a nice taste in color. Scenery, buildings and animals may be done in quite fine black silk and will then

BOOKS.	AUTHOR.	PUBLISHER.	PRICE.	REMARKS.
Mottoes and Commentaries on Froebel's Mother Play	Susan E. Blow	D. Appleton & Co.	$1.50	New free translation; more readable than old editions.
Froebel's Mother Songs and Games	Susan E. Blow	D. Appleton & Co.	1.50	
Froebel's Poems and Pictures for Songs and Games	Susan E. Blow	D. Appleton & Co.	2.00	For the children.
Kindergarten Papers (in preparation)	Sara M. Kirby	Butterick Pub. Co.	1.00	Explaining gifts, etc.
Child and Child Nature	Baroness Marenholtz-Bülow	E. Steiger & Co.	1.00	Exposition of Froebel's theory.
Reminiscences of Froebel	Baroness Marenholtz-Bülow	E. Steiger & Co.	1.50	Froebel's life and times.
Contents of Children's Minds	Dr. G. Stanley Hall	E. L. Kellogg & Co.	.25	Explains development of child's mind.
In the Child's World	Emilie Poulson	Milton Bradley Co.	2.00	Stories and morning talks for all the year round. References for collateral reading.
Finger Plays for Nursery and Kindergarten	Emilie Poulson	Lothrop Pub. Co.	1.25	Songs and finger games.
Merry Songs and Games	Mrs. E. B. Hubbard	Balmer & Weber	2.00	
Songs and Games for Little Ones	Misses Walker and Jenks	Oliver Ditson Co.	2.00	
Paradise of Childhood	Ed. Wiebe		2.00	Practical work with gifts and occupations.
Kindergarten News	Editor, Henry W. Blake	Milton Bradley Co.	.50	Devoted to stories, programmes, specimen lessons, news concerning Kindergarten work. More practical than the Kindergarten Magazine.
Seven Little Sisters Who Live on the Round Ball that Floats in the Air	Jane Andrews		.50	

The following list of supplementary readers for children will also be found useful to Kindergartners and mothers for story telling:

BOOKS.	AUTHOR.	PUBLISHER.	PRICE.	REMARKS.
Child's Christ Tales	Andrea Hofer	Kindergarten Literature Co.	$1.00	
Fairy Tales	Hans Christian Andersen	Ginn & Co.	.50	
Leaves and Flowers, or Plant Studies for Young Readers	Mary N. Spear		.30	
Seaside and Wayside	Julia McNair Wright			In three parts.
Skyward and Back	Lucy M. Robinson	School Education Co.	.30	

These books may be purchased through almost any dealer. If purchased for a club, a liberal discount should be obtained.

MATERIALS FOR THE HOME KINDERGARTEN.

In preparing for a home or other small Kindergarten, first secure a catalogue from some firm dealing in Kindergarten supplies. As there is such a variety of materials offered for some of the gifts and occupations, it is difficult for the inexperienced to decide just what to purchase. The following list includes only what is most practical. For a large class of children divided into groups, one group having an occupation while another has a gift lesson, supposing there are two or more teachers, it is usually sufficient if only one-half or at most two-thirds as many gifts of each number are bought as there are children. For example, if there are thirty children, buy from fifteen to twenty gifts of each number, unless there is only one

resemble pen and ink sketches. I've worsted needle having long eyes and blunt points. If it be necessary to use worsted, buy "split zephyr." The wrong side of the card must be used.
WEAVING.—Mats 8¼x8½ inches, strips either ½ or 1-6 inch wide. It is best to order several packages of different color combinations and not to waste ours or have crude combinations. Mrs. Hailmann's mats are used for the babies.
FOLDING PAPERS.—Squares 4x4 engine color, assorted.
PEAS WORK.—Dried Montsies from the grocery or seed store will answer. Soak and use them with wires of sticks.
CLAY.—Buy at a pottery or use fire-brick clay from the stove store.
BEADS FOR STRINGING.—Buy 1000 of Mrs. Hailmann's ½ inch beads, spheres, cubes and cylinders.
PEG BOARD.—Make at home, either using a wooden board or paper box lid, perforating the holes and using shoe pegs, colored by Diamond Dyes. See the illustration in THE DELINEATOR for April, 1895.
COLOR TOPS.—Valuable and inexpensive.
TABLES.—These are not necessary for home use. If desired, buy 4 feet long, 18 inches wide. Squared enameled cloth or ruled unbleached muslin tied over any low table is sufficient. For schools, use a table 6 feet long and 19 inches wide.

Made-up boxes of Kindergarten materials advertised "for home use" are generally unsatisfactory.

NEW STYLES IN SLEEVES, COLLARS, ETC.

LADIES' CIRCULAR-PUFF DRESS SLEEVE. (TO BE MADE IN ELBOW OR FULL LENGTH.)

No. 1040.—A soft variety of woollen dress goods was selected for this sleeve, which is in coat shape, with a puff above the elbow. The puff is circular in shape to pro-

1040

1040 1040

LADIES' CIRCULAR-PUFF DRESS SLEEVE. (TO BE MADE IN ELBOW OR FULL-LENGTH.) (COPYRIGHT.)

duce great fulness at the lower edge and only slight fulness at the upper edge, this giving the sloping effect of the 1830 modes at the top and a full, bell-like flare at the elbow. The sleeve may be made up in full length or in elbow length, as desired.

1023

LADIES' TWO-SEAM COAT-SHAPED SLEEVE, WITH MELON PUFF IN THREE SECTIONS. (FOR COATS, JACKETS, ETC.) (COPYRIGHT.)

sleeve, which is fashionably called the Amy Robsart sleeve. The lower part of the sleeve is plain and close-fitting and is extended in three straps over a large gathered puff that is widest at the top and stands out prettily between the straps. A coat-shaped lining supports the sleeve, and silk soutache forms an attractive decoration.

Combinations are required to bring out the features of this mode. Trimming is also desirable and may be contributed by jet or spangled gimp, lace insertion or edging, small buttons, etc.

We have pattern No. 1020 in eight sizes for ladies from nine to sixteen inches, arm measure, measuring the arm about an inch below the bottom of the arm's-eye. To make a pair of sleeves for a lady whose arm measures eleven inches as described, requires three yards and five-eighths of silk twenty inches wide, with seven-eighths of a yard of dress goods forty inches wide. Of one material, they need four yards and a half twenty-two inches wide, or three and three-eighths thirty inches wide, or two and seven-eighths thirty-six or forty-four inches wide. Price of pattern, 5d. or 10 cents.

LADIES' TWO-SEAM COAT-SHAPED SLEEVE, WITH MELON PUFF IN THREE SECTIONS. (FOR COATS, JACKETS, ETC.)

No. 1023.—This sleeve is sufficiently wide at the top to slip on easily over the dress sleeves; it is shown made of plain cloth. It is in coat shape and over it above the elbow is arranged a melon puff

1020

Silk and woollen goods are equally appropriate for this sleeve, which is a favored style.

We have pattern No. 1040 in eight sizes for ladies from nine to sixteen inches, arm measure, measuring the arm about an inch below the bottom of the arm's-eye. To make a pair of sleeves for a lady whose arm meas-

1020

LADIES' DRESS SLEEVE. (KNOWN AS THE AMY ROBSART SLEEVE.) (COPYRIGHT.)

ures eleven inches as described, requires four yards and a half of material twenty-two inches wide, or three yards and an eighth thirty inches wide, or two yards and three-fourths thirty-six inches wide, or two yards and five-eighths forty-four inches wide. Price of pattern, 5d. or 10 cents.

LADIES' DRESS SLEEVE. (KNOWN AS THE AMY ROBSART SLEEVE.)

No. 1020.—Camel's-hair and silk are united in this fanciful

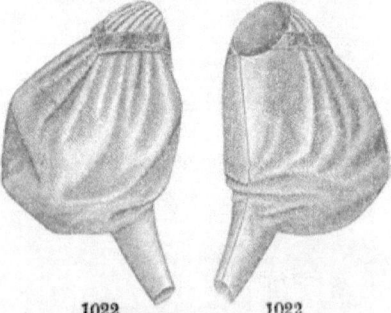

1022 1022

LADIES' DRESS SLEEVE, PLAITED AT THE TOP. (IN 1830 STYLE.) (COPYRIGHT.)

consisting of three sections. The puff, which is gathered at the top and bottom, spreads broadly and all of its seams are pressed

THE DELINEATOR

open and stitched flatly at each side in regular tailor fashion. Coats and jackets of any length or style may be completed with sleeves of this description in a like or contrasting goods.

1036

LADIES' PUFF DRESS SLEEVE. (TO BE MADE IN FULL LENGTH OR IN A SHORT PUFF-SLEEVE WITH BAND.) (COPYRIGHT.)

1036

We have pattern No. 1023 in eight sizes for ladies from nine to sixteen inches, arm measure, measuring the arm about an inch below the bottom of the arm's-eye. To make a pair of sleeves for a lady whose arm measures eleven inches as described, will require four yards and a half of material twenty-two inches, or three yards and an eighth thirty inches wide, or two yards and three-fourths thirty-six inches wide, or two yards and a fourth forty-four inches wide, or a yard and seven-eighths fifty inches wide. Price of pattern, 5d. or 10 cents.

LADIES' DRESS SLEEVE, PLAITED AT THE TOP. (IN 1830 STYLE.)

No. 1022.—This picturesque sleeve is illustrated made of soft woollen dress goods and velvet. It is in one-seam leg-o'-mutton shape with its great fulness collected at the top in side plaits that are tacked at cap depth from the top to the coat-shaped lining under a pointed strap of velvet. Two downward-turning plaits at the seam just above the elbow give the drooping puff effect.

Such a sleeve will be appropriate for any style of blouse or waist, and the straps may be covered with jewelled trimming or lace.

We have pattern No. 1022 in eight sizes for ladies from nine to sixteen inches, arm measure, measuring the arm about an inch below the bottom of the arm's-eye. To make a pair of sleeves for a lady whose arm measures eleven inches as described, requires four yards and a fourth of material twenty-two inches wide, or three yards thirty inches wide, or two yards and a fourth thirty-six inches wide, or two yards and an eighth fifty inches wide, with a fourth of a yard of velvet twenty inches wide for the strap. Price of pattern, 5d. or 10 cents.

LADIES' PUFF DRESS SLEEVE. (TO BE MADE IN FULL LENGTH OR IN A SHORT PUFF-SLEEVE WITH BAND.)

No. 1036.—This fashionable sleeve is shown made of camel's-hair. It is in coat shape, fitting the arm closely, and a full short puff is arranged upon it, the puff being gathered at the top and bottom and standing out prettily. The sleeve may end at the bottom of the puff and have a band at the lower edge, as illustrated, for evening wear.

Plain and fancy silks, cashmere, cloth, velvet and most of the dress goods in vogue will make up stylishly in this manner.

We have pattern No. 1036 in eight sizes for ladies from nine to sixteen inches, arm measure, measuring the arm about an inch below the bottom of the arm's-eye. To make a pair of sleeves for a lady whose arm measures eleven inches as described, needs three yards and five-eighths of material twenty-two inches wide, or two yards and three-fourths thirty inches wide, or two yards and a fourth thirty-six inches wide, or two yards forty-four inches wide, or a yard and three-fourths fifty inches wide. Price of pattern, 5d. or 10 cents.

MISSES' AND GIRLS' PUFF DRESS-SLEEVE. (TO BE MADE IN FULL-LENGTH OR IN A SHORT PUFF-SLEEVE WITH BAND.)

No. 1037.—The sleeve here pictured made of serge is in coat-shape and fits the arm closely. A short balloon puff arranged on it at the top is gathered at the top and bottom and stands out with pleasing effect. The sleeve ends at the puff and is completed with a band when a short puff sleeve is desired, as shown in the small engraving.

The sleeve is suitable for full dress and for house and street costumes and all fashionable dress goods are appropriate for it.

We have pattern No. 1037 in eight sizes from two to sixteen years. To make a pair of sleeves for a miss of twelve years, needs two yards and

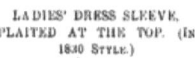

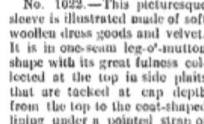

1037

MISSES' AND GIRLS' PUFF DRESS SLEEVE. (TO BE MADE IN FULL LENGTH OR IN A SHORT PUFF SLEEVE WITH BAND.) (COPYRIGHT.)

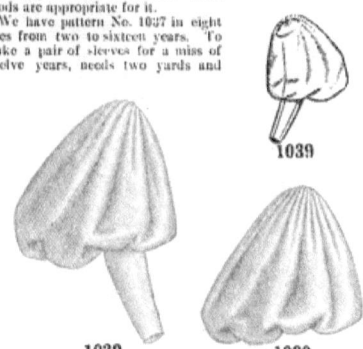

1039 **1039**

MISSES' AND GIRLS' CIRCULAR-PUFF DRESS SLEEVE. (TO BE MADE IN ELBOW OR FULL LENGTH.) (COPYRIGHT.)

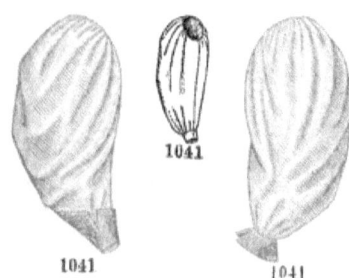

1041

1041 **1041**

MISSES' AND GIRLS' ONE-SEAM BISHOP DRESS SLEEVE. (TO BE MADE WITH OR WITHOUT A FITTED LINING AND WITH A CLOSE-FITTING CUFF OR WITH AN UPTURNED CUFF ROLLED PART WAY DOWN AND FLARING OR WITH AN UPTURNED GAUNTLET CUFF THAT MAY BE SLASHED OR NOT.) KNOWN AS THE PAQUIN SLEEVE. (COPYRIGHT.)

seven-eighths of goods twenty-two inches wide, or two yards and a half thirty inches wide, or two yards thirty-six inches wide, or a yard and five-eighths forty-four or fifty inches wide. Price of pattern, 5d. or 10 cents.

MISSES' AND GIRLS' CIRCULAR-PUFF DRESS SLEEVE. (To be Made in Elbow or Full Length.)

No. 1039.—The sleeve here shown made of dress goods is

1042

decidedly picturesque in effect. The large puff is circular in shape with great fulness at the bottom and slight fulness at the top, thus giving the sloping-shoulder effect of the 1830 styles. It is gathered at the top and bottom and arranged on a coat-shaped sleeve, which will be cut off below the puff when an elbow sleeve is desired.

All seasonable goods are available for the mode and trimming, such as lace, rows of gimp or fancy braid and small gilt or silver buttons may be added.

We have pattern No. 1039 in seven sizes from four to sixteen years of age. For a miss of twelve years, a pair of sleeves requires three yards and three-eighths of material twenty-two inches wide, or two yards and five-eighths thirty inches wide, or two yards thirty-six or forty-four inches wide. Price of pattern, 5d. or 10 cents.

MISSES' AND GIRLS' ONE-SEAM BISHOP DRESS SLEEVE. (To be Made With or Without a Fitted Lining and with a Close-Fitting Cuff, or with an Upturned Cuff Rolled Part Way Down and Flaring, or with an Upturned Gauntlet Cuff that may be Slashed or Not.) KNOWN AS THE PAQUIN SLEEVE.

No. 1041.—This sleeve is shown made of dress goods and velvet and is among the most comfortable and stylish of recent fashions. It may be made with or without a coat-shaped lining. The sleeve is shaped by one seam and its fulness is collected in gathers at the upper and lower edges and droops in innumerable soft folds. The pattern provides a close-fitting cuff, an upturned cuff rolled part way down and flaring and an upturned gauntlet cuff that may be slashed or not, as preferred. These different styles of cuffs are shown in the engravings and are equally fashionable. The sleeve is suitable for shirt-waists, and for dresses made of challis, silk and sheer fabrics, and the cuff may be of velvet or contrasting goods, or it may be of the sleeve material.

We have pattern No. 1041 in seven sizes, from four to sixteen years of age. For a miss of twelve years, a pair of sleeves calls for three yards and a half of goods twenty-two inches wide, or two yards and three-fourths thirty inches wide, or two yards and a fourth thirty-six inches wide, or a yard and seven-eighths forty-four inches wide, or a yard and three-fourths fifty inches wide, with three-eighths of a yard of velvet twenty inches wide either for the rolled or gauntlet cuff. Price of pattern, 5d. or 10 cents.

GIRLS' FANCY MUFF AND RIPPLE CAPE-COLLAR.

No. 1042.—Dark-green velvet was selected for this pretty muff and collar, changeable silk being used for lining. The collar consists of a high flaring storm collar and a round cape that is shaped in circular style with a center seam; it lies smoothly at the front and back but ripples deeply on the shoulders, and is prettily trimmed with frills of écru lace edging in two widths.

The muff is shirred to form pretty frills at the sides, a frill of lace being arranged inside of these frills; a rosette of lace and ribbon completes the dainty ornamentation. A suspension ribbon is passed through the muff and its ends are tied in a bow. These fashionable accessories are usually made of velvet, silk or some fancy material or of cloth to match a special garment.

We have pattern No. 1042 in three sizes for girls from four to twelve years of age. For a girl of eight years, the muff and collar call for a yard and five-eighths of material twenty inches wide, or seven-eighths of a yard thirty-six inches wide, or three-fourths of a yard forty-four or more inches wide. Price of pattern, 5d. or 10 cents.

LADIES' MARIE ANTOINETTE HOODS, ONE PLAIN AND THE OTHER GATHERED AT THE OUTER EDGE. (To be Made With or Without a Neck Ruff and to be Added to Capes, etc.)

No. 1044.—Two styles of hoods that will supplement opera cloaks and various evening wraps are here shown made of cloth and lined with figured silk. A deep edge frill distinguishes one hood, the lining and

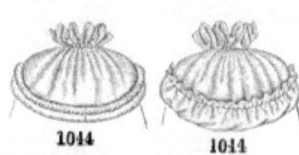

LADIES' MARIE ANTOINETTE HOODS, ONE PLAIN AND THE OTHER GATHERED AT THE OUTER EDGE. (To be Made With or Without a Neck Ruff and to be Added to Capes, etc.) (Copyright.)

outside being sewed together a short distance from the outer edge to form a casing for a wire upon which the hood is prettily shirred. The other hood is plain at the edge, which is bordered with fur and a short dart at the center of the back rolls it slightly. The ends of both hoods are reversed at the bottom and the neck is gathered and sewed to a band that fastens at the throat, the band being covered with a deep, very full neck ruff that is doubled and gathered. A twisted ribbon covers the neckband, its ends terminating under dainty ribbon bows. The hoods may be worn over the head or fall over on the wrap, as preferred.

The hoods are protective and stylish and may be made of velvet, plush and cloth, and silk of contrasting hue may be effectively used for the lining. Fur will provide a pleasing decoration for the plain hood.

We have pattern No. 1044 in three sizes, small, medium and large. In the medium size, the plain hood needs a yard and five-eighths of material twenty-two inches wide, or a yard thirty or thirty-six inches wide, or seven-eighths of a yard forty-four inches wide, or five-eighths of a yard fifty-four inches wide. In each instance a yard and five-eighths of silk twenty inches wide will be needed to line, and a yard and a half of silk twenty inches wide for the ruff, etc. The gathered hood calls for two yards and an eighth twenty-two inches wide, or a yard and a fourth thirty or thirty-six inches wide, or a yard forty-four inches wide, or seven-eighths of a yard fifty-four inches wide, with two yards and a fourth of silk twenty inches wide to line, and a yard and a half of silk twenty inches wide for the ruff, etc. Price of pattern, 5d. or 10 cents.

LADIES' PLAITED AND RIPPLE POINTED PEPLUMS.

No. 1043.—A peplum is an effective addition to a waist and the two styles here illustrated made of cloth are popular and attractive. Each peplum is in two sections that are circular in shape, their pointed ends meeting at the center of the front and back. One peplum is smooth at the top and ripples prettily over the hips, while the other has fulness laid in three backward-turning plaits at each side. Each peplum is joined to a belt that is to be adjusted about the waist.

Accessories of this kind are made up in silk, velvet and all kinds of dress goods and may either match or contrast with the bodice with which they are to be worn.

We have pattern No. 1043 in nine sizes for ladies from twenty to thirty-six inches, waist measure. For a lady of medium size, the plaited peplum requires a yard

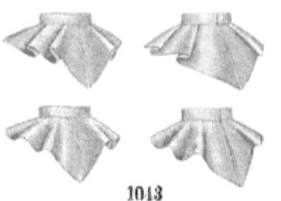

1043
LADIES' PLAITED AND RIPPLE POINTED PEPLUMS.
(COPYRIGHT.)

and an eighth of material twenty inches wide, or seven-eighths of a yard thirty or more inches wide. The ripple peplum calls for one yard twenty inches wide, or seven-eighths of a yard thirty or more inches wide. Price of pattern, 5d. or 10 cents.

MISSES' WAIST DECORATIONS. (TO BE MADE HIGH OR LOW NECKED.)

No. 986.—These attractive decorations may be made high or

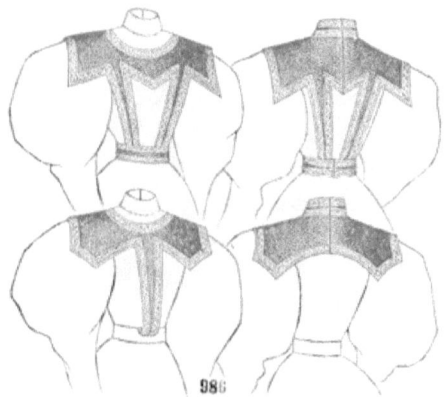

986
MISSES' WAIST DECORATIONS. (TO BE MADE HIGH OR LOW NECKED.)
(COPYRIGHT.)

low necked, as preferred. Velvet is here used for them with an effective edge trimming of passementerie. One decoration is in pointed yoke style shaped at the sides to form deep epaulettes that are pointed at the corners both back and front. The yoke is extended to form a strap at each side of the front and back, the straps being joined to a belt that encircles the waist.

The other decoration is in fancy yoke shape hollowed in a curve at the lower edge and shaped to form fancy epaulettes over the sleeves. It is extended at the center of the front in a strap that droops at the waist-line and has the effect of a box plait. Both decorations are closed at the back. A standing collar finishes either decoration when made high-necked.

Silk, satin or velvet are employed in making such decorations, and lace or a double frill of chiffon may follow the edges. An especially attractive decoration would consist of a row of insertion followed at each side by a frill of narrow lace.

We have pattern No. 986 in six sizes for misses from six to sixteen years of age. The waist decoration with a belt for a miss of twelve years, needs a yard and three-eighths of material twenty inches wide, or seven-eighths of a yard thirty-two or more inches wide, while the waist decoration without a belt calls for three-fourths of a yard twenty inches wide, or three-fourths of a yard thirty-two or more inches wide. Price of pattern, 5d. or 10 cents.

ORIENTAL RUGS.

India and the Sultan's dominions have been impoverished by misrule, palaces, mosques and harems have been made to yield up their treasures, and enterprising Europeans and Americans have taken advantage of existing political conditions to cater for their home market many rare old gems of the Oriental looms. They have also re-established spinners and weavers, who—where they loyally refuse to abandon their inherited good taste in favor of Occidental crudities in color and design—are patiently turning out attractive and durable carpets that need only the softening touches of time to make them truly beautiful. For no one need expect to see a really good new rug at its best during its own lifetime. He should be content to know that his children's children will bless his memory because he wisely chose and set rugs to ripening for them.

By the time the rugs have mellowed into the full maturity of their color harmonies it is possible that their possessors may be able to interpret the symbols they bear—illustrating, perhaps, the older conflicts between good and evil, death and life, truth and error, and their promises of Paradise to the Faithful.

Many rugs bear emblems that are supposed to arrest the evil eye and bring good luck. Many are specially intended for prayer rugs, it being an Oriental practice to stand or kneel upon such rugs at those periods of the day when the Faithful are regularly summoned to worship. It is a characteristic of prayer rugs that one end usually differs from the other either in pattern, colors or both. The design frequently suggests a temple, niche or altar. Prayer rugs are both modern and antique, religious forms in the Orient having changed but slightly with the lapse of centuries.

The costliest modern rugs are made of silk, the looms of Japan furnishing those usually esteemed the finest and heaviest in texture and the most beautiful in design and color. A silk rug only four by seven feet in size lately on view in New York is valued at twenty-five hundred dollars.

The Persian rugs, called Tennachs, have five hundred threads drawn through each square inch of web, and as each thread is tied in by a hard knot years of toil and painstaking attention are necessary to complete a carpet or a rug of any considerable size. Some Persian rugs show a combination of silk and wool, and the same union is found in not a few old Daghestan rugs.

Youruck or Bedouin rugs are highly valued when fine because they are thought to display the shifting hues of the Sahara in sunlight and twilight, the Spring and Autumn of the skies and the shimmer of its infrequent lakelets. Their pile is long and loose and gives less pleasure to Occidental eyes than the more compact work and intricate patterns of the Persians.

There was a time in Cashmere when there were a hundred thousand girls and women spinning the silky hair of the mountain goat and as many men who did the designing, weaving, dyeing and sorting of wools for rugs. The girls began spinning and the boys weaving when they were just ten years of age. But the boys were not compelled to continue this beyond a certain age, while for women it was perforce a life work. As a result, the women of Cashmere now do most of the weaving and all the spinning. Among certain tribes when a girl is a weaver and a man wants her for his wife and worker, he is compelled to pay for her to her nearest male kinsman the equivalent of three hundred dollars. If she becomes a widow after a few years of experience at the loom, her price is double her first cost. Every subsequent re-marriage adds something like a hundred dollars to her cost, the money going to the man who inherits her. Sad as such a fate appears to us, whenever we contemplate the products of these women's hands we are furnished with food for humiliating reflection. We have not and cannot acquire the exquisite skill in coloring, designing and weaving of these people we esteem pagans and barbarians.

From Samarcand (Russia in Asia) and China come many beautiful rugs, collected by wandering buyers and resold to western connoisseurs. Samarcand rugs are seldom large enough to be called carpets. Their centers are usually of a soft brown, dark or light, and their patterns are worked out in blues that are exquisitely lovely. Their surfaces are highly lustrous and their colors blend well with all sorts of woods and wall hangings. There are few if any modern Samarcands in the market. Antique Daghestans are among the best rugs obtainable at any but prohibitive prices, and very beautiful and enduring they are. Modern rugs from the same looms are good, though the buyer should carefully select those not made with the metallic and analine dyes which western dealers have persuaded a few Orientals to use.

Kelim rugs, both new and old, are at once beautiful to look upon and interesting in the methods of their making, their threads being wound in peculiar fashion about the small cords that serve as their web. These rugs are alike, or very nearly so, on both sides and have almost always a long, knotted fringe at one end. This fringe is intended to serve as a finish when the rugs are employed as hangings, a use to which they are often put when not specially intended for prayer rugs. It is a curious fact that the Kelim rugs made by women invariably show designs differing slightly from those made by men. Those made by women are called Kis-Kelims. Connoisseurs can, it is said, declare the sex of the makers by a glance at these rugs and hangings, just as keen-eyed critics sometimes assume to tell the sex of the artist when viewing paintings and sculptures.

Persian silk rugs, while not very old, are beautiful and expensive and in their own country rank in cost with fine goat's-hair antique rugs.

Shirvans are great favorites with rug collectors. They are very enduring and grow more and more beautiful as time softens their hues. With ordinary treatment upon a library or drawing-room floor, a Shirvan rug shows no wear after a hundred years of use. They are usually not quite straight across either their ends or edges, this evidence of the inexactness of hand craft usually being considered a proof of genuineness.

To advise anyone what sort of an Oriental rug to buy is difficult when all are so good and, at first class importing houses, sold at reasonable prices. One might with just as much reason advise another what pictures to purchase. Every house ought to possess at least one good picture and one good Oriental rug, because one picture establishes an irresistible craving for another just as the first rug demands a fellow. Better matting or a painted floor and an Oriental rug or two, than a carpet, which, if good, costs more than a rug of moderate size and wears out much sooner.

In choosing Oriental rugs the buyer who is not an expert should purchase only of a thoroughly reputable dealer and carefully consider his statements in regard to their relative merits before making a selection. He should insist that the rugs sold him must have no analine dyes, because such colors are an abomination when new and detestable after a little wear. Prices range from five to two hundred and fifty dollars, or one to fifty pounds, according to size, age, origin, fineness and design. These rugs are for the practical use of persons with moderate incomes. For rugs of rare artistic beauty and very ripe age large sums must often be paid. Such costly specimens are usually hung upon the wall and are as effective when thus displayed as Flemish or French tapestry. An Iran rug recently exhibited for sale in New York was wrought entirely of silk and silver thread, its design representing an Oriental idea of the Tree of Life. In its center was the curious trunk and at the top of each branch was the head of a bird, beast or fish. Under this design were men mounted and unmounted and about the borders of the rug were inscriptions, one of which, being translated, ran thus: "The best qualities in human beings are charity and a belief in God. Those who do not possess these should not exist." Such inscriptions, often hardly distinguishable to the untrained eye, are written in Chinese, Japanese, Sanskrit, Hindoo, Arabic or Persian, according to the country from which the rug comes.

Among the recent products of the Japanese are attractive woven rugs of cotton and jute, the colorings and designs being very artistic. The Miyota weave is the closest and these rugs will endure more usage than the less expensive but equally effective and pretty Yodatsu. These latter floor covers cost no more and wear as long or longer than the ingrain rugs called Kensington squares, and they are far more artistic and attractive. They have the quality common to all Oriental rugs of adapting themselves to every other furnishing in a room. They are especially suited to well appointed bed chambers and to the Summer furnishing of country houses. Miyota stair covers two feet wide are sold by the yard and are delightfully barbaric in their designs and harmonious in their color blendings. Little Miyota rugs suited to rest before a much used chair, a wash-stand, a dressing-table or a bath-tub are so inexpensive as to be within the reach of very moderate purses. Any importer or dealer in these rugs will send illustrations of them when requested. These illustrations show only the designs and those who order should not forget to mention what leading or ground colors they require.

Very many of the superb old rugs that have been brought to us from the deserted temples and decaying palaces of the far East afford evidence that their makers possessed a far higher culture, a fairer civilization and a purer religion than are now theirs. This conviction is what sensitive and imaginative people feel and respond to when studying these beautiful works of art.

THE SOCIAL CODE.
BY MRS. ROGER A. PRYOR.

TWELFTH PAPER—THE ART OF SUCCESS IN SOCIETY.

[Copyright 1895 by THE BUTTERICK PUBLISHING CO., (Limited). No unauthorized use of these Articles will be permitted.]

We are living in a country and in an age of possibilities. We may not be born to greatness, but we may all achieve it. It is the consciousness of this fact that stamps a certain bearing as distinctively American. Foreigners marvel at the ambition of young people in this country. When the mighty hunters from abroad seek their favorite pastime in the wilds of the Far West, they are prone to record in some corner of their diaries their surprise at finding the daughter of a wayside lodging-house manicuring her nails, crimping her hair, suggesting in her dress and address a faint echo of the society garb and manners of the Eastern Metropolis. This is because the girl not only supposes—she *knows* that it is possible she may some day enter that charmed circle. She reads eagerly the newspapers left by travellers at her father's little hostelry. What has happened may happen again. Marriage with a prosperous miner or speculator is just as possible to her as to another and *au reste*—well, she is as fairly good-looking as that girl whose picture she has seen in the paper, and not so dull or so old but that she may learn.

One must needs ignore what has been done time and again to declare that this young lady is ridiculous. The history, one generation back, of many members of Society proves that the pathway upon which she is venturing is already well beaten. It is because Society has not disdained to admit so many not to "the manner born" that it presents the strange inconsistencies which make it the legitimate theme for satire. It is a kaleidoscope which at one turn shows the beholder a design in royal purple, at another aesthetic mauve or blue, at another silver and gold, at yet another violent contrasts of glaring reds and greens.

Plutocratic society affects to be aristocratic and yet receives into its bosom the obscure of birth and the insignificant in character. It poses as an exclusive organization, barring its doors in front only to open them the wider at the rear. It takes high ground as to vulgar notoriety, but gladly gives the faces of its tenderest maidens to adorn the columns of the daily newspapers. Its private homes, viands, decorations—nay, the very innermost garments it wears—are eagerly yielded to the journalistic illustrator. These are only a few of the inconsistencies of Society at the present day in the United States. Nor must it be supposed that these remarkable departures from traditional ideas are peculiar to America. It is enough to make a conservative American's hair stand on end to see the wholesale demolition of social barriers in England! I think we may say the same thing of France. Possibly in Rome and in Vienna the old order may still prevail.

"LITTLE BROTHERS OF THE RICH."—Of one thing we may rest assured; however anomalous may be the doings of Society, it will always take to itself whatever it needs or finds agreeable. It will invariably supplement its own deficiencies by utilizing whatever of gift or grace it finds in others. Does it wish for an amiable, accomplished dancer to lead its cotillons? If such a one be not found within its gates, it will stretch out a long arm, and reach him somewhere along the highways or hedges. Does it need an instructor in matters of horses and hounds? An adaptable outsider will be welcomed and given the warmest corner of the fireside. Any talent for "making things go" that any man or woman possesses will win for that one a place in society—provided always that the possessor be endowed with a certain adaptability, tact, humility! Society does not expect to be criticised or satirized. Candidates must be amiable. As to not understanding rules of etiquette—that does not signify. These things can be learned. A lapse or two will be forgiven in a good, useful fellow who knows his place and puts on no airs. The number of well-known young men who illustrate the truth of these assertions swells year after year. Truly these "Little Brothers of the Rich" have no cause to complain. They receive a Benjamin's portion from the Joseph they bow down to. Society is not mean about money.

Altogether it seems to be a fortunate arrangement for both sides. Of course, it would be much more complimentary if I could, in discussing American Society, base my conclusions upon a definition given years ago by an accomplished English writer. "By Society," he said, "I wish to be understood as meaning company in the highest degree polished—company which (being or not being aristocratic as respects its composition) is aristocratic as respects the standard of its manners and usages—company controlled by the *instincts*, as well as the rules, of good breeding." Now, when this noble paragraph fell under my eye (while I was searching the past for wisdom to guide me in preparing this article) I felt like heaving a mighty sigh, a sigh in all the languages I know. Remembering that such things could be—and were before these degenerate days—I was reminded of Du Maurier's lament over past joys, and, like him, I could only say, "Hélas! Ahimé! Ach weh! Ay de mi! Eheu! In point of fact *alas!*"

However, we must take the world as we find it. We are bidden to leave the winnowing of the tares from the wheat to a stronger hand than our own. "Let all grow together until the harvest!" Who knows but the tares may become less unlovely, rough, prickly, aggressive, by reason of growing alongside the wheat? And who knows how soon they may die out of themselves and no longer blur and deface the landscape?

THINGS TO AVOID.—To my task then: the art of success in really good society—clever, refined and fastidious society—cannot be learned from rules of etiquette. Still these must not be ignored nor transgressed. A clever woman has recently declared that the strongest laws in all the world are the laws that govern etiquette. While it is no great accomplishment to possess them, it is fatal to ignore them, just as it is small honor to spell well but dire disgrace not to. Yet, however punctilious may be the observance of these laws, this obedience will not of itself include all that is demanded by good breeding. "Good breeding!" exclaims De Quincey, "What is it? It is made up chiefly of negative elements. It shows itself far less in what it *prescribes* than in what it forbids." It consists less in the doing of those things which we ought to do, than in the leaving undone those things which we ought not to do. It is much more dreadful to do disagreeable things than to omit doing pleasant things. For instance, it is much worse to shake hands the wrong way than not to shake hands at all: or to be that most awful of bores, the man who illustrates everything with a long story, than to be the silent man who neither talks nor illustrates. The silent man is pretty sure of being credited with wisdom. He is apt to be spoken of as a thinker, "a deep man," one who has too much dignity to prattle and chatter for the amusement of Society. It is amazing to see the terror with which Society regards the creature it has chosen to designate as "a bore." I have never quite understood it. He is dreaded far more than a pestilence. And his high priest, prince, grand vizier—what not?—is the teller of long stories. In no age has Society found time to listen. "Of all the bores," says De Quincey (who liked a chance to talk himself), "whom man in his folly hesitates to hang, the most insufferable is the teller of 'good stories'—a nuisance that should be put down by cudgelling, or submersion in horse-ponds, or any mode of abatement, as summarily as men would combine to suffocate a vampire or a mad dog!"

There are a thousand disagreeable things that people can do which will make them unpleasant companions and there are types of unpleasantness peculiarly offensive to some people. The too deferential man is never agreeable, nor is the man or woman who lies in wait to flatter you and springs a compliment upon you at every corner. Nothing is more irritating. Then there are the people who insist upon thrusting themselves and their private affairs upon your notice, who are so indelicate as to make you presents upon a short acquaintance, who write you effusive notes which you cannot answer in kind, or talk personalities until you are in terror lest you get into hot water—all these are unpleasant, to say the least.

Now, good breeding demands the effacement of self, the power to entertain by discussing subjects of common interest, the intelligent perception of the tastes of others, and the grace to respect them after they are perceived—in short, the avoiding of disagreeable things and skill in pleasing every companion as far as possible. Moreover, good breeding demands a solid foundation in character and culture. Indeed, when exterior polish is affected by a person of innate coarseness, the polish itself becomes inappropriate; an offence instead of an ornament. We want the solid building as well as the decoration. The structure must have a firm foundation, sound walls, and meet the needs of the inhabitant before we give attention to the graceful arch, carved traceries and delicate furnishings of embroidery and gold.

It requires tact and keen perception to understand the world around us and a vast amount of self-abnegation to live usefully in it. Success in the world, the power to make it wiser and better and to get happiness from it, depends upon ourselves. "If we crave friendship," says Emerson, "we must show ourselves friendly." If we would please, we must be pleased. Some people are too indifferent or too dull, or too indifferent to desire to please. They aim at nothing better than neutrality, inoffensiveness. They are simply innocuous. For these Society never had—never will have—the smallest use.

THE CHARM OF MANNER.—One of the most powerful influences in Society is—not beauty, grace, wealth, nor even character and learning. It is manner. "Manner," says Lord Chesterfield, "is of far more importance than matter—just as grace is a higher influence always than beauty. Now, what are the requisites of a charming manner? Something more than courtesy, or refinement, or tact, or observance of the rules of polite Society, and yet all of these. Manner has been defined as "the involuntary or incidental expression given to our thoughts and sentiments by looks, tones and gestures." Clearly then, the sentiments should be of the highest—and the thoughts strictly of "whatsoever things are lovely, pure and of good report." The character must be pitched to a high key and, over and above all things, the temper must be generous and genial. It is marvellous how much subtle malignity lurks in much that is said and done in Society. Half the censures we so conscientiously launch against the foibles of our fellows are inspired by our own ill humor, while we fancy we are fulfilling a virtuous mission to reprove folly and correct faults. A quick-tempered person is always ready to take offence and always offending. It does not atone that he is usually always repenting. Wounded feelings can no more be salved by apologies than the heavy foot can be forgiven for treading a lady's train or crushing her delicate toes. "A man," says George Eliot, "who uses his balmorals to tread on your toes with much frequency and an unmistakable emphasis may prove a fast friend in adversity, but meanwhile your adversity has not arrived and your toes are tender. The daily sneer at your remarks is not to be made amends for by a possible defense of your understanding against deprecators who may not present themselves, and on an occasion which may never arise." So when some good-natured friend has torn you to pieces, at a time, perhaps, when you were tolerably happy, by telling you of some horrid thing somebody has said about you and, having thus gratified an evil disposition, proceeds to patch you up again by repeating a compliment, the soothing plaster refuses to adhere. The wound may not bleed outwardly, but is smart until the circumstance is forgotten.

Maladroit people, however, often offend and thus become unpopular, less from want of heart than from want of thought. Here, too, repentance, as a cure for the wound is ineffectual. If you are dreadfully outraged and are assured the offender "didn't mean it," you cannot be certain that he is not apologizing without meaning it. How can you tell which was sincere, the involuntary action or the second thought? The presumption is rather in favor of the former.

We cannot, if we wish to succeed, be too careful to avoid wounding people's amour propre or irritating them by contradiction or rudeness. Besides, apologies are humiliating. The retrograde movement is always painful and embarrassing. Dear

knows, we have enough ado in this world to attain any vantage ground, without wasting time and force in retracing our steps.

CHEERFULNESS.—Cheerfulness is one of the sure elements of success in Society. The world flees from the hypochondriac, from the woman whose talk is a recital of her aches and pains and domestic worries, and from the man who proves that we are going to destruction nationally, and, of course, individually. Society has no use for tragedies, except, occasionally, on the stage. It thrusts aside the man who stands in its sunshine. Among the cruelties of which we have heard—Inquisition and what not—I place the cruelty of having life spoiled by persistent gloom dispensers. We have no right to darken the sky for other people simply because we refuse to bask in the sunshine ourselves. We can bear ourselves bravely, even in great trouble, so as to lighten our own hearts, and we absolutely must unless we are willing to become a nuisance to our friends. Since the art of pleasing consists in being pleased, how can we expect to please by Jeremiades? The greatest and wisest man I ever knew always met me with some pleasantry, some smile-provoking trifle. We talk about the still running of deep waters, their silence, their value, but whoever saw waters so deep that their surface could not sparkle like diamonds in blue enamel? "Good temper," says Hazlitt, "and animal spirits are everything. They are of more importance than sallies of wit or refinements of understanding. They will give a fool the advantage over a wise man." Who has not seen a company chilled, as if a fog had descended upon it, by some one sour, taciturn but magnetic individual? In his presence laughter is quenched, the jest dies upon the lips and pleasant talk can no more flourish than flowers can bloom or birds sing in the dark.

GRACE.—Next to good temper and cheerfulness, grace of manner—a subtle quality—is most important to insure social success. Women excel in this. Everybody knows that beauty is less irresistible than grace in women. "Petrarch's description of Laura answers exactly to this idea, and Titian's portraits are full of it. They seem sustained by sentiment, or as if the persons whom he painted sat to music. One in the Louvre is wonderful; it does not look downward; it looks forward, beyond this world"—marvellous power of gracefulness in pose! General Robert E. Lee possessed this grace in a most remarkable degree. It was his gift to sit in perfect quiet and impress one as having been eloquent. His silence was golden with the import of the fine things he could have said. Grace, as defined by a great writer, is only the outward expression of the harmony of the soul. But this definition is not wholly true. Bodily grace and grace of expression can be acquired by persons whose souls are most inharmonious, whose characters are most unsymmetrical. Lord Chesterfield says of the first Marlborough: "Of all the men I ever knew (and I knew him extremely well) the late Duke of Marlborough possessed the graces in the highest degree, not to say engrossed them. I ascribe the better half of his greatness and riches to those graces. He was eminently illiterate, wrote bad English, and spelt it worse. He had no share in what is commonly called 'parts'—that is, brightness, nothing shining in his genius. True, his figure was beautiful, but his manner was irresistible to either man or woman. It was by this engaging, graceful manner that he was enabled, during all his wars, to connect the various and jarring powers of the grand alliance, notwithstanding their private and separate views, jealousies and wrongheadedness."

The attainment of a gracious demeanor, of graceful manners and of gracefulness in pose and gesture, is not enough sought in this country. It should be made a part of education, as it is in Court circles abroad. No class of people lead more laborious lives than the men and women of fashion abroad who are conspicuous for elegance of manner. Young women deny themselves freedom and ease to acquire accomplishments. An English writer says that a professional reviewer does not drudge as a fine lady does, nor a political candidate go through half as much vexation of spirit. These fine ladies study grace, then study to make it appear unstudied, and thus attain the wonderful ease and tact for which—especially in the French salons—they become famous. It is said that the American lady who has recently become Mrs. George Curzon (Miss Leiter) is a shining example of the grace of manner which is acquired by culture. We have reason to lament that she was taken across the water and so lost to America.

It is absolutely necessary, in order to succeed in Society: first, to wish to please; then to study in what manner we can be most agreeable to those around us; finally, to neglect no small particular in behavior or dress that will tend to make us attractive and acceptable—to return the courtesies paid us, to answer all letters punctually, to appear cheerful and willing to be amused by trifles, it may be, or instructed by graver people than ourselves; to submit to being *bored* without impatience, to tolerate even the teller of stories and anecdotes, to be everlastingly vigilant not to wound or neglect others. This is the training that Royalty gives its children.

HOW MRS. CLEVELAND PLEASES.— The late Mr. Hjalmar Hjorth Boyesen was once so eloquent, in a little talk I had with him, about the charm of the gracious present mistress of the White House, that I said: "Tell me exactly wherein the *special* charm lies. Give me facts. What did she say? How often have you seen her?" "What did she say?" repeated Mr. Boyesen musingly. "Very little. I stood in line at one of her receptions. When I was presented she smiled—and her smile is a rare one—and she said 'Oh, Mr. Boyesen, I have read one of your books. Are all your heroines, I wonder, as charming as the one I know?' I told her she must be the judge of that, and I asked permission to send her my stories, and then passed on." "Was that all?" I asked. "Could you hear what she said to the man behind you?" "Dr. McCosh immediately followed me. 'Oh, Dr. McCosh!' said Mrs. Cleveland, 'I was at your lecture yesterday. I will not say I enjoyed it—that would be presumption on my part—, but I was honored by being present.' 'Madam,' said the old philosopher and divine, 'I will send you my lecture that you may learn it better.'" I assured Mr. Boyesen that he need say no more. I was answered! I reminded him of the old saying that when you fill a man's cup with sweet words, all that runs over will be yours.

I think this is the root of the whole matter. The world is a looking-glass. The face that you present to it will look back at you. If you make people happy, they will like you—if you are neglectful or disagreeable, they will not. It is very simple. Of course, our motives should be higher than merely to win good things for ourselves—the good things that come with success in Society. Chesterfield's matchless code of rules for polite behavior were all inspired by the common instinct of self-preservation. Do thus and thus, he says to his son, and you will be admired, you will be popular, you will be envied. The rules were good—the principle rotten to the core. No wonder that his son, who was an honest, sincere fellow, should have despised these rules, and elected for himself the untrammeled, slouchy, unconventional life of an easy-going country squire, with no "graces," no manner and no polish.

But I am exceeding the limits allotted for this, the last of my series of papers on the Social Code. I cannot hope that I have said all that might have been said, but of one thing I feel sure : A life ordered upon the lines I have suggested cannot be a failure. It must be a success, even if there be no social *entourage* capable of appreciating it. It is not given to every gem to be blessed with a fitting setting, nor to every song to have a harmonious accompaniment. The business of each one of us, I take it, is to make our own character and manners as perfect as possible, and trust to kind fortune for our surroundings.

FOR PLUMP WOMEN.

A despairing plump woman once said to me : "All the fashions are made for you thin people. We who are inclined to embonpoint fare hardly indeed." In many cases I fear this conclusion is arrived at because our heavyweight sister does not know how to dress. She is too often a patron of the huge boas, two yards long and of gross thickness, a purchaser of plethoric shopping or chatelaine bags that hang at the belt as if to weigh their wearer down, a buyer of large hats over-trimmed with feathers, etc. All these adjuncts emphasize her weight. A stout woman cannot wear too plain clothing. In no color does she appear so well as in black, but even this must not be black satin, essentially a material for the slender. Huge hats are not for her, nor double-breasted coats, large ruchings, heavy stock collars nor much bodice trimming. She will also do well to avoid bulky *lingerie* and jewelry. Rough cloths will increase her apparent size and horizontal lines will make her appear shorter. But there are many pretty things she can wear.

NECK RUCHES.

There is likely to be a return to the soft neck ruchings in vogue many seasons ago, for its forerunners in the shape of quillings and plaitings of ribbon or net are seen on the latest French dresses. Stock collars, while universally becoming, have been but for her who could replace them as soon as soiled, and that was always distressingly soon. With the new quillings these collars may be kept clean, and that means much to her whose income is modest. The pretty ruche about the neck gives an air of dainty refinement to the wearer and it will be welcomed back to favor without doubt.

RIBBON STOCKS.

In the new *lingerie* are shown stocks of various colors, but these are no longer made of velvet. Ribbon fully two inches wide is used, being folded in the middle to make it of the required depth and having in front a tapering plait that shapes the stock to the collar. This plait is half an inch wide at the top, narrowing to nothing at the bottom. The bow at the back is large and has many loops so drawn in at the center as to give them a very bouffant effect. One end of the stock hooks over the other, and with the addition of a cleverly concealed pin at the back and a stick pin at the front, these collars are adjustable to any frock. The lace-pin must be inserted quite at the bottom of the stock where it joins the bodice.

LACE COLLARS.

It is such accessories of dress as these ribbon stocks and their kind, the minor pomps and vanities dear to the feminine heart, that make up the changes in many a wardrobe. A lace collar made of a full ruffle of pretty lace ten or twelve inches deep, the ruffle sewed to a ribbon foundation, will brighten and change many a gown of which the owner has grown weary. These collars are none too full when made with four yards of lace, and the deeper the lace the more elegant is the collar. The lace is gathered evenly to a ribbon shaped as for a stock, and over this one of the pretty stocks is worn. The lace hangs straight all round and is caught up in two or three places in front with pretty lace or stick pins. One such collar with two or three stocks will make a variety of changes possible. Among the stocks there should be a white one, one of plaid ribbon showing a good deal of green and one of a dainty Persian or Dresden ribbon.

This is clearly a lace year, for even the advent of Winter has not entirely banished the warm yellow lace so much in favor during the Summer. There was no place which it could decorate except the face veil, so

ABOUT VEILS.

here it is, and two or three rows of it, too. These new veils are not cheap, but the clever woman buys a length of veiling and the lace and joins them herself.

The cost of veils causes any woman to whom economy is an object to take good care of these beauty pieces. In buying a veil she has learned that the quality which does not contain too much stiffness will give better service than the wiry veiling. The latter soon creeps up on the face, the tying at the back seeming to pull it all that way. But even when veils have shrunk into a veritable string, they may be restored to a useful condition by slightly dampening them and winding them upon a covered rolling pin. The round stick is covered first with wadding and then with sateen or a bit of old silk to provide a sufficient foundation upon which to pin the veiling. Carefully stretch the dampened veil around this roller, pinning it so as to secure the original width on both sides. After being left to dry for a couple of days on the roller the veil will be found quiet fresh.

It is a matter for congratulation that all millinery effects have disappeared from the refined dinner table. The use of satin and silk center-pieces was in questionable taste always and has fortunately seen its day. Any article that cannot bear a visit to the laundry is out of keeping on the dinner table. The handsome center-pieces now seen on elegantly appointed tables are of a variety of shapes, the circular form, however, being held in highest favor. The finest linen is the material used and the designs are most artistic. The worker in these pretty articles has long since learned the wisdom of using only the best of silk for the embroidery, silk that will bear all the visits to the laundry that its use will entail. There are, curiously enough, always certain patterns that are considered "the latest" and just now the flowers are stamped to look as though some of the petals were floating loosely from the blossom across the cloth. Bows and streamers of ribbon also frequently appear in these designs. Honiton lace button-holed to the linen is used in regular clusters about the border, the linen being cut from under the lace. There will be a cluster of three links of the lace, then a space, then three more links, and so on. Such a border is quite new and very effective. When a simple pattern has been chosen for the embroidered part, the lace seems to atone for any scantiness of the work.

The happy possessor of many such pretty bits of embroidered linen is sure to always launder them with her own hands, for she would not trust her treasures to the mercy of the laundress. Lukewarm water is used and a slight lather is made of white soap, no soap being used directly on the linen. After washing, the pieces are rinsed in lukewarm water. No bluing is used unless the linen has commenced to grow yellow, and even then but a slight tinge is given to the water. Bluing has a persistent way of clinging to the fringe and sometimes to the embroidery. The linen is squeezed as dry as possible without twisting, then laid in a towel and clapped between the hands to dry it as much as possible and finally ironed at once. The board on which embroidered articles are ironed should be thickly padded with a soft old quilt having a thickness of white flannel for the outer covering. Upon this the linen is laid, wrong side up, and a flat iron, not too hot, is used to bring out the beauty of the other side, ironing with the weave of the linen to keep it in shape. Fringe is brushed out with a whisk-broom, or a coarse comb, sold for this purpose, is used to untangle it.

DINNER-TABLE CENTER-PIECES.

QUIET REIGNS.

It is a sociological fact, my dears, that gentleness is an outward sign of inward civilization. The more uncivilized the home the heavier the steps of its inmates, the harsher their voices, the louder are the doors banged. In a well-ordered home of these last-of-the-century days the servants are trained to do their work with the least possible noise, a boisterous maid being less tolerated than an incapable one. The dinner bell has been discarded and the maid announces the meals. The bell for the rising call in the morning is soft and low in tone, awakening the sleepers to music, as it were. A novelty in the way of a breakfast call has several sweet-toned silver bells sounding different notes suspended from oxidized silver brackets mounted on fancy shields of mahogany or oak. These are favorite wedding gifts.

Quietness in the home has much to recommend it, but good form just now demands repression at every point if one would be considered quite refined. This repression of the emotions is likely to yield a rich harvest of broken up women when the nerves drawn just a little too tightly snap. But, despite all this, Good Form places her sign manual upon many commendable things. Certain is it that the girl she most highly approves is not she whose voice is the loudest, whose laugh makes one wince by its boisterousness, whose constant effervescing takes the life out of the beholder, but rather she who is lively without being noisy, whose laugh is merry as a bird's song yet never jars, who, talking well and happily herself, is a good listener, who is gentle and refined always. She it is who is urged to come often to afternoon tea.

EDNA S. WITHERSPOON.

AMONG THE NEWEST BOOKS.

Among books specially issued for the holiday season, but which reached us too late for review in the last issue, are the following:

With spirited little black-and-white etchings on its broad margins and full-page colored plates here and there, with rubricated initials, net and scene divisions and with its heavy plate paper, gilt edges and olive-green and gold binding, the holiday edition of *The Merry Wives of Windsor*, illustrated by J. Finnemore and F. L. Emanuel and published by Raphael Tuck and Sons, is a delight. The text is from the folio of 1623 and the brief preface repeats the tradition first promulgated in 1702 by John Dennis (in connection with his own unsuccessful attempt to improve upon Shakspere's version) that the comedy was dashed off in a fortnight at the request of Queen Elizabeth, who had expressed a wish to see Falstaff in love. Coming exactly a century after the publication of the first folio (1602) this oft-repeated story is more entertaining than authentic, but any one who will take the trouble to compare the text of the first folio (a capital fac-simile of which has been published by Mr. Augustin Daly) with that printed in this sumptuous edition may easily see for himself that the comedy was written in a hurry and revised in most thorough fashion.

In *Westminster*, a companion volume to his *London*, Sir Walter Besant boldly attacks the hitherto accepted theory that the place on which Westminster Abbey stands was chosen deliberately as a fitting place for a monastic foundation because of its seclusion, silence and remoteness from the haunts of men. He proves conclusively that it was the site of a Roman station and ford across the Thames long before London existed and that a temple of Apollo preceded the first Christian church there erected. He restores the vanished palaces of Westminster and Whitehall, portrays the life of the Abbey with its services, its Rule, its Anchorites and its Sanctuary, and shows the connection of the place with Caxton, the first of English printers. In this learned exposition of what he calls "a city without citizens" Sir Walter has had the valuable assistance of William Patten, the artist, the book being generously illustrated with careful drawings of the archæological and architectural features described. Coming from a popular novel writer, the work is a marvel of patient research and painstaking accuracy. [New York: Frederick A. Stokes Company.]

It would seem that the iconoclastic spirit of modern progress over which antiquarians lament is felt even in conservative and landmark-reverencing Boston, for it is both the plaint of, and the excuse for, Henry R. Blaney's *Old Boston*. The author's spirited etchings of famous old buildings in the New England metropolis have long been known to the cultured few, but they are here carefully reproduced in a form placing them within the reach of all. A few words of explanation precede each plate, and the book as a whole forms a handsome and valuable record of vanished and vanishing mementoes of days that tried men's souls. [Boston: Lee & Shepard.]

Apropos of the discussion in regard to Lord Tennyson's official successor, comes Kenyon West's *Laureates of England*. It comprises an introduction, dealing with the origin and significance of the office, and biographical sketches, portraits and selections from the works of these fourteen men who have held it: Johnson, Davenant, Dryden, Shadwell, Tate, Rowe, Eusden, Cibber, Whitehead, Wharton, Pye, Southey, Wordsworth and Tennyson. Mr. West points out that the laureate, an officer of the crown, had primarily to be in sympathy with monarchy and friendly to the sovereign, conditions which excluded men like Coleridge, Byron and Shelley and no doubt had to do with the refusal of the laurel by Gray and Scott. [New York: Frederick A. Stokes Company.]

In Martha C. Oliver's gift-book, *A Year's Good Wishes*, a page for every day in the year is filled with words of kindly good will and conjuration to hopefulness and noble endeavor. The compiler's work has been done with good judgment and F. C. Price's twelve colored plates are better than the usual run. Upon a like general plan and of similar excellence, but distinctively religious in character, is the same compiler's *A Year of Sacred Song*. The twelve colored plates in this volume are flower studies by C. Klein. [New York: Raphael Tuck & Sons.]

There are 366 pages in Mrs. C. S. Derose's *A Daily Staff for Life's Pathway*, each dated and headed by a scriptural quotation and containing comforting religious and moral bits from famous authors. [New York: Frederick A. Stokes Company.]

Gleanings Pure, Pointed and Practical is a little book of brief selections from the writings of Henry Drummond, John Ruskin, Charles Kingsley, Thomas à Kempis and others compiled especially for the use of members of the Christian Endeavor and Epworth League. [Philadelphia: George W. Jacobs & Co.]

The daintiest of dainty little volumes is the new edition of Owen Meredith's *Lucile*, just issued by the Frederick A. Stokes Company. Frank M. Gregory's illustrations are capital; in size the book is just right for the pocket; the type is clean, the paper superfine and the white and gold cover with its panel of pansies makes it, neatly boxed, an ideal gift.

Mary Berri Chapman's *Lyrics of Love and Nature* is a collection of gracefully phrased verses of a more or less ardent character, rather huffily illustrated by the author. [New York: Frederick A. Stokes Company.]

The Men of the Moss-Hags, by S. R. Crockett, is a semi-historic romance bristling with fierce purposes or their natural conclusions. It is a story of the times of Roundheads and Cavaliers, and what butchers of men they were—one side striking down men, women and children in the name of Religion, and the other butchering them in the name of the king! The Presbyterians were conscientiously cruel and fervently bloodthirsty, but oh, how tenderly loyal and loving to sweethearts and wives! Crockett compels us to believe—quite inadvertently, without doubt—that these destroyers of the bodies of men are less vicious than those who furnish certain poisonous mental foods that we have lately been fed upon. His story throws side lights upon the influence of Cromwell and the currents of religious, political and social evolution in his time. [New York: Macmillan & Co.]

An Old Convent School, by Susan Coolidge, includes five papers, the initial one giving title to the volume, others being "The Countess Patochi," "Miss Eden" and "The Duc de Saint Simon." They are biographical, historical and critical and, like everything she does, carefully wrought and finished by delicate touches evidencing a fine and full comprehension of her materials and a grace to omit where good taste requires silence and the courage to express truths where justice asks for testimony. [Boston: Roberts Brothers.]

A Bid for Fortune, by Guy Boothby, is a story of adventure strangely intricate and of the detective order of romance, its scenes alternating between Australia and London. Its material includes hypnotism and the unexplained potency of a little black stick covered with Chinese characters. It may be trusted to carry readers far beyond a consciousness of drudgery and dulness. [New York: D. Appleton & Co.]

The Adventures of Captain Horn, is as might have been expected from its author, Frank R. Stockton, a combination of comedy, tragedy, courage and droll love-making. It is a sea story, giving a modern version of Robinson Crusoe and, as befits the century, there are women in it. In this story woman's position is idyllic but by no means silly. The author does not set his heroine adrift without a chaperon, a young brother averting as a compromise between society's exactions and the exigencies of shipwreck. [New York: Charles Scribner's Sons.]

The sketches in *Private Tinker and Other Stories*, by John Strange Winter, are wholesome, entertaining and brief. It shows us American methods of discussing matters in the heart of the household, also un-American results, thus sparing us a study of foreign, domestic and social sentiments. Besides, it is diverting. [New York: Frederick A. Stokes Company.]

The theme of *A Singular Life*, by Elizabeth Stuart Phelps, is the differences of opinion as to those dogmas which are held to be essential at the Andover Theological Seminary. It explains why there have been so many bitter dissensions in Presbyteries and such perplexing condemnations of men who, to the unknowing, seem to have committed no wrong by casting new light upon old truths. For such a reason its hero is refused ordination and he gives thenceforth his life to befriending the ignorant poor and letting sunshine and sympathy into dark and chilly places. [Boston: Houghton, Mifflin & Co.]

The heroine of Miss F. F. Montressor's story *The One Who Looked On*, is a charming actuality to the reader, who more than half believes she sits in the chair opposite and is relating a true story in which she had a part which modesty makes as insignificant as truth permits. It is a clean, heart-warming story. [New York: D. Appleton & Co.]

In *The Sale of a Soul*, F. Frankfort Moore tells the story of a husband too busy to burn hourly incense at the little feet of a wife who is pretty and in a way—a morbid way—intellectual. She puts her soul on sale and her husband interrupts a bargain. It is not a probable story, but the conversations are brilliant and the ending satisfactory. [New York: Frederick A. Stokes Co.]

The Wise Woman is a well-told story by Clara Louise Burnham of social distinctions as they are graded and valued by men and women—especially women—who have no firm position of their own to stand upon and vary their attitudes according to the opinions of their betters. Its pages are clear and its denouement is a happy one. [Boston: Houghton, Mifflin & Co.]

That the provincial people of Maine differ materially in their social, grammatical and exclamatory practices from other New Englanders made known to the readers of Sarah Orne Jewett and Mary Wilkins may be readily seen from *The Village Watchtower*, a collection of curiously realistic stories by Kate Douglas Wiggin (Mrs. Riggs). In their telling there is the charm of novelty and much grace and facility of expression. [Boston: Houghton, Mifflin & Co.]

In *Lakewood*, by Louise L. Houstin, people well acquainted with the famous New Jersey resort will very likely recognize some of their acquaintances and will certainly find a close and clever description of the social life of that village. The record is for the most part an amiable one, though the grammatical lapses and vulgar ambitions of one rich woman who figures among its characters are turned to diverting advantage. [New York: Frederick A. Stokes Company.]

The Princess Sonia, a story of student life in Paris, by Julia Magruder, while silly, is not uninteresting, its silliness being of so uncommon a variety that it is really worth reading if one has time to kill and desires to do it painlessly. As a specimen of its style it may be mentioned that a wife who has senselessly separated herself from a worthy husband calls wildly upon the Deity six times in fifteen lines of self-accusation. Its illustrations by Charles Dana Gibson are artistic and fascinating. [New York: The Century Co.]

The White Baby is a dramatic but extremely unpleasant story by James Weish. It would seem to teach that a bad negro is more vicious and cruel than it is possible for a white person to be, but that when the African is loved and tender he is more loyal and tender than a man of any other race. The wild excesses of cruelty and angelic endurance it describes may stir the flagging emotions of sensation-surfeited novel readers. [New York: Frederick A. Stokes Company.]

Dead Man's Court, by Maurice H. Harvey, is not an alluring story for the ultra-refined reader. While its heroes are from the better classes, their manners, morals and language befit the title. It is daintily printed and bound. [New York: Frederick A. Stokes Company.]

Under title of *Margaret and Her Friends*, Caroline H. Doll makes report of a series of talks at Boston in 1841 by Margaret Fuller on Greek mythology and its expression in art. They show a much less advanced knowledge of the subject than is common to-day among classical scholars. [Boston: Roberts Brothers.]

Those who have imaginations still alive and who are still fond of wild adventure and unrewardable devotion will be thrilled and fascinated by the fervid and daring way in which William Le Queux describes the superb woman for whom the hero of his *Zoraida, a Romance of the Harem and the Great Sahara*, defies death and surmounts difficulties until he installs his Oriental bride in a Kensington flat, dressed in tailor-made gowns and Paris bonnets. [New York: Frederick A. Stokes Company.]

Macmillan & Co. reissue in paper covers *The Delectable Duchy*, a collection of delightful stories, pathetic, idyllic and tenderly human, by Arthur T. Quiller Couch, reviewed at length in these pages upon its first appearance.

A Chosen Few is the happy title of a collection of Frank R. Stockton's ingenious and diverting stories republished by Charles Scribner's Sons in handy pocket size, with dainty, cameo-decorated binding.

Washington, or The Revolution, a drama by Ethan Allen, is a timely publication that will receive a hearty welcome from the many patriotic organizations which like to rehearse the scenes that made us a free nation. [New York: F. Tennyson Neely.]

The Making of the Nation, by Francis A. Walker, President

of the Massachusetts Institute of Technology, has to do with that most critical and important epoch of United States history between 1783 and 1817, when our country's chaos was being transformed into a concrete and dignified republic. The events leading to the purchase of Florida and Louisiana are fully discussed. The maps and appendices add greatly to the value of a volume which is as fascinating as a romance and as crowded with trustworthy information as a political encyclopædia. [New York: Charles Scribner's Sons.]

In *Defiance of the King*, by Chauncey C. Hotchkiss, helps one to understand the animus of the patriotic societies, Sons of the Revolution *et al.*, which are organized to keep green the memory of the sacrifices which the ancestors of their members made to wrest America from the dominion of George III. The story begins at Harvard College and ends with the close of the Revolutionary War, giving vivid and realistic pictures of many of the scenes of that momentous struggle. The historic narration is enlivened by a thrilling love story. [New York: D. Appleton & Co.]

J. S. Fletcher's *Where Highways Cross* is an idyl, a beautiful and wholesome story. It tells of a tragedy out of which is born a noble deed that will keep the memory of its hero alive and sacred. [New York: Macmillan & Co.]

Like her other books, Rhoda Broughton's *Scylla and Charybdis* is brightly written, natural in characterization and satisfactory in conclusion. There is a shock in the story, a shock that chills one's marrow, but healing comes with the processes of the years and Rhoda Broughton knows how to graduate recoveries of mental and spiritual health. [New York: D. Appleton & Co.]

A Comedy in Spasms, by "Iota," author of *A Yellow Aster*, is not a comedy nor should its episodes be called spasms. Its characters are, for the most part, so incapable and selfish that comedy is not with or for them. The hero is married by a breezy Australian girl because she wants to provide a home for her mother, brothers and sisters, but she learns to love him and so all ends well. [New York: Frederick A. Stokes Company.]

Katherine's Yesterday is the title of a book of stories written by Grace Livingston Hill, author of *A Chautauqua Idyl*. The book has a distinctly moral purpose, giving the experiences of a Christian endeavorer who hopes her example may encourage others who are timid about, or uninstructed in the ways of, doing good to others. [Boston: Lothrop Publishing Company.]

The Hon. Emily Lawless' novel *Grania*, just republished in paper covers by Macmillan, is a tale of the wild west coast of Ireland, with its equally wild inhabitants. Descriptions of its bleak, ocean-lashed cliffs and islands and of the sturdy and superstitious people who inhabit them make up a large part of the book.

A reprint by Roberts Brothers of John Galt's *Annals of the Parish* and *The Ayrshire Legatee*, written in the early part of the present century, affords an excellent reminder and measurement of our social growth. The heroes and happenings described are curiously remote from the people and events of to-day. The love making and mating here pictured is so practical and so conscientiously limited to convenience and the worldly well-being of the contracting parties and their kinsfolk that it is worth while to study the processes of thought that lead up to so sensible and unromantic a development.

Gorham Sylvia's story *The Worm that Ceased to Turn* is both painful and offensive. It tells how a kind, easy-going, well-to-do man of middle age went to the almshouse to find a wife. He takes the first woman he sees and she lives out her wicked impulses with him and transmits them to her children. [New York: T. S. Ogilvie Co.]

Sound Money, written by I. A. Frazer Jr. and Charles Sergel and published by the latter, is a discussion in popular style of current financial issues and will doubtless assist its readers to make up their minds upon one of the most important issues of the hour.

JUVENILE BOOKS.

Doubtless many youngsters have experienced the perplexity of those described in the preface to *The Children's Shakspere*, by E. Nesbit. They pore over the "Midsummer Night's Dream," but cannot understand a word of it. Then their mama tells them the story in a simple, direct way, dwelling upon the points likely to appeal to the youthful fancy and understanding. They decide that Shakspere is a splendid story teller, and insist upon having a great deal more. The result is this volume in which an even dozen of the plays calculated to interest children are told in a simple manner. Frances Brundage and others contribute colored plates and black-and-white illustrations. [New York: Raphael Tuck and Sons.]

Though she did not write for children, the great heart of George Eliot had loving place for them and what she wrote about them was well worthy of being called for their reading, as Julia Magruder has done in *Child Sketches from George Eliot*. Here are Tom and Maggie Tulliver, Eppie and Lilo and the Garth children and little Jacob Alexander Cohen, all with a few words of graceful introduction by the compiler. But, alas! Where is the pathetic story of the pet dog drowned by his heart-broken little mistress because her father had decided that he ate too much? [Boston: Lothrop Publishing Company.]

Madame Eugénie Foa's delightful *Boy Life of Napoleon*—written forty years ago for the children of France and now translated, revised and brought up to date historically for those of America—is a good book for the young people to read who think of the famous Corsican only as a laurel-crowned Emperor. It will tell them of his troubled and tempestuous boyhood, of his battles with playmates, of his escapades at school, of the humiliations which poverty caused him. Without seeking to excuse or gloss over all his subsequent acts, it gives him due credit for his life-long and unswerving loyalty to family and friends. [Boston: Lothrop Publishing Co.]

In so far as athletics can be taught and fostered by a book, these objects are accomplished by *The Book of Athletics and Out-of-Door Sports*, edited by Norman W. Bingham, Jr. Every branch of the subject is discussed by a recognized authority. Mr. Bingham was himself captain of the Harvard track team of 1895, and Harvard's famous football captain, Arthur J. Cumnock, Yale's baseball captain, Lawrence T. Bliss, tennis champion James Dwight, cricket expert Ralph Cracknell, crew trainer Mayor Bancroft, Kirk Monroe, founder of the L. A. W., Harvard's champion jumper E. B. Bloss, hurdler Herbert Mapes and experts in skating, swimming, yachting and a lot of other athletic diversions discuss their respective sports with a zest that lacks nothing of technical accuracy to render their remarks as helpful as they are entertaining. A host of illustrations by Pinckney, Ogden and others help to make clear the instruction given. [Boston: Lothrop Publishing Co.]

Boys passing through that awkward and uncomfortable transitional period between childhood and manhood, when they grow so fast their friends and relatives do not recognize them and when their treacherous voices break from bass into falsetto without warning, should be deeply grateful to Belle C. Green for *The Hobbledehoy*, which she dedicates presumably to one of their number whom she designates as "a boy I know." The story shows at once the trials and the essential nobility and heroism of one boy passing through this ordeal and is specifically intended for the hitherto-much-neglected class to which he belongs. [Boston: Lothrop Publishing Co.]

A very human sort of girl is the central figure of *Kyzie Dunlee*, by Sophie May. Kyzie is winsome and upright in a charmingly childlike way without being the least little bit goody-goody, and she will help other nice little girls to become nicer still. [Boston: Lee and Shepard.]

In *The Ocola Boy* Maurice Thompson relates the adventures of two lads who made a Winter journey to the Land of Flowers and searched for the "Boy" alluded to in the title. The reader must not be told who the "Boy" is. To find him is to learn one of the secrets of Florida, and to hunt for him is a fascinating occupation. The story will answer very well as a guide book for those who propose visiting Florida. [Boston: Lothrop Publishing Co.]

Albeit a trifle preachy—as is natural, perhaps, in a story having a clergyman as one of its central figures—*Little Daughter*, by Grace Le Baron, is a good story for girls who can digest the moral instruction it contains. [Boston: Lee and Shepard.]

In *Young Master Kirke*, Penn Shirley, author of *Little Miss Weezy*, takes the Rowe family from Massachusetts to Southern California, where the impetuous Kirke gets into and out of much fresh trouble and Weezy continues to make bright and unexpected remarks. [Boston: Lee and Shepard.]

My Honey, by the author of *Miss Toosey's Mission*, is a sweet and gentle love story, as placid and kindly in tone as is the home of the dear old English rector in which its scenes are laid—just the book to give to a sentimental girl of sixteen. [Boston: Roberts Brothers.]

Contentment better than riches, is the moral of Sarah G. Connell's story, *The Little Ladies of Ellenwood and their Hidden Treasure*. It relates the vicissitudes but final comforting of a family reduced from affluence to very moderate circumstances. [Philadelphia: George W. Jacobs & Co.]

Lillie F. Wesselhoeft has added yet another to the list of her charming animal stories for children, *Frowzle the Runaway*, being the account of a vivacious and rather naughty mongrel dog who has a variety of exciting adventures and converses with cats, monkeys and ponies just like a person. Though of subordinate interest, the human figures of the fable are pleasantly drawn. [Boston: Roberts Brothers.]

In one volume the Lothrop Publishing Company, of Boston, has combined *The Young Cascarillero*, by Marlton Downing, the story of a boy's exploits while hunting quinine bark in Ecuador, and *Colonel Thorndike's Adventures*, by Harry W. French, a series of hair-breadth escapes told two credulous nephews by an uncle skilled in drawing the long bow.

In *The Mushroom Cave* Evelyn Raymond tells the story of a dear, unworldly old Quaker scientist, his high-minded twin grandchildren, a devoted but tearful servant and a cross-grained but warm-hearted showman who has a pet eagle, a zebra and more money than he needs. A stone-quarry cave furnishes the scene for sundry thrilling adventures, as well as the means of finally rescuing the Quaker family from its financial difficulties. [Boston: Roberts Brothers.]

Girls Together, by Amy E. Blanchard, is a chatterboxy story of a lot of nice young people from the country who come to New York and study art and music and fall in love with each other and get married, as nice young people are wont to do with unfailing regularity. It is a story for girls, sprightly and entertaining without being either very original or deeply intellectual. [Philadelphia: J. B. Lippincott Company.]

THE SOFT ANSWER.

Self-assertion, if expressed in a kindly manner, is more agreeable than martyr-like self-denial. Every conscientious person possesses certain standards and convictions by which his or her life is governed, but the standards should not be inflexible nor the convictions aggressive. There is no justice in judging everyone by our own rule, and there is nothing to warrant our thrusting our beliefs and principles upon friends and acquaintances. Deeds and manners announce their own charm and purity or their own unsatisfactoriness; and that is enough. Answers are unnecessary regarding the most disturbing matters between persons who truly care for one another.

Hospitality is by no means limited to the sharing of one's bread and shelter with other people. It also includes, among other things, courtesy to the opinions of those about us. This is expressed by receiving their statements and arguments with kindly civility, even when their ideas cannot be accepted. The will and the ability to do this constitutes one of the most desirable traits of a truly hospitable person's character. Adverse opinions are doubly impressive and convincing when couched in gentle language and calmly delivered, but biting sarcasm does not convince, and flippant answers are an unkindness. Indeed, there are times when frivolous words are more cruel than those that are deliberately harsh and cutting, because they jar with the speaker's real sentiments, producing a mental discord which is highly disagreeable to any sensitive soul.

"A soft answer turneth away wrath," said King Solomon; and this is true of all times and all conditions, except when the person who speaks first is possessed of an unjust and unrestrained temper. A soft answer, if insincere, or if spoken as though dictated by policy rather than by kindliness, is exasperating to the last degree. "Seek the spirit of kindliness and with it sweeten the words of an answer," wrote somebody long ago. An answer thus sweetened and softened will subdue and disarm, if aught can, the fierce brutality of unbridled anger.

Self-forgetfulness in its higher significance may inspire a soft answer to irritating words, but in its lower sense it may permit the temper to become rampant; and self-remembrance, which ought to bring self-respect, too often suffers torrents of intemperate language to reply to an unintentionally wounding remark or to follow some untoward occurrence that in itself is trifling. Perhaps the most aggravating form of unkind language is that which is spoken with a precise gentleness which veils its unpleasant meaning from immediate comprehension. This satirical method of expressing displeasure, anger or difference is the most cutting although the most refined species of vituperation; and when such language is received in a kindly spirit, the offender must be singularly unfeeling if he can bring himself to repeat the blow. He must be wholly lacking in self-respect if a soft answer after such an offense fails to turn away his wrath.

Sarcasm and satire in the family are venomous enemies of peace and good fellowship. Either is quite capable of snapping the tenderest ties and parting life-long friends. Ridicule is equally mischievous, particularly to children, who cannot realize that, in the majority of cases, it arises, not from a spirit of unkindliness, but from a desire on the part of its author to display his own doubtful wit. Derision of a child's opinions, tastes, misfortunes, blunders, raiment, emotions or, in fact, anything that seems serious in the little one's estimation, cuts deep into his tender heart, inflicting a wound that is sometimes years in healing, and even then leaves a sore spot in the recollection that causes many a twinge in after life.

Unjust and ungenerous words freeze the fountains of human affection. Well-bred persons may and do maintain the courtesies of life, in the first place because they would live up to their grand motto, "*Noblesse oblige*," and in the second place because self-respect demands that they should be outwardly civil; but that which makes life worth living is not ice, that cannot or does not melt. Sometimes it is by an open grave that the old love comes back, for we there gain a clearer and a truer insight into the life that has just closed and realize our own shortcomings and active faults when it is too late to be helpful or comforting. And after all, it is only anger let loose when it should have been chained and mastered that brings the bitterness of gall and wormwood into life.

If one could look at life steadily and see clearly its end from its beginning, there would be few harsh words between those who are near and should be dear. Cruel words are seldom spoken save with the intention of hurting, and their rebound, when they miss their mark, is not nearly so unpleasant as to the offender as a mildly worded answer would be; and yet no good and tender soul desires revenge. A man once confessed to his mother that he had long since broken himself of the habit of making sharp, hasty answers to his wife, because, instead of repaying him in kind when he thus forgot himself, she simply looked at him with an expression of surprise and grief upon her pretty face. "Had she treated me as I deserved," said he, "I suppose I should have been resentful and grown worse. I am quite ashamed to remember how petty I was and with what self-contained endurance she bore, in addition to her own cares and vexations, the wearied brain and irritated nerves carried home each evening for her to soothe. Her patience and fortitude made a man of me; and yet I see no justice or propriety in allowing a wife to reform the bad manners and vicious tempers of her husband. This should be the duty of his mother while he is yet a boy. Mothers should teach their sons how to be good husbands just as they instruct their daughters in the duties of true wifehood." An experienced wife once said: "I began married life impressed with the silly and mischievous idea that my husband ought to be pleased with whatever I did and said, simply because he was a man and I a woman. His chivalry and my sex was to tide me over all my ill tempers and inconsiderate habits of speech. On one occasion, during which I goaded him to righteous anger, he confined his conversation with me to bidding me good morning and good evening and answering necessary questions. After a week of this treatment the silence became intolerable and I begged him to speak to me and be merry as formerly. To this he replied, without the faintest display of anger and reproach, that he had been so wounded by my unkind answers that he dared not venture upon frank conversation. This lesson worked a great change in me, for from that time I ceased to be silly and whimsical. I am my husband's comrade and friend, and his adviser as well. I return him soft answers when he is vexed and worried, and he guards his speech with equal care. The same lesson has served me with the children; the first sentence I taught them to say when they displayed anger was, 'A soft answer turneth away wrath.'"

THE CARE OF THE TEETH.

FIRST PAPER.

The teeth are essential to thorough mastication and distinct utterance. When white and even they reclaim a face otherwise decidedly plain. Irregularities and malformations in the development and growth of the teeth produce disfiguring deviations and distortions of the alveolar arches (those portions of the upper and lower jaw into which the teeth are fixed). As the lower of these two arches forms the bony framework of the mouth and chin, it follows that these expressive portions of the countenance undergo decided changes in contour and in functional usefulness when the teeth suffer from any of the said irregularities or malformations. Often the causes of disorders affecting the system as a whole lurk in the dental organs unsuspected by either the sufferer or the physician. Conversely the teeth, in common with all the other organs of the body, are influenced by conditions of general ill health, hereditary taint, etc. The stigmata of certain hereditary affections, even though transmitted in attenuated form, are unmistakably visible upon the teeth of children. While he should be able to diagnose a case of this kind, the treatment of such affections does not properly fall within the province of the dentist. They require the careful consideration of a competent physician. One should not censure a reputable dentist without first inquiring of the family physician whether there is not some underlying constitutional cause for the black tracings, irregularity and disproportion that the teeth of a child may show.

The importance of preserving the teeth cannot be overestimated. Discolored or decayed teeth are an unprepossessing sight, conveying the impression of indifference to the care of the person. But in cases where Nature has been economical in her endowments, science and art can often make amends. Imperfections in form and structure may be corrected, dental diseases successfully treated and lost teeth replaced by well made substitutes with comparatively little pain, if attention be given the disturbance at an early stage. A self-respecting person will naturally respect the feelings of others and will as carefully avoid offending the sight by badly kept teeth as by unkempt locks or untidy attire. Cleanliness is of vital importance in the care of the teeth. It will often avert disease by preventing the deposition of foreign substances, chemical or otherwise, which upon the teeth and gums, as elsewhere in the body, act as irritants.

Brushing the teeth regularly after each meal should be made a matter of discipline with children as soon as they are able to care for themselves. The habit will thus be formed early and the care of the teeth will become a necessity to the child's comfort. Many parents pay too little heed to the preservation of the temporary or milk teeth. The fallacy of the oldtime theory that the milk teeth require no filling has been repeatedly exposed. Upon the timely care of these teeth largely depends the regularity and strength of the permanent set.

The various parts entering into the construction of the mouth make up an important and complicated portion of the digestive apparatus. They are associated by anatomical contiguity and direct nervous connection with the entire series of phenomena which constitutes life. The tongue, gums, lips and mucous membranes of the mouth at once show changes in response to any disorders of the stomach, larynx or other adjacent organs.

FORMATION.— Each tooth consists of three portions, viz: the crown or body, which projects above the gum; the root or fang, which is entirely concealed within the alveolus (the socket in the bone), and the neck or constricted portion, which lies between the crown and the root. The roots of the teeth are firmly fixed in their sockets. Each tooth contains a little cavity at the base of the crown. This cavity terminates in a little canal which traverses each fang, ending at its extremity. This is called the pulp cavity and contains a highly sensitive substance called the dental pulp, familiarly known as the nerve. The solid portion of the tooth comprises three structures, viz: the dentine or toothbone which forms the larger portion of the tooth; the enamel which covers the exposed part or crown, and the cementum which thinly coats the surface of the fang. The dentine consists of onefourth animal and three-fourths earthy matter, the latter containing phosphate and carbonate of lime, phosphate of magnesia and other substances. The enamel is the densest and hardest structure in the body. It is thickest on the grinding surfaces of the teeth until worn away by long usage. It contains about 96 per cent. of earthy and 4 per cent. of animal matter. Its chemical constituents being about the same as those of dentine, though somewhat different in arrangement. The cementum resembles bone in its structure and composition; it is very thinly spread over the surface of the fangs down to the apices, where it is thicker; it increases in thickness with age, often thereby causing difficulty when teeth are to be extracted.

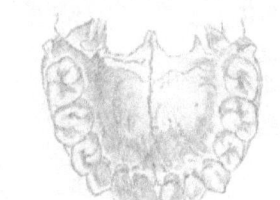

TEMPORARY TEETH.

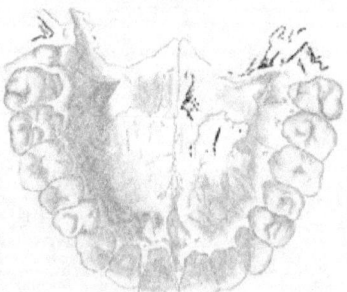

PERMANENT TEETH.

CHILDREN'S TEETH.— Two sets of teeth are provided each human being, both of which make their appearance in early life, though at different periods. The first teeth are developed in infancy and are called the temporary, deciduous or milk teeth; the second or permanent set appears later and continues until old age, if properly cared for. The first set consists of twenty teeth, which erupt in the following order: two central incisors, which usually appear between the fifth and eighth month; two lateral incisors, between the seventh and tenth month; two canines or eye teeth, between the twelfth and sixteenth months, two first molars, between the fourteenth and twentieth month, and the second molars, between the twentieth and thirty-sixth month, completing primary dentition. The teeth in both the upper and lower jaws are similarly named and appear in the same order, though not simultaneously, the lower teeth usually preceding the upper by a short interval. The time and order of the appearance of the first teeth are subject to considerable variation, their progress being hastened or delayed sometimes six or seven months. A lateral incisor or even a molar or canine tooth may pierce the gum before the eruption of the central incisors. The condition of the health very markedly affects the appearance of the teeth, any disorder accompanied by deficiency of the salts of lime in the body retarding their growth. Parents may look upon certain diseases of children, such as measles, whooping cough, etc., as necessary visitations, but if they realized the deleterious effect of interrupted dentition involved they would take every possible precaution to prevent their children catching these diseases. The progress of dentition is apparently not continuous, for after the appearance of each successive pair of teeth a pause of one or two months generally ensues.

Between the fifth and sixth year the first anterior or true molars usually appear. They do not belong to the temporary set and should be especially guarded lest decay affect them. These teeth are really more troublesome than any others. When once removed they are never replaced by natural ones and their loss sadly mars the symmetry of the alveolar arches.

The milk teeth should be retained as long as possible—in fact, until their successors are ready to appear. During the earlier period of childhood a bony plate or partition separates the permanent teeth from the fangs of the temporary teeth. As the period approaches when the permanent teeth are to replace the milk teeth, this partition disappears by absorption and the crown of the enlarged permanent tooth makes its way into the socket of the temporary tooth's root. As the permanent tooth advances the fang of the milk tooth is absorbed, not however, from any pressure exercised by the one upon the other, for the two never come in direct contact. When the crown of the temporary tooth falls off the permanent tooth is ready to replace it, unless the temporary tooth has been prematurely lost by decay, which commences rather early in these teeth. The temporary teeth are not as compact as their successors, containing less of the salts of lime. If a child's teeth are in good condition, mastication is thoroughly performed and the food is properly prepared for digestion, the general health being thus promoted. Moreover, if proper and timely attention be given to its teeth, future suffering from that cause can in most cases be spared the child. It is essential that a dentist be consulted at least three times a year after a child reaches its third year, the necessity being all the more urgent when dark spots have made their appearance upon the teeth, especially at the fissures or ridges of the crown, which are the most vulnerable points in a child's teeth. The child should never be allowed to hear any allusions to painful experiences in the dentist's chair, nor should parents ever allow the slight pain which it may be necessary to inflict to deter them from having the child's teeth promptly attended to. A skilled dentist will not ordinarily hurt a child either when treating or extracting teeth.

Children as young as three years of age sometimes suffer from abscesses which result from decay that has been allowed to spread to the pulp or nerve of the tooth, larger in the temporary teeth than in those which follow. An abscess or gum-boil is formed near the root of the tooth, and in most cases discharges itself toward the top of the gum. Sometimes it travels through the cheek towards the skin of the face, and if permitted to break there, causes permanent disfigurement. As soon as noticed a gum-boil should be treated and when the presence of matter is detected, the boil should be pricked. A careful dentist will render this slight operation painless. With the removal of the tooth complete cure, of course, follows, and often this radical measure is necessary, since the diseased condition is otherwise likely to recur. If there is a tendency in the abscess to break externally, early extraction of the tooth is imperative. Abscesses are not only painful but they result in general physical disturbance.

Decay should no more be permitted to spread in the temporary than in the permanent teeth; as soon as a cavity is discovered it should be stopped with one of the many preparations adapted to the purpose. If decay reaches the nerve, treatment will doubtless be more difficult. Some cases require extraction, but professional advice should invariably be sought. If the tooth is filled before the nerve is touched, much suffering will be avoided. Premature loss of the first teeth frequently causes irregularity in the second teeth and consequent disfigurement of the mouth.

When it becomes necessary to extract children's back teeth, dentists frequently administer gas, but only with the approval of the family physician, as anæsthetics in certain instances prove disastrous. Gutta-percha, cement, amalgam, rubber and sometimes even gold are employed to fill temporary teeth. Gold is infrequently used, as the other fillings may be put in soft, avoiding the necessity for a rubber dam or the use of the mallet or electric hammer. If the cavity is filled while it is yet small, the process will be entirely painless. In fact, the sensation is so novel that it will rather amuse than alarm the child.

Teeth that are poorly calcified are naturally more susceptible to decay than those containing more lime salts. The fissures or ridges spread more rapidly and only by constant care and attention can decay be arrested. When the spaces between the teeth in the temporary set are wide, the permanent teeth will in all probability be regular and not crowded. Some of the temporary teeth remain until the child has reached the age of ten or twelve years. It is important that they should be kept as long as possible, so that the spaces designed to ultimately hold the permanent teeth shall not be distorted or contracted.

THE PERMANENT TEETH.—The permanent teeth are thirty-two in number, those in the lower jaw corresponding in name and position to those above. At about the time of the eruption of the first anterior molars, or at most, a few months later, the central permanent incisors appear. The lateral ones are developed at about eight years; the anterior and posterior bicuspids, at nine or ten years; the canines, from eleven to twelve; the second true molars, from twelve to thirteen; and the wisdom teeth, or third molars, from seventeen to nineteen. It will be observed that there are twelve more teeth in this set than in the first set, viz: the eight bicuspids and four wisdom teeth. When pain attends the eruption of the wisdom teeth it may be due to want of space in the jaws. Constitutional disturbances may follow, necessitating systematic treatment. Sometimes extraction of the tooth itself, or of the one in front of it, is the only remedy.

HOUSEKEEPERS' DEPARTMENT.

(This department is open to all inquirers desiring information on household topics of any description.)

C. H. C.:—Chips are delicious, but considerable skill is required to make them. Mix in a kettle five cupfuls of sugar, a cupful and a half of water and a fourth of a tea-spoonful of cream of tartar and set upon the fire. When the mixture boils add a fourth of a cupful of New Orleans molasses. This candy should be cooked until very hard, consequently great care must be observed to prevent its burning. After the molasses has been added, the stove lid should be kept continually between the kettle and the fire, and when the candy is nearly done, the heat should be lowered, to prevent scorching. Test frequently, and when a small quantity upon being dropped into water immediately becomes very hard, the candy is done and should be poured out to cool upon a well-buttered slab. When cool enough to handle, pull until of a bright, glossy yellow. Now place the candy near the fire, where it will keep warm, and, putting on a pair of old kid gloves, pull it out into a flat strip and rub it on both sides until very thin and of a satiny appearance. Here the assistance of a second person is required to break the candy into small chips as it is pulled out and rubbed by the cook. This part of the work must be accomplished as rapidly as possible, so as to allow a minimum of time for the candy to cool. These flakes or chips may be variously colored, some with chocolate, others pink and still others pale-yellow.

A. B. W.:—These are the ingredients for Princess cake:

10 eggs (whites).
3 cupfuls of powdered sugar.
1 cup of butter.
1 cup of milk.
4½ cups of flour.
1 table-spoonful of baking powder (level full).
1 tea-spoonful of lemon essence, or some sliced citron.

Bake carefully for an hour in a moderate oven. This recipe is excellent for layer cake.

Miss E. M.:—To make home-brewed beer, proceed as follows: Measure four tea-cupfuls of brown sugar, four table-spoonfuls of ground ginger, and a two-quart basinful of fresh hops. Place the hops and ginger together, cover well with water, using three or four quarts, and boil for an hour. Then strain, pour the liquor into a kettle, add half a cupful of molasses, and boil for half an hour. Put the hops, ginger and sugar in a crock holding four gallons, put in the hot liquor, fill the crock with water, and add a cupful of yeast. Set the liquor in a warm place for eight or ten hours to ferment: then skim and bottle, tying the corks securely. Beer bottles with rubber corks are best. In two days, the beverage will be ready for use. Be careful in opening, as the beer will be "heady." Beer made in this way will keep all the year round. A practical brewer will tell you how much barley and hops are required for a given amount of beer.

Mrs. J. A.:—For two large loaves of pound cake, use:

2 cupfuls of butter.	12 large eggs.
2 cupfuls of sugar.	½ tea-spoonful of mace.
4 cupfuls of flour.	½ gill of brandy.

Butter the pans and line them. Measure the sugar, flour, brandy and cinnamon. Separate the eggs, putting the whites in a large bowl and the yolks in a small one. Beat the butter to a cream, and gradually beat the sugar into it. When the mixture is light and creamy, add the brandy and mace. Beat the yolks till light, and add them to the beaten mixture. Beat the whites to a stiff froth, and stir them into the mixture, alternating with the flour. Pour the butter into the pans, and bake in a moderate oven for about fifty minutes.

For two loaves of raisin cake, use:

1 large cupful of butter.	2 cupfuls of sugar.
1 cupful of milk.	4 generous cupfuls of flour.
5 eggs.	1 gill of brandy.
2 nutmegs.	½ tea-spoonful of soda.

1 quart of boiled raisins.

Put the raisins in a small stew-pan, and cover them with cold water. Cook them slowly for half an hour, then drain and cool them. Beat the butter to a cream and beat the sugar into it; add the brandy and nutmeg, and beat a little longer. Add the yolks of the eggs, well beaten. Dissolve the soda in the milk, and add this to the beaten ingredients. Now add the flour. Stir in the well-beaten whites of the eggs. Spread the batter in thin layers in two large cake-pans, and sprinkle raisins upon each layer. Continue this until all the materials are used. Bake for two hours in a moderate oven. This cake keeps well.

Constant Reader:—In reference to preserving ginger see answer to Mrs. D. G. in this paper.

Iceland Moss Jelly:—Can any of our readers supply a recipe for Iceland moss jelly?

An Old Subscriber:—To make chocolate pie take:

1 coffee-cupful of milk	2 table-spoonfuls of grated chocolate.
½ cupful of sugar.	3 eggs.
Vanilla to flavor.	½ tea-spoonful of salt.

Beat the yolks of the eggs until light, and add to them two table-spoonfuls of the milk. Heat the chocolate and the rest of the milk together, put in the salt and sugar and when scalding hot add the yolks of the eggs. Let the mixture cook for two minutes, remove it from the fire and when partly cooled add the flavoring. Line a pie-plate with crust, turn in the filling, and bake for twenty minutes in a quick oven. Beat the white of the eggs very light, sweeten with a table-spoonful of sugar and spread them over the pie; then brown the egg slightly and serve cold.

To make oyster pie: Take seventy-five oysters, one by one to see that there are are no bits of shell upon them, and put them into a bowl in their own liquor to warm. Boil four eggs until hard; take the yolks and as much bread and three table-spoonfuls of butter and rub them up together. Put this with the oysters and let them simmer a little; season with mace, pepper and salt. When cool put them in patties, with puff paste at the top and bottom.

Mrs. D. G.:—To make Turkish fig paste: Weigh out four pounds of sugar, one pound of glucose, nine ounces of corn-starch, and two scruples of powdered citric acid, and have ready oil of lemon, orange or any desired extract. A few drops of red coloring fluid may also be used. Place the sugar and water upon the fire, and when they come to a boil, add the starch dissolved in a little cold water, and then the glucose and acid. Cook until the syrup will leave the fingers readily when tested in cold water; it is then done and should be poured out on a slab over which powdered sugar has been sifted. Smooth the top neatly and sift sugar lightly upon it. When the candy is cool, cut it into blocks and crystallize.

To preserve ginger, pare the roots of fresh, green ginger, using a very sharp knife, and place each piece in cold water as it is peeled. When all is peeled, drain it from the water. Weigh the ginger and place it in the preserving kettle, covering it with cold water. When the water is quite boiling, skim out the ginger and place it again in cold water. When quite cool, again return it to the kettle, add more cold water, and when boiling, skim out and lay in cold water as before. Do this three times, when the ginger will be tender, leaving it at the last in the cold water. Allow:

1 pound of ginger.	1 pound of sugar.
1 pint of water.	1 egg (white only).

Place the sugar and the water together in a preserving kettle and heat slowly, boiling gently until the sugar is dissolved. Beat the white of the egg until it froths, and stir it into the syrup. When it boils skim until quite clear, then stand aside to cool. This is called the clarifying syrup. Drain the ginger, wipe it dry with a soft cloth and when the syrup is cold place the ginger in it and let it stand for thirty-six hours. Drain off the syrup, let it come to a boil, take from the fire, and when again cool place in the ginger, and let it remain for twenty-four hours. Drain off the syrup again, heat to boiling and this time turn it over the ginger while hot. In a week again drain it off, boil it and turn it on hot. Cover closely and the ginger will be ready to use in two weeks. Preserved in this way it is a great delicacy.

S. E. H.:—To make three large layers of caramel cake allow:

1 cupful of butter.	3 cupfuls of flour.
2 cupfuls of sugar.	5 eggs (whites).
1 cupful of milk.	2 tea-spoonfuls of baking powder.

Place the ingredients together as for plain layer cake, adding the whites of the eggs last. Bake in three well buttered tins and when done spread between the layers caramel filling made thus:

1½ cupful of brown sugar.	1 table-spoonful (scant) of butter.
1 cupful of milk.	½ table-spoonful of vanilla.

Place the milk, sugar and butter on the fire in a saucepan set in another containing boiling water and cook until thick. Take from the fire and beat it hard until stiff. Then add the vanilla.

A Subscriber:—Extract of cinnamon for flavoring is made thus: Dissolve two drachms of oil of cinnamon in one pint of deodorized alcohol; add gradually one pint of water and then stir in by degrees four ounces of powdered Ceylon cinnamon. Agitate very thoroughly and filter through paper.

Extract of nutmeg is made by mixing two drachms of oil of nutmegs with one ounce of powdered mace; macerate thoroughly in one quart of deodorized alcohol and filter.

To make extract of ginger: Pack four ounces of powdered ginger in a percolator, moisten it with a little alcohol, then pour on alcohol until a pint and a half of tincture has passed through. Mix this with eight ounces of syrup.

Extract of rose is made by bruising two ounces of rose-leaves in one quart of deodorized alcohol; press the alcohol out, add to it one drachm oil of rose and filter through paper. If red rose leaves cannot be had, a little tincture of cochineal will impart a rose tint to the extract.

May V. H.:—"Hartford election" cake is delicious, and may be made according to the following recipe:

1½ cupful of butter.
2 cupfuls of sugar.
1½ pint of flour.
3 eggs.
1½ tea-spoonful of baking-powder
2 cupfuls of raisins, stoned.
1 cupful of currants.
½ cupful of citron, chopped.
½ cupful of lemon peel, chopped.
½ cupful of almonds, shredded.
20 drops of extract of bitter almonds.
20 drops of extract of vanilla.
1 cupful of milk.

Rub the butter and sugar to a light cream, add the eggs, and beat a few minutes longer. Then stir in the flower and baking-powder sifted together; add the raisins, citron, currants, lemon peel, almonds, extracts and milk; mix to a batter, place paper in a tin, and bake for an hour and a half in a moderate oven.

Capatolia:—Semolina is a kind of rice from which an excellent soup can be made. To make it take:

1 quart of stock.	¾ of a pint of milk.
2 table-spoonfuls of semolina.	Salt and pepper.

Put the stock on the fire to boil, and stir in the semolina gradually. Boil for fifteen minutes stirring all the time. Now add the milk, pepper and salt to taste. Serve very hot.

THE FOOD VALUE OF COCOA AND CHOCOLATE.

No better evidence could be offered of the great advance which has been made in recent years in the knowledge of dietetics than the remarkable increase in the consumption of Cocoa and Chocolate in this country. During the thirty years from 1860 to 1890 the population a little less than doubled.* In 1860 the amount of crude Cocoa entered at the Custom-house, for home consumption in this country, was only 1,181,054 pounds; in 1893 it had risen to 22,961,921 pounds. Although there was a marked increase in the consumption of tea and coffee during the same period, the ratio of increase fell far below that of Cocoa. It is evident that the coming American is going to be less of a tea and coffee drinker, and more of a Cocoa and Chocolate drinker. This is the natural result of a better knowledge of the laws of health, and of the food value of a beverage which nourishes the body, while it stimulates the brain. Some evidence on this point from the highest authorities may be of interest.

Baron von Liebig, one of the best-known writers on dietetics, says:

"It is a perfect food, as wholesome as delicious, a beneficent restorer of exhausted power; but its quality must be good, and it must be carefully prepared. It is highly nourishing and easily digested, and is fitted to repair wasted strength, preserve health, and prolong life. It agrees with dry temperaments and convalescents; with mothers who nurse their children; with those whose occupations oblige them to undergo severe mental strains; with public speakers, and with all those who give to work a portion of the time needed for sleep. It soothes both stomach and brain, and for this reason, as well as for others, it is the best friend of those engaged in literary pursuits."

* In 1860 it was 31,443,321, and in 1890 it was 62,622,250.

Jean Baptiste Alphonse Chevalier, in his treatise on Chocolate, says:

"Cocoa and Chocolate are a complete food; coffee and tea are not food. Cocoa gives one-third its weight in starch and one-half in cocoa-butter; and converted into chocolate by the addition of sugar, it realizes the idea of a complete aliment, wholesome and eminently hygienic. The shells of the bean contain the same principles as the kernels, and the extract, obtained by an infusion of the shells in sweetened milk, forms a mixture at once agreeable to the taste and an advantageous substitute for tea and coffee."

Dr. H. C. Sawyer, in his valuable little book on "Nerve Waste," says: "Baker's Breakfast Cocoa is a light preparation which can be heartily recommended; it contains only so much fat as can be digested by almost any one, and is peculiar in not cloying or palling after a time, as so many Cocoa preparations do. Such a beverage is far more wholesome, and more agreeable, after one becomes used to it, than tea, which is much over-used."

In a recent article on Coffee and Cocoa, the eminent German Chemist, Professor Stutzer, speaking of the Dutch process of preparing Cocoa by the addition of potash, and of the process common in Germany in which ammonia is added, says: "The only result of these processes is to make the liquid appear turbid to the eye of the consumer, without effecting a real solution of the cocoa substances. This artificial manipulation for the purpose of so-called solubility is, therefore, more or less inspired by deception, and always takes place at the cost of purity, pleasant taste, useful action, and aromatic flavor. The treatment of Cocoa by such chemical means is entirely objectionable. . . . Cocoa treated with potash or ammonia would be entirely unsalable but for the supplementary addition of artificial flavors by which a poor substitute for the aroma driven out into the air is offered to the consumer."

Walter Baker & Co's Breakfast Cocoa is absolutely pure and soluble. It has *more than three times the strength* of cocoa mixed with starch, arrow-root, or sugar, and is therefore far more economical, *costing less than one cent a cup*. It is delicious, nourishing, strengthening *easily digested*, and admirably adapted for invalids as well as for persons in health.

No alkalies or other chemicals or dyes are used in its preparation.

As many misleading and unscrupulous imitations of Walter Baker & Co's goods have been placed upon the market, consumers should ask for, and be sure that they get, the genuine articles manufactured by that Company at Dorchester, Mass.

Publishers Department

RECITATIONS AND HOW TO RECITE.—We have just issued (January, 1896,) a book bearing the above title. It consists of a large collection of famous and favorite recitations both for adults and children, and also includes some novelties in the way of poems and monologues sure to meet with the approval of everyone interested in elocutionary entertainments. Valuable and unique features of the pamphlet are the general prefatory remarks and suggestions and those which also precede each selection, by which the reciter is instructed not only comprehensively in the art of elocution but specially in whatever number he selects for personal recitation before an audience. The collection is an eminently satisfactory one from which to choose recitations for the parlor, for school exhibitions, Church entertainments or for benefit for individual or other charitable objects. Every scholar at school should have a copy of "Recitations and How to Recite"; every elocutionist, professional or amateur, will find it most useful; and no library can afford to omit it from the list of up-to-date books of recitations. Price 25 cents.

VENETIAN IRON WORK.—The information, instruction and designs contained in this handsomely illustrated manual will be of the utmost value to every one interested in Venetian Iron Work. The details are minute, the implements fully described, and the designs so clear and comprehensive that the veriest amateur will have no difficulty in developing the work. It offers a new field to the clever Amateur Decorator, and in the multitude of its designs will be found exceedingly useful to the skilled worker. Price, 25 cents per copy.

PARLOR PLANTS AND WINDOW GARDENING.—This is the title of an attractive pamphlet in which the Amateur Florist is told all about necessary temperatures, suitable rooms, the extermination of insect pests, and the general and special care of hundreds of plants, all of them being fully described and illustrated. Common and botanical names of flowers are given, species are described, and varieties are recommended, special attention being paid to winter window gardening. It also contains valuable information as to rose and violet culture as an employment for women. Price, 25 cents per copy.

SOCIAL EVENING ENTERTAINMENTS.—This pamphlet is issued in response to many letters asking for suggestions for entertainments that are novel, original, amusing and instructive, and not of the purely conventional types requiring full dress, dancing and luxurious refreshments. It meets every requirement of our correspondents, and at the same time will offer pleasing suggestions to those who desire to vary their grand entertainments by an occasional simpler one. A few of the many entertainments offered are: A Literary Charade Party, A Witch Party, A Ghost Ball, A Hallowe'en German, A Novel Card Party, A Midsummer Night's Entertainment, A Flower Party, A Fancy-Dress Kris Kringle Entertainment, The Bowers' Christmas Tree, A St. Valentine's Masquerade Entertainment, etc., etc., all told in conversational style and many of them handsomely illustrated. Just the thing for a neighborhood full of party-giving, fun-loving young people. Price, 25 cents per copy.

THE BUTTON-HOLE CUTTER.—Among the many minor conveniences which have of late done much toward lightening the labors of the seamstress, none has been of greater practical benefit than the button-hole cutter. Our new cutter is made of the best steel, is reliable and may be very quickly and easily adjusted to cut any size of button-hole desired. It costs 25 cents.

OUR WEDDING PAMPHLET.—"Weddings and Wedding Anniversaries" is the title of a pamphlet published by us, that treats fully and entertainingly of subjects in which the average woman is always deeply interested. It gives the rules and regulations approved by good society for the arrangement of church and house weddings, including the latest forms of invitations, announcements and "At Home" cards; illustrates the choicest and most artistic styles for the gowning of brides, bridesmaids and maids of honor; describes the most fashionable materials and garnitures for wedding toilettes of all kinds; and presents a number of unique and original sketches that contain abundant suggestions for the celebration of the various wedding anniversaries, from the first—the Cotton Wedding, to the seventy-fifth—the Diamond Wedding. In the matter of wedding anniversaries the pamphlet completely covers a field that has never before been entered upon with anything like thoroughness, and the numerous hints regarding house decorations, menus and table ornaments will be found of great value by any hostess who desires to offer tasteful hospitalities to her friends. The price of the pamphlet is 15 cents.

FOR THE MASQUERADE AND CARNIVAL.—Everyone who contemplates giving or attending a fancy-dress entertainment of any kind should possess a copy of "Masquerade and Carnival: Their Customs and Costumes," a large and handsomely illustrated pamphlet in which costumes and decorations are fully considered. A large variety of characters are represented and suggested, and careful instructions are given for their impersonation. Price, 50 cents.

MEASURING TAPES.—No dressmaker can afford to be without a tape-measure that is at once *accurate* and *legible*, for upon it, as much as upon any other implement she uses, depends the success of the garments she makes. On another page of this issue we publish an advertisement of linen and sateen tape-measures which are manufactured expressly for us, and which we guarantee superior in every particular of material, make and finish.

CANNING AND PRESERVING.—"The Perfect Art of Canning and Preserving," as issued by us, is a convenient pamphlet which we can commend to our readers and to housekeeper, generally as a complete and reliable instructor and book of reference in the branch of cookery of which it treats. Among the new subjects introduced are: Fruit Butters; Brandied Fruits; Conserved Fruits; Syrups; Spiced Fruits; Dried Fruits, Herbs and Powders; Home-Made Wines; and Flavored Vinegars. In the canning department special attention has been paid to the canning of vegetables, including corn, peas, beans, asparagus, etc. The price of the pamphlet is 15 cents.

GOOD LITERATURE FOR THE FAMILY.—The works included in our *Metropolitan Book Series* embrace so large a variety of topics and are so thorough and comprehensive in their several lines that they form in themselves a valuable library for domestic reference and instruction. They include text-books on art and artistic handiwork, works on deportment and etiquette, guides to good housekeeping and manuals of fancy work of various kinds. The following books are published at Four Shillings or $1.00 each: "Good Manners," "Needle-Craft," "Needle and Brush," "Home-making and Housekeeping," "Social Life," "The Pattern Cook-Book," "Beauty: Its Attainment and Preservation," and "The Delsarte System of Physical Culture." Those named below are sold for 2s. or 50 cents each: "Drawing and Painting," "The Art of Knitting," "The Art of Crocheting," "Fancy and Practical Crochet Work," "Drawn-Work," "The Art of Modern Lace-Making," "Wood-Carving and Pyrography or Poker-Work," "Masquerade and Carnival," and "The Art of Garment Cutting, Fitting and Making."

PATTERNS BY MAIL.—In ordering patterns by mail, either from this office or from any of our agencies, be careful to give your post-office address in full. When patterns are desired for ladies, the *number* and *size* of each should be carefully stated, when patterns for misses, girls, boys or little folks are needed the *number*, *size* and *age* should be given in each instance.

THE SYMPHONY

SELF PLAYING   **SELF PLAYING**

is an instrument upon which a person with no musical knowledge can render perfectly any piece of music ever written. **You Don't Turn a Crank,** but simply seat yourself at the instrument, insert the roll of music which you wish to play and use the pedals as in an ordinary organ.

It is an orchestra at your command.

Send for illustrated pamphlet.

| If you wish to know where THE SYMPHONY Can be seen In your locality. Drop us a line. | **WILCOX & WHITE CO.,** MERIDEN, CONN. and 123 Fifth Avenue, New York. THE SYMPHONY is represented by the leading music houses in the world. |

Royal Baking Powder

Absolutely Pure

A Lenten Hint

Satisfaction always attends the use of a genuine article. Beardsley's is the original and only Shredded Codfish.

All Good Grocers.

"Your Breakfast," is the name of a Codfish receipt book which we send for a 2c. stamp. It tells things you never knew before.

J. W. Beardsley's Sons,
100 West St., New York City.

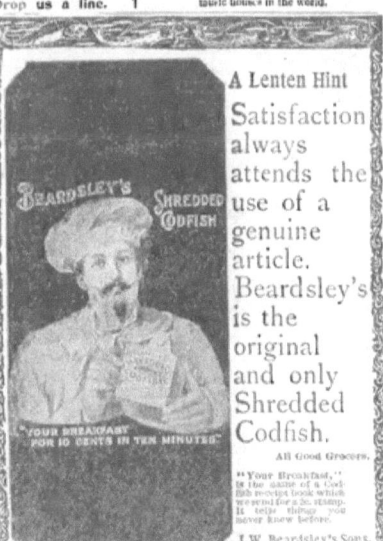

AN OPPORTUNITY TO TRY
MADAME RUPPERT'S FACE BLEACH

Almost Free. Do Not Miss This Chance.

Mme. Ruppert, the Eminent Complexion Specialist, who gave the ladies of New York a most charming lecture at the Fifth Avenue Theatre, March 13, makes the following liberal offers for this month:

OFFER NO. 1.

To every purchaser of a $2.00 bottle of her World-Renowned FACE BLEACH she will give a bar of her exquisite Almond Oil Soap FREE. This offer applies to any who live at a distance and order by mail, as well as resident patrons who purchase in person.

OFFER NO. 2.

To all who have not tried her world-renowned FACE BLEACH she offers for this month a trial bottle for 25 cents. This offer also applies to any at a distance, who will receive a trial bottle in plain wrapper, all charges prepaid, on receipt of 25 cents, either silver or stamps.

FACE BLEACH, which is an external treatment, is solely the invention of MME. A. RUPPERT and is the only preparation for the complexion that has withstood the test of time. Eighteen years it has been manufactured and during that time many millions of bottles have been used. It has never failed, if used as directed, to remove Tan, Freckles, Pimples, Eczema, Moth, and, in fact, all diseases the skin is heir to. It is used externally and when applied strikes, as it should, at the root of the trouble.

LIVING EXAMPLES.

Mme. Ruppert has proven the effectiveness of her FACE BLEACH by having patients in her office with but one side of the face cleared at a time, showing the remarkable difference between the side cleared and the side as it was before the application of Face Bleach. Miss Hattie Trainor, whose likeness is shown herewith, is now on exhibition at her Parlors, 6 East 14th Street, New York City, with one side of face cleared from dark, deep set skin Freckles, leaving the other side as it originally was, showing beyond doubt the wonderful transformation due to FACE BLEACH. Call and see for yourself, or write your friends to call and see for you. NO OTHER SPECIALIST HAS EVER GIVEN THIS ABSOLUTE PROOF.

Call or send for Mme. A. Ruppert's book, HOW TO BE BEAUTIFUL, which alone is worth its weight in gold to every woman, and should be read by all. It is given or sent FREE.

Miss Hattie Trainor, as in condition of Mme. A. Ruppert's Parlors, with one side of face bleached.

MME. A. RUPPERT, Leading Complexion Specialist,
WESTERN OFFICE: 6 EAST 14TH STREET,
235 STATE ST., CHICAGO, ILL.   NEW YORK CITY.

THE DELINEATOR.

On this and the succeeding two pages will be found some illustrations of Patterns for Ladies'

Tea-Gowns and Wrappers,

which our readers will no doubt be pleased to inspect. They represent the latest and prettiest modes available for invalid, bath and comfortable home wear. The Patterns can be had from either Ourselves or Agents for the Sale of our Goods.

In ordering, please specify the Numbers and Sizes desired.

The Butterick Publishing Co.,
(LIMITED),
171 to 175, Regent St., London, W.;
or, 7 to 17 W. 13th St., New York.

7427 — Ladies' Tea-Gown (To be Made with Long or Elbow Sleeves and with a Slight Train or in Round Length) (Copyright): 13 sizes. Bust measures, 28 to 46 inches. Any size, 1s. 6d. or 35 cents.

7097 — Ladies' Tea-Gown or Wrapper, with Eton Fronts and a Slight Train (Perforated for Round Length) (Copyright): 13 sizes. Bust measures, 28 to 46 inches. Any size, 1s. 8d. or 40 cents.

7909 — Maternity Gown (To be Made With or Without a Short Under-Body and With a Slight Train or in Round Length) (Copyright): 12 sizes. Bust measures, 30 to 46 inches. Any size, 1s. 6d. or 35 cents.

7540 — Ladies' Tea-Gown or Wrapper, with Short Train (Perforated for Round Length) (Copyright): 13 sizes. Bust measures, 28 to 46 inches. Any size, 1s. 8d. or 40 cents.

8007 — Young Ladies' Tea-Gown, with a Fitted Lining and a Star Collar Separated at the Front and Back (To be Made with Full-Length or Three-Quarter Length Puff-Sleeves) (Copyright): 13 sizes. Bust measures, 28 to 40 inches. Any size, 1s. 8d. or 40 cents.

7339 — Ladies' Tea-Gown or Wrapper, with Short Train (Perforated for Round Length) (Copyright): 13 sizes. Bust measures, 28 to 46 inches. Any size, 1s. 8d. or 40 cents.

7903 — Ladies' Tea-Gown or Wrapper (To be Made with a Short Train or in Round Length) (Copyright): 13 sizes. Bust measures, 28 to 46 inches. Any size, 1s. 8d. or 40 cents.

7933 — Ladies' Tea-Gown (To be Made with a Slight Train or in Round Length) (Copyright): 13 sizes. Bust measures, 28 to 46 inches. Any size, 1s. 8d. or 40 cents.

CLEANSES — PRESERVES — BEAUTIFIES

Sample Vial of Rubifoam MAILED FREE TO ANY ADDRESS

RUBIFOAM FOR THE TEETH.
DELICIOUSLY FLAVORED.
PREPARED AND GUARANTEED BY E. W. HOYT & CO., LOWELL, MASS. MANUFACTURERS OF THE CELEBRATED HOYT'S GERMAN COLOGNE.

7934 — Ladies' Tea-Gown or Wrapper (To be Made with a High or Square Neck and with Full-Length or Elbow Puff-Sleeves) (Copyright): 13 sizes. Bust measures, 28 to 46 inches. Any size, 1s. 8d. or 40 cents.

THE DELINEATOR.

7665
7665 Ladies' Empire House-Gown or Wrapper **7665**
(To be Made with a Plain or Tucked Yoke-Shaped Body, With or Without a Fitted Body Lining and with Full-Length or Elbow Sleeves) (Copyr't): 13 sizes. Bust measures, 28 to 46 inches. Any size, 1s. 6d. or 40 cents.

7301 **7301**
Ladies' Lounging, Dressing or Bath Robe, with Slight Train (Perforated for Round Length) (Copyr't): 10 sizes. Bust measures, 28 to 46 ins. Any size, 1s. 6d. or 35 cents.

LABLACHE FACE POWDER
Queen of Toilet Powders.

The Purest and most Perfect Face Powder that science and skill can produce. It is Invisible. It makes the Skin Soft and Beautiful. Removes all Gloss, Sunburn, Tan, Freckles, Blotches, etc.

50 CENTS.
Of all Druggists, or by Mail.
BEN. LEVY & CO., French Perfumers,
34 West Street, Boston.

7979 **7979**
Ladies' Watteau Wrapper or House-Gown (To be Made with a Short Train or in Round Length and With or Without the Fancy Collar) (Copyright): 13 sizes. Bust measures, 28 to 46 inches. Any size, 1s. 6d. or 40 cents.

7437 **7437**
Ladies' Wrapper, Outlining a Round Yoke on a Fitted Body-Lining (To be Made with a Standing or a Rolling Collar) (Copyright): 13 sizes. Bust measures, 28 to 46 inches. Any size, 1s. 6d. or 35 cents.

7994 **7994**
Ladies' Wrapper or Lounging Robe (To be Made with a Standing or Rolling Collar) (Copyright): 13 sizes. Bust measures, 28 to 46 inches. Any size, 1s. 6d. or 35 cents.

8030 **8030**
Ladies' Princess Wrapper, with Loose Fronts (Lounging Robe or Night-Gown) (Copyright): 14 sizes. Bust measures, 28 to 48 inches. Any size, 1s. 6d. or 35 cents.

Sufferers from CATARRH, ASTHMA, BRONCHITIS,
AND OTHER
Throat and Lung Troubles
know that the regulation treatment has proven unsatisfactory.

THE PILLOW-INHALER

attacks these diseases in a rational and scientific way. From reservoirs concealed in our Pillow, a healing vapor is thrown off, to mix with the air our lungs inhale whilst in bed and asleep for 6 to 8 hours every night. It is safe as wholesome and is comfortable. It brings rest and heals without loss of time. It will appeal to your good judgment.

One third of our sales comes from advertising; two-thirds from the personal recommendation of those who have used the Pillow-Inhaler, which speaks volumes as to its merit.

To know more, send for circulars and testimonials, or call and see it. Kindly be sure to mention THE DELINEATOR.

PILLOW-INHALER CO.
1406 Chestnut Street, Philadelphia, Pa.

7180 **7180**
Ladies' Wrapper or Tea-Gown, with Fitted Lining (Which may be Omitted) (Copyright): 13 sizes. Bust measures, 28 to 46 inches. Any size, 1s. 6d. or 35 cents.

7955 **7955**
Ladies' Bath or Invalid Robe (Copyright): 11 sizes. Bust measures, 28 to 48 inches. Any size, 1s. 6d. or 35 cents.

7290 **7290**
Ladies' Vapor Gown (To be used as a Wrapper, Lounging-Robe or Night-Gown) (Copyright): 10 sizes. Bust measures, 28 to 46 inches. Any size, 1s. 6d. or 35 cents.

7375 **7375**
Ladies' Bath, Invalid or Lounging-Robe (To be Made with a Standing or a Sailor Collar) (Copyright): 13 sizes. Bust measures, 28 to 46 inches. Any size, 1s. 6d. or 35 cents.

THE DELINEATOR.

ANSWERS TO CORRESPONDENTS.

Jo George:—The names of the principal hotels throughout the country can be found in The Hotel Register, published in New York, or in The Hotel Guide, published in Boston. Arsenic should never be taken except by the advice of a physician. Tetlow's Gossamer Powder imparts softness to the skin. Read answer to Miss J. regarding a foundation for face powder. Introduce your husband as you would any one else, thus: "Miss Blank, permit me to introduce Mr. Dash to you."

Forsan:—We would advise you to scan the pages of some educational magazine to obtain the address of a boarding school near your city. There are so many composers who have written classical music that it is impossible to give a definite answer on that subject. Some of them are: Beethoven, Wagner, Schumann, Mendelssohn, Bach, Handel and Chopin.

Mrs. H. H.:—Peroxide of hydrogen as a hair bleach is in no way injurious to the head, but its constant use will render the hair dry and brittle.

L. C. S. G.:—A tonic which has received universal renown relative as an efficient promoter of the growth of the hair is compounded after the following formula:

   Eau de Cologne, 8 fluid ounces.
   Tincture of cantharides, 1 fluid ounce.
   Oil of lavender, ½ fluid drachm.
     " rosemary, ½ fluid drachm.

Mix thoroughly and apply to the roots of the hair every day or two.

L. R. D.:—Five feet, five inches is the average height for a woman. A woman of that height should weigh about one hundred and thirty-five pounds. The continued use of such lubricants as almond oil, vaseline or cocoa butter will cause a growth of superfluous hair.

G. R. M.:—A cement which is said to have been used with great success in fixing basins, ornamental stones, etc., is formed of sixty-three parts well burned brick and seven parts litharge, pulverized and moistened with linseed oil. Moisten the surfaces to which it is to be applied.

LADIES of the World:
We are now at your Service.

THE "RAPID" HOOK AND EYE.

THIS EYE

SEVEN Points of Merit.

1. No sewing under the bill.
2. Takes one-third less sewing. (This is more than some people.)
3. Divides strain on the cloth.
4. Easier to hook and unhook.
5. Has a more reliable bump. (No should to catch on pipes.)
6. Gives a braver fastening.
7. Same price as common safety hook.

"RAPID" HOOK AND EYE CO.
175 Canal Street,
Grand Rapids, Mich.

IT PAYS
to do your shopping with
"The Quickest Mail Order House in the World"—
BY MAIL

Walking Suit— of all wool storm serge in Navy or Black, an exact reproduction of the newest Paris pattern-gown. Two-seam French-back cutaway leg-o'-mutton sleeves—pleated at shoulder, velvet reverses—button-trimmed with rows of tiny brass buttons—velvet trimmed collar and cuffs. The suit is band throughout and waist lined. Full velvet bound skin with new flare, gathered back; in every respect a $25.00 outfit—made in our own workrooms. Samples will show an excellence of quality that is maintained in workmanship. **$12.00**

Spring Silks— are here— the earliest of them. The reigning fabric is the "Primed-in-the-warp"—21 inches wide Glace Taffeta—in Persian and Oriental designs and colors. $1.75 quality . . . **$1.25**
$2.00 quality . . . **$1.50**
Habutai—White and Ivory White—three special values 27 in. wide at **48c** and **35c**
20 inches wide at . . **23c**
Fancy Kai Kai—plaids—stripes and checks—woven colors washable—
24 inches wide at . . . **49c**
27 inches wide at . . . **33c**
20 inches wide at . . . **23c**

Lounging Robes— a dainty as these become a necessity when coupled with such taste + merit. Exquisitely fashioned $5.00 garments, made of fine swan's-down flannel or wash-silk—with extra large sleeves and skirt of ample fulness. The entire front and V-style epaulets are trimmed with fancy silk gimp, satin bows on sleeves, pocket and at throat complete the charming effect. Samples waiting to be mailed in you will show six colors—in ordering state bust measure. Equally appropriate for traveling or for cold weather slumber robes . . . **$2.75**

Send for Sample Copy

Carson-Pirie Monthly

February Number Now Ready

72 pages handsomely illustrated. Yearly subscription 10c.

Reefer Jacket— No. 340—made of all wool Dobson Chinchilla—box front—ripple back—high storm collar—lined throughout except sleeves with fine quality of satin rhadame—sizes 32 to 44. These have been $18.00 all season until now — Black only **$10.50**

London Box Coats— No. 417—made of best IMPORTED rough Boucle—25 inches long—wide box front—full ripple back—extremely large 3 piece melon sleeves—high storm collar—4 fancy black horn buttons set with pearl—garment is lined throughout except sleeves, which are capped—with best quality black satin—this garment an honest $20.00 value, reserved exclusively for our mail-order trade at . . . **$13.50**

House Gowns— depend much upon their stylishness for their beauty. The designs shown above is becoming to one every figure. Of superior quality Flannelette in black or navy ground with white pin dots; shoulder-in, front and back trimmed with black and gray-seam to much. Full Watteau back—Marlborough collar—large leg-o'-mutton sleeves and very wide skirt. Waist made with close fitting ladies and half belt—samples waiting—sizes 32 to 44 bust measurement. We wouldn't talk about them here if they weren't worth a good deal more than . . **$1.95**

Smart Skirts Made in our own work-rooms. Over some of these stylish and thoroughly well made garments sold through our Mail Order Department already this season without a single case of dissatisfaction. Perhaps the reason is that the entire fashioning is done under the direct supervision of our own skilled skirt-builders. Black Corporon—all wool and five yards wide, stiffened around the bottom—bound with velvet—full lined and tailor finished throughout **$6.50**
The same in all wool black serge . . **$5.00**

Send for Sample Clippings

SEND FOR

YOUR MONEY BACK
if not satisfied with your purchase.

MAILED FREE!

"THE SHOPPERS' ECONOMIST"

The most complete Shopping Guide ever published — 128 pages devoted to good form in woman's wear, the correct Spring styles as shown in our seventy departments being accurately described and handsomely illustrated. Ready March 1st.

CARSON PIRIE SCOTT & Co.
93 to 107 WASHINGTON STREET

CHICAGO

BIG BARGAINS IN ROSES, PLANTS, AND SEEDS

Our **GRAND SET of 13 Elegant Ever-blooming ROSES** for only 50cts. by mail, post-paid, safe arrival and satisfaction guaranteed.

These roses are fine healthy plants and will bloom all this Summer in pots or planted out. We guarantee them to be by far the best 50 cts. you ever invested in roses, as follows:

Malacrin Augusta Victoria—(New.) Pure White, elegant. **Grace Darling**—Silvery, Peach beauty. **Clothilde Soupert**—This is everybodys favorite. **Reidsmaid**—the most charming Pink Rose. **Pearl of the Gardens**—Deep Golden Yellow. **Sunset**—Beautiful shades of Copper and Gold. **Scarlet Bedder**—the richest and brightest of all Red Roses. **Franciska Kruger**—yellow flushed pink charming. **Mad. de Watteville**—the famous Tulip Rose. **Rheingold**—deep Citron and Gold, a remarkable color. **Mad. Welche**—Amber Yellow, deepening toward the center. **Mad. Hoste**—A Pure Snow White, none better. **Duchess de Brabant**—Amber Rose, delicately tinged apricot.

What You Can Buy for 50 Cents.

Set 14—13 Ever-blooming Roses all different . . 50c.
" 25—12 Fragrant Carnation Pinks, 12 kinds, 50c.
" 30— 5 Lovely Flowering Begonias, all sorts, 50c.
" 34—13 Geraniums, all colors and kinds, . . 50c.
" 39—13 Choice Prize Chrysanthemums, . . 50c.
" 40— 4 Choice Decorative Palms, try them, 50c.
" 51— 5 Dwarf French Cannas, 5 kinds, . . . 50c.
" 41—12 Sweet Scented Double Tube Rose, 50c.
Set 6—15 Large Flowered Pansy Plants, . . 50c.
" 10—15 Coleus, will make a bright bed, . . 50c.
" 12—12 Double and Single Fuchsias, all colors 50c.
" 15— 6 Choice Hardy Shrubs, 6 sorts, . . . 50c.
" 46—20 Pkts Flower Seeds, no two alike, . 50c.
" 49—20 Pkts elegant Sweet Peas, all different 50c.
" 45—15 Pkts choice Vegetable Seeds in sorts 50c.

You may select half of any two sets for 50 cents, or 3 complete sets for $1.25, any 5 sets for $2.00, the entire dozen for $5.00; or half of each set for $2.50. Get your neighbor to club with you. Our catalogue free. **ORDER TO-DAY.** We will hold the plants and ship them any time you may desire. Address

THE GREAT WESTERN PLANT CO., SPRINGFIELD, OHIO.

ANSWERS TO CORRESPONDENTS.
(*Continued.*)

M. W.:—Write to the Numismatic Bank, Boston, Mass., Coin Dept. D, regarding the value of rare coins.

H. D., JR.:—You can have piano or violin music arranged for the guitar by a musician.

L. L. D.:—Directions for knitting pretty Afghans or counterpanes are given in "The Art of Knitting," published by us at 2s. or 50 cents. "The Art of Crocheting," which we publish at the same price, also contains tasteful designs for Afghans.

WEDDING BELLS:—All the articles of food you mention—oyster pâtés, chicken salad, jelly, turkey, cranberry sauce, celery, etc., are suitable for the wedding menu. All but the oyster pâtés (which must be brought in hot) may be placed on the table. Butter is seldom served at large dinners.

PAUL:—The use of corn meal upon the face will not cause a growth of down; only greasy preparations have this effect.

MAC:—The name Olive in French is spelled the same as in English. Sweetheart in Spanish is "novia" for the feminine gender, and "novio" for the masculine. We do not know the addresses of firms who wish employees. You might advertise for such a position as you want.

TEDDY:—The use of the electric needle is the only permanent means of removing superfluous hair. Consult your family physician in reference to the operation, which is momentarily painful but, when well performed, leaves eventually no scar and only for a short time any mark at all.

GRAND OFFER IN FLOWER SEEDS

Pansy	40 kinds	Poppy	25 kinds
Nasturtiums	10	Candytufts	5
Phlox	20	Morning Glory	15
Verbena	10	Sweet Peas	8
Pinks	5	"Mignonette"	6
Petunia	12	Alyssum	5
Asters	10	Portulaca	15
Balsam	10	Zinnias	10

(A) The above 16 pkt. Choice Annuals $1.00
(B) " 2 ounces Tall Nasturtiums, choice 50c
(C) " 2 " Dwarf " 50c
(D) " Martha Washington, 12 Bulb flower seeds 50c
(E) " 10 pkgs. (16 Kinds) Choice Vegetable Seeds (Beet, Carrot, Parsnips, Cucumber, Squash, Cabbage, Lettuce, Radish, Onion, Melon) 50c

We will send any one of the above lots postage paid for price quoted.

SPECIAL. If you wish to send us 10 cents we will send you POST-PAID all the above 5 lots, and 1-2 lb. of the finest and best named varieties of SWEET PEAS FREE. Address HILLSIDE NURSERY, So. Hingham, Somerville, Mass. ILLUSTRATED CATALOGUE FREE.

---

1 ROSE and 3 Pkts. FLOWER SEED 10c. 3 Roses 3 Pkts. 20c.
5 Roses 5 pkts. 30c.; 10 Roses 10 pkts. 50c.; 20 Roses 20 pkts. $1. Big bargain catalog & cultural directions with every order. **Wm. G. Hert, Chambersburg, Pa.**

$1,000. IN POTATOES GIVEN AWAY.

EARLY FORTUNE is the earliest potato grown, and has proved it. A potato grower writes: "Early Fortune is the earliest potato in the world. I have tested everything equality, shape, and color the best. One potato produced me over 60 lb. It is going to sell everything." We want a great hit made in 1896, and will give **Five** a barrel of them to growers of the largest potato from one potato 5c each Mass. and Territory. Instructions with potato.

One potato to wards $1.00 to any person.
ALL HEAD CABBAGE.—Very early. None so satisfied. We sent a premium to every one buying a seed hamper. Single heads have weighed over 15 lb.

JAPANESE CLIMBING CUCUMBER.—A wonderful variety from Japan, and will produce a lot of crisp cucumbers, fit for cutting. Please, all cut a wonderful culinary, Unite stores, in these large, produce several golden ears to each one, excellent for people.
GOLDEN TOM THUMB POP-CORN.—A perfect little golden, grows in lumps high, produces several golden ears to each corn, excellent for people.

$250.00 FOR EARLY TOMATOES. This wonderful Early Tomato has proved a great success, and our cashiers, bookkeepers and gardeners, Perfect ripe fruit has been gathered 80 in less than 9 days. We offer $250 to the Tomato growers in the most number of days from the seeds planted. Full instructions with each. We have it all.

We will send one whole potato (each one of Early Fortune) and one small packet each of All Head Early Scotched Cabbage, Japanese Climbing Cucumber, Early Tomato and our Easy Tom Thumb Pop-Corn, with our grand Seed Catalogue for 10c. (full of bargains) for 25c. Plant Calendar, Seeds, Free, if you send under order of above.
FAIRVIEW SEED FARM, Box 56, ROSE HILL, N. Y.

The Most Artistic Effect In Sweet Peas

is obtained by having each color by itself in a separate row. Try it. We offer one packet each of the choicest sorts: BLUSHING BEAUTY— clear as break pink; EMIGRATION—rich velvety maroon; EMILY HENDERSON—purest white; COUNTESS OF RADNOR—soft lavender; VENUS— a grand salmon buff, together with our 1896 SEED CATALOGUE, which is handsomely illustrated by direct photographs, and containing many Choice Novelties in both Vegetables and Flowers for **12c.** STAMPS. 1 oz. each of the above with Catalogue for 50c. $1.00

JOHNSON & STOKES, 217 & 219 Market St., Philadelphia, Pa.

What SHALL I PLANT? How SHALL I PLANT?

We answer these questions fully, and are the only Nursery making Planting Plans and Suggestions without cost. You can find no lower-priced

Trees · Shrubs · Rhododendrons
Roses · Hardy Perennials

than we offer and many rare novelties hard to obtain.

Our Unique Catalogue, finely Illustrated with photographs, sent for Ten Cents.

300 Acres. Largest Nursery in New England.

SHADY HILL NURSERY CO.,
102 State St., Boston, Mass.

EVERYONE interested in **PLANTS**

or Horticulture, should have our latest catalogue. New and revised. Tropical and Semi-Tropical Fruit Plants, Economic plants, Rare trees, Aquatics, Palms, Cacti, Ferns, Succulents, Orchids, and all manner of Choice Decorative and useful Plants, trees and vines, described, illustrated and honestly priced. Stock is forwarded safely to all parts of the world. Small orders by mail a specialty. Large specimens by express or freight. Lowest freight rates. **Special Offer**—10 Choice Palms $1 (delivered free) or of much larger size for $1. to Fine Decorative Plants, $1. Send to-day.

Reasoner Bros., Oneco, Fla., U.S.A.

TELL ALL YOUR FRIENDS who belong to Dramatic Clubs or get up "Shows" for Churches and Schools, that the fit for play to buy Plays at a Bargain may be. My catalogue of over FREE to anybody. Sgreatest. H. ROORBACH, 132 Nassau Street, New York, N.Y.

1896

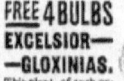

Miss Mary E. Martin,
FLORAL PARK, NEW YORK,

Will sell you **FRESH, PURE,** up-to-date

Flower Seeds and Bulbs.

When you buy of me—you save money—get bright Flowers, fashionable colors, honest measure, and **PATRONIZE**

A WOMAN. HONEST DEALING IS WANTED.

15 OF THESE VARIETIES IN FULL-SIZED PACKETS 25c.

"A WHOLE FLOWER GARDEN FOR 25 CENTS."

Alyssum Little Gem, Aster Giant Comet White, Immense, new. Dahlia Double, Large. Dianthus or Japanese Clove Pink. Dbl. Seeds. "Fairy Zinnias, Gem. Giant Phlox Drummondii, Star, fringe, &c. "Japanese Imperial" Morning Glory, New. Verbena Invincible.
Mignonette Giant Tree. Pansy Parisian Fancy 40 colors, New strain. Petunia — Pyramidal Tree, French. Poppies — Shirley and Chrysanthm., Double. Snow Queen Candytuft, Elegant. Sweet Peas, 40 kinds. Verbena — Mammoth. Bright Flowers. 20 colors.

NOVELTIES MARKED THUS ~~~

Anyone sending for 4 of these collections from 4 people, names and addresses enclosed, I will send

FREE 4 BULBS EXCELSIOR — GLOXINIAS.

This plant, of such exotic richness, is as easy grown as a Geranium. Flowers royal purple, sea shell pink, ivory throat crimson, tiger spotted.

4 Bulbs, 50c

AGENTS WANTED Little more, good pay. I pay cash, easily premium, best sellers, Genuine Diamond Rings, Watches, Fans, Gold Pens, Bosks, &c. Catalogue—Directions for Growing. Premium and Prize Books with every order.

Miss Mary E. Martin, Floral Park, New York.

ANSWERS TO CORRESPONDENTS.

(Continued.)

LUCY:— While Utah has not yet been formally admitted as a State, the preliminaries thereto are under way. The water of the Dead Sea is very salt and of a dull-green color. Very few fish are found therein, but it is not true that birds which venture into its vapors fall dead. The shores are almost barren, but hyenas and other wild beasts lurk there.

K. McH.:— We do not approve of making up your light goods in a flower suit. Basque pattern No. 8032 and skirt pattern No. 8066, which cost 1s. 3d. or 30 cents each, and are illustrated in the December number of THE DELINEATOR, would be most suitable. You cannot match the stripes in the skirt if you wish to make it up in the gored style. Skirts with box-plaits are still used. Folds of brown shot silk applied to the skirt as illustrated on the pattern, would be effective. A little borax in the water used to wash the hair will not injure it. Unless we know the style of coat you wish, we cannot tell you how much goods will be required for it. Do not have a seamless back in making up a coat of striped material. Ribbon is much used for garniture; if, however, you do not care for it, finish the basque at the bottom with a twisted fold of narrow velvet.

TRIXY:— If the nose is oily or shiny, use borax water or wash it with corn meal instead of soap.

Peter Henderson & Co's
NEW FREE DELIVERY SYSTEM
FOR 1896, DELIVERS THEIR FAMOUS SEEDS, AT CATALOGUE PRICES,
FREE
TO ANY POST OFFICE IN THE UNITED STATES.

Our New Manual of "**Everything for the Garden**" is the grandest ever issued. It not only points the way to successful gardening, but is, as well, a careful gleaning of the world's newest and best in Seeds, Plants and Bulbs. Its 160 pages, size 9 x 11 inches, are embellished with over 500 engravings, and contain, besides, 6 beautiful colored plates of Novelties in Seeds and Plants.

NOW THEN, to trace our advertising we make the following unusually liberal offer: To every one who will state where this advertisement was seen, and who encloses us 20 cents (in stamps), we will mail the Manual, and also send, free of charge, our famous 5c. Pioneer Collection of Seeds, containing one packet each of New Mammoth Mignonette, New Bonfire Pansy, New "Blue Ribbon" Sweet Peas, Succession Cabbage, Prizetaker Onion, and "Table Queen" Tomato, in a red envelope which, when emptied and returned, will be accepted as a 25c. cash payment on any order of goods selected from Manual to the amount of $1 and upward.

PETER HENDERSON & CO.
35 & 37 CORTLANDT ST., NEW YORK.

Every genuine package of our Seeds bears this Red Trade-mark stamp or label. Every genuine package of our Seeds bears this Red Trade-mark stamp or label.

Pioneer Seed Catalogue
DOUBLE SWEET PEA
(BRIDE OF NIAGARA)
The Only One in the World—True To Name.

VICK'S FLORAL GUIDE, for 1896, with Colored Plates, Hundreds of Illustrations, many Novelties, elegantly bound, and **one packet BRIDE OF NIAGARA,** for 15 cents.
JAMES VICK'S SONS, Rochester, N. Y.

Dwarf Sweet Pea "Cupid."
A New Dwarf or Bush Sweet Pea, growing only five inches high, yet spreading out and forming a large mass of foliage and flowers. Flowers pure white, extra large, three on a stem, and bloom profusely from Spring until Fall. An elegant plant for Winter and Spring. If started now, try it! It's the most exquisite novelty. Packet of 10 seeds, 15 cents, or for only 20 cents we will send all of the following art novelties:

3 Seeds CUPID DWARF SWEET PEA.
1 pkt. SCARLET PANSIES, fine red colors.
1 pkt. MARGARET CARNATION, all colors, blooms in 3 mos.
1 pkt. VERBENA GIANT WHITE SCENTED, new fragrant.
1 pkt. FILIFERA or WEEPING PALM, a grand plant.
1 pkt. DWARF GIANT FLOWERED CANNA, mixed, ex. fine.

All by mail postpaid for only 20 cents, together with my great Catalogue. These are the most valuable novelties in Flower Seeds. Order at once.

OUR CATALOGUE of Flower and Vegetable Seeds, Bulbs, Plants and Rare new Fruits is the finest ever issued; profusely illustrated with elegant cuts and colored plates. We offer the choicest standard sorts and finest Novelties. We are headquarters for all that is New, Rare and Beautiful. This elegant Catalogue will be sent for 10 cents, Free, if you order the above articles. Address,

JOHN LEWIS CHILDS, Floral Park, N.Y.

One full-sized packet of each the following choice **Eighteen Varieties of Flower Seeds, 25c**
varieties:—Adonis, Aster, Balsam, Cypress Vine, Eschscholtzia, Gaillardia, Marigold, Mignonette, Nigella, Pansy, Petunia, Phlox, Dianthus, Sweet Pea, Verbena, Whitlavia, Xeranthemum, Zinnia. Guaranteed to please or amount gold refunded. Send for most unique and attractive Catalogue, free. CROCKER FLOWER SEED CO., 125+125 S. 5th St., Minneapolis, Minn.

$250.00 FOR 4 FLOWER BEDS. The following is the greatest collection ever offered for variety of colors, and I will pay $100 to person who grows the largest number of colors from it; $75 to second; $50 to third; and $25 in fourth. It will surprise you, and make a very interesting flower bed.
1 pkt. A fine Pansy—all colors mixed, deeply grand.
1 pkt. Sweet Peas—Eckford's Mixed, over 30 kinds, splendid.
1 pkt. Chinese Pinks—mixed colors, hardy and very showy.
1 pkt. Poppies—mixed, a wonderful selection of colors.
1 pkt. Mignonette—mixed, all kinds to be found; fragrant.
1 pkt. Chrysanthemum—mixed, all choicest single sorts, bright.
1 pkt. Mixed Flowers—of over 100 kinds that grow anywhere.
1 bulb Excelsior Pearl Tuberose—extra early.
1 bulb Gladiolus, out each of White, Pink, Scarlet, Yell., mixed.
1 tuba Shallot, fancy mixed, lovely spikes, all colors.
1 tuber Gladiolus, Lemoine, earliest of all, intensely colors.
1 bulb Oxalis—new in bloom—lovely color for borders.
1 bulb Tuberose, fancy mixed, months—every color for borders.
These 13 pkts. of seed and 13 choice bulbs (worth $1.50, sold all flower this season, and make a wonderful flower bed or round 10 feet circle) (of H. O.) Order at once, and you will be sure of an interest in the prize and how to get the most colors. My large catalogue, just out for 1896. This book and a sample of our magazine free on request. "Cupid" Sweet Pea, the floral Wonder, Free with each order. F. B. MILLS, Box 105, ROSE HILL, N.Y.

Headquarters for the Choicest
SEEDS, PLANTS,
TREES, SHRUBS, VINES, ROSES, BULBS, Etc.

Elegant 168 Page Catalog, Free. Send for it before buying. Half saved by dealing direct. Everything mail size postpaid. Largest express or freight. Satisfaction Guaranteed. 42nd year. 1000 Acres. 29 Greenhouses.

STORRS & HARRISON CO.,
Painesville, Ohio. Box 11

D. & C. ROSES

How to grow and care for them, as well as all other flowers of worth, is told in the 25th annual edition of our *New Guide to Rose Culture* — a magnificently illustrated book of 116 pp., mailed free, just out for 1896. This book and a sample of our magazine free on request. The Dingee & Conard Co., West Grove, Pa.

SWEET PEAS.

Every American garden should have the best NEW SWEET PEAS in 1896. By keeping Purity and High Quality, rather than low prices, our first aim, we are now **HEADQUARTERS for SWEET PEAS.** We have thirty-two thousand pounds of the seed, and sell common Mixed Sweet Peas at 35 cts. per lb., 3 lbs. for $1.00, postpaid,—BUT we recommend as far superior the most beautiful NOVELTIES here offered:—

25 Cts. buys these Seven Superb Sweet Peas:

BLANCHE BURPEE. Exhibited "finest of all Sweet Peas." Pure white flowers of immense size; three and four on a stem. See illustration here with.
DOROTHY TENNANT. Flower of large, expanded form; a deep rosy-mauve with wings of Heliotrope.
LADY PENZANCE. Superb flowers of large size and exquisite color; beautiful laced pink, touching orange.
NEW LOTTIE ECKFORD. Remarkably beautiful, large flower; white, edged and suffused with lavender-blue.
ROYAL ROBE. The largest and best soft pink; a lovely flower of exquisite beauty.
STANLEY. The flowers are produced abundantly in fours on long stems and are of a rich, dark maroon. Exceptionally fine for bouquets,—the best dark Sweet Pea.
SPECIAL SUPERFINE MIXED. This mixture contains only the very best Eckford Sweet Peas. It is a choice blending of seventeen large-flowered new named varieties.

The Seven Superb Sweet Peas named above, in same sized packets, would have cost $1.00 in 1895, but are now sold for 25 cents. "JUST HOW TO GROW SWEET PEAS; FULL DIRECTIONS BY AN EXPERT," sent with each collection.

New SWEET PEAS at merely nominal cost. Get four friends to order and you will have a collection FREE, as we give **five collections for $1.00.** OR, for $1.00 you can have **four collections** and a regular size 25-cent pkt. of CUPID,—our little floral wonder.

ORDER TO-DAY! and ask for BURPEE'S FARM ANNUAL for 1896,—the Leading American Seed Catalogue. A handsome BOOK of 184 pages, it tells all about the Best SEEDS that Grow. It describes rare NOVELTIES of real merit, including CUPID—the first and only Dwarf Sweet Pea,—for which we received an award of merit last summer upon exhibition in both London and Paris.

W. ATLEE BURPEE & CO., Philadelphia, Pa.

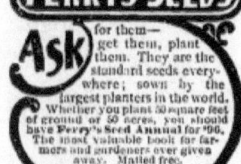

FERRY'S SEEDS

Ask for them— get them, plant them. They are the standard seeds everywhere; sown by the largest planters in the world. Whether you plant 50 square feet of ground or 50 acres, you should have **Ferry's Seed Annual for '96.** The most valuable book for farmers and gardeners ever given away. Mailed free.

D. M. FERRY & CO., Detroit, Mich.

BOWKER'S FLOWER FOOD

For house plants. Makes luxurious growth and brilliant flowers. Clean, odorless, applied occasionally to plants. Enough for 20 plants all winter, 25c.; for 100, 50c. We pay postage and send book on **Window Gardening** free with each package. Grocers and Druggists sell it—or address

BOWKER Fertilizer Co. 43 Chatham St., Boston, Mass.

WIGS, WHISKERS, Grease Paints, Spirit Gum, etc., for Masquerades, Plays, School and Stage Entertainments. MOUSTACHES, 10c., Full Beard, Skirts, Tester 97c, Wax Lips, 10 cts., Negro, Judaic 50c., Farmers, Chinese, Indian or Ladies' Wigs 75 cts. each, by mail, postpaid. Catalogue of Wigs, Veils, Novelties, etc. FREE. Costumes supplied at wholesale. **C. F. MARSHALL**, Lockport, N. Y.

WALL PAPER.

Samples Free from Largest Wall Paper concern in U.S. **KAYSER & ALLMAN** 408 Arch St., Philad'a.

ROSES, SEEDS and BULBS AT LITTLE PRICES. A FINE ROSE and pkt. beautiful mixed Flower Seeds, 50 sorts, 10 cts. 6 cts. Collection Flower Seeds, 1 pkt. each, Aster Balsam, Pansy, Petunia, Pinks, Phlox, Mignonette, Morning Glories, Sweet Alyssum, and Sweet Peas. 10 pkts., only 12 cts. 3 Bulbs Spanish Iris 10 cts.; 5 Hybrid Gladiolus, 25 cts.; 3 lovely Tuberoses, 12 cts.; Catalog with every order. **ALFRED F. CONARD**, West Grove, Pa.

THE YOUNG LADIES' JOURNAL

THE QUEEN OF FASHION JOURNALS.
Much Enlarged and Improved, and Wonderfully Attractive.
THE FEBRUARY NUMBER NOW READY.

The *New Album of Colored Fashion Plates*, made in Paris, is superb. This exquisite Album, together with the Supreme Supplement, makes the *Budget of Winter Fashions of Unequalled excellence and variety.* No lady wishing to see the very latest Correct Winter Paris Fashions should fail to ask for the February part of *The Young Ladies' Journal.*

The New Serial Story, "THE LOVE OF SIGHTS," continues in this number. There are also short sketches, articles on Fashion and Fancy Work, the Home and Cookery, Poetry, Music, etc., etc. Including the Extra Christmas Numbers. Of all Newsdealers and

Price 25 Cents. Yearly, $3.00.

THE INTERNATIONAL NEWS COMPANY,
83-85 Duane Street, New York.
(One Door East of Broadway.)

Subscription—Received for Any Periodical, Foreign or Domestic.

ANSWERS TO CORRESPONDENTS.

(Continued.)

ANXIOUS ORPHAN.—To become a good actress necessitates years of hard work. Without some exceptional ability it would not be wise to enter such a career.

ROSE M. D.—Shape the yellow satin by skirt pattern No. 7978, which costs 1s. 3d. or 30 cents, and basque-waist pattern No. 7905, price 1s. 3d. or 30 cents. Arrange the hair high.

A MONTREAL GIRL.—To arrange the Empire-Pompadour, first free the hair from tangles, so that it can easily be drawn through it evenly and freely. Then part the hair all round far back. After coiling, gather the hair up lightly to the crown of the head, twist it to the coil, being a upwards, securing it in a loop and coil. Then curl lightly round the loop which is puffed.

Miss H. J. G.—A wash-stand cover of dotted crash or pongee of pink material with yellow satin and trimmed at the edges with shirrings of yellow lace ribbon would be dainty and inexpensive. Work the pillow-shams, which may be of linen, with white floss. The pongee as a wash-stand is evidently for towels. Splashers are still in use.

Do you plant Flower Seeds? Do you Grow Flowers?

FRESH Flower Seeds

NEW SWEET PEA "AMERICA"—1½ lb., New White, with side crimson blotch. —Splendid for Bouquets.

The Best in America, and we've got to make it known in some way—guess we've tried all ways but the right one; but now—for 1896 to get our "GARDENING ILLUSTRATED" into the hands of every single flower buyer

We're going to give away Six Best Novelties

Pkt. Giant Japan Morning-glory
Pkt. New Red Pansy
Pkt. New Yellow Aster
Pkt. Double Sweet Peas
Pkt. Yellow Sweet Pea
Pkt. Verbena—Very scarlet

These six and the 32-page Book for cost of Seeds, 14c.
We're to Chicago and New York: send stamps and ask for the "Flower Girl Collection" and the book. Mention Delineator.

NEW YORK: Vaughan's Seed Store CHICAGO:
6 Barclay St. 84-86 Randolph St.

An Elegant Garden of the Best Named Varieties of **SWEET PEAS**

We will send one quarter pound to any address, postpaid, for **TEN CENTS** in stamps.

HILLSIDE NURSERY, Somerville, Mass.

NOW READY—THE JANUARY FAMILY HERALD!

Containing Four New and Complete Stories, and the opening chapters of two New Serial Stories,

"Atoned," and **"Elizabeth—A Story of Love,"**

together with much entertaining miscellany of practical value in the household. This forming one of the **MOST ATTRACTIVE** family magazines ever published, at the low price of

15 Cents monthly; $1.75 a year.

For sale by all Book and Newsdealers, and by

THE INTERNATIONAL NEWS COMPANY,
83 and 85 Duane St., (one door East of Broadway) New York.

ANSWERS TO CORRESPONDENTS.

(Continued.)

NOVICE:—To transfer the designs for embroidery, etc., which appear in THE DELINEATOR, first lay a piece of tissue paper over the design and carefully trace its outline thereon. Then place the traced tissue paper upon a piece of transfer paper and place both upon the material. When the design on the tissue paper is now retraced it will be imprinted upon the material by the transfer paper. You can purchase the latter and also a stamping outfit from J. F. Ingalls, Box D, Lynn, Mass.

W. A.:—Thomas Campbell is the author of the poem "Lord Ullin's Daughter."

TYPEWRITER:—We know of no remedy to eliminate iron from the blood. The quantity of iron in the blood determines the severity of freckles—that is, whether there are many or few—and the thickness of the cuticle is responsible for the intensity of their color.

LILLIAN VERONA:—Write to Bloomingdale Bros. 3d Avenue and 59th Street, N. Y. City, for pictures framed and unframed. Pears' soap is excellent for the complexion. Read how to manicure the nails in our publication "Beauty," price 4s., or $1.00.

THREE SCHOOL GIRLS:—Freckle remedies and whitening lotions for the skin have been frequently given in these columns during the last few months, as have suggestions for coiffures for young girls. Protruding eyes which are not due to disease cannot be changed by artificial means.

BAKE A BATCH OF BISCUITS

Sift one quart of flour, two rounding teaspoonfuls of baking powder, and one teaspoonful of salt into a bowl; add three tablespoonfuls of COTTOLENE and rub together until thoroughly mixed; then add sufficient milk to make a soft dough; knead slightly, roll out about half an inch thick, and cut with a small biscuit cutter. Place a little apart in a greased pan, and bake in a quick oven for fifteen or twenty minutes. These biscuits should be a delicate brown top and bottom, light on the sides, and snowy white when broken open.

The secret of success in this recipe, as in others, is to use but two-thirds as much Cottolene as you used to use of lard. Cottolene will make the biscuit light, delicious, wholesome. Better than any biscuit you ever made before. Try it. Be sure and get genuine *Cottolene*. Sold everywhere in tins with trade-marks—"*Cottolene*" and *steer's head in cotton-plant wreath*—on every tin.

THE N. K. FAIRBANK COMPANY, Chicago, St. Louis, New York, Boston, Philadelphia, San Francisco, Montreal.

MADAM ROWLEY'S TOILET MASK
(OR FACE GLOVE)

Trade Mark Registered.

Is a natural beautifier for bleaching and preserving the skin and removing complexional imperfections.

It is soft and flexible in form, and can be easily applied, and worn without discomfort or inconvenience.

It is recommended by eminent physicians and scientists as a substitute for injurious cosmetics.

COMPLEXION BLEMISHES may be hidden imperfectly by cosmetics and powders, but can only be removed permanently by the Toilet Mask. By its use every kind of spots, impurities, roughness, etc., vanish from the skin, leaving it soft, clear, brilliant and beautiful. It is harmless, costs little, and saves many dollars uselessly expended for cosmetics, powders, lotions, etc. It prevents and removes wrinkles, and is both a complexion preserver and a beautifier.

Illustrated Treatise, with full particulars, mailed free. Address, and kindly mention THE DELINEATOR.

To be Worn Three Times in the Week.

THE TOILET MASK CO.,
1164 BROADWAY, NEW YORK.

There are two classes of bicycles—

COLUMBIAS
and others

Columbias sell for $100 to everyone alike, and are the finest bicycles the world produces. Other bicycles sell for less, but they are *not* Columbias.

POPE MFG. CO., HARTFORD, CONN.

You See Them Everywhere

★ THE FAULTLESS QUAKER ★
★ **DISH WASHER** ★
Will make your wife smile, your daughters rejoice, your house happy & bright. You don't have to wait... [illegible]
The Quaker Novelty Co. Salem, O.

HAIR ON THE FACE, NECK, ARMS OR ANY PART OF THE PERSON
QUICKLY DISSOLVED AND REMOVED WITH THE NEW SOLUTION

✦ MODENE ✦

AND THE GROWTH FOREVER DESTROYED WITHOUT THE SLIGHTEST INJURY OR DISCOLORATION OF THE MOST DELICATE SKIN.

Discovered by Accident.—In Compounding. An incomplete mixture was accidentally spilled on the back of the hand, and on washing afterward it was discovered that the hair was completely removed. We purchased the new discovery and named it MODENE. It is perfectly pure, free from all injurious substances, and so simple any one can use it. It acts mildly but surely. You will be surprised and delighted with the results. Apply or rub on where hair should be, and the growth will be destroyed in a few minutes without the slightest pain or injury when applied or ever afterwards. MODENE supersedes electrolysis. Recommended by all who have tested its merits—Used by people of refinement.

Gentlemen who do not appreciate nature's gift of a beard, will find it a priceless boon to Modene which does away with shaving. It dissolves and destroys the life, growth of the hair, leaving the skin soft, smooth and natural. We never fail, no matter how long the growth. So harmless any child can use it. Lasts a lifetime. If the growth be light, one application will remove it; permanent the heavy growth such as the beard or hair on moles, may require two or more applications before it is permanently destroyed. Although all hair will become dark and dry applied at each application, it is without injury or injury of whatsoever kind. Modene applied at once afterwards, renders re-appearance to prevent new growth.

Postage prepaid by us if you have tested its merits—Used by people of refinement. We offer $1,000.00 for failure or the slightest injury. EVERY BOTTLE GUARANTEED.

Price, $1.00 per bottle, sent by mail, safely sealed in plain. $ Cor. in advance cashier's gold... Postage stamps received the same as cash. [We want live, active agents and local representatives.] Cut this ad out and send with order.

LOCAL AND GENERAL AGENTS WANTED. MODENE MANUFACTURING CO., CINCINNATI, O., U.S.A. Manufacturers of the Highest Grade Hair Preparations. You can register your letter at any Post-office to insure its safe delivery.

FREE STAMPING OUTFIT. 75 PATTERNS

New and beautiful, for every kind of embroidery, conventional, floral, Kensington and outline designs for doilies, splashers, tray-cloths, etc. This alphabet for monogramming and stamping, one color. Symbols, Compound, and instructions for stamping without cost, powders or stencils. Every thing new and desirable; and if in value to add to stores, and all that I FREE to every one who sends 10c. for 3 months trial subscription to our new Grand, illustrated magazine, contains 52 pages and the bee-hive house hold and fancy-work departments. Address, POPULAR MONTHLY, 178 Federal St., BOSTON, MASS.

THE DELINEATOR.

AMERICA'S FAVORITE.

Will give the wearer satisfaction every time. If not for sale at your dealers, send $1.25 to
BRIDGEPORT CORSET CO.,
FITZPATRICK & SOMERS,
85 Leonard St., New York.

ANSWERS TO CORRESPONDENTS.
(Continued.)

MARIE:—Brown and green are both popular shades; the adoption of either is simply a matter of taste.

JESSICA:—Directions for crocheting Afghans, rugs and slumber-robes are given in the Art of Crocheting, which we publish at 2s. or 50 cents.

BLANCHE D.:—Buttermilk, plain or mixed with grated horseradish, is a familiar remedy for a tanned skin. The proper age at which to marry depends entirely upon circumstances and the views held by the parents of the couple.

READER:—Gray hair cannot be restored to its original color. It may be dyed, but no dye is permanent and none is advisable.

MARGARET:—Munsey's Magazine is published at 155 Fifth Avenue, N. Y. It is certain that, if used too often, cocoa butter will cause a growth of down upon the face.

AN OLD SUBSCRIBER:—You should consult a physician in reference to a remedy for "blood that is too rich."

C. S. B.—We do not know of any "Civil Service Examination for Kindergarten teachers." Teachers in private or mission schools are appointed on the merits of diplomas they hold and their reputation as teachers. Teachers of public school Kindergartens must pass the usual "County Examinations" to teach in small towns, or the "School Board Examinations" for cities.

3 Everblooming Tea Roses

The Finest Kinds, White, Pink and Yellow

FOR 10c

Send 10c for the above three beautiful roses.

The Big Six Rose Offer for only 25c.
A Beautiful Hardy Moss Rose.
A Charming Everblooming Rose.
A Lovely Sweet Scented Tea Rose.
A Fine Perpetual blooming Hardy Rose.
A Magnificent Hardy Climbing Rose.
A Dainty Fairy or Polyantha Rose.
Think of it, the above collection of roses for only 25c.

6 Charming and Sweet Scented Tea Roses, lab'ls, 25c
6 Splendid Double Geraniums all colors, labeled, 25c
6 Beautiful Single Geraniums, fine assortment, 25c
6 Sweetest and Best Carnations, choice colors, 25c
6 of the Loveliest Fuchsias, Double and single, 25c
15 Plant Prize Chrysanthemums, all the colors. 25c
The Grand African Blue Lily, 25c

Send 10c for our beautiful catalogue full of original illustrations. Our Special Bargain edition is free to all.

McGREGOR BROS., Springfield, O.

An Automatic Chef
that will help you get up the daintiest meals without bother and at trifling cost—
NEW PERFECTION CHOPPER.

"Kitchen Knacks" with recipes by Mrs. S. T. Rorer tells you all about it. A postal brings it to you. **NORTH BROS. MFG. CO., Phila'd.**

MOTHER AND BABE.

A Book of Priceless Value for EXPECTANT MOTHERS, by Mrs. JENNESS MILLER, with Patterns for Maternity Dress, Adjustable Underarments, and for Baby's entire outfit, all for $1. Send bust measure for Mothers' patterns.
Book-list of 16 pages free.
JENNESS MILLER BOOK DEPT.,
141 Fifth Ave., New York.

DRESSMAKING SIMPLIFIED.

Any Lady Can now Learn to Cut Perfect-Fitting Dresses
with The McDowell Garment-Drafting Machine.

[illustrations of pattern pieces]

The ONLY improvement in the Tailors' Square ever Invented.

Easy to Learn. Rapid to Use. Follows Every Fashion. All first-class Dressmakers are adopting this Wonderful Garment-Drafting Machine.

ITS SUCCESS HAS NEVER BEEN EQUALLED.
You can test it at your own house for 30 days Free. Write now for Illustrated Circular and Liberal offer.

THE McDOWELL GARMENT-DRAFTING MACHINE CO.,
6 West 14th Street, New York.

ESTABLISHED **Dr. Scott's** 1878
GENUINE
ELECTRIC CORSETS.

Prefect in fit, durability and comfort possessing strong electro-magnetic curative powers, and is Nature's own remedy, affording instant relief in cases of Rheumatism, Lumbago, Debility, Liver and Kidney Affections, Spinal Troubles, Headache, Indigestion, Palpitation and Nervousness. They cure as the entire nerve system. The bust and hips will never wear any other. Our sale represents over Fifty City Corsets, made of fine Jean sateen cloth, in colors drab, white, in sure fit. We warrant it to be generally strong and durable article and a perfect fit.

GIVEN AWAY!

PRICE, $1.25. To introduce this Corset to the trade of Ten dressmakers, we will, until further notice, make the following inducement: send $1.10 for one of these beautiful Corsets and postage, and we will send you FREE, with the Corset postpaid, one of our

Dr. Scott's Electric Hair Curlers.

[illustration of hair curler]

Including all 50c. (one more than Corset sell) if the offer is good for one family.) This offer is made for a limited period only. As do not refuse sending on once, the book, **"THE DOCTOR'S STORY,"** giving full information concerning all our goods. Free on application.
GEO. A. SCOTT,
Agents Wanted. Room 1, 846 Broadway, N.Y.

HOW OFTEN DO YOU LOSE YOUR KNIFE?

Once usually—then it's gone for good. Not so with our

Novelty Knife

It tells the finder who you are and where you can be found. Also identifies you in case of accident. The handle is made of an indestructible, transparent composition, more beautiful than pearl. Beneath the handle are placed your name and address, photo of mother or friend, society emblem, lodge, etc. Blades are hand forged from the finest razor steel, workmanship perfect and a printed warranty is sent with each knife.

Two-bladed knife, men's $1 or $1.75, ladies, $1.50 to $1.75. Three bladed, boys' 75 cents, ladies $1 to $1.50. For each photo 25 cents additional. Handsome Christmas presents. Catalogue free. Send cash with order.
Agents Wanted, All-or— retail department.

NOVELTY CUTLERY CO., Box 107, Canton, O.

CARMEL SOAP

For the Toilet and Bath.
Made only from Sweet Olive Oil, by a mission society in Palestine, Syria. An absolutely safe soap for the nursery. No injurious substances. Recommended by physicians as the purest form of castile soap.
Sold by druggists and grocers. Imported by
A. KLIPSTEIN & CO., 122 Pearl St., New York City.

SPOONS FREE!

[illustration of spoons]

To introduce our goods quickly I make this liberal offer: I will give any lady One Dozen Tea Spoons, Heavy Silver plated, latest artistic design, warranted to wear, who will dispose of 1 dozen boxes of Hawley's Corn Salve (more warranted) among friends at 10c a box. I ask no money in advance, simply send your name; I mail you nice packages paid. When sold you send the money and I will mail you the 1 dozen handsome Tea Spoons. I also carry back if you can't sell. I run all the risk. Address

O. D. HAWLEY, Chemist, Berlin, Wis.

DRESS

Sample Copies, 15c.

The Newest and Brightest Fashion Publication ever offered to the American Public. It not only contains a choice selection of the Best and Most Practical Fashions for all Classes, but it Illustrates and Shows How to Cut Out the Latest Designs from Month to Month. This is the information LADIES SO MUCH DESIRE and NEED. Sample copies, 15 cents. $1.50 per year.
DRESS PUB. CO.,
132 W. 23d St., N. Y.

THE DELINEATOR

ANSWERS TO CORRESPONDENTS.
(Continued.)

LYSIA:—Your hair is a pretty shade of brown and we would certainly not advise bleaching it. Try inodorous castor oil for accelerating the growth of the brows and lashes.

ROSEBUD:—A lady neither talks to nor recognizes a man to whom she has not been formally introduced.

A SUBSCRIBER:—Do not wear a black dress trimmed with crape at a home wedding. On such an occasion young women in mourning have the alternative of wearing white, heliotrope or gray. Astrakhan or Persian lamb muffs are suitable during the mourning period.

L. A. S.:—Canary seed purchased from a seed merchant should be steeped in very hot water for twenty-four hours in order to soften the outer shell of the seed, which is very hard, before sowing. It would also expedite germination should either end of the seed be pared down until the white interior shows itself. Without these preliminaries the seed would take nearly six months to sprout. If the seed should be taken off a growing plant, and sown at once, without scooping in hot water, germination takes place within three or four weeks, according to circumstances.

MARION:—You will ascertain how to grow palms and other foliage plants successfully by reading "Parlor Plants and Window Gardening," which we publish at 1s. or 25 cents per copy.

(My mamma used Wool Soap)   (I wish mine had)
WOOLENS will not shrink if

Wool Soap

is used in the laundry.
Wool Soap is delicate and refreshing for bath purposes. The best cleanser. Buy a bar at your dealers. Two sizes; toilet and laundry.
RAWORTH, SCHODDE & CO., MAKERS, **CHICAGO.**
3 Chateau Street, Boston.
63 Leonard St., New York.   207 Chestnut St., St. Louis.

EMBROIDERY SILK HALF PRICE
Factory ends or waste embroidery silk at half price. Ounce package (assorted colors) sent post-paid for 40 cts. (One-half oz. package, 25 cts.) All good silk and good colors, 100 every stitches in each package. With an order for 4 oz. we give one extra ounce **FREE.**
Brainerd & Armstrong Silk Co.,
5 Union Street, New London, Conn.

The Help of

ANHEUSER-BUSCH'S

Malt-Nutrine

TRADE MARK.

turns weakness into strength, nourishes the nursing mother —vitalizes the debilitated.

Malt-Nutrine is the ideal Food Drink—the palatable nutriment of malt and hops.

To be had at all druggists' and grocers.

Prepared by
Anheuser-Busch Brewing Ass'n,
S'. Louis, U. S. A.

Send for handsomely illustrated colored booklet and other reading matter.

Cures While You Sleep
Whooping Cough Croup, Asthma, Catarrh
Prevents the spread of contagious diseases by acting as a powerful disinfectant, harmless to the youngest child. Sold by druggists. Valuable booklet free.
Vapo-Cresolene Co., 69 Wall St., N. Y.

Hall's Bazar Forms.

 **INDISPENSABLE IN THE HOUSEHOLD AND INVALUABLE TO DRESSMAKERS.**
Send for Catalogue showing large assortment and giving full particulars. Prices from $2.00 to $7.00.
Complete Form, as shown in this advertisement, adjustable to any size and when not in use folds like an umbrella, sent on receipt of $5.00.
The R. R. Appleton Co., 78 Franklin St., New York.
Complete Form, $5.00.   Mention Delineator.

Jackets $4, Suits, $8 and $9.

If you desire a stylish Suit or Cloak you should see our Winter Catalogue and samples. Write for it and we will also send our Bargain List of reduced prices on seasonable garments. Every lady should take advantage of this on e.
Suits at $8 and $10, reduced from $18 and $20. Jackets $4, reduced from $10 and $12. Capes $3, reduced from $6 and $8. Fur Capes $7, were $12.
We will also send a full line of samples of the goods from which we make our garments, to select from. We pay all express charges. Be sure to say that you wish the Winter Catalogue.
Our Spring Catalogue of Suits, Dresses, Silk Waists, Shirt Waists and Skirts will be ready February 15th. Write now and we will mail you a copy with samples as soon as issued. Be sure to say that you wish the Spring issue.
THE NATIONAL CLOAK CO.,
152 and 154 West 23rd St., New York.

Faces Fair

are made fairer with a touch of Tetlow's Gossamer Powder. It corrects the little mistakes of nature—imparts a delightful softness and a delicate beauty to the skin without becoming visible to the eye. Pure and harmless. Makes the skin *feel* well cared for. Be sure and get

HENRY TETLOW'S
Gossamer Powder.

Price 25c. by mail, or at druggists. Send to stamp for sample.
HENRY TETLOW,
Cor. 10th & Cherry Sts.,
PHILADELPHIA.

VELUTINA

Wonderfully Like Silk Velvet, is always Stamped on the Selvage.
"VELUTINA WEAR GUARANTEED."
See that the Name is Spelled:
V·E·L·U·T·I·N·A.

Warner's
Safe Cure

Ask your friends and neighbors about it

EMERSON PIANOS
60,000 SOLD
43 YEARS BEFORE THE PUBLIC.   MODERATE PRICES. TERMS REASONABLE.
SWEET TONED,   Every Instrument Fully Warranted.
SOLD ON MERIT.   *Catalogues Free.*
EMERSON PIANO CO., 92 FIFTH AVE. NEW YORK.
116 BOYLSTON ST., BOSTON, MASS.
218 WABASH AVE., CHICAGO, ILL.

REMEMBER that no Stocking will wear well or look well that does not fit well.

THE *Shawknit* IS THE **Best-Fitting**

IT IS THE ONLY STOCKING THAT IS

=KNITTED TO THE SHAPE OF THE HUMAN FOOT=

☞ THE TRADE-MARK *Shawknit* IS STAMPED ON THE TOE.

Descriptive Price-List, free, to any applicant.
Beautiful Castle Calendar, free, to any applicant mentioning this publication.

Shaw Stocking Co.
LOWELL, MASS.

In Buying a Piano or an Organ

do not fail to examine the latest Mason & Hamlin models. Recent improvements together with time-tested points of superiority render them instruments par excellence. Old pianos or organs taken in exchange. Instruments sold for cash or easy payment.

Catalogues and full information sent free.

Mason & Hamlin Co.
BOSTON. NEW YORK. CHICAGO.

Corticelli Sewing Silk.

Established 1838.
Unequalled for hand or machine sewing. This brand has been a winner of First Prizes for 57 years, having already been awarded

Fourteen Gold Medals

for Superiority.

Prudent buyers exercise care in selecting sewing material. If you find the name Corticelli on each spool of Silk, Twist and Worsted Braid, you need not hesitate, for it is reliable.

NONOTUCK SILK CO., New York, Boston, Philadelphia, Chicago, St. Louis, Cincinnati, St. Paul and San Francisco.

Purchasing Agency, Etc.

MISS C. F. MORSE, who refers by permission to THE BUTTERICK PUBLISHING CO. (Limited), wishes to announce that she is prepared to receive orders from those desiring her to purchase goods, her arrangements enabling her to fill orders, whether for large or small quantities, with despatch and at reasonable prices.

Dress Goods, Cloakings, Ladies' Infants' Wardrobes, Millinery, Trimmings, Publications, Stamping Patterns, Hand-made Laces, Accordion-Plaiting and Wall Paper, Netting and Lace Samples. Materials and Implements. In fact, all Materials and Implements for Fancy Work are Specialties in her business; but orders for other articles will be as punctually attended to and as carefully executed.

Parties who anticipate giving an order are requested, when writing for information as to prices, to enclose a 5c. stamp for reply and state the expense to which they wish their purchase limited. Those desiring a collection of samples must enclose 50 cents in payment for the time taken to procure them. As purchases can be made more satisfactorily with ready funds than upon terms of credit, no order will be accepted unless the full amount be sent with order. Address, with stamp,

MISS C. F. MORSE, 40 East 14th Street, New York, N. Y.

CORPUS LEAN		ABSOLUTELY HARMLESS.	
FAT	reduces fat at rate of 10 to 15 lbs. per month without injury to health. Send 4c. stamps for sealed circular containing testimonials. Le E. Marsh Co., 2815 Madison Sq., Philada., Pa.	MADE	Simply stopping the fat-producing effects of food. The supply being stopped, the natural working of the system draws on the fat and reduced weight at once. Sold by all Druggists.	LEAN

"Gives Such Comfort."

G-D

Chicago Waist

Price $1.00

Wear one and discover what real comfort means.
It allows perfect freedom of movement and perfect development of the body, gives grace to the form and imparts to the entire person a sense of absolute ease. Made of Sateen, white, drab or black. All dealers, or sent postpaid for $1.00.

GAGE-DOWNS CO., 268 Fifth Ave., CHICAGO.

Dress Your Walls

in tasteful clothes. Are you looking for artistic wall paper at the usual price? Give description of rooms and price you wish to pay, and we'll send dainty and attractive samples. Our little book tells you the practical side of home decoration—FREE on request. Large sample book for paper hangers, $1.00.

CHAS. M. N. KILLEN, 1231 Filbert St., Philadelphia, Pa.

ANSWERS TO CORRESPONDENTS.
(Continued.)

JUNIORITY:—The following treatment may benefit the spot left on your skin by a fly blister: Get your druggist to dissolve as much corrosive sublimate as will rest on a nickel in as little alcohol as will dissolve it. When dissolved, add eight ounces of soft or distilled water. Use the preparation according to the following directions, and strictly observe them, as the mixture is both poisonous and caustic. Apply with a bit of linen or flannel drawn over the tip of the finger, being careful not to wet the skin around the spot; apply two or three times a day. When the spot begins to burn, apply less often, but continue the treatment until the spot becomes rough and sore, as if it were blistered by the sun. The spot will for a few days look very much worse, and much darker, but the roughened skin will gradually scale off, and if the discoloration is simply on the under side of the outer cuticle, it will disappear, or become much lighter, in which case another course of the same treatment may entirely dispel it. The treatment will probably require three weeks, and afterward it will be advisable to occasionally apply the lotion—not to blister, but to bleach the spot. Perhaps the proportions given will make a mixture either too strong or too weak for your skin. If it burns too much at first, dilute a portion with water, and experiment until it is of the right strength for your case. If it does not burn at all, add half the original quantity of corrosive sublimate to the mixture and try it again. If the spot is over a scar, you may have to make the lotion stronger. Have the druggist put a poison label on the bottle, which should be kept where no one but yourself can get it.

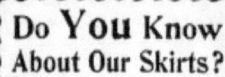

Do You Know About Our Skirts?

Our "Serpentine" Lustre Skirt

Is the neatest thing you ever saw. Made of "Lustre" Wool Sheeting—very latest texture, 3½ yards wide at bottom. Will not shrink, crush or wrinkle—Fits perfectly—hangs perfectly—wears perfectly. Price (as shown) $3.00: with Silk Shell edge, $3.50. Colors—Black, Navy Blue, Havana Brown.

Merritt's Skirts

Our "Cassimere" Felled Flannel Skirt is heavier than the Lustre Skirt. Made with French Lids and silk shell edge. Latest and most fashionable Flannel Skirt. Will not shrink—dust and mud do not stick. Colors—Black, Navy Blue, Cardinal and Gray. Price—(as shown), with silk shell edging..........$3.50
Without edging..........$2.00

Our Skirts are Guaranteed. Money refunded if not satisfactory. Merritt's Skirts are sold by all dealers. Ask to see them. Insist on getting them. They are "The Best." Badge on Catalogue free.

GEO. MERRITT & CO.
407 W. Washington St., Indianapolis, Ind.

ANSWERS TO CORRESPONDENTS.
(Continued).

AN OLD SUBSCRIBER:—Select green zibeline for your travelling costume, cutting it by pattern No. 8062, which costs 1s. 8d. or 40 cents, and is illustrated in THE DELINEATOR for December. White is always preferable for the bride's dress and satin is a safe choice. Shape it by pattern No. 8060, which costs 2s. or 50 cents. Brides still wear tulle veils, and gloves are proper.

MISS STREET:—You can restore tortoise shell by scraping it smooth and rubbing with fine sandpaper, repeating the rubbing with a bit of felt dipped in very finely powdered charcoal moistened with water and lastly with putty powder. Finish with a piece of soft wash leather moistened with a little sweet oil.

INEXPERIENCED MISS:—The hostess never accompanies a guest to the dressing-room. Some one should be appointed to direct the guests thither. She may introduce guests who happen to be near her to each other. A lady bows an acknowledgment when a man thanks her for a dance. We cannot tell you what to say on stated occasions. Reply as you think best, using the simplest language.

MARTHA:—A tailor-made gown, a few silk waists and a black crépon skirt would be sufficient wardrobe for a short trip. A travelling dress, hat and one a little more elaborate will suffice. The latter should be worn in attending the commencement exercises. If a street dress is assumed.

ONE-HALF SIZE OF BOX.

POZZONI'S
COMPLEXION POWDER

has been the standard for forty years and is more popular to-day than ever before.

POZZONI'S

is the ideal complexion powder—beautifying, refreshing, cleanly, healthful and harmless. A delicate, invisible protection to the face.

With every box of POZZONI'S a magnificent Scovill's GOLD PUFF BOX is given free of charge.

AT DRUGGISTS AND FANCY STORES.

HE WEARS COLLARS?

If you love him tell him about the Benedict Collar Button—the collar saver, time saver, temper saver.

Sold everywhere. Made by Enos Richardson & Co., 72 Malden Lane, New York.

Send postal for free Collar Book.

For SORE EYES use Dr ISAAC THOMPSON'S EYE WATER

CATALOGUE
FREE

Now is the time to buy a **PIANO** or **ORGAN** from the largest manufacturers in the world, who sell their instruments direct to the public at wholesale factory prices.

TERMS ...

REFERENCE ...

BUT DON'T BUY UNTIL YOU Write Us. BEETHOVEN PIANO & ORGAN CO., P. O. Box 801, WASHINGTON, N. J.

LE BOUTILLIER BROTHERS,
14th STREET, NEW YORK.

SPECIAL REDUCTION IN SILKS PRIOR TO STOCK TAKING.

BLACK SILKS.

Satin Duchesse, all silk, worth 99c.	65c.
Brocade Satin, new designs, $1.50 grade	69c.
Armure Royal, latest weaves, $1.25 grade	79c.
Satin Pékin Stripes, 7 different effects	79c.
Peau de Soie, heavy lustrous qual., $1.25 grade	89c.
Moiré Antique, very rich, $1.50 grade	89c.
Brocade Gros Grain, heavy quality	98c.

EVENING SILKS.

Brocade Silk, new designs, 59c. grade	39c.
China Silks, 60 different shades, 89c. grade	39c.
Brocade China, neat effective designs, 69c. grade	49c.
Moiré Taffeta, all color, 98c. grade	59c.
Brocade Satin, rich designs, $1.50 grade	69c.
Printed Warp Satin, latest novelty	85c.
Brocade Satin, extra heavy quality, $1.50 grade	98c.

COLORED SILKS.

Fancy Taffeta, changeable effects, 89c. grade	59c.
Faille Française, all pure silk, $1.00 grade	69c.
Moiré Française, heavy quality, $1.25 grade	79c.
Satin Duchesse, heavy lustrous quality, $1.75	89c.
Brocade Satin, changeable effects, $1.50 grade	$1.00
Printed Warp Taffeta, very stylish	1.39
Trimming Velvets, all shades	49c. to 2.00
Black Cooking Velvets	$1.75 to 4.50

DRESS GOODS, CLOTHS AND CLOAKINGS.

40-inch Autumn Novelties, Mohair, Silk-and-Wool, Exclusive Styles	49c.
46-inch French Cashmeres, Full Colorings	59c.
46-inch Imperial Serges, latest shades	39c.
35-inch Mohair and Worsted Novelties	59c.
45-inch Silk-and-Wool Novelties	$1.25
40-inch Silk-and-Wool Lansdowne	89c.
52-inch Scotch Tweeds, Heather Mixtures	69c.
54-inch Bouclé Novelties	$1.00, $1.25, $1.50
50-inch French Broadcloths for tailor suits and capes, unsurpassed by any $2.25 in the market, per yard	$1.25
54-inch Novelty Cloakings, 98c., $1.25, $1.75 to $3.50
50-inch Silk Seal-Plush for Capes and Jackets	$2.98 to $3.98
50-inch English Astrakhans	$2.98 to 6.50

BLACK DRESS GOODS.

56-inch English Storm Serges	85c.
44-inch French Jacquards	79c.
44-inch Worsted Storm Serge	98c.
50-inch Mohair and Worsted Novelties	$1.00
50-inch Fancy Worsted Suiting	85c.

In addressing us, direct all letters to **14th Street.**

LONG SUÉDE GLOVES.

SPECIAL OFFERING of Ladies' Long Suède Mousquetaire Gloves. Importers entire stock at about one-half value.

8-Button Length, White, black emb'd backs, 16-Button or Elbow Length, White, Grey, Pearl	88c.
Tan, Nile, Rose, etc., worth $2.50	$1.19
20-Built-in Length, Tans, Gray, Pearls, Modes or White, worth $3.00	1.50
24 and 30-Button Lengths, on evening tints	2.50
4 Pearl-Button, or Foster 7-hook, Kid	.79
Glacé Kid, embroidered back or Paris print	.93
Pique Seam Kid Gloves, 4-button	.98
Men's Dog-Skin Gloves, worth $1.00	.79
Misses' Kid Gloves, Tan and Red	.69

New Winter Jacket of Rough Bouclé Cloth, shield front, ripple back, full sleeves, value $7.98. **$4.98**
Same Style, finer cloth, reduced to...
$6.98, $7.48, $9.98 and $12.48

$4.98 $9.98

English Seal Plush Cape. Silk Lined.
Fur Trimmed, Full Sweep, was $15.00 **$9.98**
For Capes, plain and fur trimmed,
$4.98, $5.98, $7.98, $12.48 to $19.98

New Separate Skirts in Serge	3.98 4.98
New Separate Skirts in Crépons	3.98 to 12.98
All-Wool Moreen Under-skirts, full Ruffle	$1.98, $2.49, $2.98 and $3.98

UPHOLSTERY DEPARTMENT.

Nottingham Lace Curtains, per pair, 79c. to	$3.50
Antique and Cluny Lace Curtains, $2.98 to	25.00
Real Tambour Lace Curtains	4.98 to 24.98
Real Irish Point Lace Curtains	2.50 to 15.00
Marie Antoinette Lace Curtains	8.98 to 15.00
Brocade Silks, 50-inch wide, per yd., 1.69 and 1.75
French Tapestry, silk stripes	1.25 and 1.50
Turkish Tapestry for Couch Covers, 50c. to	9.98
Flax Velvet Covers, 1½ yard square	$2.98
Bagdad Couch Covers	$1.98 to 4.98
Turkish Kis Kilm Rugs	3.98 to 7.50

CLEAN HANDS.

Every body buys a STOVE POLISHING MITTEN at sight. Polishes the stove better and quicker than a brush. Sample by mail, 25 cents, 5 sets, $1.00. New England Novelty Mfg. Co., 249 Portland St., Boston, Mass.

AGENTS can make $3 to $5 per day. Circulars free.

xiv THE DELINEATOR.

On this and Page 16 is illustrated an Assortment of Patterns for

INFANTS' GARMENTS,

which many mothers will no doubt be pleased to inspect.

The Patterns can be had from Ourselves or from Agents for the Sale of our Goods. In ordering, please specify the Numbers desired.

The Butterick Publishing Co. (LIMITED), 171 to 175, Regent St., London, W.; or 7 to 17 W. 13th St., New York.

7479 7479
Infants' Cloak, with Cape Sewed to a Yoke (Copyright). One size: Price, 10d. or 20 cents.

8054
8054
Infants' Cloak (To be Made with or Without a Ripple Pointed Collar) (Copyright). One size: Price, 10d. or 20 cents.

W.B. CORSETS

Gracefully Fitting Corsets

W. B. Corsets add beauty and grace to any variety of figure and can be had as easily as the awkward, uncomfortable kind. Made with 4, 5 and 6-hook clasps and in short, medium, long, and extra long waists.

Prices, $1.00 to $5.00 per pair. Insist on having W. B. Corsets. If your dealer does not keep them, write to

W. B., 62 Walker St., New York.

6851 6851
Infants' Cloak (Copyright). One size: Price, 7d. or 15 cents.

8055 8055
Infants' Pompadour Yoke Dress, having a Straight Lower Edge for Hemstitching (Copyright). One size: Price, 10d. or 20 cents.

7354 7354
Infants' Dress (Copyright). One size: Price, 10d. or 20 cents.

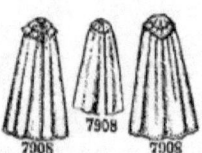

7908 7908
Infants' Long Cape (Copyright). One size: Price, 10d. or 20 cents.

7592 7592
Infants' Dress or Slip, with Straight Lower Edge for Hemstitching (Copyright). One size: Price, 7d. or 15 cents.

7656 7656
Infants' Present Dress or Slip (In Dress Reform Style) (Copyright). One size: Price, 7d. or 15 cents.

7895 7895
Infants' Yoke Dress (Copyright). One size: Price, 10d. or 20 cents.

Infants' Wrapper (Copyright). One size, 7d. or 15 cents.

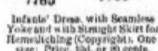

7785 7785
Infants' Dress, with Seamless Yoke and with Straight Skirt for Hemstitching (Copyright). One size: Price, 10d. or 20 cents.

7803 7803
Infants' Dress, with Round Yoke and with Straight Skirt for Hemstitching (Copyright). One size: Price, 10d. or 20 cents.

7534 7534
Infants' Dress, with Straight Lower Edge for Hemstitching (Copyright). One size: Price, 10d. or 20 cents.

897 897
Infants' Tucked Slip or Night-Gown (Copyright). One size: Price, 7d. or 15 cents.

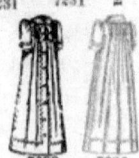

7030 7030
Infants' Wrapper (Copyright). One size: Price, 7d. or 15 cents.

THE TRUMPETER'S CALL

is obeyed by the soldier who hears its note no more implicitly than the call of fashion is followed by those who are socially correct.

The Whiting Paper Co.

are the largest manufacturers of fine correspondence papers in the world, and their product is recognized by society everywhere as being the highest grade and most suitable for polite correspondence.

Your dealer will show you samples; if not, write us.

WHITING PAPER COMPANY,
Holyoke. New York. Philadelphia. Boston. Chicago.

898 898
Infants' Night-Gown or Slip (Copyright). One size: Price, 7d. or 15 cents.

7391 7391
Infants' Slip or Night-Gown (Copyright). One size: Price, 7d. or 15 cents.

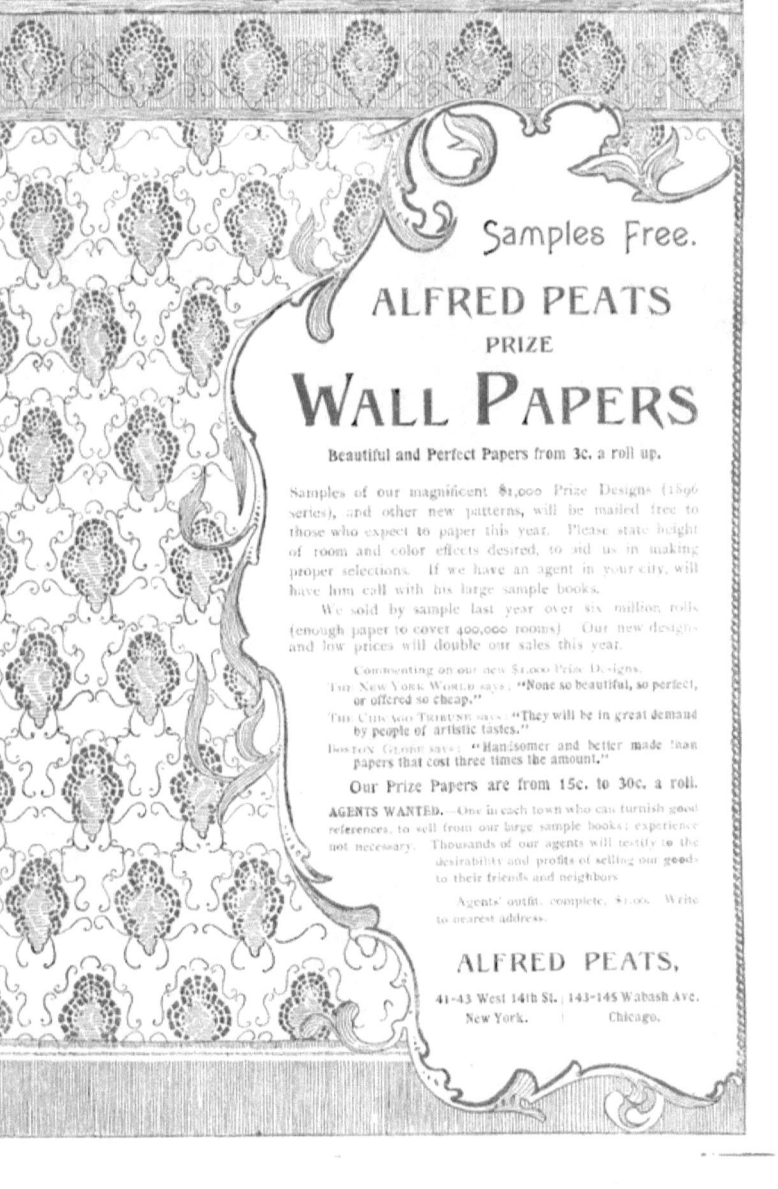

Ostrich Feather Collar.

$2.98

Ladies' 20-inch black ostrich collar. A wonderful bargain at the price, postage included, $2.98. extra full feather

Jordan, Marsh & Co.
Boston, Mass.

A HELPING HAND

WOMEN suffering from any form of female weakness are requested to communicate promptly with Mrs. Pinkham, at Lynn, Mass. All letters are received, opened, read and answered **by women only**. A woman can freely talk of her private illness to a woman; thus has been established the eternal confidence between Mrs. Pinkham and the women of America. This confidence has induced more than 100,000 women to write Mrs. Pinkham for advice during the last few months.

Think what a volume of experience she has to draw from! No physician living ever treated so many cases of female ills, and from this vast experience surely it is more than possible she has gained the very knowledge that will help your case.

She is glad to have you write or call upon her. You will find her a woman full of sympathy and a great desire to assist those who are sick. If her medicine is not what you need, she will frankly tell you so, and there are nine chances out of ten that she will tell you exactly what to do for relief. She asks nothing in return except your good will, and her advice has relieved thousands.

Surely any ailing woman, rich or poor, is very foolish if she does not take advantage of this generous offer of assistance. Read the following illustration:

DEAR MRS. PINKHAM:
In March I wrote you the following letter, asking you if your remedies would aid me:—"I am twenty-eight years old, and have three children. I suffer terribly with pain in the small of the back, dizziness, kidney trouble, nervousness, burning sensation in my stomach, and I am unable to do anything." I received a reply, a very kind helpful letter. I followed your advice. To-day, I am glad to be able to write that I am a well woman. I wish all women in my way afflicted would do as I did, and they will find relief. I think any woman who will continue to suffer with any of these trying diseases peculiar to our sex after hearing what Lydia E. Pinkham's Vegetable Compound has done in so many cases, is responsible for her own sufferings.
MRS. JAMES J. HAGAN, 3842 Clinton St., Nicetown, Phila., Pa.

Three Books Worth Getting—"Guide to Health," "Woman's Beauty, Peril, Duty," "Woman's Triumph."—These are FREE

Lydia E. Pinkham Medicine Co., Lynn, Mass.

GOOD HEALTH

is a blessing. Worms cause more sickness of a serious nature, especially in children, than any other known disorder. They cause sleeplessness, irritability, loss of appetite, convulsions and are often the cause of death of

CHILDREN

If your little ones are ailing without apparent cause, you may be sure they are afflicted with worms. To obtain immediate relief and get rid of stomach, seat and pin worms, use

KICKAPOO
Indian Worm Killer

It is purely vegetable, absolutely harmless and positively effectual. To convince you of its merits we will mail you a package FREE if you will mention this paper.

Healy & Bigelow, New Haven, Conn.

FREE.

GIVEN TO EVERY LADY
A New Book on Fancy Work containing 50 handsome Illustrations. Among them are designs for Sofa Pillows, Table Covers, Scarfs, Tray Cloths, Doilies, Celluloid Work, Tapestry Painting and Embroidery; also another book giving directions how to make all kinds of Rugs and Mats, &c., &c., &c. These two books we'll send you free if you will send 10¢ for a 3 months' trial subscription to The Home, a 20 page paper containing stories, fashions and fancy work illus'd. Send to **The Home, 113 Milk St., Boston, Mass.**

VOSE
ESTABLISHED 1851
PIANOS

OVER 34,000 SOLD.
Distinctly Superior and Up to Date.

Highest Award Columbian Exposition, 1893, for Tone, Touch, Scale, Action, Design, Material, Construction.

MONTHLY PAYMENTS TAKEN.
Delivered, Freight Prepaid, at your home.
Send for Handsome Illustrated Catalogue, FREE.
VOSE & SONS PIANO CO.
174 Tremont Street, Boston, Mass.

THE DELINEATOR.

ANSWERS TO CORRESPONDENTS.
(Continued.)

N. F. B.:—Relative to a course in shorthand, write to W. G. Chaffee, Oswego, N. Y., quoting THE DELINEATOR in your letter.

MILLARD:—There are many prettily figured silks of subdued shades that are far more appropriate for elderly ladies than those of plain white. Hair jewelry is entirely out of date. Machine poetry is verse without poetic significance—rhymed platitudes, doggerel.

JAMES:—Mandolin and Paquin sleeves are likely to remain in vogue for some time. The blue serge dress is quite seasonable for travelling.

L. P. E.:—White satin duchesse will make a pretty bridal costume. Drape the bodice with a fichu of Brussels point and continue it to the waist with a belt of satin. The bridesmaids' gowns could be of white China silk adorned with lace and baby ribbon, and they may wear Gainsborough hats of white velvet turned up at one side with pink roses and white plumes. The bride may carry white and the bridesmaids pink roses. The travelling dress may be of green cloth trimmed with white cloth and mink fur. The coat may be of the same material. The pulpit may be decorated with ferns and smilax.

The New Manhattan Mohair Skirt Binding

Yarn Dyed, Steam Shrunk and Fast Color.

Guaranteed for Quality and Durability.

If you cannot obtain this Braid from your dealer, send us 20 cents for a 5-yard piece of any color.

Manufactured by

THE CASTLE BRAID CO.
15 & 17 MERCER ST.
NEW YORK.

Windsor BICYCLES

The American Beauties For 1896
Win love at first sight and hold it. Bicycling should be pure happiness. It's sure to be if you ride a

Windsor... $85 and $100.
For Catalogue, Address
SIEG & WALPOLE MFG. CO., Kenosha, Wis.
Branch Houses:
Chicago—Milwaukee—Portland, Ore.
Address all correspondence to Kenosha, Wis.

C. C. WETHERELL,
122 and 124 Wabash Avenue, Chicago.

RIBBONS.

A beautiful Satin and Gros Grain Ribbon, full widths, and quality superior at the low prices: No. 5, 5¢; No. 7, 6½¢; No. 9, 8½¢; No. 12, 9½¢; No. 16, $1.75; No. 22, $2.80 per piece of ten yards. Write for samples of any ribbons you want. Terms net cash.

DURKEE'S SPICES & MUSTARD

**Guaranteed
Absolutely Pure
Highest Strength
Richest Flavors
Finer Goods
Cannot be Made**

E. R. DURKEE & CO.
NEW YORK
Your Grocer Keeps Them

TOOTH SENSE

Your address on a postal will bring a sample of Wright's Antiseptic Myrrh Tooth Soap. Gives beautiful teeth and sweet breath. Heals sore gums. Prevents decay. Large china box for 25¢ in stamps, postpaid, which includes a complete edition of Webster's Pocket Dictionary and Guide to Spelling.
Chas. Wright & Co., Chemists,
DETROIT, MICH.

FEMININE BEAUTY

PRESERVED. All blemishes of the face or form quickly removed by my celebrated Preparations. Brows and hair colored and restored. Flesh reduced or increased. Interesting book sent sealed for 2¢. With sample Creamolia Powder, 10¢. **Mme. EDITH Velaro**, 220 W. 80th St., N.Y.

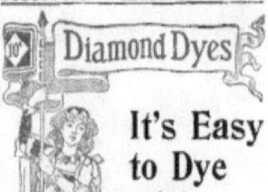

Diamond Dyes

It's Easy to Dye with Diamond Dyes

36 dyed samples of cloth and Book of Directions for Home Dyeing sent free; also beautiful lithograph card to any baby under two years.

WELLS, RICHARDSON & Co.,
BURLINGTON, VT.

SLEEP AND REST
For Skin Tortured
BABIES
And Tired
MOTHERS
In One Application of

Cuticura

SPEEDY CURE TREATMENT.—Warm baths, with CUTICURA SOAP, gentle applications of CUTICURA (ointment), and mild doses of CUTICURA RESOLVENT (the new blood purifier).

Sold throughout the world, and especially by English and American chemists at all principal cities. British depot: F. NEWBERY & SONS, 1, King Edward-st., London. POTTER DRUG & CHEM. CORP., Sole Props., Boston, U. S. A.

Mrs. ELEANOR GEORGEN, Private and Class Lessons in Delsarte Physical Culture, Development of the Voice, Elocution. Holland Building, Broadway & 40th Street, N. Y.

FREE PINS

Send your address on a postal, and we will mail you free, enough Puritan Pins, and a booklet about them, to forever convince you that they are the only pins that don't bend.

American Pin Co., Waterbury, Conn.

FLAVOR
For Soups
Gravies, Sauces, etc., can always be depended upon to be the best when cooks use pure, rich Extract of Beef like

Cudahy's Rex Brand

The Cudahy Pharmaceutical Co., South Omaha, Neb., send free copy of "Lunch Book," and for 4 cents in stamps valuable of CUDAHY'S REX BRAND.

CUDAHY'S
REX BRAND

THE DELINEATOR

ANSWERS TO CORRESPONDENTS.
(Continued.)

PAULINE:—We would not advise lightening the color of your hair and brows. Your writing shows character.

INQUIRER.—When peroxide of hydrogen is used to render superfluous hair brittle, so that it may be brushed away, it should be applied daily.

REINE:—Cone-shaped chicken croquettes obtain their shape from the use of a croquette mould. You can purchase individual jelly moulds.

R. M.:—A man may find pleasure in a woman's society and comradeship and may plainly show that he does, without wishing to marry her. It will be well for you to treat your friend exactly as you have heretofore.

L. E. H.;:—"Little Gem" calla requires the same treatment as the older variety of calla lily—that is, an alternate season of rest and growth. When at rest, water must be withheld. The bulbs you have used for Winter flowering in the house may be transferred to the open ground in the Spring. If not too much exhausted by the forcing process, they will rapidly increase in numbers; but in order to have them do this, they must be left undisturbed for several seasons.

SQUIRES' SOFA BEDS Are Standard.

The Leading Sofa Bed on the market for years.
Nothing but the best materials are used, and we guarantee our goods superior to all others for comfort, elegance and durability. Cut By Taken All Apart by Anyone. WE PAY THE FREIGHT.

SIDNEY SQUIRES & CO., Manufacturers,
329 Tremont Street, Boston.
Write for Catalogue and Prices.

Don't be backward
about saying
" I don't want it "
when the clerk tells you that some other kind is just as good as the

BIAS VELVETEEN SKIRT BINDING

If your dealer will not supply you, we will.

Send for sampler showing labels and make this sure S. H. & M. Co. P. O. Box 699 New York City.

BEDTIME
I TAKE
A
PLEASANT
HERB DRINK

THE NEXT MORNING I FEEL BRIGHT AND NEW AND MY COMPLEXION IS BETTER.
My doctor says it acts gently on the stomach, liver and kidneys, and is a pleasant laxative. This drink is made from herbs, and is prepared for use as easily as tea. It is called

LANE'S MEDICINE

All druggists sell it at 50c. and $1 a package. If you cannot get it, send your address for a free sample. Lane's Family Medicine moves the bowels each day. In order to be healthy this is necessary. Address ORATOR F. WOODWARD, LeRoy, N.Y.

"1847"
Rogers Bros.
Silver Plate that Wears

Make sure of the "1847" if you wish the genuine original Rogers Silverware.

Meriden Britannia Company

MERIDEN, CONN.
and Fifth Ave., NEW YORK.

New EMBROIDERY.
We send this the fine Linen Doily for the new "Jewel" work with assorted wash silk & Printed Instructions to work. Also a new Stamping Outfit which has Patterns for the new kinds of Embroidery—on Tiny Centerpieces and Kits, Doily for Lawns, others for Delft, Button-hole lace, Honiton and Scalloped edge work. Stamping Materials & Fancy Work Book, all for **40c.**
Walter P. Webber, Lynn, Mass., Box M

The "LINENE" are the best and Most Economical Collars and Cuffs made, they are made of fine cloth sides finished alike, and being reversible, one collar is equal to two of any other kind.
They fit well, look well and wear well. A box of ten Collars or Five Pairs of Cuffs for Twenty-five cents. A Sample Collar and Pair of Cuffs by mail for six cents. Name style and size. Address,
REVERSIBLE COLLAR COMPANY,
27 Franklin St., New York. 27 Kneeland St., Boston.

Eclipse Bicycles

are the net result of combining the choicest materials, the most skilful labor, an immense factory just completed and fitted with the latest machinery, almost human, ample capital and many years of experience, with an honest, persistent endeavor to give the public, for their hundred dollars, the very finest bicycle possible to build. We are justly proud of our wheels—they are highest possible grade and

Stand the Test.

Send for Catalogue.

Eclipse Bicycle Company
Elmira, N.Y. Drawer A.

THE AIR .... WE BREATHE Contains Oxygen and Nitrogen in the proportion of one to five.

Doctors Starkey & Palen's COMPOUND OXYGEN

contains Oxygen and Nitrogen—the former greatly in excess—ozone, and is very soluble in water. Heat liberates it. It is taken into the lungs by inhalation, absorbed by the blood, which it purifies and so goes directly to the seat of all diseases.

It has been in use for more than twenty-five years; thousands of patients have been treated; and over one thousand physicians have used it and recommend it—a very significant fact.

Send for our 200-page Treatise. Sent free.

Drs. STARKEY & PALEN,
1529 ARCH STREET,
PHILADELPHIA, PA.
SAN FRANCISCO, CAL. TORONTO, CANADA.

FREE! If sick or ailing, send name, age, sex, symptoms, 2-cent stamp, and I will send a Scientific Diagnosis of your disease and tell you what it will cure you. Address, J. C. Batdorf, M.D., Grand Rapids, Mich.

A 25c. GAME FOR 5c. "Johnny, Pipe the Puzzling, Amusing Game mailed FREE with catalogue for 5c. to cover postage, etc. Six Games for only 25c. M. C. BURKEL, 478 Nelson Ave., Jersey City, N.J.

YOU can now grasp a fortune. A new guide to rapid wealth, with 240 fine engravings, sent free to any person. This is a chance of a lifetime. Write at once. Lynn & Co., 48 Bond St. New York

PILLOW-SHAM HOLDERS. A full set of 3 for 15c. or 2 full sets for 25c. to any address, postpaid. Agents wanted. Directions and agreement with every set. **15 CENTS.** T. M. CANDY, Chester, Conn.

OLD COINS $5 to $500 reward for every old coin. Examine all coins received before 1878, and send 2 stamps for fully illustrated circular on the American and Foreign Coins. Agents wanted. National Coin Co., Cort St. Boston, Mass. **WANTED**

McPHAIL PIANOS

For 56 Years Made on Honor, Sold on Merit.

A Piano with a Reputation. Remarkable Singing Quality.

Inspection Invited.
Comparison Challenged.

CATALOGUE ON APPLICATION.

On account of the many applications from Poster Collectors for our Prize Poster, same will be sent in tubes (avoiding creasing) for 10c. in stamps.

A. M. McPHAIL PIANO CO.
520 Harrison Avenue,
Factory, Dept. C. BOSTON, MASS.

PERFECTION CAKE TINS.

Delicate Cake easily removed without breaking. Require no greasing. All style—round, square and oblong. Proof-free for prices. CAUTION—see Trade Mark. "Perfection" on all Improved Tins. Can't buy better. Made with a guarantee. Look for it.
Agents Wanted. RICHARDSON MFG. CO. 9-31 Bayv, N.Y.

ANY SHOES THAT YOU SELECT FROM OUR

Catalogue

Will Surely Please Your Feet.
Send for it. 14 pages, illustrated, and booklet, "Short and How to Wear Them," sent FREE, showing large variety of styles and prices for Men, Women and Children.

$3.50 THE FIT Kid Lace or Button. Many Shoes sold at $4.00 no better, **Fine Quality, Fine Fit,**

ALL SHOES DELIVERED FREE. Your money refunded if not satisfied with fit, quality and style. **Stylish, Easy.**

MANUFACTURERS' SHOE CO., 146 Mulu St., Jackson, Mich.

Ladies

Wanting permanent position with reliable house can do it, in doing sewing, knitting, etc., in their own homes, on machines such as they have or use, will make from $5 to $12 a week, where most of our workers are located. Reply with stamp. The Pelissier Co., South Bend, Ind.

LADIES. NO CHAPPED OR ROUGH HANDS in cold Winter weather, if you will send two cent stamp for information to MRS. H. N. BRIGGS, Lock Box 977, New Philadelphia, Ohio.

$500.00 REWARD for any case of CATARRH Treatment mailed FREE. London Analytical Association, Dept. 27, Cincinnati, O., U.S.A.

BOYS AND GIRLS who wish to make money out of school, send name, and we will tell you how; no money wanted. Dan'l Stayner & Co., Providence, R.I.

$100.00 in cash prizes for the best advertisement of our weak rubber-dye silks. Full particulars on application. Address, The Brainerd & Armstrong Co., Union Street, New London, Conn.

ANSWERS TO CORRESPONDENTS.
(Continued.)

M. E. W.:—You may impersonate a tambourine girl, Illyrian lady, Marguerite, Pocahontas, Portia, Desdemona or Amy Robsart at the ball. Suggestions for these costumes will be found in "Masquerade and Carnival," published by us at 2s. or 50 cents.

TAFFY:—To mould the face of a person in wax: take one pound of new wax and one-third of a pound of rosin; melt them over a slow fire and let them cool until you can endure some of the preparation on your hand without burning it; then, having thoroughly oiled the face with olive oil and covered the eye-lashes and eyebrows with paste, with a brush nimbly spread upon the face a coat of wax of about the thickness of a quarter of a dollar, being careful not to stop the nostrils, and that the eyes are not closed firmly enough to wrinkle the face. When cool enough, take the wax mask off gently and strengthen it with clay at the back, that it may not give way. In this way one may cast all kinds of faces—laughing, weeping or wry faces—also fruits or anything else, dividing the mould of any object entirely enclosed into two pieces with a warm knife and, after fortifying them with clay, rejoining them.

A Perfect Complexion ASSURED BY USING "CHARMANT" TURKISH WONDER BALM AND SOAP.

Absolutely harmless. Guaranteed to remove freckles, pimples, black-heads, moles, or money refunded. Used for centuries in Turkey and Throughout the continent. Well-known remedies from eczema at once. It renders the skin smooth and velvety and gives a natural, rosy complexion. Not a cosmetic, but composed of herbs and balms. Price, Balm, $1; soap, $1. Sent free by mail. Should be used together for best results. Remit by Postal or Express Order or Registered Letter. Send stamp for circular. Imported and sold Agents for C. TURKISH BALM CO., 19 Union Square, New York.

HOW TO MAKE WOMEN BEAUTIFUL

Many women with fair faces are deficient in beauty owing to undeveloped figures, flat busts, etc., which can be remedied by the use of

ADIPO-MALENE.

It is impossible to give a full description in a newspaper, and in answer to a description we color, with full particulars, will be sent you, sealed, by return mail.

L. E. MARSH & CO., Madison Sq., Phila., Pa.

THE DELINEATOR.

ANSWERS TO CORRESPONDENTS.
(Continued).

RENA:—You can order henna or alkenna through any druggist.

ALOETHES:—You might register your name at a dramatic agency or apply to the managers of theatres in person with reference to securing a chance to act. But unless you have phenomenal gifts or a fortune to spend, the chances of obtaining a hearing are discouragingly small. The Dramatic Mirror and Freund's Musical Weekly, both published in New York, are devoted to music and drama.

M. L. M. R.:—People of culture always thank others, of whatever station, for any service rendered.

A SUBSCRIBER:—Pretty designs for shawls to be made of ice wool are given in our new book entitled "Fancy and Practical Crochet-Work," which we publish at 2s. or 50 cents.

CLARA P.:—You can easily enlarge the sections of the sofa-pillow illustrated in THE DELINEATOR for November by adding an equal amount of material to each edge.

The woman pinned down

to one or two uses of Pearline will have to be talked to. Why is she throwing away all the gain and help that she can get from it in other ways? If you have proved to yourself that Pearline washes clothes, for instance, in the easiest, quickest, safest way, you ought to be ready to believe that Pearline is the best for washing and cleaning everything. That's the truth, anyway. Try it and see. Into every drop of water that's to be used for cleansing anything, put some Pearline. 61

Mothers Should
SEND FOR SAMPLES OF OUR . . . . .

Boys' Knee Pants.

We take remnants of **Fine Woolens** from our Merchant Tailoring Department and make them up into **BOYS' KNEE PANTS**, which we retail for **50 cts., 75 cts.** and **$1.00.**

SEND FOR SAMPLES.

MILLS & AVERILL,
BROADWAY and PINE ST.,
St. Louis, Mo.

The modern ready-to-use stove paste.

A bright gloss in half the time of other polishes. No dust, no dirt, no trouble. See that you get the genuine.

All dealers.

CREATES A PERFECT COMPLEXION

Mrs. Graham's **Cucumber and Elder Flower ..Cream**

It cleans, whitens and beautifies the skin. It feeds and tones up tissues, closes banishing wrinkles. It is harmless as dew, and as nourishing to the skin as dew is to the flower. Price $1. at drug stores and sent anywhere prepaid. Sample Size Bottle 10c. Hair-dresser's book "How to be Beautiful" free. Agents Wanted! Mrs. GERVAISE GRAHAM, 103 Michigan Av., Chicago. Eastern Branch: 21 W. 14th St., New York.

Something New and Good for
WOMEN
Pearl Corset Shields made without steels or bones. Do not enlarge the waist. They heal finely prevent Corsets Breaking and will make a Broken Corset as good as new. Sold everywhere. Prepaid on receipt of 25c. and corset size.

LADY AGENTS make $3 to $5 a day. Send at once for terms. **Eugene Pearl, 23 Union Square, New York.**

L. SHAW
Established 35 years.
**THE LARGEST
Hair and Toilet Bazaar in America.**
Perfect fitting WIGS, and WAVES, SKELETON BANGS, the latest styles. NATURAL WAVY SWITCHES, COCOANUT BALM for complexion; cures pimples, makes the skin soft, fresh and fair as a child's, price 50c. and $1.00. EXTRACT TURKISH ROSE LEAVES, for the lips and face, imparts the natural bloom of youth, $1.00 and $1.50. MAGIC TONIC, softens and beautifies the hair, prevents it from falling out, 50c. and $1.50. HAIR DYES of all colors of hair. Book "How to be Beautiful," mailed free.

54 W. 14th St., near 6th Ave., N. Y.

MENNEN'S
BORATED TALCUM
TOILET POWDER

Approved by highest medical authorities as a Perfect Sanitary Toilet Preparation for Infants and Adults. Positively relieves Prickly Heat, Nettle Rash, Chafed Skin, Sunburn, etc. Removes Pimples, Pimples and all Skin Blemishes. Delightful after shaving. Recommended by The Ben, Sprinkler Top. Sold by Druggists or mailed for 25 cents. (Name this paper.) Sample by mail.

FREE

Gerhard Mennen Co., Newark, N. J.

STAMMERING.
GIBBON'S STAMMERING SCHOOL.
Room 66, Mass. Building, Kansas City, Mo.

BUTTERFLY PANSY
Table Mat, stamped on Fine White Linen, and Illustrated Catalogue of Centerpieces, Table Mats, etc. all for 15c. Address, J. F. Ingalls, Lynn, Mass., Box D.

EUREKA TAPES.
Our New, Low-Priced, Durable and Accurate Tape-Measures.

WE GUARANTEE THE QUALITY!   NOTE THE PRICES!

Each 60 inches long, and numbered both sides in inches.

No.		Each. Per doz.
1,	Linen, Stitched,	5c. 40c.
2,	Super-Linen, Wide, Stitched,	10c. 60c.
3,	Sateen, Sewed,	20c. $1.50
4,	Super-Sateen, Sewed,	20c. 2.00
5,	Super-Sateen, Wide, Sewed,	25c. 2.50

Order by Numbers. Cash to accompany all orders. Tapes ordered at the retail rates will be sent by mail, prepaid, to any address in the United States, Canada, Newfoundland or Mexico. When ordered at dozen rates, transportation charges are to be paid by the party ordering, at the rate of 3 cents per dozen. Rates by the gross furnished on application. We cannot allow dozen rates on less than half a dozen of any style ordered at one time, nor gross rates on less than half a gross.

THE BUTTERICK PUBLISHING CO., (Limited), 7 to 17 West 13th Street, New York.

LADIES WE WILL SEND FREE

our unique and interesting pamphlet, giving some interesting points on Wringers etc. How important it is to get our soft rubber rolls, etc. We are the largest makers of Rubber Rolls and Wringers in the world.

Capital $4,500,000. When you are warranted on rolls you you know your wringer will give good service and wear well. Send postal for pamphlet.

AMERICAN WRINGER COMPANY, 52 Chambers Street, New York.

THE DELINEATOR.

ANSWERS TO CORRESPONDENTS.
(Continued.)

R. E. B.—A wooden wedding could be postponed on account of illness.

MAE.—Violet sachet powder is largely composed of powdered orris or Florentine iris and this alone put among the linen in bureau drawers will impart a faint but very sweet odor of violets.

A WONDER.—Walnut stain comes in liquid form and is simply applied to the hair with a sponge. It can be procured ready for use from any druggist or through Miss C. F. Morse, 40 E. 14th Street, N. Y.

A DEVOTED READER.—There have been cases on record where lead palsy, lead colic and brain troubles have ensued from using certain hair dyes, but we have heard of no worse results from the use of peroxide of hydrogen than the color which it imparts to the hair.

INK SPOTS.—Ink stains are of two kinds, analine and nut galls. Many inks now made are analine, so it is always best to treat all ink stains first with diluted tartaric acid, increasing its strength until the spot begins to disappear. Should this acid, however, have no effect, then treat as for ink made from nut galls. The material containing the spot is spread out tightly over a bright, hot tin plate and rubbed with a hot solution of oxalic acid, using a piece of iron to rub with—an iron key for instance. It often happens that in silk goods nothing can be done to remove the stain.

Its Graceful, Intelligent Construction
makes the
Ben-Hur Bicycle
lightest, strongest, swiftest of all. It represents the highest art in bicycle construction—graceful design and splendid finish. Four elegant models—$85 and $100. Catalogue free. Write

CENTRAL CYCLE MFG CO.,
99 Garden St., Indianapolis, Ind.

Going to Build a Home?
If you are, begin right. Get our beautiful book of Designs and Plans.

"ARTISTIC HOMES No. 2"
richly illustrated—entirely new. The most unique book published. Ten Cents in silver pays for it.

GEO. F. BARBER & CO., Architects, Box 26, Knoxville, Tenn.

A STOCKING FOOT PATTERN
for footing worn-out stockings, and cut so that the seams will not hurt the feet, will be mailed you on receipt of 10 cents

ECONOMY PATTERN CO.
P. O. B. 457. Reading, Pa.

You Dye in 30 minutes
if you use Tuck's French Dyes. No other dye like them. Dye cotton as permanently as wool. Our turkey red for cotton won't wash, boil or freeze out—all others will. Carpets, dresses, capes and clothing of all kinds had to look like new. No failures with Tuck's dyes; any one can use them. Send 6c. for 6 pkg. or 10c. for 10c—any color. Big pay to agents. Apply now and mention this paper.

FRENCH DYE CO., Vassar, Mich.

LEADING POINTS ABOUT THE FAMOUS MACHINE MADE Ceylon TEA

Ceylon TEA AROMA, FLAVOR, PURITY, STRENGTH
"TWO CUPS IN ONE"

SEWING MADE EASY.
The... **Lightning** TRADE MARK **Needle.**

Lightning Needles are tapped from centre to eye, one push is sufficient to pass the entire needle through the fabric. Try it once and you will use no other. The eyes of Nos. 4, 5 and 10 are as large as those in 5, 6 and 7 of other makes. If you cannot get them from your merchant, send 5 cents for each paper desired to

THE LIGHTNING NEEDLE CO.,
16 to 22 Washington Place, New York City.

Mme. McCABE'S CORSETS
Ladies, if you would have the most perfect corset made, try this style. Endorsed by thousands now wearing them. SIDE UNBREAKABLE. Handsomely illustrated catalogue of Corsets and Health Waists, with prices, free **St. Louis Corset Co., Mfrs.,** by mail. 19th and Morgan Sts., Department C. ST. LOUIS, MO.

Lady Agents Wanted.

Bone your dresses with R. & G. Festina Dress Stays.

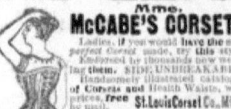

FREE TO BALD HEADS
We will mail on application, free information how to grow hair upon a bald head, stop falling hair and remove all dandruff.
Address,
Altenheim Med. Dispensary,
132 East Third Street,
Cincinnati, O.

THERE'S NO EXCUSE
For having freckles, blackheads, tanned, red, spotted, scaly, oily or muddy skin, pimples, boils, eczema, rashes, etc., when

Derma-Royale —banishes—

easily, quickly and forever removes and cures every blemish and makes the skin clear, soft and beautiful. There is nothing like it. Leading actresses, professional beauties, society ladies and people of refinement everywhere eagerly unite in its praise. Hundreds of testimonials with portraits will be sent free to anyone who writes for them. Derma-Royale is the best skin preparation in the world. We will give $500 cash for any case it fails to cure. Wherever it is once tried everybody wants it, so we are determined to introduce it everywhere, and will send you a full-sized

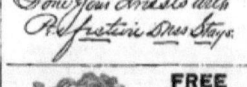

$1 BOTTLE FREE
if you will talk it up among your acquaintances. Send us your full post-office address today.
The DERMA-ROYALE CO., Cincinnati, O.

The Quarterly Report of Metropolitan Fashions
Includes a Collection of Beautiful Colored Plates Illustrating the Incoming Styles for Ladies and Children.

THE dates of issue of the QUARTERLY REPORT are for the months of March, May, September and November. Each number includes a handsome CHROMO-LITHOGRAPHIC PLATE, 24x30 inches in size, illustrating Fashions for Ladies, **Three Small Plates of Ladies' Figures** and a Magazine containing descriptions in **English, Spanish** and **German.**

Subscription Price of the Quarterly Report, as described above, **5s. or $1.00** a Year.
Single Copies of the Quarterly Report, comprising all the Plates and Descriptive Book, ... **1s. 6d. or 37 Cents.**
Any of the small Plates, 5d. or 10 Cents.

"THE QUARTERLY REPORT," sent by mail to any part of the United Kingdom, United States, Canada, Newfoundland or Mexico, is post-paid by us. When the Publication is ordered to be sent on Subscription to any other country, 10d. or 20 cents extra for postage must accompany the Subscription Price.

Revista Trimestral de las Modas Metropolitanas
incluye una colección de Hermosos Grabados Iluminados Mostrando los Últimos Estilos para Señoras y Niños.

LA REVISTA TRIMESTRAL se expide para los meses de Marzo, Mayo, Setiembre y Noviembre.

Cada número contiene las descripciones en **Inglés, Español** y **Alemán.**

Precios de Suscripción á la Revista Trimestral, según doctrina, **$1.25, oro, ó 6 Pesetas** 25 Centimos al Año.
Un Ejemplar de la Revista Trimestral, incluyendo todos los Grabados y el Libro con las Descripciones, **50 Centavos, oro, ó 2 Pesetas 50 Centimos.**
Cualquiera de los Grabados Pequeños, 10 Centavos, oro, ó 50 Centimos.

Der Quartal-Bericht über Moden
enthält eine Sammlung von hübschen kolorirten Modebildern, welche die neu hinzukommenden Moden für Damen und Kinder bringen.

DER QUARTAL-BERICHT erscheint im März, Mai, September und November.

Die Modebilder begleitet ein Journal, welches Beschreibungen in **englischer, spanischer** und **deutscher** Sprache enthält.

Abonnementspreis des Quartal-Berichts, wie oben beschrieben, ... **6 M. Per Jahr.**
Einzelner Exemplare des Quartal-Berichts, aus allen Modebildern und dem Buche der Beschreibungen bestehend, ... **2 Mark.**
Jedes der kleinen Modebilder, . . . 40 Pf.

THE BUTTERICK PUBLISHING CO. (Limited),
7 to 17 West Thirteenth St., New York, U. S. A.   171 to 175, Regent St., London, England.

ANSWERS TO CORRESPONDENTS.
(Continued.)

ROWENA:—In paying formal visits wraps are not removed. Jellies are served on jelly dishes and eaten from a fork. Use the old velvet again on the hat, freshening it by the steaming process. Half-shell oysters are eaten from a fork. Suède gloves are undressed kid. The word is pronounced "swade."

FLUSH:—If rice powder is lightly applied to a face habitually red, it will cool the skin and reduce and conceal the redness to some extent, but the better recourse is proper diet, plenty of exercise and a general observance of all hygienic laws.

SWEET SIXTEEN:—Iron is the tonic generally given to strengthen the blood. If your pallor results from ill health, place yourself under the care of a good physician.

AN ACTRESS:—A very small amount of pure, refined, white coppers dissolved in a pint of water is an excellent wash for inflamed eyelids; but it must be carefully used, as taken internally it is a deadly poison. Use a bit of linen to bathe the eyes, getting some of the lotion under the lids. Cocoa butter applied to the lashes is said to make them grow.

N. M. P.:—If simple remedies have failed you might, as you suggest, investigate some of the methods for developing the bust advertised in THE DELINEATOR.

TRIXY:—A lady who visits her fiancé without her chaperon when no other members of the family are at home makes herself liable to much criticism.

STARVED TO DEATH in midst of plenty. Unfortunate, yet we hear of it. The Gail Borden Eagle Brand Condensed Milk is undoubtedly the safest and best infant food. *Infant Health* is a valuable pamphlet for mothers. Send your address to the New York Condensed Milk Company, New York.

When you see the stamp B. & H. on a lamp, you can rest assured that you are getting the best. Our reputation for making the finest possible work will always be maintained.

"Little Book" sent free on application, telling more about the lamps and also giving an idea of our very complete and beautiful line of Gas and Electric Light Fixtures, Art Metal Goods, etc.

BRADLEY & HUBBARD MFG. CO.,
MERIDEN, CONN.
New York. Boston. Chicago. Philadelphia.

GOLD!!

Ladies and Gentlemen investing $10 per month for ten months in our 5 per ct. bonds receive $1000 in Gold as a premium. No risk. Loss impossible. Highest references. Particulars free. WILCOX & CO., Brokers, 529 Broadway, New York City.

The Quarterly Report of Juvenile Fashions

is issued for March, May, September and November, and comprises a handsome Lithographic Plate, and a book containing Illustrations of the Latest Styles of Juvenile Clothing, with Descriptions in **English, Spanish** and **German.**

The terms on which the Publication is furnished are as follows:

Subscription Price, ... 4s. or 75 Cents.
Single Copy, ... 1s. 3d. or 25 Cents.

Comprising the Plate and Descriptive Book.

Postage prepaid by us to any address in the United Kingdom, United States, Canada, Newfoundland or Mexico. When the Publication is ordered to be sent on Subscription to any other country, 10d. or 20 cents extra for postage is charged in addition to the Subscription Price.

La Revista Trimestral de Modas Juveniles

Se expide para Marzo, Mayo, Setiembre y Noviembre, y comprende una hermosa Lámina Litográfica y un Libro conteniendo Ilustraciones de los Últimos Estilos en Ropas para Niños, con Descripciones en **Inglés, Español** y **Alemán.**

Las Condiciones para obtener la Publicación son las siguientes:

Precio por Suscripcion, $1.00, oro, ó 5 Pesetas.
Cada Ejemplar, 30 Centavos, oro, ó 1 Peseta 50 Céntimos.

Incluyendo el Grabado y Libro Descriptivo.

Der Quartal-Bericht über Kinder-Moden

erscheint im März, Mai, September und November, und besteht aus einem prachtvollen Modebild und einem Buche, welches Abbildungen aller Moden-Neuheiten in Kinder-Kleidung, mit Beschreibungen in **englischer, spanischer** und **deutscher** Sprache, enthält.

Die Bedingungen unter welchen die Ausgabe erscheint sind folgende:

Abonnementspreis, - - 4 Mark.
Einzelne Exemplare, - M. 1.20.

Für Modebild und Buch der Beschreibungen beifolgend.

THE BUTTERICK PUBLISHING CO. (Limited),
7 to 17 West Thirteenth St., New York, U. S. A.   171 to 175, Regent St., London, England.

THE DELINEATOR.

EARN A BICYCLE! We want to introduce our Teas, Spices and Baking Powder. They are good and the prices reasonable. Sell 75 lbs. for us and we will give you a Safety Bicycle (Pneumatic Tire, A Solid Silver Watch for 25 lbs. sold or a Solid Gold Ring for $5 lbs. sold. These articles are within reach of bright boys and girls. Write for particulars to W. G. BAKER, 356 Main Street, Springfield, Mass.

BUGGIES SLEIGHS & HARNESS AT HALF PRICE. We Can the Prices & consult) $30 2-Pas.Sleigh $14.00 $20 Top Buggy... $9.97 1 Pas. Top Surrey $47 Buy at factory prices. $45 Road Buggy $23.00 $30 Road Buggies, $12.50 $10 Harness --- $4.75, some FREE. New Buggy Wheels painted and tired only 3-4 each U.S. BUGGY & CART CO., Clx, 1 Cincinnati, O.

PHOENIX BICYCLES
8th Year They Stand the Racket
High-grade in name and reality. We omit to be critical, and guarantee EVERY wheel Send for the catalogue. Stover Bicycle Mfg. Co., Freeport, Ill. Eastern Branch, 575 Madison Ave. New York, N.Y.

ANSWERS TO CORRESPONDENTS.
(Continued).

LACE-MAKER.—A few of the designs contained in our publication, "The Art of Modern Lace-Making," are of working size. Most of them are, necessarily, reductions.

MRS. S. W. R.—Black crepon will make a more stylish gown for your thin black hair. Cut it by pattern No. 8067, which costs 1s. 3d. or 40 cents, using either silk or percaline for lining. Capes will doubtless remain fashionable for a long time.

BEATRICE:—There is no process known to science which will harmlessly lessen the size of finger nails.

KAROS:—Any physician will remove superfluous hair by the use of the electric needle. Electrolysis is simply the administration to the root of the hair of the negative current of the galvanic battery by means of a needle.

PERPLEXED:—Make the dress by maternity gown No. 7669, which costs 1s. 3d. or 30 cents. It provides for lengthening the skirt as you desire.

WIDOW:—A widow uses her husband's Christian name upon her card. She is, for instance, Mrs. John Blank, just as when her husband was living.

M. V. L. K.:—Neither a tea-gown nor a blouse of the outer order is suitable for wear at breakfast in the dining-room of a hotel. Either a neat street dress or a fitted silk waist would be proper. In travelling, wear any plainly made suit of seasonable material that will not crush easily.

WOMEN WHO WHEEL
should seek a light bicycle, yet one in which strength is not sacrificed for light weight. The STEARNS Model C weighs but 22 pounds, yet is as staunch and graceful a wheel as one could wish for. The STEARNS Model B is of diamond frame pattern, built expressly for those who use the rational costume. Ease of running is another attribute of the STEARNS which all ladies appreciate. Send for beautiful new catalogue.
E. C. STEARNS & CO., Makers, Syracuse, N.Y. Buffalo, N.Y. Toronto, Ont. San Francisco, Cal.

Stamping Patterns Free. Stamping Outfit, 91 patterns, including original designs for napkins, doylies, etc. etc.

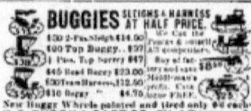

Marshall's Catarrh Snuff
the instant relief of Catarrh, Cold in the Head and Headache. Cures Deafness, restores lost sense of smell. Sixty years on the market. All Druggists sell it. 2c. per bottle. F.C. KEITH, Mfr., Cleveland, O.

THE ANCHOR ELECTRIC BELT.
AGENTS WANTED, BOTH SEX.

Goods sent to reliable persons to be paid for after arriving. W. H. Palmer, Glasgow, Conn., has sold 4,000 Belts, and as much as 30 in one day. The electricity from the batteries will turn a needle through your table, or hand. No one but who has worn them, Cures rheumatism, Liver and Kidney Disease, Weak and Lame Back, and other diseases. Prevents Cold Feet and taking Cold. Gives a comfortable glow of warmth all over the body, which shows that it is acting on the circulation. For advertising purposes we will give one Belt Free of Any Cost to one person in each locality. Address E. J. SMEAD & CO., Dept. M, Vineland, N. J.

How to Take Measures for Patterns.

Non-Breakable Corsets and Corset Waists
The finest in the world. We invite correspondence with every lady who reads this. Lady Agents wanted in every city and town. Our agents have wonderful success.
Price Lists and Retail Guide free.
RELIANCE CORSET CO., Merton Tin Delaware, Jackson, Mich.

Agents Local or travelling, ladies or gents, make good wages selling
National Patent Dish Washer.
National Patent Dish Washer, best made, simple, durable, low price, well and honestly made, washes and dries dishes in two minutes, no muss, slop, scalded fingers or broken dishes, a child can operate, every one warranted, one in a locality means a sale to all the neighbors, sells on merit, every family uses, permanent situation, write for agency. World Mfg. Co., 420-25 Columbus, Ohio.

SORE EYES Dr. ISAAC THOMPSON'S EYE WATER

To Measure for a Lady's Basque or any Garment requiring a Bust Measure to be taken:—Put the measure around the body, over the dress, close under the arms, drawing it closely—NOT TOO TIGHT.

To Measure for a Lady's Skirt or any Garment requiring a Waist Measure to be taken:—Put the measure around the waist, over the dress.

To Measure for a Lady's Sleeve:—Put the Measure around the muscular part of the upper arm, about an inch below the lower part of the arm's-eye, drawing the tape closely—NOT TOO TIGHT.

☞ Take the Measures for Misses' and Little Girls' Patterns the same as for Ladies'. In ordering, give the ages also.

To Measure for a Man's or Boy's Coat or Vest:—Put the measure around the body, under the jacket, close under the arms, drawing it closely—NOT TOO TIGHT. In ordering for a boy, give the age also.

To Measure for a Man's or Boy's Overcoat:—Measure around the breast, OVER the garment the coat is to be worn over. In ordering for a boy, give the age also.

To Measure for a Man's or Boy's Trousers:—Put the measure around the body, OVER the trousers at the waist, drawing it closely—NOT TOO TIGHT. In ordering for a boy, give the age also.

To Measure for a Man's or Boy's Shirt:—For the size of the neck, measure the exact size where the neck-band encircles it, and allow one inch—thus, if the exact size be 14 inches, select a Pattern marked 15 inches. For the breast, put the measure around the body, over the vest, UNDER the jacket or coat, close under the arms, drawing it closely—NOT TOO TIGHT. In ordering a Boy's Shirt Pattern, give the age also.

Offer to Purchasers of Patterns.
To any retail customer sending us by mail, at one time, $1.00 or more for patterns, we will, on receipt thereof, send a copy of the METROPOLITAN CATALOGUE, post-paid, free of charge. Or, to any retail customer sending us by mail, at one time, 50 cents for Patterns, with 10 cents additional, we will forward, on receipt thereof, a copy of the METROPOLITAN CATALOGUE.

Rates for Packages of Patterns.
On orders for **Packages of Patterns** the following Discounts will be allowed, but the Entire Amount must be ordered at one time. In ordering, specify the Patterns by their Numbers.

On Receipt of $3.00, we will allow a Selection to the Value of $4.00 in Patterns.
" " 5.00, " " " " " " 7.00 "
" " 10.00, " " " " " " 15.00 "

Patterns at Package Rates will be sent, Transportation Free, to any part of the world.

Our Patterns, with Labels Printed in Spanish or German.

To meet a constantly increasing demand for our goods in Spanish-speaking and German-speaking countries, we have had translated into **Spanish** and **German** the Labels giving directions for using our Patterns; and beg to announce that any Pattern of our manufacture can be obtained with either a **Spanish** or **German** Label from our General Office, or through any of the Branch Offices or Agencies for the sale of our Goods, at the price of the same Pattern containing a Label printed in English only.

Though Agents in English-speaking countries do not carry in stock Patterns containing Labels printed in Spanish or German, they will be pleased at any time to order the same for customers who may desire them.

THE BUTTERICK PUBLISHING CO. (Limited), 7 to 17 W. 13th St., N. Y.

THE DELINEATOR.

The pleasure and safety of **BICYCLE RIDING** depend largely upon the Tires used.

..Great G. & J. Tire..
"*The most Reliable Tire on Earth*"
has added much to the reputation of that most popular of all wheels, the

Rambler Bicycle

Any Bicycle Dealer will supply G. & J. Tires on any wheel, if you insist.
GORMULLY & JEFFERY MFG. CO.
Chicago. Boston. Washington. New York.
Brooklyn. Detroit. Coventry, Eng.

DEAFNESS

and Head Noises relieved by using Wilson's Common Sense Ear Drums. New scientific invention; different from all other devices. The only safe, simple, comfortable and invisible Ear Drum in the world. Helps where medical skill fails. No wire or string attachments. Write for pamphlet.
WILSON EAR DRUM CO.,
 1147 Front Bldg., Louisville, Ky.
 1162 Broadway, New York.

INCUBATORS
Our 160 page, finely illustrated Combined Poultry Guide and Catalogue will tell you what you wish to know about
PROFITS IN POULTRY
We manufacture a complete line of Incubators, Brooders and Poultry Appliances. Guide and Catalogue 10c. in stamps or silver. Worth one Dollar. Reliable Incubator & Brooder Co., Quincy, Ill.

AGENTS WANTED—MEN and WOMEN
Any man or woman can earn $100.00 a month with
OUR JOURNEY AROUND THE WORLD
By Rev. Francis E. Clark,
Pres't United Soc. Christian Endeavor. 720 engravings, a perfect library of art and entertainment, and the bargain of the century. One Agent has sold 300, another 235, and others from 25 to 100 copies a month; all our making money. Agents Wanted. Now is the time.
"Dickens no hindrance, for we Pay Freight, Give Credit, Premium Copies, Free Outfit, Extra Terms and Exclusive Territory. Write for terms and specimen engravings free, to
A. D. WORTHINGTON & CO., Hartford, Conn.

....**SUVIO**....
FIRE GLOBE GAS HEATER.
For warming rooms with ordinary Gas Billings. The heat of the Gas Flame is increased 500 per cent.
Economical—Efficient—Pure Radiant Heat.
No Odor, No Flue, No Fittings.
PRICES: Black Japan, $1.00; Brass or Nickeled, $1.50.
Enclose 15 cents for postage.
MANUFACTURED BY
SUVIO HEATER CO.,
10 Dey St., N.Y. City.
Agents wanted everywhere.
Send for DESCRIPTIVE CIRCULAR.

Who want to make money must Send for Sample Copy of EVERY MONTH, contains $3.00 worth of latest and most Popular Music. Motives of all in Teaching Music and Illustrations. Liberal Commissions and Prizes to Clubs or Agents. Sample, 10c. Yearly, $1.00.
Howley, Haviland & Co., Publishers,
4 East 20th St., New York.
Reference: Any music store in the United States or Canada.

THE IMPROVED VICTOR INCUBATOR
Hatches Chickens by Steam. Absolutely self-regulating. The simplest, most reliable, and cheapest first-class Hatcher in the market. Circulars free.
GEO. ERTEL & CO., Quincy, Ill.

A Hundred Dollars for a Wheel!
NONSENSE!!

The man or woman who pays that amount for a bicycle, no matter what the name, or who the maker, when for $75 he can buy the ENVOY, or she can buy the FLEET-WING, might just as well throw $25 into the ocean.

We have made cycles for Ten years, and know whereof we speak. So will you, if you will send for our catalogue.

BUFFALO CYCLE CO.,
Buffalo, N.Y.

ANSWERS TO CORRESPONDENTS.
(*Continued.*)

MARIE VINETTE:—Write to Madame Josephine Le Fevre, 1208 Chestnut Street, Philadelphia, Pa., in reference to developing the bust. To prevent and cure chapped hands, wash them with fine soap, and before removing the soap scrub the hands with a table-spoonful of Indian meal, rinsing thoroughly with soft, tepid water, using a little meal each time except the last. Dry the hands thoroughly, then rinse in a very little water containing a tea-spoonful of pure glycerine, rubbing the hands together until the water has evaporated. This is an excellent remedy, but the glycerine must be pure or it will irritate.

LE:—Cancelled American postage-stamps of current issues have no face value and we know of no one who desires to purchase them.

SUFFERER:—Carbuncles show debility in the blood. They are very dangerous and the person affected should summon medical aid at once.

G.:—For travelling by rail or boat, lounging and blanket robes are indispensable. They are made from wool blankets and English and French flannels.

TOPSY AND PEGGY:—Eighteen hundred and ninety-six is a leap year. Pretty costumes for young girls have been given many times in these columns. Young girls should not wear many ornaments; a few tasteful pieces that seem to serve a purpose is a good rule for the selection of jewelry.

To Parties Desiring Addresses Changed on our Subscription Books: Subscribers to our Publications, when notifying us of a change of Address, are particularly requested to give their full former Address, together with the new Address, and state the name of the Publication, and the Month and Year in which the subscription to it began. Thus:

"THE BUTTERICK PUBLISHING Co. (Limited):
"Mrs. John Martin, formerly of Smithville, Bullitt Co., Ky., whose Subscription to THE DELINEATOR began with October, 1895, desires her address changed to Manchester, Delaware Co., Iowa."

To Parties Complaining of Non-Receipt of Magazines: To avoid delay and long correspondence, a subscriber to any of our Publications not receiving the publication regularly, should name in the letter of complaint the Month with which the subscription commenced. A convenient form for such a complaint is as follows:

"THE BUTTERICK PUBLISHING Co. (Limited):
"Mrs. John Martin, of Smithville, Bullitt Co., Ky., has not received the December number of THE DELINEATOR, for which she subscribed, commencing with the number for October, 1895. She knows of no reason for its non-receipt."

To Secure Specific Numbers of The Delineator: To secure the filling of orders for THE DELINEATOR of any specific Edition, we should receive them by or before the tenth of the month preceding the date of issue. For instance: Parties wishing THE DELINEATOR for February will be certain to secure copies of that Edition by sending in their orders by the Tenth of January.

To Parties Ordering Patterns or Publications by Mail: In sending money through the mail, to us or to agents for the sale of our goods, use a Post-Office Order, an Express Money-Order, a Bank Check or Draft or a Registered Letter. Should a Post-Office Order sent to us go astray in the mails, we can readily obtain a duplicate here and have it cashed. An Express Money-Order is equally safe and often less expensive.
A Registered Letter, being regularly numbered, can be easily traced to its point of detention, should it not reach us in ordinary course. To facilitate tracing a delayed Registered Letter, the complaining correspondent should obtain its Number from the local postmaster and send it to us.
Bank Drafts or Checks, being valuable only to those in whose favor they are drawn, are reasonably certain of delivery.

THE BUTTERICK PUBLISHING CO. (Limited),
7 to 17 West Thirteenth Street, New York.

Six Spools Best Six Cord **THREAD**
Or Solid Silver (any size) **THIMBLE** **FREE**

Cut the "Terra Cotta" label as shown here from One box of Sterling Dress Stays, send to us, and we will mail you your choice of above articles FREE.

DRESS STAYS

This stay is Guaranteed to outlast the garment.
CROTTY & MITCHELL, Woodsport, N.Y.

Are Your Shears Dull?
Our sharpeners will keep them always sharp—can do it in 3 minutes—25c each. Agents wanted.
PERFECTION NOVELTY CO., Cleveland, O.

SORE EYES Dr. ISAAC THOMPSON'S EYE WATER

The Dressmaker and Milliner

A NEW MAGAZINE ILLUSTRATING IN COLORS AND TINTS THE LATEST MODES IN COSTUMING AND MILLINERY.

THIS MAGAZINE is published Quarterly, for March, May, September and November, representing the Fashions for Spring, Summer, Autumn and Winter respectively. It contains the Finest Presentation of Modes and Millinery ever offered to the public, with accompanying Descriptions in English, Spanish and German.

**Subscription Price, $1.00 or 5s. a Year.
Price of Single Copies, 35 cents or 1s. 6d.**

ORDERS may be placed through any of our Agents, or sent direct to the General Office. THE DRESSMAKER AND MILLINER, sent on Subscription or by Single Copy from our New York Office to any Address in the United States, Canada, Newfoundland or Mexico, is post-paid by the Publishers. When the Magazine is ordered sent on Subscription to any other country, 25 Cts. for Extra Postage must be remitted with the Subscription Price.

La Modista de Vestidos y de Sombreros.

Se Publica por Trimestre. Es un Nuevo Periódico, Ilustrando en Colores y Tintes las Ultimas Modas en Trajes y Sombreros.

El Precio de Suscripcion al Año, $1.25 cts. oro.
El Precio por cada Entrega Sencilla, 50 cts. oro.

Se pueden hacer pedidos por cualquiera de Nuestros Agentes, ó enviar directamente a la Oficina General.

...DIE... Modistin und Putzmacherin.

Eine neue Zeitschrift, welche die neuesten Moden für Garderobe und Putz in farbigen Illustrationen darstellt und vierteljährlich herausgegeben wird.

Abonnementspreis, per Jahr, M. 6.
Einzelne Exemplare, - · M. 2.

Bestellungen nehmen unsere Agenturen entgegen oder werden direkt von unseren Haupt-Geschäft ausgeführt.

**THE BUTTERICK PUBLISHING CO. (Limited),
7 to 17 West 13th Street, New York, U.S.A. | 171 to 175, Regent Street, London, England.**

The Juvenile Outfitter

IS A NEW QUARTERLY MAGAZINE DEVOTED TO THE NEEDS OF YOUNG FOLKS.

Published in March, May, September and November, for Spring, Summer, Autumn and Winter respectively. It contains a series of Colored Plates showing the latest Styles of Clothing for Misses, Girls, Children, Boys and Infants; Plates of Fashionable Hats, Caps and Bonnets, and many additional illustrations of Figures and Patterns showing Seasonable and Practical Garments. The Descriptions are in English, Spanish and German.

**Subscription Price, 75 Cents or 4s. a Year.
Single Copies, 25 Cents or 1s. 3d. Each.**

EL PROVEEDOR JUVENIL

es un Nuevo Periódico Trimestral, Dedicado á las Modas de Niños.

Publicado en Marzo, Mayo, Setiembre, y Noviembre para Primavera, Verano Otoño, é Invierno respectivamente. Contiene una série de Grabados Iluminados, mostrando los Ultimos Estilos en Ropaje para Señoritas, Niños y Bebés. Las Descripciones están en Inglés, Español y Aleman.

Precio de Suscripcion, $1.00 oro, al Año.
Precio por Entrega, - 30 Centavos, oro.

DIE KINDER-AUSSTATTUNG

ist eine neue Quartalschrift, die das ganze Gebiet der Mode für Knaben und Mädchen umfasst,

und wird im März, Mai, September und November für die Frühjahrs-, Sommer-, Herbst- und Winter-Moden herausgegeben. Sie enthält eine Serie von kolorierten Modenbildern, welche die neuesten Moden für Mädchen, Kinder, Knaben und auch für kleine Kinder zeigen. Die Beschreibungen erscheinen in englischer, spanischer und deutscher Sprache.

Abonnementspreis, per Jahr, 4 M.
Einzelne Exemplare, M. 1.20.

**THE BUTTERICK PUBLISHING CO. (Limited),
7 to 17 West 13th Street, New York, U.S.A. | 171 to 175, Regent Street, London, England.**

Atlanta's

New Cotton Mill. Take stock. Every monthly payments. Write for our prospectus, showing that Atlanta's cotton mills now in operation are making larger profits than any to the known world. Address PRESIDENT COTTON MILL, Atlanta, Ga.

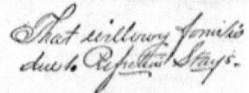

ANSWERS TO CORRESPONDENTS.
(Continued).

DAISY BELL:—The Judic corset, imported by Simpson, Crawford and Simpson, 6th Avenue and 19th Street, New York, is said to lengthen the waist without lacing. It can be had in models to suit all figures. Let an explanation of your friend's coolness come from him; treat him as you have done heretofore. Black satin is pretty for church wear.

L. C. M's.:—A ring worn on the third finger of the left hand does not necessarily indicate an engagement. The engagement ring varies with the circumstances of the groom; it may be set with a solitaire diamond or a less costly jewel. A foreign custom is to choose a plain gold ring for the emblem of betrothal and to use it also for the wedding ring.

JAPAN LILY:—You write a good business hand. We think a child of six too young to take vocal instruction. Madame Ruppert's Face Bleach has been advertised in THE DELINEATOR for several years and it is said to be an officious preparation.

R. H.:—Turpentine is used for thinning paints. Outfits containing a complete assortments of oil colors can be bought of any dealer in artists' supplies.

LARA:—Silver gifts for the bride that are to be marked must bear the initials of her maiden name, but it is not best to mark ordinary pieces that are likely to be duplicated.

NEW RAGS or old rags colored with "PERFECTION" Dyes will make beautiful carpets and rugs, and are guaranteed not to fade. We will send you a package each of "PERFECTION" Turkey Red, Black, Green, Medium Brown, Yellow and Orange dyes, or six packages, any colors, for button or wool, for 6 cents. Single packages, 10 cents. W. CUSHING & CO., Dept. 4, FOXCROFT, Maine.

MAKE MONEY! selling BEVERIDGE'S Automatic Cooker. Best cooking utensil. Food can't burn. No odor. Saves labor and fuel. Fits any stove. Agents wanted, either sex. Good Pay. One lady sold 2385 in one town. Write (F. O. 725.)
BEVERIDGE MFG. CO., Baltimore, Md.

New Idea in Trunks

The Stallman Dresser Trunk is a portable dressing case, with drawers instead of trays; the bottom is as accessible as the top. Costs no more than box trunk, shipped C. O. D. with privilege to examine. 2c. stamp Illustrated catalog.
F. A. STALLMAN, 49 W. Spring St., Columbus, O.

WINDSOR DOLL HEADS.
Indestructible. Beautiful.

These heads are intended for fitting to bodies made at home, but will fit almost any kind of a body 14 to 16 inches long. They are handsomer than the expensive French heads and will stand roughest handling. The wigs used are the finest imported, have natural eyes and make a most beautiful doll. Mailed anywhere on receipt of $1.25. **WINDSOR DOLL CO.,**
P. O. BOX 248, Brooklyn, N. Y.

THE DELINEATOR.

SILVERWARE, CUT GLASS and CHINA.

Your Dealer has or can procure OUR WARES.

"Pairpoint"

IS THE NAME.

Pairpoint Mfg. Co.,
NEW BEDFORD, MASS.
CHICAGO. NEW YORK.

FREE! Our Booklet, "Utility in Silver and 1896 Novelties" sent to your address. Mention DELINEATOR.

A LADIES' PRESENT.

FOLDS UP AND GOES INTO THIS CASE.

PIANOS! ORGANS! FREE!!

Test trial for 30 days in your own home. NO MONEY REQUIRED.
PIANOS-ORGANS FROM $25.00 UP.
Including a Complete Musical Outfit. CASH or EASY PAYMENTS.
NEW SOUVENIR CATALOGUE a work of art illustrated in colors.

ANSWERS TO CORRESPONDENTS.
(Continued.)

SUBSCRIBER'S DAUGHTER:—You can purchase walnut stain from any druggist.

IGNORANCE:—High noon is still the fashionable hour for weddings. You can serve a wedding breakfast at that time. The services of a caterer will, of course, greatly lighten your responsibilities. If you forward us an addressed envelope, we will send you the name of one in New York. As you do not mind expense, decorate the house with roses, lilies and orchids. Sometimes wedding rings are worn by both bride and groom, but this is not usual. A bride's dress should have a long, sweeping train. Invitations to a wedding must reach the guests exactly two weeks before the event. To those whom you do not wish to invite send announcement cards. The bride and groom always go to the table with the wedding guests. The withdrawal of the bride to change her bridal toilette for a traveling dress follows, and goodbyes are quickly said. You may have bridesmaids or a maid of honor or both, or you may dispense with all.

The Berkshire Hills Sanatorium,

An institution for the scientific treatment of

Cancer,

Tumors, and all forms of Malignant Growths,

Without the Use of the Knife.

We have never failed to effect a permanent cure where we have had reasonable opportunity for treatment. Book and Circulars giving a description of our Sanatorium and Treatment, with terms and references, free.

Address: **DRS. W. E. BROWN & SON, North Adams, Mass.**

WHAT 10 CENTS WILL DO.
$100.00 WORTH OF FUN.

See what you get: a three months' Subscription to Modern Stories, a 16 page, 64 column family and story magazine, and a package of games, &c., as follows:

1 fine set of Dominoes, 1 Checker Board and Men, 1 game of Authors (48 cards in pack), 1 game Fox and Geese, 11 Parlor Games, 1 game Nine Men Morris, 1 game Fortune, 1 game Forfeits, 12 Magic Tricks, 1 game Clairvoyant, 1 game Shadow Buff, 1 game Tableaux, 1 game Pantomimes, 275 select Autograph Album Verses, How to tell a Person's Age. A System by which you can write to another person and no one can read it without the key, 50 charming Conundrums with answers. All sent nearly packed for 10 cents. Address, **Modern Stories, 111 Nassau St., N.Y.**

18c. STAMPING OUTFIT. 18c.

This Outfit has the newest patterns. Doilt Designs, Violet Mats, Butterfly, Pansy, Bluet Alphabet, Stamping Tablet and Ingalls' Fancy-Work Book, over 100 Illustrations. Latest things in Fancy Work. All for 18 cents. Stamps taken.
Address, J. F. INGALLS, Lynn, Mass., Box D.

HERE AGAIN!
SHOEMAKER'S POULTRY ALMANAC FOR 1896.

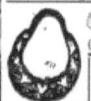

It is a bright, larger and better than ever, nearly 200 pages filled with new and useful information. Finely illustrated with finest engravings of several breeds. A valuable Reference Book. Postage 15 cents. Address,
C. C. SHOEMAKER, Box 43, Freeport, Ill., U.S.A.
P. S.—Incubators and Brooders. Hot water, pipe system, the best in the world, a fine 32 page Catalogue free.

LADIES!

Do you like a cup of Good Tea? If so, send this "Ad" and 15c. in stamps and we will mail you a ½ lb. sample Best Tea Imported. Any kind you may select. Good Incomes, Big Premiums, etc.
Teas, Coffees, Baking Powder and Spices. Send for terms. Cash Book Free to Patrons.
THE GREAT AMERICAN TEA CO.
P. O. Box 289, 31 and 33 Vesey St., New York.

THE JEWELRY GRANDMOTHER CASH FOR WORE...

We buy broken Plated Jewelry, gold or silver Watches, Jewelry, Spoons, &c. Also unused Diamonds and Gems. Send by registered mail or express. We remit immediately. Free, a beautiful double-heart Pin with each box of our Turkish Incense for cleaning Jewelry. Price 25c. postpaid.
H. HARTE, Rochester, N. Y. Established 1869.

WE PAY

This $70 High-Grade New Folding Cabinet "Kenwood" Sewing Machine $22 WITH COUPON HIGH ARM.

$27.00 is our special Wholesale Price, never before sold for less. To quickly introduce this latest style Folding Cabinet we have decided to make a special Coupon Offer giving every reader of this paper a chance to get a strictly high grade sewing machine at the lowest price ever offered. On receipt of $22.00 and coupon we will ship this machine anywhere and prepay all freight charges to any railway Station east of the Rocky Mountains. Money refunded if not as represented after 30 days trial. We will ship C.O.D. with privilege of industrial on receipt of $1.00. The "Kenwood" is the best machine ever made, regardless of price. Twice to three times the money has been paid for machines not as good. It has all the latest improvements, including every pound of superiority over other family machines. It sews faster, runs easier, makes less noise and lasts longer than any other. Ten years written warranty. Complete set of best attachments free. The Folding Cabinet is beautiful in design, oak or walnut, highly polished, elegantly finished, strong and simple in construction, will not get out of order, can be opened or closed by a child. When not in use the machine head is tipped down out of the way and the extension leaf folds over, forming a neat table. Altogether it is the most simple, convenient and satisfactory machine ever sold. Buy the "Kenwood" and get the best. If you prefer thirty days trial before paying, send for our large Illustrated **CATALOGUE WITH TESTIMONIALS**, explaining fully how we ship sewing machines anywhere to anyone at lowest manufacturers' prices without asking one cent in advance. We are headquarters and have all makes and kinds in stock from cheapest to the best. Over $2 differences in styles. Such "Arlington" machines $11.00 and $15.00, guaranteed better than machines sold by others at $25.00 to $27.00. We also sell new Singer machines at $8.00, $11.50, $13.00. If you want a sewing machine now is the time to get one at a bargain direct from the manufacturers. This is a chance of a lifetime, and you cannot afford to take the opportunity pass.
REFERENCES: Dun's or Bradstreet's Commercial Agency. First National Bank, Chicago, whose capital is $2,000,000. This ad. will not appear again; better write today.
Address (in full) **CASH BUYERS' UNION,**
158-164 West Van Buren St., Dept. O, Chicago, Ills.

JANOWITZ'S DUPLEX EAGLE DRESS BONE
BETTER THAN WHALEBONE
for FREE SAMPLE ADDRESS JULIUS JANOWITZ, 135 GRAND ST N.Y.

ME-GRIM-INE

A positive and permanent cure for MEGRIM (Sick Headache) and all other forms of Headache or Neuralgia.

Headache Cured Free

by sample mailed you if this paper is mentioned. The more promptly headaches are relieved the less frequent will be their return, until permanently cured. Sold by all druggists. 10 CENTS A BOX.
The Dr. Whitehall Meg. Co.
South Bend, Ind.

BROWN'S French DRESSING

For Ladies' and Children's Boots and Shoes

It is the most reliable dressing upon the market, and more of Brown's French Dressing is sold throughout the world than any other make.

Ask your dealer for it and accept no substitute; take only **BROWN'S French Dressing.**

Send 10c. to us, and receive the most beautiful music and fashion book in the world. It has 32 pages, full sheet music size, and has a very handsome cover on which is a large and beautiful portrait of an actress. It contains from 10 to 12 pieces of vocal and instrumental music, also four or five portraits of leading actresses.
The New York Musical Echo Co., Broadway Theatre Building, N. Y. City.

Money Saver. Young or old have fun and make money printing cards for others. Type-setting easy by full printed instructions. Press $3. Print your own cards &c. Larger foot-reach circular, small newspaper. Catalogue type, presses, type, paper, cards, &c. from makers KELSEY & CO. Meriden, Conn.

PRINTING OUTFIT 10c.

Crazy Patchwork

Sixty elegant pieces, enough to make a crazy quilt 400 square inches, of silk and satin, assorted bright, rich colors, 25 cts. 5 packages, $1. If plush and velvet pieces, 25 cts. If you are not fully satisfied with every package, you may return it and we will refund your money.
The BINGHAM Co., New London, Conn.

FLY SHUTTLE RAG CARPET LOOM
Weaves 40 yards an hour.
100 Yards a Day. New FREE Catalogue and Price List.
Address THE NEWCOMB LOOM CO., 149 West 5th Street, Davenport, Iowa.

MAGIC LANTERNS

Also STEREOPTICONS, all prices for PUBLIC EXHIBITIONS, etc. Pays well. A profitable business for a man with a small capital. Also Lanterns for Home amusement. 152 page Catalogue, free.
McALLISTER, Mfg. Optician, 49 Nassau St., N.Y.

THREE YARDS OF FLOWERS

In all their BEAUTIFUL COLORS, PANSIES, CHRYSANTHEMUMS, POPPIES, etc., 25 Cents EACH. SPECIAL OFFER—We will send you the Three Yards of Flowers for 50c.
Address, J. F. INGALLS, Lynn, Mass., Box D.

SELF THREADING THIMBLE.

Teeth and eyes saved. Needle threading conquered at last. This patent thimble combines a needle threader through which a needle can be easily threaded. Also a thread cutter, which never dulls. Two ingenious attachments saving teeth, lifting thread, and eyes threading needle while sewing. The thimbles are highly polished and plated and resemble coin silver. The threader is the most perfect ever produced. The combination thimble and threader retail for 10 cts. though they have been sold as high as a dollar a piece. Agents make $5.00 a day. Sample by mail postpaid 10 cts., one doz. 50 cts.

H. T. ROOT & CO.,
34 Park Row, New York.

INCUBATOR.

NOT A CENT

until after you try it.
Highest Award, World's Fair, 1893.

A CHILD CAN RUN IT.

Book Incubator, 5 cts.
VON CULIN INCUBATOR CO., Box F, Delaware City, Del.

Baby's Health Demands the Use of

"THE BEST" NURSER

Prevents Wind-Colic and Bowel Trouble. See how easily cleansed!
Nipple cannot collapse. At druggists, 25c., or by mail 27c. postpaid. Safe delivery guaranteed. "Clingfast" Nipples warranted pure gum, 50c. doz. The Gotham Co., 94 Warren St., N.Y.

ANSWERS TO CORRESPONDENTS.

(Continued.)

ALICE:—To restore black silk, proceed thus: To oxgall add boiling water sufficient to make it warm, and with a clean sponge rub the silk well on both sides; squeeze it out well and proceed again in like manner. Rinse it in clear water and change the latter until perfectly clean; dry it in the air, then dip the sponge in gum water and rub it on the wrong side; spread it on a table, pin securely and dry before a fire.

MOTHER:—Little girls who are chosen as bridesmaids at weddings precede the bride and her father. They carry baskets of roses, which are strewn down the aisle along which she walks after the ceremony. Dealers are the only ones to whom we make a discount on our publications.

MRS. LIZZIE D.;—A lotion composed of best Cologne, 4 ounces and corrosive sublimate, 8 grains, has been productive of very satisfactory results in cases of muddy or sallow skin. Trim your gray cashmere with appliqué embroidery applied on silk or velvet.

AMABA:—A unique booby prize is a small colored doll with a great many flannel petticoats, to be used as a pen-wiper.

PYROGRAPHY
OR
BURNT WORK

F. W. DEVOE & CO'S. Outfit
for producing this pleasing, artistic and profitable work, so fully explained in THE DELINEATOR.
(Pamphlet Free.)
Outfit contains Platinum Point, Handle, Bellows, Lamp, Tubing, etc.
All of Superior Quality.
Complete, in Wood Box, **$7.50**

By mentioning THE DELINEATOR, this Outfit will be delivered free of charge on receipt of price.

F. W. DEVOE & C. T. RAYNOLDS CO.,
Dealers in Artists' Materials,
Fulton and William Streets, New York.

"Read Your Life in the Stars."

The Influence of the Zodiac Upon Human Life.
By ELEANOR KIRK.

This work, one of the best from the pen of the gifted authoress, will be found of absorbing interest to the general reader, as well as to the student.
It treats of a subject older than the Pyramids and concerning which innumerable books have been written, but none from the standpoint of profound research, combined with simple and concise arrangement, such as characterize this work.
The heretofore mystic science of Astrology, whose disciples and believers date from the earliest ages of the world, is made plain and the influence of the Stars upon Human Life and Destiny is depicted so clearly that the reader is compelled to admit that through so mere guesswork could such accurate relationship be shown as is found in this book.
The peculiar characteristics in general of persons born under the different signs, which are described with wonderful accuracy, and the directions for the education and training of children as shown to be the most advantageous in their relationships to the influences of the stars that prevail at time of birth, are evidence of a research and adaptation that cannot fail to prove of the greatest interest.
In short, the scope of this work is so great and the subject so admirably handled that it cannot fail to become one of the most popular as well as instructive books published.
Winter evening Zodiac parties are the craze in Eastern social circles; as a drawing-room entertainer this work is unexcelled.

Price, $1 and four 2c. stamps.

WORLD DISTRIBUTING CO.,
Room 52, Potter Building, N. Y. City.

NO DIRT LEFT

in clothes washed with the "DOTY" RUB WASHER; rub presses in one body and no hard work done. Try the record. AGENTS WANTED. Exclusive territory given. Write for terms.
Lake Erie Mfg. Co., 131 E. 12 St., Erie, Pa.

MUSIC SALE To reduce our stock we send by mail 50 pieces, full sheet music size, all parts complete, all for 12c.; or 4 lots, 45c. Money back if not suited. Only One girl in the World for 5c, and 10 songs with music, 5c. D. Holloway, 20 Wash. St., Boston, Mass.

BIRD MANNA Makes Canaries sing like a Nightingale. If given, with seed, makes them the steadiest new layer. FREE Sample of Manna. 15 cents. Bird Book, 10 cents. Philadelphia Bird Food Co., 400 N. 3d St., Phila., Pa.

THE MONITOR
INCUBATOR, self regulating. Large Ill. 64 page catalogue for 4 cts. in stamps. **Buy the Best.**
A. F. WILLIAMS, 32 Race St., Bristol, Conn.

NEW MAMMOTH

Poultry Guide for 1896. Finest book ever published, contains nearly 100 pages, all printed in colors, plans for best poultry houses, sure remedies and recipes for all diseases, and how to make poultry and gardening pay. Sent post paid for 15c.
John Bauscher, Jr., box 55 Freeport, Ill.

A POPULAR OR CARE, DISEASES and BOOK on TREATMENT, by DR. J. N. HATHAWAY, 129 2d Ave., etc., Cloth, bound, $1.50. Send for circulars.
Diseases, Hatfield Medical Jour. Co., Publishers, Detroit, Mich.

Rupture Cured

WITH our Improved Elastic Truss. Worn with ease night and day. Retains the rupture under the hardest exercise or severest strain. Examination free. Lady in attendance for ladies. Send for pamphlet.

IMPROVED ELASTIC TRUSS CO.,
822 & 824 Broadway, Cor. 12th St., N. Y.

ANSWERS TO CORRESPONDENTS.
(Concluded).

USEFUL:—Advertisements offering home employment will be found each month in THE DELINEATOR.

ROSE, M. K.:—You failed to send a stamp for a reply by mail. Friends are not debarred from sending gifts on the occasion of a party if they choose to do so.

HIS SWEETHEART:—There are many white persons who can understand the language of Indians. Braid your hair loosely and tie it with a ribbon.

A. G.:—On damp days, or when the hair is naturally too moist or oily, a fine, tinted drying powder may be dusted over the locks with a puff after they have been curled so that they may retain their fluffiness. Only an occasional use of this powder is advisable since frequent applications would affect the scalp.

MISS J.:—Glycerine diluted with rose-water and applied to the face will, when dry, form a good foundation for face powder. Consult an oculist about your eyes.

ELLEN:—"Charmant," the Turkish Wonder Balm, is a reliable remedy for faulty complexions and kindred skin troubles. "Charmant" does all it claims to do. We would suggest a trial of it to all sufferers. It can be obtained of the Turkish Balm Co. (Importers), 19 Union Square, New York.

Tobacco-Weakened Resolutions.

Nerves irritated by tobacco, always craving for stimulants, explains why it is so hard to *swear off.* No-To-Bac is the only guaranteed tobacco habit cure because it acts directly on affected nerve centres, destroys irritation, promotes digestion and healthy, refreshing sleep. Many gain 10 pounds in 10 days. You run no risk. No-To-Bac is sold and guaranteed by druggists everywhere. Book free.

AD. STERLING REMEDY CO.,
New York City or Chicago.

♦♦♦♦♦♦♦♦♦♦♦♦♦♦♦♦♦♦
COMPLIMENTARY.

Cut this out, write name and address plainly on bottom, enclosing with 15 cts. to pay for packing and postage, send to METROPOLITAN and RURAL HOME, Box 383, New York City, and you will receive a handsome present worth $1.00.

Name....................
Address in full.....................
♦♦♦♦♦♦♦♦♦♦♦♦♦♦♦♦♦♦

ALOGUE FREE!
We give the following premiums with TEA.
Watches, Solid Gold Rings, Banquet Lamps, Banjos, Autoharps, Air Guns, Tea, Dinner and Toilet Sets.
Liberal Tea Co., 109 Cross St., Boston, Mass.

CUT THIS OUT
and return it to us with the 10c for a trial subscription to new 64-pp. Illustrated Magazine just being issued, and we will publish your name free in our Agents Directory. You will get hundreds of Papers, Cards, Magazines, Novelties and Music from Publishers and Manufacturers who want agents. Send at once. All for 10c. (This limits reliable.—Ed.) Address Pub's Pop. Monthly, 14 Federal St., Boston, Mass.

OILY SKIN, Moth, Tan, Freckles, Blackheads, Pimples, removed by Mrs. Bradley's FACE WASH.
Agents Wanted. Testimonials and Millions sent for circulars. Wash 25 cts., post-paid.
MRS. C. S. BRADLEY, Omaha, Neb.

COFFEE, SPICES, EXTRACTS. For 5 years largest dealers in this country. 170-page Premium List Free. We are importers and offer best inducements with pure and honest goods. **LONDON TEA CO.,** 19 Congress Street, Boston. **CLUBS.**

The LUNGS CATARRH, BRONCHITIS, ASTHMA,
and the earlier stages of CONSUMPTION, be successfully treated at Home, by the New Andral-Broca Discovery. Not a Drug, but a New Scientific Method of Home Treatment. Cures Guaranteed. Sent FREE to all who apply. Try it FREE, and pay if satisfied. State age and full particulars of your disease. Address,
NEW MEDICAL ADVANCE, 42 E. 14th St., Cincinnati, O.

---

40 VALUABLE BOOKS FREE!

Read this Gigantic Offer by an Old-Established and Reliable Publishing House!
Two Dollars' Worth of Splendid Books Absolutely Free to All! During the next three months we are determined to double the circulation of our large and handsome Illustrated literary and family journal, **Good Literature**, and to accomplish this object, regardless of expense, we now make to the reading public of America the most astounding offer ever made by any reliable publishing house in the world. **Good Literature** is one of the most charming family papers published. Each number consists of 16 large pages, in connection with the most delightful reading matter and beautiful illustrations; it is filled with charming serial and short stories, sketches and poems by the most popular authors, David Munrimer, Fanny Ward, Hawthorne, Homer, and Juvenile Departments, etc., etc. Everybody is delighted with **Good Literature**, and those who are now subscribers are always subscribers, hence for the purpose of introducing this charming periodical into as many homes as we can afford to lose money upon each subscription at the outset. To secure, therefore, immediately, the new subscribers to **Good Literature**, we now make the following special, limited and extraordinary offer: *Upon receipt of only Twenty-five Cents in postal stamps, silver or money order, we will send* **Good Literature for Six Months**, *and to every subscriber we will also send,* **Free and post-paid, Forty Valuable Books, as follows:**

How to Make and Save Money on the Farm. A valuable compilation of useful facts, hints and suggestions for farmers and gardeners.
Wonders of the Sea. A description of the many wonderful and beautiful things found at the bottom of the ocean. Illustrated.
Manual of Etiquette for Ladies and Gentlemen. A guide to politeness, giving the rules of modern etiquette for all occasions.
Winter Evening Recreations, a large collection of Acting Charades, Tableaux, Games, Puzzles, etc., for social gatherings and evenings at home. Illustrated.
The Book in Itself. A practical work, pointing out a way by which all may make money, easily, rapidly and honestly.
Famous Detective Stories. A collection of thrilling narratives of Detective experience and adventures.
Humorous Sketches, by Josiah Allen's Wife. Comprising some of the most laughable sketches ever written by this popular author.
The Home Cook Book and Family Physician. Containing hundreds of excellent cooking recipes and hints to housekeepers; also telling how to cure all common ailments.
Guide to Needle Work, Knitting and Crochet. Containing designs for all kinds of Fancy Needle-Work. Diagrams.
Fishing, Boating and Hunting, a large and choice collection for sport and recreation, public and private undertakings.
Wild Oats Comic Book. A Novel. By Mrs. Alexander.
Monday on Tramp Girl. A Novel. By Florence Warden.
Mamie's Secret. A Novel. By H. Rider Haggard.
A Troublesome Girl. A Novel. By "The Duchess."
Mad Orange. A Novel. By Mrs. Henry Wood.

*The Story of a Wedding Ring. A Novel. By Charlotte M. Brazene, author of "Dora Thorne."
Her Manifest Destiny. A Novel. By Amanda M. Douglas.
Claude and Gabrielle. A Novel. By Charles Reade.
The Lawyer's Secret. A Novel. By Miss M. E. Braddon.
The Romantic Adventures of a Milkmaid. A Novel. By Hardy.
Two Kisses. A Novel. By Charlotte M. Yonge.
The Countess of a Street. A Novel. By Mary Cecil Hay.
Sir Noel's Heir. A Novel. By Mrs. May Agnes Fleming.
The Track of the Comet. A Novel. By Sylvanus Cobb, Jr.
From the Earth to the Moon. A Novel. By Jules Verne.
Mildred Trevanion. A Novel. By "The Duchess."
An Island Pearl. A Novel. By E. L. Fargeon.
Wolf Farm. A Novel. By Marian Harland.
The Lady of the Rocks. A Novel. By Miss Mulock.
The Strange Case of Dr. Jill, and Mr. Hyde. A Novel. By Robert Louis Stevenson.
Felicity's Voyage. A Novel. By Mrs. Ann S. Stephens.
A Fake Hero. A Novel. By Mrs. Alexander.
A Modern Cinderella. A Novel. By Charlotte M. Braeme.
The Pitman Woman. A Novel. By Wilkie Collins.
Current College. A Novel. By Mrs. Henry Wood.
The Prince of Ayr. A Novel. By Florence Marryat.
The Little Old Man of the Batignolles. A Novel. By Gaboriau.
I who the Lilies. A Novel. By Charlotte M. Braeme.
Her Lost Lover. A Novel. By "The Duchess."
Gilded Sin (an). A Novel. By Margaret Blount.*

The above books are published in neat pamphlet form, many of them handsomely illustrated, and they are printed from clear, bold, readable type on good paper. Each book contains a complete, first-class novel or other work by a well-known and popular author, published in the handsome and unabridged editions by reading and preserving. It is not a large number of novels or stories bound together in one book, but forty separate and distinct books. And we agree to send to you each one on the receipt of only the whole forty splendid books absolutely free. In each particular of which is worth at the regular rates of books in 22 cents on each of the two months' subscription to **Good Literature**. Our readers prices for these books are fifty cents on each of the four subscription to **Good Literature**, so of these as a bonus will find the sets valued above as 25 cents each. In addition we shall, on our own hand, no doubt, present to you a most popular **Good Literature** actually give you, absolutely free, nothing less than that amount's worth of splendid books in addition to our fine LITERATURE. Your readers prices for these books are forty cents on each of the forty, so the unbleached of any of the popular "Literature" or "Review" you will find this sale book offered in 12 cents each. Talk about our world of Sparrows here to have a total rule offer to **Good Literature**. This is the most gigantic, the most startling offer ever made by any responsible and reliable publishing house in the world. We lose money on every subscription, but only we are willing to do so. Because we believe that those who become our subscribers now through this offer will become permanent subscribers to **Good Literature**, and our profit will come in the future. This big offer is made from one of the leading publishing houses of the U. S.—there are houses that have been established over twenty years, and has a national reputation for honesty and reliability. It must not be compared with the fraudulent offers of irresponsible parties. We refer to the Mercantile Agencies and to all the leading newspapers as to our reliability. We guarantee perfect and entire satisfaction to every one who shall take advantage of this offer, and we now guarantee that if you are not satisfied and fully satisfied, we will return your money and make you a present of full books and paper. This is a special limited offer, and only good May 1st, but, if as advantage of it before that date, for the dollar we will send you subscriptions, with the forty books free to each, therefore by putting four of your neighbors in with you your own subscription and books free. Address,

V. M. LUPTON, Publisher, 106 and 108 Reade Street, New York.

WOULD YOU
Like a permanent position and $150 monthly, also write as we can.
We will send you full particulars **Free,** also a sample and receipt for making six **Sterling Silver** spoons on receipt of **Five Two-cent stamps** for postage, etc. Address
Standard Silver Ware Co., Boston, Mass.

SAVE TWO PROFITS
We are sold direct from factory to Consumers. Special offer to agents free. **Diamond Cutlery Co.,** 60 Broadway, N. Y., & 140 State St., Chicago.

HATCH CHICKENS BY STEAM.
MODEL EXCELSIOR INCUBATOR.
Simple, Perfect and Self-Regulating. Thousands in successful operation. Lowest priced first-class Hatcher made. Circulars Free.
GEO. H. STAHL, 114 to 122 S. 6th St., Quincy, Ill.

YOUR WEIGHT REDUCED
15 lbs. a month by a new harmless herbal remedy—safe, sure and speedy. Trial package sent FREE on application. Give it a trial, it costs you nothing. Chase Remedy Co. Dept. P, Chicago

DEAFNESS CURED! THE EAR VAPORATOR.
Deafness relieved by self-application, Satisfaction guaranteed. Circulars free. KEY VAPORATOR CO., 195 Marietta St., Chicago.

Shorthand
for note-taking in a few HOURS: requires no previous knowledge, no teacher, equally adapted to all ages, all positions. Exclusive World's Fair Award. Authors and users write H. M. Pernin, Author, Detroit, Mich.

STUDY AT HOME
and prepare for a good position in business. Bookkeeping, Arithmetic, Penmanship, Shorthand, etc. By Mail, is a modern, practical way. A place is always opened. Ten years' Success. Endorsed free of cost, Catalogue free. Trial lesson 10 cents.
BRYANT & STRATTON'S COLLEGE, No. 20 College Bldg., Buffalo, N.Y. BY MAIL.

LEARN the WATCH TRADE.
JEWELRY AND ENGRAVING. | PARSONS' INSTITUTE, BARKER AVENUE, CATALOGUE FREE. | PEORIA, ILLINOIS.

CURE RUPTURE.
Send for book of particulars and learn how.
I. B. SEELEY & CO., 25 S. 11th St., Phila., Pa.

Ideal Spring Beds.
Our booklet, "Wide-Awake-in-Sleeping," describing and illustrating them, Happy Thoughts and a beautiful color map of your State, Free on receipt of two 2-cent stamps.
Foster Bros. Manufacturing Co., 80 Clay Street, Utica, N.Y.

WE PAY
Cash, $5 to $100, a thousand for Newspaper Clippings and your subscribers' addresses and ideas. Particulars for stamp.
News Clipping Co., Dept. DA, 3rd W. 125th St., N.Y.

INVALIDS, if you can't find at home what's what you need in all things as Rolling, Reclining, Carrying and Commode Chairs, Tricycles, Invalids' Lifters, Beds, Bed Rests, Bed Trays, Tables and Invalids' conveniences generally, you may as well give it up. While staking just what you want, No charge. Address, Geo. F. Sargent Co.,
814 Broadway, New York.
Mention THE DELINEATOR in your letter when you write.

LADIES
Make big money, quick sales and keep customers selling our Mackintosh suits and rubber hot goods. Perfect in every way. Fresh territory. Catalogue free.
LADIES SUPPLY CO., 3118 Forest Ave., Chicago.

STOUT ABDOMENS AND LARGE HIPS
Are reduced by my Own Methods. Safe, Easy, Permanent. For full information, Address, with stamp,
Dr. Edith Berdan, 111 Ellison St., Paterson, N. J.

SAMPLES
of Knitted, Tatted, Crocheted Laces. Also doilies, squares, etc., or Lace for the Yard, made to order. Materials and implements for all kinds of Fancy Work also supplied. Terms, Cash in Advance. Address, with stamp for information,
MISS C. F. MORSE,
651 Lafayette Avenue, Brooklyn, N. Y.

HARTMANN'S WW'S (Women's Napkins.)
CANVASSERS WANTED.
Send 4 cts. for sample and circular.
Hygienic Wood Wool Co., 56 Broadway, New York.

Asthma
The African Kola Plant, discovered in Congo, West Africa, is Nature's sure cure for Asthma. Cure Guaranteed or No Pay. Export Office, 1164 Broadway, New York. Home Large Trial Case, FREE by Mail, address
KOLA IMPORTING CO., 132 Vincent., Cincinnati, Ohio.

THE BUTTERICK CUTLERY.

☞ Order these Goods by Numbers, Cash with Order. Cutlery, ordered at the retail or single-pair rate, will be sent prepaid to any Address in the United States, Canada, Newfoundland or Mexico. When ordered at dozen rates, transportation charges must be paid by the party ordering. If the party ordering desires a mail package registered, 8 cents extra should be remitted with the order. Rates by the Gross furnished on application. Dozen rates will not be allowed on less than half a dozen of one style ordered at one time, nor gross rates on less than half a gross.

THE CHAMPION CHEAP SCISSORS.

☞ Made of English Razor Steel, full Nickel-Plated, and Neatly Finished.

No. 11.—LADIES' SCISSORS (5¼ inches long).
25 Cents per Pair; $2.00 per Dozen Pairs. Postage per Dozen Pairs, 20 Cents.

No. 12.—POCKET SCISSORS (3¼ inches long).
20 Cents per Pair; $1.50 per Dozen Pairs. Postage per Dozen Pairs, 15 Cents.

No. 13.—POCKET SCISSORS (4 inches long).
25 Cents per Pair; $2.00 per Dozen Pairs. Postage per Dozen Pairs, 20 Cents.

No. 14.—POCKET SCISSORS (4½ inches long).
30 Cents per Pair; $2.50 per Dozen Pairs. Postage per Dozen Pairs, 20 Cents.

No. 15.—RIPPING OR SURGICAL SCISSORS (5 inches long).
25 Cents per Pair; $2.00 per Dozen Pairs. Postage per Dozen Pairs, 10 Cents.

No. 17.—SEWING-MACHINE SCISSORS and THREAD-CUTTER (4 inches long).
(With Scissors Blades 1½ inch long, having File Forcep Points to catch and pull out thread ends.)
35 Cents per Pair; $3.00 per Dozen Pairs. Postage per Dozen Pairs, 10 Cents.

No. 18.—TAILORS' POINTS and DRESSMAKERS' SCISSORS (4½ inches long).
25 Cts. per Pair; $2.00 per Dozen Pairs. Postage per Dozen Pairs, 20 Cts.

No. 19.—TAILORS' POINTS and DRESSMAKERS' SCISSORS (5½ inches long).
35 Cts. per Pair; $3.00 per Dozen Pairs. Postage per Dozen Pairs, 25 Cts.

No. 20.—TAILORS' POINTS and DRESSMAKERS' SCISSORS (6½ inches long).
50 Cts. per Pair; $4.50 per Dozen Pairs. Postage per Dozen Pairs, 30 Cts.

The "Ideal" Skeleton-Frame Silk Scissors.

These Scissors are made of the finest English Razor Steel, and are designed especially for Cutting Silk and other fine fabrics in such a manner as not to unravel the warp of the material. They are full finished, full ground and nickel-plated. Being extra hard-tempered, they will retain their cutting edge for many years. While very delicate and dainty-looking in construction, they are really very strong, which makes them Ideal light-cutting Scissors.

No. 26.—(4¾ inches long).
40 Cts. per Pair; $3.75 per Dozen Pairs. Postage per Dozen Pairs, 10 Cts.

No. 27.—(5¾ inches long).
50 Cts. per Pair; $4.50 per Dozen Pairs. Postage per Dozen Pairs, 15 Cts.

No. 28.—(6¾ inches long).
60 Cts. per Pair; $5.25 per Dozen Pairs. Postage per Dozen Pairs, 25 Cts.

Rates by the Gross furnished on application.

FIRST QUALITY STRAIGHT & BENT SHEARS.

☞ Made of Solid Razor Steel throughout, full Nickel-Plated, with Finger-Shaped Bows and Screw Adjustment. In lots of Half a Dozen or more, these Shears can generally be sent more cheaply by express.

No. 16.—DRESSMAKERS' or HOUSEKEEPERS' STRAIGHT SHEARS (7¾ inches long).
50 Cents per Pair; $4.50 per Dozen Pairs.

No. 21.—DRESSMAKERS' or HOUSEKEEPERS' BENT SHEARS (7¾ inches long).
(With Patent Spring that forces the Shanks apart and the Edges together making the Shears cut evenly, independent of the Screw.)
75 Cents per Pair; $6.50 per Dozen Pairs.

No. 22.—DRESSMAKERS' or HOUSEKEEPERS' BENT SHEARS (9½ inches long).
(With Patent Adjusting Spring, as in No. 21.) $1.00 per Pair; $9.00 per Dozen Pairs.

The Banner Button-Hole Cutters.

These various Cutters are of Solid Steel throughout and full Nickel-plated.

No. 1.—ADJUSTABLE BUTTON-HOLE CUTTERS, with Outside Screw (4 inches long).
25 Cents per pair; $2.00 per Dozen Pairs. Postage per Dozen Pairs, 15 Cents.

No. 1.—In these Cutters the size of the Button-Hole to be cut is regulated by an Adjustable Screw, so that Button-Holes can be cut of any size and of uniform length.

No. 2.—ADJUSTABLE BUTTON-HOLE CUTTERS, with Inside Gauge-Screw (4 inches long).
50 Cents per Pair; $4.50 per Dozen Pairs. Postage per Dozen Pairs, 20 Cents.

No. 2.—These Cutters are of English Razor Steel, full Nickel-plated, and Forged by Hand. The Gauge-Screw being on the inside, there is no possibility of it catching in the goods when in use.

No. 3.—ADJUSTABLE BUTTON-HOLE CUTTERS, with Sliding Gauge on Graduated Scale (4½ inches long).
75 Cts. per Pair; $6.50 per Dozen Pairs. Postage per Dozen Pairs, 20 Cts.

No. 3.—These Cutters are of English Razor Steel, Full Nickel-plated and Hand-forged. They are regulated by a Brass Gauge, with a Phosphor-Bronze Spring sliding along a Graduated Scale, so that the Button-Hole can be cut to measure.

If the above Cutlery cannot be obtained from the nearest Butterick Pattern Agency, send your Order, with the Price, direct to Us, and the goods will be forwarded, prepaid, to your Address.

THE BUTTERICK PUBLISHING CO. (Limited), **7 to 17 W. 13th Street, New York.**

THE BUTTERICK CUTLERY.
(CONTINUED.)

The Butterick Manicure Implements.

The goods here offered are Low-Priced and of High Quality and Superior Designs, having the approval of Leading Professional Manicures and Chiropodists.

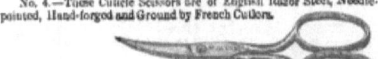

No. 4.—MANICURE CUTICLE SCISSORS (4 Ins. long).
50 Cents per Pair; $4.50 per Dozen Pairs. Postage per Dozen Pairs, 10 Cents.

No. 4.—These Cuticle Scissors are of English Razor Steel, Needle-pointed, Hand-forged and Ground by French Cutlers.

No. 5.—BENT NAIL-SCISSORS (3½ ins. long).
50 Cts. per Pair; $4.50 per Doz. Pairs. Postage per Doz. Pairs, 10 Cts.

No. 5.—These Bent Nail-Scissors are of English Razor Steel, Forged by Hand, with Curved Blades and a File on each side.

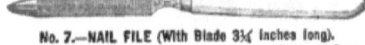

No. 6.—CUTICLE KNIFE (With Blade 1¼ Inch long).
35 Cents per Knife; $3.00 per Dozen. Postage per Dozen, 10 Cents.

No. 6.—The Handle of this Cuticle Knife is of White Bone, and the Blade is of Hand-forged English Razor Steel, the connection being made with Aluminum Solder under a Brass Ferrule.

No. 7.—NAIL FILE (With Blade 3½ inches long).
35 Cents per File; $3.00 per Dozen. Postage per Dozen, 15 Cents.

No. 7.—The Handle and Adjustment of this Nail File are the same as for the Cuticle Knife, and the Blade is of English Razor Steel, Hand-forged and Hand-cut.

No. 8.—CORN KNIFE (With Blade 2¼ inches long).
50 Cents per Knife; $4.50 per Dozen. Postage per Dozen, 10 Cents.

No. 8.—The Handle, Blade and Adjustment of this Corn Knife are the same as the Cuticle Knife.

TRACING WHEELS.
☞ These Articles we Specially Recommend as of Superior Finish and Quality.

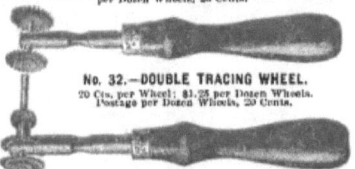

No. 31.—SINGLE TRACING WHEEL.
15 Cts. per Wheel; $1.00 per Dozen Wheels; $10.00 per Gross. Postage per Dozen Wheels, 20 Cents.

No. 32.—DOUBLE TRACING WHEEL.
20 Cts. per Wheel; $1.25 per Dozen Wheels. Postage per Dozen Wheels, 20 Cents.

No. 33.—DOUBLE ADJUSTABLE TRACING WHEEL.
25 Cts. per Wheel; $1.60 per Dozen Wheels. Postage per Dozen Wheels, 25 Cents.

Scissors for the Work-Basket.

The Gloriana Scissors are of Razor Steel, with Nickel and Gold embossed Bows fluted along the sides, and polished and nickeled Blades having a convex finish along the backs and full regular finish to the edges. They are also fitted with a patent Spring, which forces the shanks apart, making the blades cut independently of the screw.

No. 23.—GLORIANA SCISSORS (5½ inches long).
50 Cents per Pair; $4.50 per Dozen Pairs. Postage per Dozen Pairs, 20 Cents.

The Gloriana Embroidery and Ripping Scissors are made of English Cast Steel, well tempered and full Nickel-plated. The handles are embossed in gilt and nickel, and the Blades are carefully ground.

No. 25.—GLORIANA EMBROIDERY AND RIPPING SCISSORS (4 inches long).
50 Cents per Pair; $4.50 per Dozen Pairs. Postage per Dozen Pairs, 10 Cents.

The Embroidery Scissors are made of English Razor Steel, Nickel-plated and Double-pointed. They are used as Lace and Embroidery Scissors and Glove-Darners, being Dainty and Convenient Implements of the Nécessaire and Companion.

No. 9.—EMBROIDERY SCISSORS (3½ inches long). No. 10.—EMBROIDERY SCISSORS (2½ inches long).
20c. per Pair; $1.60 per Doz. Pairs. Postage per Dozen Pairs, 5 Cents.   15c. per Pair; $1.25 per Doz. Pairs. Postage per Dozen Pairs, 5 Cents.

The combined Folding Pocket, Nail and Ripping Scissors are made of the finest grade of German Steel, full Nickel-plated. The Handles are hinged on the Blades so as to fold when not in use. The inside of the Handle contains a phosphor-bronze Spring which keeps the blades firm when open, making an indispensable pair of Pocket Scissors. The Blades are filed on each side for Manicure purposes, and are ground to a point for Ripping purposes. Each pair is packed in an Imitation Morocco case.

No. 24.—Open (4 inches long). Closed (2¼ inches long).
30 Cents per Pair; $2.50 per Dozen Pairs. Postage per Dozen Pairs, 15 Cents.
Rates by the gross furnished on application.

Lamp-Wick Trimmers.

No. 29.—LAMP-WICK TRIMMERS (5½ ins. long).
35 Cts. per Pair; $3.00 per Doz. Pairs. Postage per Dozen Pairs, 30 Cts.

No. 29.—These Trimmers are carefully designed to trim wicks evenly, and are of fine Steel, full Nickel-plated and neatly finished.

☞ Order by Numbers, Cash with Order. Ordered at the retail or single-pair rate, these Goods will be sent prepaid to any Address in the United States, Canada, Newfoundland or Mexico. When ordered at dozen rates, transportation charges must be paid by the party ordering. If the party ordering desires a mail package registered, 8 cents extra should be sent with the order. Rates by the gross furnished on application. Dozen Rates will not be allowed on less than half a dozen of one style ordered at one time, nor gross rates on less than half a gross. If the Goods cannot be procured from the nearest Butterick Pattern Agency, Send your Order, with the Price, direct to Us, and the Goods will be forwarded, prepaid, to your address.

THE BUTTERICK PUBLISHING CO. [Limited], **7 to 17 W. 13th Street, New York.**

THE DELINEATOR.

Agreeable

Preventives in season are much surer than belated drugs. A healthy condition of the Kidneys, Liver and Bowels is the strongest safeguard against Headaches, racking Colds, or Fevers.

Syrup of Figs

Acts as a perfect laxative should, cleansing and refreshing the system without weakening it; permanently curing Constipation and its effects.

Mild and Sure

Pleasant to the taste and free from objectionable substances. Physicians recommend it. Millions have found it invaluable. Taken regularly in small doses, its effect will give satisfaction to the most exacting.

MANUFACTURED BY
CALIFORNIA FIG SYRUP CO.
Sold everywhere in 50c. and $1 bottles.

SHORTHAND

WIFE $9.00

RUPTURE

CANCER

FREE

MAGIC LANTERNS

PATENTS FRANKLIN H. HOUGH

RUBBER GOODS BY MAIL

STRANGE INDEED THAT A PLAIN THING LIKE
SAPOLIO
SHOULD MAKE EVERYTHING SO BRIGHT, BUT "A NEEDLE CLOTHES OTHERS, AND IS ITSELF NAKED."

FILL YOUR OWN TEETH. DR. TRUMAN'S CRYSTALINE

 **It's Gone**

$2.75 Buys Baby Carriage

"TOO STOUT" ZETCOLACCA BERRY TABLETS

HARD WOOD DOORS

COINS

PILLOW SHAM

PLAYS ... **PLAYS**
AND DIALOGUES

PROGRESSIVE EUCHRE PLAYERS

SUPERFLUOUS HAIR.

THE OLD COUNTRY STORE

Ladies Wanted

A Perfect Picture,

I WILL

BUST DEVELOPMENT ASSURED

Over Half Million in Use.

A NEW ART

NO MORE GRAY HAIR.

FANCY WORK.

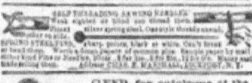 **DROPSY** TREATED FREE

WITCH HAZEL BULLETS
are a positive and guaranteed cure for all forms of
PILES AND CONSTIPATION.

SILK

GUNS

POULTRY

7 CENTS PER COPY **SHEET MUSIC!**

Grow Lovely Moustache

Fat People

I lost 135 lbs.

MRS. STELLA LEWIS,

The Metropolitan Catalogue of Fashions

The Metropolitan Catalogue of Fashions is 15x19 inches in size, and contains from 125 to 150 pages of beautifully printed large Illustrations, representing the Latest and Reigning Fashions for Ladies', Misses' and Children's Wear. It is published Semi-Annually, in February and August, with Ten Monthly Supplements, the latter containing the New Styles that have become fashionable between the time of publication of each volume and that of its successor.

☞ The Price of the Publication places it within the reach of every Dressmaker, Milliner and Housekeeper.

TERMS FOR THE METROPOLITAN CATALOGUE.
Popular Edition. Printed in English.

Price of Subscription, including Two Volumes (in Pamphlet Binding), issued respectively in February and August, and Ten Supplementary Sheets, issued monthly, Transportation Charges Prepaid by Us, ... **75 Cents**.

NOTE—If One Volume is delivered over the Counter, an allowance of Ten Cents is made on the Subscription Price.

Price of Subscription, when the Two Volumes are delivered over the Counter and the Supplementary Sheets are delivered by mail or otherwise, **50 Cents**.

Price of Single Volume, over the counter, **20 Cents**.

Price of Single Volume, by mail, **30 Cents**.

FREE TO ALL.

THE... METROPOLITAN FASHION SHEET, Illustrating the Latest Fashions for Ladies, Misses and Children, can be obtained, Free of Charge, by ordering the same from Us or any of our Agents.

We do not accept Subscriptions to the METROPOLITAN FASHION SHEET, but are always pleased to furnish, Free of Charge to Any One applying for the same, a Copy of the Current Issue, as above stated.

THE METROPOLITAN FASHION SHEET consists of eight pages, 11 x 16 inches in size, and is a handy index of the latest styles of Patterns issued.

If there is no Agency for our Patterns in your vicinity, send a Postal to us for the Fashion Sheet. If you desire Sample Copies sent to any of your friends, we shall be pleased to fill such orders.

El Periódico De Las Modas Metropolitanas.

Muestras las Ultimas Modas para Señoras, Señoritas y Niños. Consiste de ocho páginas, 11x16 pulgadas en tamaño, y es un índice muy conveniente de los últimos estilos. Envíenos una Tarjeta Postal por una copia muestra, la cual surtiremos **Libre de Gasto**. Si desea V. suscribirse á la publicación, tendremos sumo gusto en enviarle un número mensual, por doce meses sucesivamente, al recibo de sellos ú otros fondos sobre los cuales podemos realizar 25 centavos, dinero de los Estados Unidos, ó un shilling Inglés.

OFERTA ESPECIAL.—A cualquiera Señora que nos envíe una lista de doce ó más direcciones de sus amistades, que ella crea garantizan la recepción del Periódico de las MODAS METROPOLITANAS, enviaremos la publicación, libre de gasto, por un año.

The Metropolitan Catalogue of Fashions.

(Cosmopolitan Edition) is a reproduction of the above, with the descriptions in English, Spanish and German. Subscription Price for this Edition, including Two Volumes, etc., as above, Transportation Charges Prepaid by Us, **$1.00**.

NOTE.—If 1 Volume is delivered over the Counter, an allowance of 10 Cents is made on the Subscription Price.

Price of Single Volume, over the counter, **25 Cts.** Price of Single Volume, by mail, **35 Cts.**

EL Catálogo Metropolitano
(Edición Cosmopolitana)

es una reproducción, impresa en Español, Alemán é Inglés, de la Edición "Popular." Es 15 á 19 pulgadas en tamaño y contiene de 125 á 150 páginas de ilustraciones, hermosamente impresas, representando las Últimas Modas para Ropas de Señoras, Señoritas y Niños. Se publica Semi-Anualmente, en Febrero y Agosto, con Diez Suplementos Mensuales.

Precio de Suscripción á la Edición Cosmopolitana, incluyendo 2 Tomos, y Diez Suplementos Mensuales, Cargos de Porte, pagos por la Casa, **$1.00 oro**.

Precio por Un Tomo en el mostrador, **30 Centavos, oro**.

Precio por Un Tomo por correo **40 Centavos, oro**.

..DER.. Grosse Katalog
(Cosmopolitische Ausgabe)

ist eine, in spanischer, deutscher und englischer Sprache gedruckte Reproduction der unter dem Namen "Popular Edition" bekannten Ausgabe des "Metropolitan Catalogue." Derselbe ist 25x48 cm. gross und enthält 125 bis 150 Seiten prächtig ausgeführter Illustrationen, welche die neuesten und herrschenden Moden für Damen, Mädchen und Kinder darstellen. Er erscheint halbjährlich und zwar im Februar und August, ausserdem gehören zu demselben zehn monatliche Beilagen.

Abonnements-Preis der Cosmopolitischen Ausgabe, zwei Bände und zehn monatliche Beilagen enthaltend, Versendungs-Kosten von uns bestritten, **M. 4.**

Einzelne Exemplare, am Verkaufstisch, - - - **M. 1.20.**

Einzelne Exemplare, per Post, **M. 1.60.**

BUTTERICK'S MODENBLATT

bringt die neuesten Moden für Damen, Mädchen und Kinder. Es besteht aus acht Seiten 28 x 41 cm. gross und ist ein Verzeichniss aller herrschenden Moden. Nach Erhalt einer Postkarte werden wir Jedem eine Probe-Nummer **gratis und franco** zustellen. Jedem, der auf dieses Blatt zu abonniren wünscht, werden wir gern gegen Einsendung von Freimarken oder Geld, im Werte von 25 Cents (Geld der Vereinigten Staaten) oder 1 Mark, monatlich für zwölf auf einander folgende Monate eine Nummer zuschicken.

SPECIELLE OFFERTE.—Jeder Dame, welche uns eine Liste von zwölf oder mehr Adressen von betreundeten Damen zuschickt, eine Probe-Nummer unseres Modenblattes (denen solchen werden wir diese Publication) auf ein Jahr gratis zuschicken.

THE BUTTERICK PUBLISHING CO.
(Limited),
7 to 17 West 13th Street, New York.

The Butterick Publishing Co.
(Limited),
7 to 17 West 13th Street, New York.

www.ingramcontent.com/pod-product-compliance
Lightning Source LLC
Chambersburg PA
CBHW030318170426
43202CB00009B/1047